Handbook
of College and
University
Trusteeship

A Practical Guide for Trustees,
Chief Executives, and Other Leaders
Responsible for Developing
Effective Governing Boards

Richard T. Ingram
and Associates

Foreword by *Mary Louise Petersen*

Handbook
of College and
University
Trusteeship

Jossey-Bass Publishers
San Francisco • Washington • London • 1980

HANDBOOK OF COLLEGE AND UNIVERSITY TRUSTEESHIP
A Practical Guide for Trustees, Chief Executives, and Other Leaders
Responsible for Developing Effective Governing Boards
by Richard T. Ingram and Associates

Copyright © 1980 by: Association of Governing Boards
of Universities and Colleges
1 Dupont Circle, Suite 720
Washington, D.C. 20036

Jossey-Bass Inc., Publishers
433 California Street
San Francisco, California 94104

Jossey-Bass Limited
28 Banner Street
London EC1Y 8QE

Library of Congress in Publication Data

Ingram, Richard T
  Handbook of college and university trusteeship.

  Bibliography: p. 481
  Includes index.
  1. College trustees—United States. 2. Univer-
sities and colleges—United States—Administration.
I. Title.
LB2341.I533   378'.1011   79-92465
ISBN 0-87589-450-X

Manufactured in the United States of America

JACKET DESIGN BY WILLI BAUM

FIRST EDITION

Code 8011

*The Jossey-Bass
Series in Higher Education*

Foreword

We trustees have long called for a solid and comprehensive resource of authoritative information on all aspects of trusteeship, a unique institution in American higher education. At last we have it. The *Handbook of College and University Trusteeship* offers a new synthesis of what we now know about how governing boards function and how they should function. It dispels myths and misconceptions about the proper roles of trustees and provides guidance for today's board members in fulfilling their obligations to their institutions and to the public.

The authors assess both traditional and new responsibilities of the 38,000 volunteers who serve on the nation's 2,300 boards of public and private higher education. Through their own service to twenty-four colleges and universities as current or recent trustees, or as chief executives and other administrators, the authors bring many years of varied experience to their proposals for advancing the effectiveness of governing boards. For the first time in a single volume, the full range of complex trustee responsibilities is clarified and translated into alternative policies and practices.

Richard T. Ingram and his colleagues assess the pressures of the remainder of the century as they are likely to affect trustees, regents, curators, overseers, visitors, and governors in their difficult and sometimes painful decisions. The book addresses the issues of board membership, organization, and development programs and examines policies affecting presidential search, institutional planning, academic program review, academic tenure, faculty negotiations, and relationships with faculty, students, and outside constituencies. It explains trustee roles in procuring, monitoring, and managing resources and offers valuable advice on issues of liability and conflicts of interest. Finally, it presents alternative approaches to periodic assessment of board and presidential leadership and institutional performance, including a collection of proven resources developed by the Association of Governing Boards of Universities and Colleges (AGB).

Founded in 1921, AGB expanded its mission and membership in 1964 to include all types of institutions. Since then it has grown rapidly both in membership and in its capability to assist the thousands of men and women trustees who voluntarily serve higher education and their communities, states, and nation. From the beginning, a paramount AGB purpose has been to provide a forum for the free exchange of ideas about trustee roles and responsibilities. This book, published under the auspices of the association, is an important contribution to that end as a source of ideas, of suggestions, of alternatives.

The opinions of the individual contributors are their own. At the same time, the reader will find wide unanimity among the authors on the principles of trusteeship, such as the need to strengthen the relationship between administrators and trustees. Today, the increasing vulnerability of trustees and regents parallels that of presidents and chancellors. Only through mutual trust and joint effort will those who carry the rewards and burdens of leadership steer their way through the difficulties for public and private higher education in the next decades.

I believe that this handbook will prove of exceptional value as a reference for new and experienced trustees, chief executives, and other administrators who recognize the importance of effective governing boards to the future of American higher education. Every institution, every board chairman, every president, every board secretary, and every trustee who takes his or her job seriously will want to read it and keep it handy. Academic officers, business officers, development officers, librarians, professors of education, researchers, and many others will also find it indispensable.

The members of the AGB board of directors join in expressing thanks to the nineteen distinguished contributors and especially to our vice-president and friend, Richard T. Ingram, for the thought and effort that went into creation of this significant addition to the literature of governance.

Washington, D.C.　　　　　　　　　　MARY LOUISE PETERSEN
February 1980　　　　　　　　　　　　　Chairperson
Association of Governing Boards
of Universities and Colleges

Preface

More has been written about the roles and responsibilities of trustees, regents, curators, overseers, visitors, and governors of colleges and universities within the past ten years than was written during the thirty-four previous decades of American higher education. The central aim of this handbook is to offer a new synthesis of what is now known about how governing boards function, how they should function, and how they can be helped to fulfill their legal, moral, and public obligations.

Four assumptions provide the philosophical foundation for the book:

First, lay trustees should participate actively in determining policy for higher education rather than remain the underdeveloped resource they have been in the past.

Second, the success of volunteer trustee participation will remain a function of three interdependent elements—the competence of those selected to serve on boards, the ability of the chief executive officer of the institution to cultivate an effective board, and the manner in which the board is organized to meet its responsibilities.

Third, a systematic approach to the development of a dedicated and motivated board is possible, provided that such an approach is given priority by both the chief executive and its members.

Fourth, all boards of higher education share fundamental similarities in function, however various the natures and purposes of their respective institutions.

The *Handbook of College and University Trusteeship* is divided into six sections, based on the purposes and assumptions just noted:

Part One, "Significance of Trusteeship," provides background perspectives on an institution unique to the United States, with emphasis on recent events that have helped to push boards into public view and have given them a new sense of purpose.

Part Two, "Effective Board Management," highlights principles of effective board organization, including trustee selection, orientation, and continuing education.

Part Three, "Effective Institutional Oversight," discusses major policy issues confronting trustees, from selection and appointment processes for chief executives to the board's role in faculty negotiation.

Part Four, "Resource Development and Management," provides advice for strengthening the board's role in the acquisition, management, and monitoring of institutional resources, including the board's responsibilities in light of new exposures to liability.

Part Five, "Performance Assessment," offers guidelines and criteria to help boards take stock of themselves, their institutions, and chief executive leadership.

The resources in Part Six include a trustee audit, a self-study instrument for private college and university boards, an illustrative set of bylaws, a model conflict-of-interest policy statement with disclosure forms, and references to further readings keyed to each of the preceding chapters.

In one way or another everyone in the Washington office of the Association of Governing Boards of Universities and Colleges (AGB) extended a helping hand to make this book possible. Special appreciation goes to Robert L. Gale, AGB president and my constant source of inspiration and encouragement, and to Joseph C. Gies, the editor's Editor. Joyce Fitzpatrick Hartley, AGB's associate editor, kept the contributors on track along with the able help of Linda Einstein. Lynda L. Kost and Enid R. Nolan were especially helpful in shaping the pieces of the puzzle and keeping them from wandering.

And to my mentors, J. L. Zwingle, AGB president for ten years until 1974, and John W. Nason, education's dependable colleague, statesman, and friend, go continuing appreciation for their guidance.

The contributors are due special thanks for their thoroughness and their responsiveness to editorial suggestions. Their labor of love will surely strengthen trustee and chief executive relationships and help to preserve the precious national resource that trustees have become in what Martin Meyerson calls the "fascinating thicket" of higher education. Finally, to my own precious resources, Mollie, Kirsten, and David Ingram, go my love and affection for their understanding and patience.

It is unlikely that a book on this subject would have been widely welcomed as recently as ten years ago. The fact that there is need for it now gives testimony to how far the volunteer trustees of higher education have come in their desire to live up to complex and sometimes ambiguous responsibilities. It is dedicated, therefore, to the nation's 38,000 trustees, whose boards seek the right balance between the exercise of authority and the exercise of restraint.

Washington, D.C.   Richard T. Ingram
February 1980

Contents

Part Two: Effective Board Management

Part Six: Resources

The Authors

RICHARD T. INGRAM is vice-president of the Association of Governing Boards of Universities and Colleges in Washington, D.C. Prior to joining the Association in 1971, he held positions in the Department of Student Life at the University of Maryland, served with the U.S. Army as admissions and personnel officer at the U.S. Military Academy Preparatory School, and taught high school.

Ingram was awarded his bachelor's degree in social sciences education from Indiana University of Pennsylvania (1963), his master's degree in secondary education from the University of Pittsburgh (1964), and his doctorate from the University of Maryland (1969), with higher education being his major field.

Active in higher education for more than fifteen years, Ingram is a trustee of the University of Charleston, an advisory commissioner of the Education Commission of the States, and a member of the advisory board for the Center for Mediation in Higher Education. He has been a teacher and lecturer with the University of Virginia, the University of Southern California, and the Washington International Center in the District of Columbia. His past affiliations include memberships on the National Advisory Board of the Students and Collective Bargaining Project and on the Technical Advisory Group for the Maryland Commission on the Structure and Governance of Higher Education. He has served as a consultant to the U.S. Office of Education as well as to public and private colleges and universities.

GEORGE W. ANGELL is a consultant to colleges and universities in the area of collective bargaining. Previously, he served as director of the Academic Collective Bargaining Information Service and as president of the State University of New York College of Arts and Science (Plattsburgh). He has written forty articles and is co-editor of the *Handbook of Faculty Bargaining* (with E. P. Kelley, Jr., 1977).

RICHARD P. CHAIT is assistant provost and affiliate associate professor of education at Pennsylvania State University and consultant to various colleges and universities. Previously, he served as education chairman of the Institute for Educational Management and assistant professor in the Graduate School of Education at Harvard University. He has also served as assistant to the president of Stockton State College (Pomona, New Jersey).

JOHN J. CORSON is a trustee of George Mason University (Fairfax, Virginia) and of Marymount College (Arlington, Virginia) and is also a consultant to colleges and universities. Previously, he was president of the American Blood Commission; a consultant to the directors general of UNESCO, International Labor Organization, and the Organization of the American States, as well as to San Salvador, Panama, Iran, and Turkey; director, McKinsey and Co.; and professor of public and international affairs at Princeton University. He is the author of *The Governance of Colleges and Universities* (1960; rev. ed. 1975).

RHODA M. DORSEY is president of Goucher College (Towson, Maryland) and has also been a professor of history, dean, and vice-president at the college. She is president of the Women's College Coalition and first vice-chairman of the Commission on Higher Education, Middle States Association of Colleges and Schools.

ROBERT L. GALE is president of the Association of Governing Boards of Universities and Colleges and a trustee of Carleton College (Northfield, Minnesota). He has served as president of Gale Associates; director of public affairs for the Equal Employment Opportunity Commission; director of recruiting and of public affairs, U.S. Peace Corps; and vice-president of Carleton College.

ALFRED M. HALLENBECK is a partner in the law firm of Nixon, Hargrave, Devans, and Doyle (of Rochester, New York; Washington, D.C.; and Palm Beach, Florida) and a trustee of Monroe Community College (Rochester, New York), Rochester Institute of Technology, and Syracuse University.

HARVEY K. JACOBSON is assistant to the vice-president for university relations and development at the University of Michigan, Ann Arbor, and former director of university relations, University of North Dakota, Grand Forks. He is editor of *Evaluating Advancement Programs* (1978) and has written articles on evaluation, management, and research.

EDWARD P. KELLEY, JR., is associate director of the Academic Collective Bargaining Information Service and former assistant to the president for employee relations, State University of New York College of Arts and Science (Plattsburgh). He is co-editor of the *Handbook of Faculty Bargaining* (with G. W. Angell, 1977).

DAVID M. LASCELL is a partner in the law firm of Nixon, Hargrave, Devans, and Doyle (of Rochester, New York; Washington, D.C.; and Palm Beach, Florida) and is trustee and chairman of the board at Wells College (Aurora, New York).

MARTIN MEYERSON is president of the University of Pennsylvania. Previously, he served as president of the State University of New York, Buffalo; acting chancellor at the University of California, Berkeley; Williams Professor at Harvard University; and director of the M.I.T.-Harvard Urban Studies Center. He is a consultant to many nations and the author of numerous books, articles, and reports.

JOHN D. MILLETT is executive vice-president of the Academy for Educational Development, Washington, D.C., and a trustee of DePauw University (Greencastle, Indiana). He has also been chancellor of the Ohio Board of Regents, president of Miami University (Oxford, Ohio), and a trustee of the College Entrance Examination Board and the Educational Testing Service. He is the author of numerous articles and books, including *Politics and Higher Education* (1974) and *New Structures of Campus Power* (1978).

BARRY MUNITZ is chancellor of the University of Houston's main campus. Previous positions include vice-president and dean of the faculties, University of Houston; vice-president for academic development and coordination, University of Illinois; staff associate, Carnegie Commission on Higher Education; and assistant professor, University of California, Berkeley. He is a consultant to private firms and government agencies and the author of *Leadership in Colleges and Universities* (1977).

JOHN W. NASON serves as a consultant to colleges and universities, is a foundation trustee, and recently directed the Association of Governing Boards' Project on Presidential Selection and Assessment. He previously was president of Swarthmore College and Carleton College and a trustee of Vassar College. He is the author of *The Future of Trusteeship: The Role and Responsibilities of College and University Boards* (1975), *Trustees and the Future of Foundations* (1977), *Presidential Search* (1979), and *Presidential Assessment* (1980).

CHARLES A. NELSON is principal of Peat, Marwick, Mitchell, and Co. in New York City and a consultant to colleges, universities, and other nonprofit institutions. He is also chairman, board of visitors and governors, St. John's College (Annapolis, Maryland); a member of the National Council on Educational Research; and former director of the Liberal Arts Program and of the World Politics Program, University of Chicago.

JAMES G. PALTRIDGE is research educator emeritus, Division of Higher Education Policy and Administration at the University of California, Berkeley. Previously, he served as associate director of the Center for Research and Development in Higher Education at Berkeley and as assistant to the president, California Statewide System. He is the author of *Self-Study Guidelines and Criteria for Governing Boards* (1976).

JOHN W. POCOCK is trustee and board chairman of the College of Wooster in Ohio and a member of the board of directors, Association of Governing Boards of Universities and Colleges. He has previously served as chairman of the AGB/NACUBO steering committee on financial responsibilities of governing boards; chairman, Associated Consultants International; partner, director, and senior vice-president of Booz, Allen, and Hamilton; and president and chief executive officer of Booz, Allen Applied Research, Inc.

MICHAEL RADOCK is vice-president for university relations and development and professor of journalism at the University of Michigan, Ann Arbor, and a trustee of Westminster College (New Wilmington, Delaware). Formerly, he was educational relations representative for the Ford Motor Company; president of the American College Public Relations Association; and founding trustee of Greenhills School in Ann Arbor. He is one of the divisional editors of the *Handbook of Institutional Advancement* (A. W. Rowland, Gen. Ed., 1977) and author of *The Fund-Raising Role* (1977).

J. L. ZWINGLE is a member of the Commission on Higher Education, Middle States Association of Colleges and Schools. Previously, he was president of the Association of Governing Boards of Universities and Colleges, president of Park College (Parkville, Missouri), and vice-president of Cornell University. He is the author of *Effective Trusteeship: Guidelines for Board Members* (1979).

Handbook
of College and
University
Trusteeship

*A Practical Guide for Trustees,
Chief Executives, and Other Leaders
Responsible for Developing
Effective Governing Boards*

1

Richard T. Ingram

Toward Effective Trusteeship for the Eighties

The lay governing board has never lacked outspoken critics. Francis Wayland, upon his retirement from the presidency of Brown University in 1855, sounded this testy note: "How can colleges prosper, directed by men, very good men to be sure, but who know about every other thing except about education. The man who first devised the present mode of governing colleges in this country has done us more injury than Benedict Arnold" (Rudolph, 1965, p. 172). Despite its imperfections and occasional misuses, however, the lay governing board remains higher education's best hope for coping successfully with the challenges that lie ahead for our colleges and universities. As the next chapter emphasizes, the alternatives to lay trusteeship are clear but much less desirable.

The contributors to this book agree that an important place for the governing board has been carved in the academic landscape and that trustees can contribute significantly to the security and diversity of educational enterprises for the benefit of the society that supports them. Even though they have few illusions about the magnitude of the job that trustees will face, along with their presidents and chancellors, in the difficult years ahead, the authors do not succumb to pessimism about the outcome; indeed, their chapters constitute a practical guide to building more effective governing boards.

If trustees are to function as effective overseers of change during the 1980s, they will need to be alert to certain key trends and new dilemmas that will differentiate this decade from the 1960s and 1970s. Some of these changes are already being faced squarely by many boards and administrators; others have been avoided, sometimes wisely but more often not. However, all such changes warrant attention as an introduction to the later chapters of this book.

Agenda for the Eighties

The 1960s brought strife from within the campus. The number of Americans aged fourteen to twenty-four grew more than in the seven preceding decades. This huge one-time change in the age cohort required a massive expansion of education, and more of the responsibility for the passage of these young people from childhood to adulthood fell on the shoulders of schools and colleges than on those of any other social institution except the family. College and university governance came under severe attack—an attack that on the whole it weathered well, partly because of, sometimes in spite of, boards of trustees.

The 1970s brought demands from without, including challenges from government at all levels, the national economy, the courts, statewide coordinating commissions and boards, and accrediting agencies. Accountability and efficiency became watchwords as institutions attempted to assure funding agencies that they were making proper, cost-effective use of resources. As a result, governing boards were forced to assume, if they had not already done so, a more active role in choosing among competing demands for limited funds and weighing the consequences of wrong choices.

The 1980s promise a different, but no less critical, set of problems. Internal dissent and external pressures will continue, but in addition competition for funds and students among institutions will increase notably. Degrees of freedom will be fewer, tolerance levels tighter, and margins for error narrower, especially for small institutions. Those colleges and universities that have (or can regain) flexibility in their responsiveness to new consumer needs and other pressures of the eighties will fare the best.

Planning to Weather Enrollment Decline. The 1980s are expected to end with a nearly 25 percent drop in the number of 18-year-old youths. And the scramble for students, domestic and foreign, has begun: *marketing* is now an acceptable term; "life-long learners" are being cultivated; student retention efforts have been intensified; off-campus centers have proliferated with attractive but sometimes controversial programs. It is well known that enrollment declines will not equally affect every institution, although the rural state colleges and less visible private liberal arts colleges are likely to suffer the greatest losses—particularly in the industrial belt of the Northeast. Interstate migrations and varying birth rates may allow some states to claim small increases, particularly in the sunbelt, but all sectors of higher education and virtually every institution will feel the impact of decline in the traditional college-age cohort, which currently provides about 50 percent of undergraduate enrollments.

For all but the most prestigious, highly selective institutions, the question is not whether but when and how serious the impact will be. Some institutions have already closed or merged or taken other significant steps in the face of enrollment decline caused by reasons other than the forthcoming shift in national and state demographics. Further decline will intensify pressures on administrations and boards to guard against unfounded optimism, reluctance to ask the hard questions, and failure to engage faculty and student leaders in dialogue about the economic and political facts of institutional life. Contingency plans as part of longer-term planning processes are required to avoid prospects for a kind of purgatory for hundreds of institutions.

Trustees have a *monitoring role*—more acutely needed now than ever before—over the assumptions that underlie enrollment projections, over financial trends and budget controls, over marketing strategies, and over the quality of academic programs on and off the campus. Trustees have an urgent responsibility to continuously review all institutional policies, including the administration of such policies, to see that such policies insulate the institution from, rather than expose it to, the prospects of a decade of nasty weather. Most current institutional policies were adopted a decade or more ago when a very different set of circumstances prevailed. A clear schedule of review now, in concert with the academic community where appropriate, will minimize the likelihood of crisis revision later. Chapter Nine makes a case for greater trustee participation in institutional planning, and Chapter Fifteen details how boards can improve their abilities for tracking institutional finances. Several other chapters are also particularly useful for looking at institutional responses to stress.

The board's role in planning for the possibility of enrollment decline begins with a simple question and ends somewhere else: What must be done if enrollment decreases by factors of 10, 15, or 20 percent over the next four or five years? Do existing board or administrative policies preclude or hamper institutional flexibility? Have the board, administration, and faculty achieved consensus on actions to be taken in response to specified and agreed upon warning signals? Has legal counsel helped the board to look at viable alternatives: refinancing; cooperative arrangements with other institutions; change of sponsor, mission, or clientele; merger or adoption by another independent or state-owned institution; or orderly closing, with ample time for students, faculty, and alumni to be convinced that all possible alternatives were employed as part of a well-conceived and conducted schedule of contingency budgeting and planning. Some institutions have already begun employing an annual practice of adopting two or three balanced budgets contingent upon actual fall enrollment figures.

A number of public policy issues at the state level will be resolved in the 1980s—issues of coordination, of finance, and of control. There may be need to clarify, for example, whether the governing board has the authority to close, merge, or change the purpose of an institution, or whether higher legal authority must be petitioned for approval of any departure from the existing charter. Whatever the circumstances, however, the trustees should be mindful of their collective responsibility to document deliberations of alternatives, remedial actions, and adherence to a schedule of contingency plans—to demonstrate awareness of their responsibility to protect the human (as well as financial and physical) capital that they hold in trust.

It is a time for scores of institutions to consider more frequent board and committee meetings with markedly different agendas—agendas that are less crowded with the trivia of well-worn reports and more concerned with inseparable issues of the quality of academic programs, the adequacy of existing policies, and the responses to a declining traditional-age market. Trustees who meet only two, three, or four times annually and who serve institutions already experiencing wide disparities between projected (or optimum) enrollments and actual enrollments leave themselves vulnerable, as well as those who look to them for leadership and direction. The same fate is due those who rely too heavily on executive committees to avoid more frequent board meetings, who fail repeatedly to use their acknowledged expertise, or who fail to see that board policy decisions are carried out expeditiously.

Litigation and the Courts. The 1980s will bring more judicial intervention. When administrators and trustees are named defendants in suits brought against their institutions, serious dangers threaten. A poorly conducted defense by a single institution because of inadequate funds or weak counsel can adversely affect all higher education. A college or university managed irresponsibly by an uninterested board of trustees will unfairly expose other boards to greater threat of liability.

More care should be taken to see that institutional policies are sound, current, and administered properly. There is also need for better communication between institutions facing potential precedent-setting lawsuits and their national resources, especially the educational associations in Washington, D.C. It is far more effective to seek broad and comprehensive advice when a legal issue first emerges than to ask for help on subsequent appeals. The

American Council on Education (ACE) and the National Association of College and University Attorneys (NACUA) are two organizations that can serve a valuable clearinghouse function.

Government Regulation. State and federal governments will continue to attach burdensome strings to tax dollars. Without reference here to the administrative cost of compliance or to the merits or demerits of existing regulations, it can be said that trustees and their chief executives must become more vigilant. They should determine in advance what role, if any, they should assume and what mechanisms may be used to express positions on legislative and bureaucratic proposals. Some boards of large public institutions have already established special committees to deal with governmental relations. Others will no doubt do so.

In the past, responsibility for expressing opinions on local, state, or federal proposals fell to the chief executive, with minimal trustee involvement. The 1980s will require greater participation of carefully selected and influential trustees as legislative advocates. Trustee skills in the halls of government need to be sharpened. Further centralization and bureaucratization at federal and state levels will tax the vigilance of boards in protecting the integrity and independence of individual institutions and higher education as a whole.

Self-regulation is the best hope for reducing governmental intrusion. Important here is the governing board's responsibility for ensuring that the college or university delivers what it promises. This means, in part, ensuring that the institution is not overcommitted, that it offers what it can do best. It also means improving relationships with statewide agencies responsible for coordination, particularly in the public sector. This effort calls for much good will and initiative on both sides. Statewide coordinating and planning agencies, charged initially to deal with the problem of growth and more recently with the problem of retrenchment, have a legitimate and difficult role for which institutional trustees should provide support. In return, such agencies should demonstrate their own competence and good judgment through more careful consultation with boards and institutions affected by decisions at the state level. They should also show respect and appreciation for the difficult and vital role of institutional boards in maintaining a balance between the legitimate interests of state authorities and institutional freedom.

Private Gifts and Tax Reform. The public institution's search for private dollars will keep pace with the independent school's search for tax dollars. The trustees and regents of public institutions will eventually have to undertake fund-raising efforts little different from those now required of independent college trustees. Efforts of tax reformers to remove the tax-deductible status of gifts to colleges and universities are likely to recur, and these pose serious threats to independent *and* tax-supported institutions. Given higher education's dependence on private philanthropy, few issues will demand more trustee attention and response.

Note should also be made of the fact that increasing numbers of Americans are using the standard deduction rather than itemizing deductions on their federal income tax returns—an estimated 75 percent of all taxpayers in 1979. As the ceiling for the standard deduction is raised, the number of taxpayers who itemize their deductions decreases, resulting in a decline in the percentage of personal income contributed to nonprofit organizations. Until taxpayers are permitted to deduct charitable contributions, whether or not they use the standard deduction, colleges and universities will be among those charitable organizations likely to experience declining gift support. For all these reasons, trustees should be alert to proposals to amend state and federal tax laws that could affect their institutions.

Academic Tenure. Governing boards are being forced to reassess their role in review of faculty tenure policies and practices, a particularly troublesome area in a period of retrenchment. Chapter Twelve of this handbook urges greater recognition of the need to set tenure policies that are within the larger context of institutional needs in order to exercise maximum influence and leverage. The security of the faculty and the security of the institution will require some intricate balancing in the years ahead if the board's heavy responsibility to guarantee academic freedom is not to be sacrificed. Some new understandings among boards, administrations, and faculties will become necessary.

Faculty Unionization. It is likely that collective bargaining will continue to flourish even in the private sector. Thus, Chapter Thirteen calls for more informed trustee awareness of the *causes* (and consequences) of faculty unionization, sounder institutional management, and an effective role for faculty in campus governance.

Interinstitutional Cooperation. Most consortia organized on a local or regional basis provide for little or no trustee participation at policy levels. But this picture seems to be changing as a result of growing recognition that genuine trustee involvement can bring greater objectivity and more cooperative ventures. The usefulness of interinstitutional cooperation—with or without formal consortial arrangements—will surely be tested in the intense competition of the 1980s.

There are increasing examples of programs where cost savings have been realized and expensive program duplication avoided. Consortia and other forms of institutional cooperation will always have more potential for good than they can fully realize, however, until trustees express greater interest in them.

Deferred Maintenance. There is no documented national estimate of the extent of deferred maintenance, but the figure is surely staggering. One private university reports a $9 million maintenance and building rehabilitation shortfall, about 33 percent of its total current funds (and six percent of its investment in plant). But at least this institution knows the magnitude of its problem and what must be done. Many other boards have no idea of their total maintenance needs, or they have ratios of deferred maintenance to current funds, or to investments in plant, more severe than the example just noted.

Most institutions of higher education have aging physical plants, and all face rising energy and other utility costs. In the next decade a large number of campus buildings will have to be completely renovated or simply bulldozed. Many boards will be forced to concur with recommendations to remove buildings to realize savings rather than to "mothball" them for possible future use. Good planning is needed to provide answers to trustee questions in this area, so that institutions will not be unprepared for future requirements.

Accreditation. Until recently, institutional and program accreditation have largely escaped trustee attention. But when board members *have* asked questions, they have found that budgets have escalated for accreditation groups for specialized programs. Proliferation of such groups continues without abatement, and dissatisfaction with their accrediting processes is growing, especially with regard to a seeming lack of responsiveness to new issues, sensitivity to requests for wider participation and consultation, and maintenance of academic quality.

Accreditation processes have traditionally been a concern of administrators and faculties to the exclusion of governing boards. Both trustees and accrediting groups should address the question of whether such exclusion should continue into the next decade. The federal government, through the Division of Eligibility and Agency Evaluation of the U.S. Office of Education, and some state governments see a responsibility for establishing their own criteria for program and institutional review. The future of nongovernmental accreditation may be in jeopardy, and for that reason alone trustees should be more informed and involved in the continuing debate. In addition, trustees have a legitimate role in accreditation because program and institutional review standards and practices affect the mission of the institution. Presidents and chancellors should help ensure that trustees are cognizant of accrediting groups, their purposes and activities, and their cost-benefit ratios.

Public Image. A recent poll (Harris, 1978) reported that not a single national institution had the confidence of a majority of the public, though higher education placed at the top of the list—just below medicine and well ahead of local, state, and federal government. Until recently, there has been little need for colleges and universities to influence public opinion except to make cases for their own support. But the next several years will require a stronger trustee voice in speaking to the purposes and value of higher education itself.

Trustees should help to ensure the preservation of our dual system of higher education by speaking out for it. The voice of a state university board chairman, who on behalf of his or her board, publicly supports proposed legislation to aid private liberal arts colleges can carry a hundredfold the influence of spokespersons from the private sector. The same holds true for the private university president or trustee who speaks out for tax-supported higher education.

Public and private sector advocates disagree about the validity of statistics on the net closings and mergers of private colleges in the preceding decade—additional evidence of the growing competition among types of institutions (Magarrell, 1979). Although the debate may be moot except for the researcher's need to get the facts straight, what may yet come to pass is not without frightening precedent. Of 500 colleges founded in 16 representative states before the Civil War, an 80 percent mortality rate was attributed to unfavorable location, financial disaster, internal dissension, and other effects (Brubacher and Rudy, 1968, p. 73). Although the most pessimistic observers are not predicting a mortality on this scale, declining enrollments, high inflation, and a widening tuition gap between private and tax-supported institutions are bound to take their toll in the current decade. If private institutions are to remain part of a healthy, diverse system that provides real alternatives in the pursuit of education, board members everywhere should become involved—not as trustees of a particular institution or category of institution, but as *trustees of higher education.*

Trustee Interdependence and Power

These trends and dilemmas suggest an important point: colleges and universities will be more interdependent in the 1980s than they have been in the past. The successful or unsuccessful resolution of an issue at one institution will affect others, just as state and national policies directed toward a particular kind of institution will be felt elsewhere by other types of institutions.

The nation's 38,000 trustees of higher education are increasingly recognizing not only this interdependence of colleges and universities but their own mutual interest and interdependence as trustees. Until recently, they have perceived themselves as buffers among competing interest groups. There are signals now that they themselves could become a special-interest group. Currently, some fifteen state trustee associations exist across the country—a movement apparently begun and sustained thus far by community college boards, which seem to have more zeal for political activism than do boards of other institutions. Although such groups vary in degree of organization, staffing, and activity, one significant characteristic is shared: they exist to promote the interests of a particular type of *public* institution. Exactly how this phenomenon may affect the future of the academy is unclear.

Some efforts continue in the private sector to form separate trustee organizations at state levels, but the going there seems to be more frustrating. Even less likely to emerge, unfortunately, are state associations for *all* trustees—public, private, two-year and four-year. United fronts on key issues are a long way from reality as long as institutional self-interest prevails at the expense of cooperation, and funding patterns differ so widely. One can only hope that trustees and chief executives of all institutional species will eventually find common ground in comprehensive and unified groups at the state level.

At the national level, the Association of Governing Boards of Universities and Colleges (AGB) presents a useful role model for similar coalitions at the state level. The diversity of its membership demonstrates how a greater good—the protection of the higher education enterprise itself—can and must be served. AGB's mission is to advance higher education by strengthening the organization and performance of its governing, coordinating, and advisory boards. As a forum for the exchange of ideas and information on issues that affect the health and welfare of all types of colleges and universities, the association is one of the very few on the national scene that brings together the top leaders from all sectors. By doing so, AGB enables trustees and chief executives to bring their collective insights to the resolution of issues that would otherwise be divisive. It is time for trustees to temper their natural and necessary inclinations toward institutional self-interest by joining with their peers from other types of institution at the local, state, and national levels. Their agenda should be to help ensure the best possible outcomes from public policy debates yet to come—debates that will surely affect the increasingly delicate fabric of postsecondary education.

The president of Stanford University has observed a movement among trustees that he sees as analogous to other movements of individual or institutional self-assertion: "I know of no one who is in touch with developments around the country who does not see growing tendencies towards assertion of trustee rights and prerogatives. Sometimes these tendencies conflict with the true role of governing boards, by threatening to involve trustees in detailed academic decision making. That must be resisted for the good of all concerned. . . . On the other hand the surge for "trustee power" is not to be dismissed as merely self-serving or frivolously imitative of all other "power" movements we find ourselves having to cope with. It is related to the uneasiness many people feel about the responsiveness of institutions, including institutions of higher learning" (Lyman, 1973, p. 7). Lyman's observation may be disconcerting to some—perhaps the word *power* causes alarm. And for trustees and presidents alike there is considerable concern about how trusteeship will evolve as boards become more active. Will the Rip Van Winkle who has suddenly awakened become overzealous to make up for his long sleep? Will he go back to sleep when the thunder stops? Or will he be sensible, deliberate, and responsible in his new life?

Building the Board

There are presidents who somehow expect their boards to be effective while being kept at arm's length from the institution's central purpose, its reason for being. There are other chief executives who keep their boards in the mainstream of institutional life by keeping them fully informed. These are in a sense the brave souls, the risk takers, but they are also the chief executives most likely to see trustees respond appropriately rather than dangerously.

The successful chief executive works at making trustees effective. He or she, more than any other individual, is responsible for developing a knowledgeable, sensitive, and dedicated board. If a board and its president have confidence in themselves and in one another, a sense of timing and, most of all, a sense of purpose, exciting changes can occur. Fewer eleventh-hour policy decisions will be made in response to economic pressure or other crises. Gardner (1965) once wrote: "University people love to innovate away from home" (p. 76). But a successful board development program requires the kind of innovation that can *only* begin at home.

The first and most significant step in any board development effort is a candid, open assessment of the board's roles and responsibilities by the trustees and president; its membership, organization, and performance; and its relationships with the chief executive and various publics. Trustees should conscientiously pursue such a course to ensure that the board is functioning responsibly and to set an example for others. The *process* of self-assessment, the *findings* from a self-study, and an *agenda* of steps to be taken to meet apparent needs will contribute to renewal of purpose and faith in the board, the president's office, and the institution itself. Such initiatives have been repeated time and time again throughout the nation in the past decade. Effective boards have been built on the results.

The trustee's job is much tougher now, one that is not for the faint of heart. America is fortunate to have women and men who are welcoming the challenges of the next decade rather than withdrawing from them. Notwithstanding concern about personal liability, disclosure, and sunshine laws, even unreasonable intrusions into their lives, thousands of capable citizens come forward to take their places as new trustees each year. Their informed commitment to the future of the academy through the exercise of responsible trusteeship will help to reverse what many have called an erosion of the authority of the presidency and the lay board.

In his annual report as president of Georgetown University, T. S. Healy (1978) noted: "For anyone deeply involved in a University, holding a steady angle of vision on it is extraordinarily difficult. So many things get in the way: immediate plans and problems, pressures from various constituencies, above all the intricate beauty of its people with all their complexity, cussedness, talent, and power. It's like living in the middle of a kaleidoscope and trying to keep a fix on the horizon" (p. 2). Trustees exist to help their institutions keep a fix on the horizon and hold a steady angle of vision. The remaining chapters of this handbook aim to help trustees and administrators increase the effectiveness of the governing board in accomplishing this task.

2

J. L. Zwingle

Evolution of
Lay Governing Boards

Two features of American education immediately strike even the most casual observer: first, the magnitude of the enterprise; second, its form of control.

In providing educational opportunity, the United States has gone far beyond anything attempted elsewhere. In sheer numbers it is an impressive achievement: more than 3,000 postsecondary institutions enroll more than 11 million students, including half the nation's high school graduates. Two great innovations—the land-grant colleges, stemming from the so-called Morrill Act of 1862, and the public community colleges, stemming from the junior college movement of this century—dramatically expanded Americans' access to higher education and drastically changed the population on campuses, both in type and numbers of students. These innovations brought into the classroom and laboratory students who could benefit from postsecondary education but who would have remained outside the reach of traditional colleges and universities. As a result, enrollments on some campuses are today counted in the tens of thousands, and campus administration has become the equivalent of city management. Whatever the shortcomings of the system, the very attempt to offer education on such a scale is little short of astounding.

Equally impressive is the fact that the responsibility for this vast enterprise rests upon citizens who claim no special competence as educators and who serve without compensation. Education is not alone among American institutions in this respect, of course, since other institutions that serve the public good, such as hospitals, museums, orchestras, and foundations, are governed in the same style. But the trustees of colleges and universities have played a special part in the development of the nation. The flexibility and adaptability of American higher education that have aided its evolution, and the growth of other institutions, are due in large part, to the involvement of responsible citizen-trustees in each stage of its development. For this reason, the origins, composition, functions, and prospects of lay governing boards are worthy of serious reflection not only by trustees, administrators, and faculty members but also by students and members of the public at large; the latter, after all, are the chief beneficiaries of the trust held by these boards.

Origins of Academic Trusteeship

Even though history in itself may not prove anything, failure to understand the evolution of a system such as trusteeship can lead to false expectations about it or to misconceptions of alternatives to it. Thus, the importance of lay trusteeship for American higher education arises from certain underlying principles that were present at the beginning of the American story and that bear on the future of education and the nation itself.

The first of these principles is that unchecked monopoly is a threat to the public good, no matter how benign the monopoly. For education, monopoly of power is especially threatening, whether that power be vested in church or state or in any one individual, whether a commissioner of education, a governor, or a campus administrator. A related principle is that education is too important to the public interest for the public to rely totally for its governance on the faculty, whose self-interest, as with any professional group, is ever present.

These principles and the resulting reliance on external boards of control in education and other social institutions did not originate in the New World, as is sometimes alleged. Prototypes are to be found in Italy as early as the twelfth century, where city-states appointed boards of citizens as liaison between university students and their instructors, and in the Netherlands and Scotland, where, following the Protestant Reformation, control of religious and educational policy was no longer vested in the clergy itself but became the responsibility of lay elders. The American colonists followed these precedents, in contrast to those of Oxford and Cambridge, whose colleges were governed by senior faculty members, who in turn relied on a single "visitor" from outside the college to adjudicate irreconcilable disputes. In the fledgling society of the New World in 1636, the questions were: Who would take the first steps toward the founding of a college? Who would be responsible for its charter? And when the clergyman John Harvard left his library as an initial endowment for a college, the question became: Who would assure its continuity? It could hardly be the members of a faculty—something yet to be created. But royal charters formed a model, and the holders of the charter could be drawn from local citizens—mainly clergymen, to be sure, but lay persons too. Thus Harvard operates to this day under a "board of overseers," who approve the decisions of its president and fellows and who are responsible for its ultimate governance and well-being.

In other colonies, other colleges were established with lay boards—William and Mary in 1693, Yale in 1701, and many more along the eastern seaboard and eventually across the mountains, farther and farther west as the population increased and spread. Because of church sponsorship, clergymen dominated the governing boards of many of these colleges, and close legal ties to the sponsoring denominations led to later conflict over their academic independence. But the pattern was set: the beneficiaries of a trust, in contrast to Oxford's and Cambridge's senior fellows, could not themselves serve as trustees of the trust.

When state universities began to receive charters—the University of Georgia in 1785, North Carolina in 1789, South Carolina in 1801, and Ohio in 1804—the states followed the example of existing colleges and provided for lay governing boards. In some instances, as in Michigan, they went beyond mere legislation and adopted constitutional provisions as a means of protecting these institutions from political influence.

Not insignificantly, while many American colleges were transforming themselves into universities during the second half of the nineteenth century with the aid of their lay trustees, Oxford and Cambridge were proving incapable of adapting themselves to the needs of a changing English society. Parliament had no mechanism to reform them except a series of royal commissions appointed by the crown, and every British university established since then has involved laymen and alumni in their governance from the beginning.

Composition of Today's Boards

The citizens who serve as trustees of America's colleges and universities today represent a significant cross section of American life. A recent survey conducted by the American Council on Education (ACE) and the Association of Governing Boards of Universities and Colleges (AGB) reveals the following facts about them (Gomberg and Atelsek, 1977):

In terms of occupational background, the largest single group (34 percent) is composed of active executives (not retirees) in business or industry. Of these executives, over half are either presidents of corporations or chairmen of corporate boards, and all but a few are at least members of corporate boards. The professions of law, medicine, and the ministry contribute 25 percent of the total number of trustees, while teachers and administrators in education constitute 13 percent.

Women make up 15 percent of the total, and minorities account for 7 percent. The figures for distribution by age show 10 percent of all trustees to be under forty years of age, while 67 percent are fifty or older. In terms of educational background, 90 percent hold the baccalaureate, while 32 percent hold a professional degree or a doctorate.

Some 19 percent of the total serve on more than one collegiate board. Their multiple membership may produce benefits to their institutions, but casual observation would suggest that institutional benefits result largely from the personal commitment of an individual to one particular institution. Thus duplicate memberships may not prove to be as great a value to their institutions as is commonly supposed. Furthermore, as Chapter Seventeen points out, multiple trusteeships may present conflicts of interest.

Changes in the personal characteristics of trustees over the past decade are revealed by comparing these figures with figures from a 1968 survey of collegiate boards conducted by the Educational Testing Service (ETS) (Hartnett, 1969). Although the 1977 ACE-AGB survey was not organized in precisely the same way as the ETS survey, the questions were similar enough to indicate the following shifts:

In the nine-year period between the two surveys, there has been a 5 percent increase in the number of trustees who are presidents of companies or chairmen of corporate boards (from 14 percent to 19 percent). A 12 percent increase has occurred in the number of trustees who are members of corporate boards (from 20 percent to 32 percent). The proportion of women has increased only slightly—2 percent, from 13 to 15 percent; but the representation of blacks has risen 5 percent, from 1 percent in 1968 to 6 percent in 1977. In age, the most marked change has been in the increase of those under forty years of age (5 percent), with comparable shifts downward in each of the older groupings. In educational achievement, the major change is a 13 percent increase in the number of trustees holding the baccalaureate, with no significant changes in other degree categories.

If the composition of collegiate boards follows recent trends in membership on corporate boards, the academic boards are likely to be increasingly diverse, particularly in representation of women and minorities. Among a sample of members of corporate boards of directors who have been appointed within the past five years, fully 41 percent are women and 25 percent are black (Research and Forecasts, 1978). Moreover, the newly appointed directors tend to believe that, while personal qualifications should come first in the choice of new members, boards should elect still more members from among women and minorities. These new directors are about the same age as those elected six or more years ago, but 82 percent of them have completed baccalaureate programs and 57 percent of them hold professional degrees or doctorates. Three quarters of these directors hold positions on more than one board, and nearly one fifth of them are members of four or more boards. These surveys indicate that both the business world and the world of education are responding to pressures for change in board membership. One can assume with considerable certainty that more change and diversity will be forthcoming.

Regarding the distribution of membership of college and university boards, trustees for private colleges and universities outnumber those of public institutions by a large proportion: seventeen to one. Regarding the size of these boards, those for private colleges and universities average twenty-six members, in sharp contrast to the average of nine members on boards of public institutions. In terms of special representation, three out of every ten trustees must be selected from designated constituencies or special groups, such as alumni. (Six percent of all trustees are selected from alumni groups alone.)

Some 3400 positions stand empty at any one time, largely in the private sector, where boards usually have some latitude under their charters in the actual number of positions required to be filled. One prevailing notion is that a few seats should be left unfilled just in case some especially desirable person becomes available, but the record of trustee selection does not indicate that this presumed advantage is often well utilized. In fact, the whole issue of selection is one of the most delicate problems of the structure of trusteeship in both the public and private sectors. Extraneous factors are frequently dominant in the selection process, and this weakness constitutes one of the areas in greatest need of reform (see Chapter Five).

In terms of span of control, 164 boards govern multicampus systems of institutions rather than individual colleges or universities. Within these multicampus systems are 886 institutional units. Significantly, by now fully one half of all students are enrolled in these institutions. The ability of these boards to govern such mammoth systems effectively has major implications for the quality of education these students receive, and it deserves particular study.

Responsibilities of Boards

The legitimacy of collegiate governing boards has been seriously challenged over the decades, most recently during the 1960s and 1970s when various groups have strongly urged the virtues of "participatory democracy" for the members of all organizations and social institutions. In recent years, many colleges have revised their structures of academic governance, and these changes have had serious effects on the role and function of trusteeship. For example, a number of institutions have created campus-wide senates that include representatives not only of faculty, students, and administrators but also of nonacademic staff. Have these new structures of campus governance undercut the need for lay trustees? One answer is provided in a study by Millett (1978b) in which he traces the origins and consequences of these new campus bodies. Principal among Millett's conclusions is that these structural changes in campus governance have not accomplished much and that effective trusteeship and administrative leadership are in even greater demand today than before. A second comes from Epstein, a political scientist at the University of Wisconsin who has studied academic government at that university and other similar institutions and who returned to teaching after a period of frustration as an administrator. Arguing against the idea of disposing of lay trustees in favor of a system of internal governance, Epstein (1974) concludes that the lay governing board is the best alternative among any suggested so far, despite its need for improvement in personnel and in practice.

Colleges and universities will always face the conflicting demands of special-interest groups, and they require more than campus senates, no matter how representative, to respond to these demands. Whether one group calls for specialized training and indoctrination or another for basic research and experimentation, some part of the public will inevitably become indignant and look for culprits to condemn. There is always some kind of vested interest that will feel imperiled by unorthodoxy, whether ecclesiastical, economic, or political; and the problem of intellectual integrity under these pressures is as old as civilization: How can eleemosynary institutions, dependent as they are on benefactions, be both sufficiently separate from and yet mutually supportive of their benefactors?

It is not a simple problem. On the one hand, there must be at least a minimal level of self-determination for an academic institution to function. On the other hand, the institution must be in tune with its supporting community, whether this community is a municipality, a state, a region, the nation, or simply a group of interested persons. A constituency that is too demanding will suffocate an institution, but an institution that is too freewheeling will not sustain a following.

The problem is how best to meet apparently opposing demands, such as independence versus reasonable control, pluralism versus irresponsible individualism, accountability versus flexibility, and self-determination versus responsiveness. Even the demands of such professions as medicine or the military appear to conflict at times with the broader needs of society, and the conflict poses a problem not merely for the profession but for the citizenry. Consider the additional pressures on educational institutions from influential individuals—the would-be donor of an endowed professorship who wishes the privilege of naming the holder of the chair or prescribing the qualifications of the holder; the business executive who encourages his counterparts in industry to withhold gifts from institutions that appear to be unsupportive of "free enterprise," however defined, or at least to harbor scholars who seem overcritical of business practices; the federal official who interprets federal legislation as prohibiting a father-and-son banquet; members of the council on higher education of a state who seek to dominate the process of accreditation; the governor who calls upon the state legislature to make the terms of all trustees of state institutions conform to the schedule of gubernatorial elections so that his office will be able to control the institutions by appointing all their trustees. Who can best represent the interests of the public, of past benefactors, and of future students and citizens under these conditions?

The fate of the German universities during the Nazi era points to the lay governing board as an answer. These universities, traditionally nonpolitical and autonomous, became an easy prey to national power gone wrong because they were operated as agencies of the government through Germany's ministry of education. Without the buffer of any intervening board, they became entirely dependent on the government for policy determination and support.

In short, a corollary of the principle stated earlier about the danger of monopoly is that, where educational policy arises from any one single-interest group, including the government, the long-range results are likely to be bad for everyone. Thus, the giving of financial support to an institution cannot justify domination over its program. Although for some organizations the power of the purse may represent ultimate power, for education the power of ideas must remain the ultimate power and the search for knowledge the central motive. The external governing board exists, among other reasons, to protect this principle.

In this regard, one of the encouraging changes currently affecting trusteeship in the private sector of higher education is the increasing independence of colleges from their founding religious groups, a fact to be observed among Catholic institutions as well as among Protestant ones. This change can in no small part be attributed to the effect of a broadened base of financial support for these institutions—a base that includes alumni, the general public, the business community, philanthropic foundations, and state and federal government.

Prospects for Lay Trusteeship

If external governing boards thus perform essential functions for their institutions, how can they best meet their responsibilities? The answer does not lie in modeling themselves on a corporate board of directors. The development of business corporations during the nineteenth century resulted in confusing the boards of trustees or regents of educational institutions with the boards of directors of profit-making corporations. Directors of business corporations are in principle delegates of the stockholders, chosen to protect the investors and, if possible, enhance their investment—and often chosen to represent special expertise because of overlapping responsibilities in other similar enterprises. Their corporations may incidentally serve the public good in some sense and certainly must operate within the law, but their prime purpose is production at a profit.

As commerce and industry expanded during the nineteenth century, the business corporation became the avowed or assumed model for other organizations, including colleges and universities. The assumption grew that the college was composed of a skilled work force, whether the skills lay in medicine or engineering, in economics or political science. The model for the successful college president, given this assumption, was that of the successful corporate manager, with college presidents having the same relationship to their boards as did their corporate counterparts. And from this perspective, professors were employees whose work was directed and determined by administrators and the board, rather than professionals whose expertise warranted their establishing academic policy and fulfilling their responsibilities subject to trustee review.

These ideas resulted in a belief that college trustees should concern themselves primarily with financial matters—with property, institutional growth and stability, public relations, intercollegiate athletic spectacles, and other issues of interest to the public but not of particular importance to higher education. At the center of this misconception was a false distinction between fiscal matters and educational matters. The college does not function for the financial benefit of investors, as does a business corporation, and its effectiveness cannot be judged primarily on financial grounds. Financial soundness is not an index of academic vitality. Fiscal realities cannot be avoided, of course, but for the academy the really important facts are those that surround financial data. The effectiveness of teaching and learning is the result of many intangible factors beyond money, including institutional goals that are widely understood and shared and a sense of personal aspiration. These priceless intangibles are not available on requisition, but they provide the intellectual and spiritual energy to be observed in productive academic institutions.

As a consequence, the lay governing board in higher education is responsible for a process as well as for property, for activities as well as for assets. Trustees or regents must accept the educational functioning of the institution as their concern, along with its fiscal operation. In fact, the fiscal operation cannot make sense apart from the educational function, including goals, experimentation, and those controversies that seem inherent in the academic enterprise.

To grapple with this range of responsibilities, the board needs to concentrate on three special functions as they bear on the total institution. First is the planning function. The board should not be the planning body but rather should require adequate planning for all aspects of the institution. Planning is never static, never finished, but must undergo periodic revision as experience dictates. Given competent planning; the board can perform its next function, that of authorization. Here it must rely heavily on the professional leadership of the president, other administrators, and the faculty. The third stage is review—independent oversight, evaluation, and assessment of administrative and faculty performance as well as of general institutional achievement.

Planning, authorization, and review must each be applied to specific aspects of the institution: enrollment, curriculum, obtaining of resources, and the whole range of support activities that can make or break the institution—make it if consistently carried out or break it if performed haphazardly.

Academic trustees must avoid another parallel with corporate boards of directors, namely, the tendency, conscious or otherwise, to perceive each trustee as a delegate or representative of some constituency, especially when representation is thought to be more important than competence. If an individual board member is to represent some special group or interest, the board itself cannot fulfill its responsibility to the whole public. Rather than being forced to establish formal representation for any group that can muster support for special treatment, boards must insist that all members represent the general interest. This is true even of students and faculty members from the institution, who as members of the board are almost certain to be expected by their colleagues to be special pleaders, even if they themselves have a broader view of their role.

In this regard, academic boards should conceive of themselves in the way that Edmund Burke in the eighteenth century conceived of Parliament, and trustees should see their role as he viewed his own responsibility as a member of Parliament from Bristol (1774): "Parliament is not a *congress* of ambassadors from different and hostile interests; which interests each must maintain, as an agent and advocate, against other agents and advocates; but Parliament is a *deliberative* assembly of *one* nation, with one interest, that of the whole; where, not local purposes, not local prejudices ought to guide, but the general good, resulting from the general reason of the whole. You choose a member indeed; but when you have chosen him, he is not member of Bristol, but he is a member of *Parliament*."

Many faculty members and students are suspicious of lay trustees, and they fear the intrusion of noneducators into educational matters and trustee interference with day-to-day administration. These fears seem particularly well founded within public community colleges, many of which have grown out of secondary school roots. Here board members are elected from the local community and are directly exposed to pressures of fellow townspeople. Because of the intimacy of this local relationship, community college boards seem to cross into the territory of administrators more frequently than do those of four-year colleges and universities. But is the cure for board meddling to recruit more heavily from academic circles for membership on such boards? Not at all. The potential for the lay governing board will not be realized by adding faculty, student, staff, or other "representatives" of the institution itself but instead by devising means for more effectively educating lay trustees about educational concerns and their distinctive duties as trustees.

Currently there appears to be a lessening of confidence in education and in educators, as in other professions and professionals. For such a time, the potential value of the lay governing board may be higher than at any former period. In such an era, the citizen-trustee has unrivaled opportunity, whether in a public or a private institution. Tax dollars and governmental agencies form a poor alternative to the voluntarism so deeply rooted in American history and in the American view of effective social institutions. Even if government agencies continue to increase their role in higher education, it is not therefore inevitable that colleges and universities must surrender a significant degree of self-determination. The lay governing board can assure the self-determination of its institution if its volunteer trustees set themselves this task. The outcome will depend upon those who hold this unique responsibility.

3

John W. Nason

Responsibilities
of the Governing Board

Colleges and universities are corporations or associations formed
for the purpose of providing education and related services. They
are governed by boards of trustees or of regents who are primarily
lay persons rather than professional educators or government
bureaucrats. These boards hold in trust the physical and financial
assets of the institutions over which they have legal control, and
they have the power to direct and supervise operations and programs in the best interests of the intended beneficiaries.

Three aspects of the role of trustees deserve emphasis. First,
trustees hold and control assets and programs *in trust,* that is, for
the benefit of others. Theirs is a fiduciary role. Second, although it
is often said that the trustees control and manage the affairs of the
institution, their direct involvement in the management of programs has gradually declined to the point where it is more appropriately described as direction and supervision (see Chapter
Seven). Trustees are policy makers, not managers or administrators. Third, the beneficiaries can vary widely according to the

27

institution's charter as amended or modified by board decisions, state laws, government regulations, and even popular demand. Beneficiaries can be the general public (open admissions) or those who qualify on academic, religious, or residential criteria; they can be business and industry or the general welfare, as in the case of agricultural extension programs of land-grant colleges or research programs of major universities. To understand the increasingly important role of governing boards, we must examine their major responsibilities.

Appointing the President

Since the president is the central and normally the most powerful figure in the life of an institution, selection of the right man or woman is a critical matter. Faculty, administrative officers, students, alumni, and others will want a voice in the decision, but the choice—let there be no doubt about it—is a board responsibility. Often the various groups are united on the kind of leadership the college or university needs, but this is not always the case. Faculty will want a scholar who understands teaching and research; students may prefer someone who is sympathetic to their youth culture; administrative officers may want a captain to run a tight ship or, conversely, a nonadministrator who will leave the ship to them; some alumni will emphasize the value of an outgoing person who favors admitting the children of alumni, who recognizes the importance of winning football games, and who will increase the alumni fund. The responsibility of the trustees is to see the institution as a whole and to decide what kind of individual will on balance serve it best as president.

This is no easy task. The choice of the new president ought to depend on the needs of the particular institution at this particular point in its history. The analysis of institutional needs is not a job for the trustees alone. It should be the joint product of faculty and staff, alumni and students, but it is not likely to be undertaken, as we shall see later, unless the board demands it. Then follows the often protracted process of search and screening. Some small boards, particularly among community colleges, prefer to carry out the whole process by themselves, but most boards set up one or more committees of search and selection to which they delegate the work of developing a list of qualified candidates. The step-by-step process is discussed in detail in Chapter Eight. It is sufficient for our present purposes to reiterate that the trustees must play a decisive part in selecting a president. And no other decision will have quite so profound and far-reaching an impact on the institution.

Supporting the President

To say that the president is the board's man, or woman, is to imply a degree of emotional or ideological commitment to the trustees that most presidents would deny, especially those who have risen from the ranks of the faculty. Some would say that their interests and loyalty lie with the faculty; many would insist that their commitment is to the whole institution. But the trustees—not the faculty or the students—have hired the president, and they delegate to him or her the responsibility and authority for running the institution. Whatever else he or she may be, the president is their agent, and the trustees have a vested interest in, as well as a moral responsibility for, doing all they can to help their agent succeed. Academic communities have been likened to organized anarchies, and whatever the president does will please some and offend others. Every president will suffer criticism for not doing well what the critic insists should be done better. It is important for trustees to understand the president's role with its built-in conflicts and often unreasonable demands—important because the president will need the support and encouragement of the board. Where else can the president turn for friendly counsel and sometimes even for a place to blow off steam?

A wise board chairman can save a president from serious mistakes and even catastrophe by thoughtful and sensitive coaching. It may be a case of calling to the president's attention areas in which he is doing less well than he thinks and where more time and attention would correct the situation. Or it may be a case of recognizing that the president is simply not good at certain things— glad-handing the alumni or controlling departmental expenditures, for example—and pointing out that his administration needs to be buttressed by the addition of new staff, administrative reorganizations, or by a shift in priorities.

The nurture of presidents includes a concern for their physical and emotional well-being. Some board members, and particularly the chairman, should keep a watchful eye for signs of presidential exhaustion. The volume of work going through the president's office often precludes, or seems to the occupant to preclude, much in the way of relaxation. The board should insist in its own self-interest that the president take a yearly vacation as well as short holidays from time to time. Indeed, the board should insist that the president take a sabbatical leave every so often to restore institutional perspective and professional competence. Kauffman (1974) states the situation bluntly: "Given the substantial investment a governing board makes in finding a president, it is simply good management for the board to conserve this important resource. Leadership is a scarce and precious asset that should not be taken for granted" (p. 61).

It is extremely difficult, and sometimes quite impossible, for multicampus boards and boards of statewide systems to watch over all their chief executives. The board of governors of the University of California has nine different and geographically scattered institutions under its egis; the trustees of the State University of New York have seventy-three. Such boards can stand *in loco parentis* to the chancellor, president, or chief administrative officer of the system. But they must leave to that officer and to such local boards as may exist responsibility for looking after the welfare and effectiveness of the presidents of member colleges and universities. All presidents need help (though not all presidents want it!), and those are fortunate who have sympathetic and understanding boards.

Monitoring the President's Performance

Closely related to the board's role in providing nurture and support for the president is its responsibility to keep a constantly watchful eye on the quality and performance of the institution's administration. Is the administration efficient? How can it be improved? Colleges and universities are no different from hospitals, charitable organizations, social clubs, and businesses in lapsing from time to time into sloppy, careless, or inefficient habits. Sometimes the president is unaware of this situation because it has developed by imperceptible degrees; sometimes he or she knows that the business office, the counseling service, or the athletic department is poorly managed but is reluctant to take corrective steps because people would be hurt. Private but firm counseling of the president may be required.

Are the policies approved by the board being faithfully carried out? Educational policies are proposed and shaped in the often sharp and sometimes protracted debates among faculty, administration, students, alumni, and state education officers. They become official when finally adopted by the board, which then has the duty of making certain that they are honored. Strong-minded presidents have been known to follow their own inclinations regardless of the wishes of the trustees. The board may permit this as the wiser course or may decide that the issue is not important enough to merit confrontation; but it should know what is happening and be prepared, when the issue is one of real importance, to insist that its policies be followed.

In doing this, the trustees must be careful not to interfere with management. The line between making and carrying out policy is a fine one. The business and professional experience of individual trustees can often be used to great advantage by administrative officers. A trustee who is a physician, for example, might be very helpful with advice on setting up or reorganizing a college or university health service; bankers and businessmen have regularly been called upon to assist with the investment of capital funds. However, it should not be trustees who decide which faculty members receive tenure. That is a faculty and administrative decision. The board's role is to insist that there be clear institutional regulations regarding the conferring of tenure and that these be followed in every case. The board should approve an athletic policy for the institution; it should not get involved in the choice of the athletic director or football coach.

College and university presidents are public figures. At even the smallest and most private institutions the president makes decisions and takes actions that affect the lives of faculty and students, as well as administrative, clerical, and maintenance staff and that influence the response of parents, alumni, donors, and friends of the institution. Whether he or she likes it or not, the president's performance is judged, day in and day out, by those with whom he or she comes in contact. The trustees likewise make their own assessment of the quality of the president on the basis of what they hear from the various constituencies and what they observe at board meetings and through other channels. Many boards set aside time once a year for an informal or semiformal evaluation of the president, the results of which are discussed by the chairman with the president.

In recent years the trend has been to appoint presidents for fixed terms, and along with this has grown the practice—still the exception rather than the rule—of conducting a formal appraisal of the president's office or the president's performance. (The methods of this procedure are discussed in Chapter Eighteen.)

Whether the assessment is informal or formal, the president has every right to know the criteria by which he or she is to be judged, and the frequent failure of boards to be specific in setting forth their expectations is a serious flaw in our present system. Not only do presidents often not know what is expected of them but they are also too often judged on inconsistent or contradictory standards. One of the arguments for term appointments is that they give board and president the opportunity to review the situation and to decide whether circumstances have changed to such a degree that different criteria should be established for the president. Trustees think that they make clear to the presidents-elect what is needed and expected, but the presidents report that they are too often left in the dark (Nason, 1979).

Assessment may result in termination, either by request of the board or by mutual agreement that the president is not the right person for the job. Its major purpose and value, however, are not negative but constructive. Assessment provides a better perspective for both trustees and president, a fresh analysis of strengths and weaknesses, and an opportunity to reorder priorities of time and energy. It is an expression of the board's concern for the president and his or her success. It epitomizes the close cooperation and understanding that should exist between president and board.

Clarifying the Institution's Mission

Every college and university was created to serve one or more specific purposes: to provide an educated ministry in colonial days; to prepare citizens who could cope with the problems and prospects of a new democratic society; to train young people in the arts and skills necessary for an honest living; to safeguard the true faith; to train schoolteachers; to carry on research in science and technology; or—simply stated but not so simply achieved—to encourage young men and women to explore and develop their inherent potentialities. Over the years and under the pressure of changing circumstances, these original purposes or missions have frequently been modified. Locally centered institutions have become regional or national. Church-founded and controlled colleges have sought to break the dominance of the denominations and the limitation in clientele. Normal schools have become full-fledged institutions of arts and sciences. Teaching colleges aspire to become research-oriented universities. Sometimes these changes take place because of a sharp awareness of new social needs, sometimes because of a general institutional urge to improve its position in the academic pecking order.

There has been both loss and gain in the churning movement of institutional purpose. The drive for upward mobility has raised the level of postsecondary education in America. The zeal that spawned so many small denominational colleges in the nineteenth century was often accompanied by limited vision and woefully inadequate resources. The struggling institutions had to enlarge their scope to survive. But the marks that distinguished one college from another tended to disappear in the process. An unconscious process of homogenization set in, as some institutions sloughed off what made them distinct while others added new programs and services in the struggle for students and funds.

Someone must ask: What is the mission of this particular college or university? What makes it distinct from other institutions? What difference would it make—and to whom—if it ceased to exist? Does it serve a special clientele? Does it include subject matter not normally taught? Are its instructional methods different? Does it have unique facilities for instruction or for research?

Does it fill a real gap and meet real needs? "The first thing an institution needs to do to start on a conspicuously higher course," writes Greenleaf (1974, p. 25) "is to state clearly where it wants to go, whom it wants to serve, and how it expects those served directly, as well as society at large, to benefit from the service" (p. 22).

The formulation of a statement of mission is a joint enterprise involving trustees, faculty, and administration. In public institutions, legislators, the governor's office, and the state office or council of higher education may also have an important voice. In private colleges and universities alumni and donors will frequently have something to say. But faculty, deans, and presidents—the professionals of the academic world—must carry the chief burden of articulating a statement of mission. It is unlikely, however, that there will be a clear consensus on mission unless the trustees insist that a concise formulation be written. For the most part faculty members are not much concerned with the broader aspects of educational purpose; their attention is understandably focused on their own fields of teaching and research, and they become exercised over ultimate goals only when institutional purposes interfere with their work. Presidents and deans, who are concerned with the larger issues of education, are likely to be so preoccupied with the immediate problems of institutional life that they postpone consideration of what may be the more important but seemingly less urgent issues.

The board should not try to write such a statement of mission, but it should insist that administrative officers, faculty, and others do so. The board can then approve the statement, draft its own version for consideration by faculty and administration, or send it back for revision. Once agreement among the participating groups has been reached, the statement should be published for all to read. (If there is a stalemate, the board's decision should be final.) If the mission includes primary emphasis on teaching undergraduates, faculty can no longer demand extensive support for research and graduate programs. Students will be warned in advance what subjects will be taught and can pick their institutions accordingly. With changes in society the time may come when the mission of the college or university should change. Hence, the trustees should see that it receives periodic review.

Approving Long-Range Plans

Long-range plans are the strategies for achieving the institution's mission. As in the formulation of the mission itself, the responsibility of the board is not to draft the long-range plans but to insist that the administration do so.

We all make short-range plans—next week, next month, next year—and any sensibly managed organization will have projections for the near future of volume of business, income and expenditures, capital outlays, anticipated shortages, and the like. Important as these are, they are not enough. For some institutions the short run may be so critical that looking beyond immediate survival makes no sense. For most colleges and universities, however, the prospects are not so desperate. The short-run projections are essential for developing plans for staffing, for housing students, for balancing the budget, for focusing the development program, for making the case for appropriations from public funds. But long-range plans are equally important. They provide direction, vision, and the goals toward which the institution should be moving.

Consider the financial crunch that all colleges and universities, public and private, are experiencing. Is this a temporary phenomenon? Are there signs or portents on the social, economic, or political horizons to suggest that things will get better or worse? Given the present configuration of a particular institution's income and expenses, how will these change over the next five years? The next ten years? What forces besides inflation will affect both its income and outgo? What will the budget look like ten years from now? What steps will need to be taken in this long-range perspective to keep the institution viable? There may not be enough thumbs to plug all the holes in the dike. Certainly, without a constructive and forward-looking plan, the institution will face a losing battle.

Or take the enrollment problem. Where will the institution's students come from? What changes in numbers and character may be necessary? What long-term plan of action should be established? Should the size of the student body be permanently reduced? If not, what new sources of students should be explored? What new

methods of recruitment? What new programs or other induce-
ments should be considered?

It would be easy to multiply examples. The preparation of
plans is the business of the president and his or her administrative
team. If wise, they will involve faculty, students, and (more important for public than for private institutions) public officials. As
emphasized in Chapter Nine, it is the business of the governing
board to see that this is done, to approve the plans if they make
sense, and to negotiate the differences when faculty and administration disagree among themselves and when the trustees hold different views from both the president and the faculty.

Overseeing the Educational Program

As colleges and universities grew more complex and educational programs burgeoned, trustees turned over their original responsibility for the content of education to the president whom
they had chosen for his or her professional competence in this
sphere. In this century pressure from faculty, along with the proliferation of managerial responsibilities, brought about a further
transfer of authority for educational programs from president to
faculty. At least faculty have felt for a long time that, as experts,
they should have the dominant voice in deciding what should be
taught and that trustees should stay clear of what is not properly
their business. Conventional practice, at least in this century, has
assigned responsibility for finances and physical plant to the
trustees and reserved responsibility for the educational program to
the president and faculty.

This is nonsense. How can trustees be responsible for their
institutions if they abdicate responsibility for the goals of those
institutions? How can they make wise decisions about buildings and
grounds if they do not know what they are to be used for? Don't
they, for example, have to know how important a new computer
center is—does it take priority over a language lab or a student
union? By common consent the trustees must approve the budget.
Unless their approval is merely a rubber stamp on the president's
recommendations, their decisions will either be arbitrary and irresponsible or will be determined by their knowledge of the nature

and importance of the various educational programs. In the last analysis, the person who sets the budget shapes the program.

Viewed from another angle, final approval of the institution's mission and its long-range plans by the trustees largely determine the educational program. What should be the ratio, for example, of the institution's emphasis on teaching and research, on technology and pure science? Who decides whether a school of business administration or a department of classical archeology should be developed? Should the college concentrate on bright students with high Scholastic Aptitude Test scores or provide instruction for students of less academic ability? The programs of many public universities are mandated by charter or law, but in most states regents still have the authority to allocate programs to different campuses under their jurisdiction and to expand or contract (within available funds) the instructional programs and public services that the university offers. Community colleges—the most recent and fastest growing addition to the postsecondary educational family—are still seeking their most useful roles. The president of a community college may be the focal point of the various, and sometimes conflicting, demands of students, their parents, and members of the local sponsoring community. The president must cope with these demands as well as possible, but it is the board that must decide the college's direction, what new programs will be added, and what old ones, if any, abandoned.

Two cautions should be noted with regard to the board's responsibility for educational programs. First, while the board has the final authority, it should listen very carefully to the recommendations of the president. One can only repeat that the president was selected for his or her competence as a professional educator. Presidents are not infallible, and they sometimes barge off in the wrong directions. Most of them, however, know more about education in general and the institution in particular than does the average trustee or regent. Their actions should be supported unless they are clearly wrong. Second, trustees should not meddle with the curriculum. The courses to be taught and their content are the responsibility of the faculty. Trustees may decide for or against a department of music. Having decided for it, they should leave the decisions on what should be taught to the faculty. Chapter Ten offers more on this important subject.

Ensuring Financial Solvency

Since trustees hold the assets of colleges and universities in trust, they have always felt a special responsibility for the financial health of their institutions. In the private sector the founding trustees either gave the money themselves to start the college or university or assumed the personal responsibility for raising it. This created a direct concern among the trustees for the financial solvency of the fledgling college, and their successors have continued to feel that they must keep a close eye on its business operations. In the public sector trustees and regents are charged with the responsibility for the best use of the public funds appropriated for support of the institution. (See Chapters Fifteen and Sixteen for thoughtful discussions of these issues.)

In the long run, income must equal expenditure if the institution is to survive. Short-term deficits are sometimes preferable to the long-term damage done by sudden and drastic curtailments in personnel and programs. Bank loans or the use of capital funds such as endowment may bridge a temporary crisis. Sooner or later, however, a day of reckoning must come. Many faculty and some presidents who are sensitive to the hardships created by cutbacks are willing to let deficits continue either in the hope that some miracle will happen (a $5 million bequest) or with the conviction that the needs of the present outweigh those of future generations. The trustees must decide the relative claims of the present and the future. It is a responsibility that stems directly from their title.

When a budget is out of balance, the trustees must find ways to increase income or to reduce expenses or to do both. Retrenchment is never easy, nor will it ever be popular. One of the perennial problems of higher education is the pressure to add new programs, more staff, more equipment. Rarely is anything given up. The welfare of football players requires more expensive equipment and medical service every year, but special meals, it is argued, could not possibly be forgone. The proliferation of knowledge leads to new departments of instruction and research, but any suggestion that the institution cannot teach all subjects, must select carefully among them, and must abandon B or C when it adds X or Y provokes howls of outrage.

The president is sometimes caught in a merciless cross fire. He or she knows that retrenchment is necessary, that cutting a little bit here and a little bit there has limits, and that major surgery is the only solution. Some faculty and students will always argue that the administration itself is overstaffed and inefficient and that there is really no need for its insensitive and philistine program of curtailment. Other faculty, more realistic about the institution's plight, will agree that amputation is probably necessary but not in their fields or departments. Here the trustees can come to the support of the president, strengthening his or her hand, meeting perhaps with the most vocal dissidents, and in the end accepting public responsibility for insisting that expenditures be reduced to match income.

The other and more attractive path to follow is that of increasing income. Income cannot always be increased, at least not to a sufficient degree, but this alternative must be tried before the argument for retrenchment is proposed or at least along with such a proposal. Tuition and other charges to students can be raised, unless they are already as high as the market will bear or unless further increases would be inconsistent with the mission of the institution, as has been vigorously argued at the City University of New York. Further, one of the responsibilities of trustees, and it is an important one, is to raise money to help pay for the operations of the institution—to raise it by asking for contributions from individuals, corporations, foundations, and state governments. No trustee of a private college or university should consider himself or herself immune from the responsibility of fund raising. Private institutions cannot survive without donated funds, and every trustee should be prepared to give and to solicit money. For some the gift will have to be small, but it can still set an example for others. For some access to people with money will be limited, but that is no justification for failing to participate in fund-raising campaigns (see Chapter Fourteen).

For the trustee of a public college or university the situation is more equivocal. More and more public institutions are supplementing state appropriations with privately solicited funds. Although such funds are supplementary rather than central to the financial health of the institution, there is no reason why the public trustee or regent should not pitch in to aid the institution financially. No large sum of money is likely to be raised in this way unless the regents are known to approve of this form of fund raising and to take an active part in it. The members of some governing boards can be very influential with the governor and the state legislature, and there are times when that influence must be used. However, the growth of statewide systems, in part to prevent jockeying for funds by partisans of competing public institutions, limits the access of some trustees to the people who decide appropriations, determined and responsible boards can still work wonders.

One aspect of financial control involves the capital investment. In the American tradition, trustees have always had a special interest in and concern for the land and buildings that are the visible embodiment of the college or university. They constitute an aspect of the total enterprise with which the trustee who is a businessman can feel at home and an area where he or she can make a useful contribution. The practical sagacity and vision of many trustees have resulted in some of our most beautiful and even spectacular campuses. In addition, many an institution has profited from the involvement of practical-minded trustees who contribute their expertise and judgment in coping with problems of construction and maintenance. Furthermore, those who have been most interested and active in this area have frequently been most effective in campaigns for additional resources. There is some evidence, however, that trustees' concern for buildings and grounds may lead them to move beyond issues of general policy to areas of management. The dividing line is not always clear, but its importance should always be kept in mind.

Boards should also keep in mind the physical condition of grounds and buildings. In times of tight budgets it is tempting to make ends meet by deferring proper maintenance, but in the long pull this policy will be more costly to the institution. Here again the board has a responsibility to grasp the whole picture and properly to manage the institution's resources.

Preserving Institutional Independence

"Autonomy, in the sense of full self-governance," wrote the members of the Carnegie Commission on Higher Education (1973), "does not now exist for American higher education, nor has it existed for a very long time—if ever. Autonomy is limited by the law, by the necessary influences and controls that go along with financial support, and by public policy in areas of substantial public concern" (p. 17). And yet one of the great sources of strength for American colleges and universities, both public and private, has been their independence—more accurately, their relative independence—from outside control. Colleges and universities constitute a very special kind of organization or community, so important to the health of society that outside groups are constantly trying to exploit them and so vulnerable that only watchful and determined boards can protect them.

Simply put, one of the responsibilities of governing boards is to defend the institutions they govern—to defend their existence, their programs and operations, their right to manage their own affairs. One of the great contributions of the modern college or university is its role as a critic of society. It can perform this role only as long as it is protected from those who would silence its criticisms or twist them to serve some ulterior end. This is why academic freedom is so important, why boards of trustees must not permit outside groups or extremists within (such as the radical left during the turbulence of the sixties and early seventies) to muzzle the voices expressing unpopular positions. Colleges and universities pride themselves on teaching students to think for themselves. This cannot be done without a guarantee of academic freedom.

There are other pressures from the outside that make themselves felt on internal policies and management—pressures against which the trustees must take a resolute stand. Donors will sometimes try to attach unacceptable conditions to their gifts. Alumni will sometimes seek to change a college's or university's athletic policies. Legislators seek admission or scholarships for the sons and daughters of constituents. Governors attempt to place friends on the faculty or in administrative positions. Business interests may bring pressure to stop research in areas where they fear the results might be detrimental to their business. Trustees must be ever alert to these invasions of institutional autonomy.

The dual role of the trustees and regents of public colleges and universities presents them with subtle and acute dilemmas. As Perkins (1973) asks: "How does a regent act as an agent of the state and as a member of an autonomous organization at the same time? How does a regent conceive his role when he is appointed by the state to an office designed to protect the institution from the state itself?" (pp. 208–209). This problem is compounded when the regent is a member of a board that is responsible for more than one institution. He or she can defend the prerogatives of member institutions by defending the system against gubernatorial or legislative encroachments; but the same trustee must be impartial in judging the relative claims of Downstate U. and Upstate U.

Downstate and Upstate may have their local boards with limited and chiefly advisory powers. Presumably such boards will be sympathetic to the needs and opportunities of the local institution. They may have to do battle with the statewide board and its central administration, but it will be an uneven fight, with personal loyalty, conviction, and powers of persuasion pitted against state mandates and statewide perspectives. The preservation of the autonomy of the local institution in such a system has become difficult. It is one more example of the classic conflict between the best interests of the individual and the greatest good for the greatest number. With the relatively recent appearance of statewide coordinating and system governing boards we are still trying to work out the best formula for settling this conflict.

Enhancing the Public Image

By becoming a trustee, the individual publicly identifies himself or herself with the institution. This identification is important for the college or university, especially if the trustee is a man or woman respected in the community. And that is why governors appoint—some of the time at least—outstanding citizens to serve as regents, and why private colleges and universities are constantly seeking prominent individuals whose association will strengthen the institutions.

The public relations responsibility of trustees, however, stretches much farther than lending a name. It means active work on behalf of the institution—for example, interpreting the campus to the community at large and defending the institution against outside accusations and attacks. To fulfill this role trustees must educate themselves, or be educated by the president, about the institution—what it stands for, its mission, its programs, its problems, its future dreams. For a nation with over 3,000 postsecondary institutions and with a significant proportion (almost 50 percent) of high school graduates having some college experience, many Americans are still naive about what a university does and is. They attack the right of professors to be critical of society. They are outraged by a controversial speaker whom a student group has invited to the campus. They want the deans to tuck the boys and girls into bed each night (separate beds of course). The litany is endless. Most of the charges can be disposed of by appropriate administrative officials, but some spill over into the public press or become exaggerated rumors. Since the replies of college officials will be discounted as self-serving, this is the time for the trustee to speak up in defense of the institution and set the record straight. He or she can scotch the rumor better than anyone else. He or she can explain what lay behind some controversial policy and note that it was adopted by the board, not arbitrarily laid down by the president or dean. The trustee must know the facts, and that should not be difficult if there is constant communication and close cooperation between president and board.

Sometimes the trustee may have to defend a policy or action with which he or she does not agree. Trustees may argue as much as they like at board meetings and in private conferences with the president and staff. Indeed, they will not be doing their job if they do not raise questions, challenge decisions, debate over policies. But in public they should stand united with the institution and its programs. If the issue on which they differ is an important one of principle or if they hold such strong convictions that they cannot be comfortable with the majority decision, they should resign. Short of that, they must maintain a solid front.

Interpreting the Community to the Campus

Trustees also have a responsibility to enlarge the institution's vision by insisting that faculty and administration see their place in the framework of the larger world. Trustees, we noted at the beginning, hold the institution in trust. Their responsibility is to make certain that it is serving society in the best possible way.

Society, however, is always changing, while institutions tend to resist change. There is a kind of built-in parochialism in colleges and universities, such that left to themselves they would adjust slowly to new demands and new situations. In the nineteenth century the classical curriculum continued to dominate most educational programs long after the rise of science rendered the traditional pattern obsolete. In part this resistance to change is the result of inertia, since it is always easier to continue doing what one has always done than to venture into unknown territory. But it is also the result of the self-centeredness of most college and university campuses. Living as well as working together tends to isolate the members of the academic community. They become an ingroup that tends either to shut itself off from the outside world or to disparage that world as living by different (and inferior) values.

The result is that the forces producing long-term trends and changes in the larger world often go somewhat unnoticed. Or if not unnoticed, disregarded. The now famous Supreme Court decision of 1954 in *Brown* v. *Topeka Board of Education* foreshadowed many changes, but it took outside pressure in the 1960s to produce a significant increase in the number of blacks in our student bodies. Reference has already been made to the long-term implications of a primarily service-oriented postindustrial society, but there is as yet little reflection of what they portend for postsecondary education. Trustees bring different perspectives to the affairs of the institution. In the light of those perspectives they should ask uncomfortable questions that will keep the ultimate ends of education constantly in the forefront.

Serving as a Court of Appeal

There was a time when student discipline and faculty appointments and terminations were settled by faculty, deans, and the president. Before the Second World War it was rare for an internal dispute to be brought to the board for adjudication, and to have recourse to the courts was almost unheard of. Since then both boards and courts have become increasingly involved in the various issues that arise from our preoccupation with civil rights. Faculty claim discrimination or improper procedure if they are not promoted or given tenure or reappointed. Students or their parents challenge the right of the faculty and/or administration to expel students for disciplinary or academic reasons or to impose other penalties. In a litigious age the parties take their appeals to the boards or the courts or both.

Boards of trustees can and should insist that there be clearly established and publicized codes governing faculty status and student behavior, and these should include provisions for due process in all actions. Beyond this there is little that trustees can do but to insist that the agreed upon procedures be followed and to accept jurisdiction if settlement fails at an earlier stage. One hopes that, if the procedures are orderly and fair and if the administration acts with intelligence, most cases will be resolved before reaching the board. But when they do come to the board, the trustees must decide on the merits of the case. The president and deans may not always be right. If they are not, the board must be prepared to rule against them. If this happens very often, however, it may indicate that the time has come to look for a new president.

Assessing Board Performance

As we have seen, trustees play a central and important role in governing the institution and in determining its mission, goals, plans, and programs. They have a responsibility to evaluate the performance of the president, to assess the adequacy of the administration as a whole, to monitor the institution's progress toward agreed upon goals. They have also and finally a responsibility to assess their own contribution and performance. Indeed, the assessment of the president can be more gracefully conducted if it is made part of a review of the governance of the entire institution, the trustee role included. It sometimes develops that the cause of an institution's problems lies with the board, not the president.

Trustees ought to be asking themselves, what are our major responsibilities as trustees? This chapter attempts to answer that question. Perceptive trustees will recognize another question, namely, how well are we fulfilling our responsibilities? The self-examination needed to answer this question is the final trustee responsibility. Do we have the best possible board for this college or university? If not, why not? How can we bring about a change for the better? Are we spending our time on the right questions and issues? (Many boards, particularly those for public institutions, waste time on trivial items and routine matters when they should be discussing major issues.) Who prepares the agenda? Who schedules the meetings? Do we get the right information from the president at the right time before the meetings? Chapters Four to Six provide more detailed treatment of these issues.

There are various ways of going about this self-assessment. The chairman can take the initiative in setting aside some part of one or more regularly scheduled meetings for this kind of review. Or he can call a special meeting to be devoted entirely to the board's self-examination. The board can make use of the self-study materials prepared by the Association of Governing Boards in conjunction with or independent of the Board-Mentor Service. A special board committee can be appointed to examine the problem and make recommendations, or an outside consultant can be employed. Chapter Twenty outlines ways of doing this.

The board has no more right to be above assessment of its performance than the president or any other part of the organization. If improvement can be made, let it begin with the governing board, which thereby will set an example to the rest of the institution.

4

Robert L. Gale

Selecting and Deploying Trustees

There are two vital ingredients in building a strong board of trustees—selecting good people and educating them early and well. No amount of orientation or stimulation can make an outstanding board out of a group of poorly selected persons. Conversely, outstanding prospects may be wasted if they are not properly motivated. This chapter offers suggestions on how to identify, properly enlist, and effectively deploy board members. Emphasis is placed on sound trustee orientation.

In selection of board members, there are very great differences between public and private (or independent) institutions. Private boards have the advantage of being able to select their own members, while the members of public boards are politically appointed or elected. Once board members have been selected, however, the problems of orientation and effective early deployment differ only slightly for private and public boards.

In the private sector, the importance of involving the president in the selection process cannot be overemphasized, and the same is true for the "recommendation" process in the public sector. A board need not be made up of the president's friends, but it should include the kinds of people who can contribute significantly to the well-being of the institution and are compatible with the chief executive.

The mission, direction, and needs of the institution should influence trustee selection. These are concerns that the president and board should examine together. The board and president of a private institution, once they agree on the fundamentals of their joint enterprise, can move to the nominating committee stage, and begin consideration of board composition. In so doing they may proceed in four steps: (1) decide what specific skills are needed on the board, (2) establish a search-and-recruit procedure, (3) establish an orientation procedure, and (4) establish a procedure for terminating service.

Selecting Public Sector Trustees

The National Commission on College and University Trustee Selection, established under the auspices of the Association of Governing Boards of Universities and Colleges (AGB), has set out to convince governors, legislators, and other appointing bodies of the importance of choosing the best possible citizens for the boards within their jurisdiction. It is studying standards for and methods of selecting the right people, along with the issue of whether boards of public institutions should identify their membership needs and make these known to appointing authorities.

How can more objectivity be brought into the selection process than is often found in the public sector? Procedures for appointment or election differ from state to state and even within individual states for different categories of postsecondary institutions. Where the governor makes appointments, a board can seek appropriate channels or individuals who can present to the governor information on the skills that are needed. Some governors may welcome lists of nominees. Where boards are elected, incumbent trustees might make known the qualities and areas of expertise that are needed by those who intend to run for election.

That a problem does exist was pointed up in a 1973 AGB

survey of board chairmen. More than two thirds of the 800 respondents felt that appointive authorities do not tend to place the ablest persons on boards of public institutions. Three quarters of the respondents agreed that "there is an urgent need for a set of guidelines to assist state authorities in identifying and placing the most able people on boards" (Association of Governing Boards of Universities and Colleges, 1973, p. 1). Moreover, a survey revealed a conspicuous gap between variables that *should be* influential in trustee selection and variables that *are* influential. For example, 73 percent of the respondents agreed that leadership skills *should be* an important criterion for trustee selection while only 35 percent reported that leadership skill *is,* in fact, an important criterion (Davis and Batchelor, 1974).

Selecting Private Sector Trustees

As pointed out in the proposal establishing the AGB National Commission on College and University Trustee Selection, the self-perpetuating boards of the some 1,600 independent colleges and universities in the United States are able to control their own appointment procedures. In practice, however, another picture emerges. Many boards do thoughtfully consider the mix of skills and backgrounds needed among trustees; many other boards do not. Some boards have effective and conscientious nominating committees; many others do not. Some boards give total responsibility for trustee selection to the president; many others give the chief executive no responsibility at all. It is also noteworthy that although private institutions tend to have the largest boards, their membership is least diverse as measured by various demographic characteristics. Apparently custom and tradition often prevail over reason and preclude formal policies for effective trustee selection. Hence, the AGB National Commission will also recommend methods and procedures for selecting the best possible people for private boards.

The Nominating Committee. As one of the most vital of the standing committees, the nominating committee should have a clear statement of purpose in the bylaws or other policy document. The first step is to determine the composition of the board in terms of skills, background, residence, age, sex, and ethnic and other factors. The areas that need to be covered by new board members will then become apparent. Nominees should be welcomed from all the institution's key publics, with active solicitation by the committee for candidates from other board members. Nominating committee members should face up to the fact, however, that in practice most candidates will inevitably be identified by the committee itself.

The committee should check the credentials of candidates, cultivate good prospects, and, for those selected to join the board, issue the invitation in an appropriate fashion. It has become common in recent years for the nominating committee to assure the orientation of new members. Nominating committees are usually charged with recommending board officers and reviewing trustees for reelection. They may also recommend committee assignments.

It is vital that the chairman of the nominating committee be one of the most respected, dedicated, and thoughtful board members. No other standing committee is more important to the long-range development and viability of the board. Very often, the chairman's competence will be the decisive factor affecting the future composition of the board. The committee's size should be small, with membership made up of those who have demonstrated distinctive service to their institution and who have accessibility to good prospects.

Even a good nominating committee with well-defined duties will not operate satisfactorily unless a clear set of written practices is adopted. These should include: (1) the minimum number of meetings to be held each year; (2) the process by which nominees are solicited; (3) the method of checking qualifications; (4) the way in which recommendations are brought to the full board; and (5) the process by which newly elected board members are oriented. Recommendations for board officers and perhaps committee assignments are usually determined in consultation with the chairman and president and forwarded along with the names of new nominees to the board.

The committee should meet each time the full board meets, even when vacancies do not exist, to expand the pool of potential nominees and to keep it current. If an unexpected vacancy occurs, or if an unusually capable person is identified for possible nomination, the committee should be prepared to call a special meeting. The solicitation of nominees from the various constituencies of the institution should also be formalized. This process will vary from institution to institution, but at least once a year key groups might be encouraged to make suggestions. Because the committee must be prepared to find the majority of the prospective candidates itself, however, careful planning is necessary to ensure an adequate list of top-notch persons.

In the private sector, approximately 3,000 board seats are unfilled at any given moment (Nelson and Turk, 1974). This large number of vacancies may result in part from confusion about the most effective procedures to identify candidates best suited to the board's needs. Methods of checking on the qualifications of potential board members should parallel those used by corporate management in considering prospective high-level employees. In particular, care should be taken to ascertain how candidates have performed on other volunteer boards.

Recommendations for election to the board should never be presented at a board meeting without prior notification to all trustees. Candidates' names, with biographical information, should be supplied in advance of the board meeting, when the meeting's agenda and supporting materials are mailed. If nominating committees are properly charged with the additional duty of orienting new trustees (with staff support), a formalized procedure should be in place.

Board Composition. Board composition should be viewed in two separate dimensions: first, what we usually call diversity, that is, such personal characteristics as age, sex, ethnic and geographic background, and alumni status; second, the individual talents or professional background that a board needs for good balance.

A major question for a board to ask itself is: Are we a local, regional, or national institution? For a small college that gets the lion's share of its students and financial support from a limited area, it makes little sense to try to achieve a wide geographic representation on its board. However, a regional or national college or university should recruit more broadly.

There seems to be universal agreement on the need to continue and expand efforts to recruit women and minorities. The 1977 AGB board composition survey shows gains for both, especially minorities. Board membership for minorities grew from 1 percent to 7 percent over a ten-year period as compared with an increase of only 13 to 15 percent for women. The number of trustees over fifty years of age is still high—two out of three, down from three out of four in the previous survey. Only one in ten is under forty years of age (compared with one in twenty reported in 1968, however).

The first thing most boards and administrators want and need among their members is the ability to give and to get money. Close behind is the ability to deal effectively with the money raised, whether from tuition, endowment income, gifts, or government grants. These two talents are not always found in the same person, however. Another characteristic that a board should find among some of its members is an intimate knowledge of higher education. The obvious source for this type of trustee is the faculty or administration of another institution.

Some board members fear that placing a president of another institution on the board will cause difficulties for their own president, but this is unlikely. On the contrary, a president as board member can be very helpful to the institution's president because he or she will often raise issues that should be brought out but that the institution's president may hesitate to raise. It is not usually desirable, however, for a past president of the same institution to be made a trustee lest his or her objectivity as a board member be affected. This point also argues against selection of a president from another institution that competes for the same students.

Some board members should be knowledgeable in marketing—a word we hardly dared use in reference to education just a few years ago. Today's institutions must be able to determine their markets and use sound marketing principles for the benefit of potential students and potential donors. Once the market is determined, the college or university must be able to reach it effectively. In admissions marketing—finding the right students for a given institution—ethnic diversity on the board can be of considerable help in recruiting a varied student body. If an institution has a natural Hispanic constituency, for example, Spanish-surnamed board members can help to relate the institution's capabilities to the constituency's needs.

With the present-day involvement of local, state and federal government in both the public and private sectors, it is good to have a few people who know their way around the state capital and Washington, D.C. And, because of the escalation in the number of lawsuits brought against institutions and their governing boards in recent years, legal expertise is a desirable board attribute. Trustees who are attorneys should not, however, serve as institutional counsel, with or without remuneration. Finally, it is an excellent idea to recruit members who have expertise in real estate and physical plant management. The plant may be the institution's biggest single asset, and a good board should have the competence to protect it.

Faculty and Students on Boards. The pressure for direct board membership of faculty and students has recently diminished, but some institutions are still considering such a policy in spite of what most students of governance feel is an unresolvable conflict of interest. A faculty member from another institution, however, can supply useful perspectives without creating such a situation. Recently graduated alumni can also bring important points of view to bear on board deliberations.

In dealing with the question of board composition, the Carnegie Commission on Higher Education (1973) had this to say: "Board membership should reflect the different age, sex, and racial groups that are involved in the concerns of the institutions. Faculty members from other institutions and young alumni should be considered for board memberships" (p. 35). Another approach is to involve faculty and students on board committees, where the real work of the board should be done. Often such committee membership provides more voice and influence than full trusteeship. (See Chapter Eleven for additional perspectives on this issue.)

Board Profile. A worthwhile exercise is to try to put down on paper a profile of the board's current membership. This will show where the board is strong, where it is adequate, and where it is weak. The format for a typical profile is shown in Figure 1.

Identifying Prospects. If the board profile shows that existing needs are fairly well covered, a further question might be whether there is a new category of person who should be considered. For

Categories	Present Membership 19__	Possible Vacancies			
		198X	198Y	198Z	Total
Age					
70 and over					
60-69					
50-59					
40-49					
30-39					
Under 30					
Sex					
Female					
Male					
Race					
Black					
Other					
Minority					
White					
Occupation					
Accounting					
Advertising					
Banking					
Business					
Education					
Government					
Law					
Marketing					
Medicine/					
Dental/Health					
Nonprofit					
Religion					
Retired					
Other					
(Specify)					

Figure 1. Board Profile for Mythical National College, Winnetka, Illinois

example, is there reason to think that money could be raised with help in New York, or Chicago, or Dallas? Would it be helpful to have someone from such an area on the board? Could the board use a person who is knowledgeable about athletic programs? Or medical programs?

Does the board depend too heavily on alumni? Because they have a built-in interest, alumni and parents tend to be overre-

Categories	Present Membership 19___	Possible Vacancies			
		198X	198Y	198Z	Total
Geographical Distribution					
Winnetka					
Chicago Area					
Milwaukee					
New York					
Midwest					
East					
West					
South					
College Relationship					
Alumni					
Parents					
Other					
Financial Position					
Independent					
Salaried					
Other					
Church Affiliation (if church related)					
Length of Service					
Over 10 years					
5-10 years					
2-5 years					
1 year or less					

Figure 1. Board Profile for Mythical National College, Winnetka, Illinois (continued)

cruited. Church-related institutions naturally consider church leaders as possible trustees, but every such board needs to recruit outside its own religious community and include members of other faiths. The local community also presents fertile ground for possible nominees because they are likely to know about the institution and its value to the community.

Be wary of choosing someone who would simply like to add

the distinction of trusteeship to his or her vita. Instead, try to determine how the person stands in the community, in his or her business or professional field. Is this person a leader or a coming leader?

Generally speaking, it is not advisable to try to recruit someone who has already reached the top of the career ladder. Even if such a person accepts the invitation, he or she is likely to be too busy to contribute. It is better to look for persons who are on their way up and who are willing to work. A valuable talent for nominating committee members is the knack for identifying "comers," those who are moving up rapidly. Such persons, committed to the institution before they reach the top, become investments in the future.

The overcommitted person often proves a particular disappointment. Again and again the complaint is heard, "So-and-so was on four boards, so we were sure he would be good. But when he got on our board, he didn't do anything." My response: "If you had called the executives of those other four boards, you would have found that the reason he could take on a fifth board was that he wasn't doing anything on theirs." The time to find that out is *before* an invitation is offered. Check volunteer references, just as if the chief executive were being selected.

Because the need to raise money is so central to the problem of most private institutions today, it might be well to close this section with a quote from Edward G. Wilson (1979), long-time chairman of the Earlham College board and secretary of the AGB board: "Trustees must have deep emotional commitment to the institution to guarantee fund-raising success. Thought must be given to financial power in selecting trustees, but take a man or woman who knows what a commitment is rather than a rich person without commitment" (p. 1).

Cultivating Prospects. Once a prospective board member has been identified, how do you approach him or her? The first thing to do is to determine whether the prospect is well-enough acquainted with your institution to be invited to become a trustee immediately, or whether additional time and cultivation are necessary. If the latter is the case, a good approach is to assign an active board member, if possible an acquaintance of the prospect, to familiarize him or her with the school. Even board members who are not at home in fund raising or other areas are nearly always happy to do this kind of job. Cultivation can involve many things, including taking prospects to lunch with the president, inviting them to campus events, and touring the campus.

When it comes time for the formal invitation, don't make the mistake of being too casual. Dependence on the telephone or a letter may risk loss of a good prospect. Make a personal call and use the best team that can be put together—perhaps the president and board chairman, or the president together with a board member who is a friend or business associate of the prospective trustee.

In addition, only in a somewhat formalized setting can it be made clear that something more is wanted from the person than another name on the letterhead. If a false impression is given, subsequent assignments for committee work or requests for giving or fund raising may cause the new recruit to feel that he or she was misled: "That isn't what I was told when I was invited to join the board." A simple and effective way to minimize misunderstanding is to give the prospective board members a written statement of what is expected of the board and its trustees. Every board should develop its own document, supplemented with a few selected publications (see Resource E). Each new member should be sought for a reason: "We need you because. . . ."

Orienting New Trustees

Whether the board is public or private, a well-conducted orientation process is essential. Once new board members have been made aware that there are defined responsibilities attached to their trusteeship, they must then be shown how to go about discharging these responsibilities. Too often a good person spends two or three years on a board without ever really coming to grips with what is going on. Such a waste of time and talent cannot be tolerated in this period of challenge for postsecondary education.

Orientation should normally be the province of the nominating or membership committee in a private institution and of the orientation committee in a public institution. The committee need not perform the orientation but should oversee it. An officer of the college may be the best person to coordinate the job, with the aid of appropriate materials and one or more trustees, including the president. Avoid overloading new trustees with literature. Provide something that looks like the *Encyclopaedia Britannica* and new board members not only won't read it, they may turn and run. (See Chapter Six for suggestions.)

The new trustee should be helped to become familiar with the campus as soon as possible. An orientation session in conjunction with the first board meeting is a practical possibility. At minimum, the president, the board chairman, and the chairman of the nominating or orientation committee can conduct a tour of the campus that includes meetings with student and faculty leaders. A few institutions have a trustee-in-residence program, open to all trustees, new and old, but with emphasis placed on the new trustee, who is required to stay overnight on campus sometime in the first six months of his or her tenure. This orientation should include spending a night in a student residence and meeting with students, faculty, and key administrators.

A technique that some boards use for orientation is the "buddy system" whereby each new member of the board is assigned to a trustee who knows the ropes, can answer questions, introduce other members, go over the agenda of the upcoming meeting, serve as campus guide, and generally help break the ice and encourage participation.

Another very useful experience for new trustees is to get together with other new trustees at one of AGB's scheduled seminars. They might also be urged from time to time to attend AGB's National Conference on Trusteeship in the spring or National Trustee Workshop in the fall. Here they can get counsel from veteran trustees, raise questions, and talk things over, as well as be exposed to current issues in education.

Since new trustees are alike only in their newness, however, orientation programs should be personalized as much as possible to take advantage of their unique interests, whether vocational or avocational.

Finally, new board members should be encouraged to read the regular AGB publications: *News Notes,* a monthly newsletter; and *Reports,* a bimonthly journal. A subscription to the *Chronicle of*

Higher Education will also help them to keep abreast of general issues in higher education, as will education articles in newspapers and newsmagazines.

Deploying New Trustees

New trustees, excited about being on a college's board, may experience a sense of anticlimax if they find themselves with nothing to do. A good solution is to assign new members immediately to active committees. An ideal assignment might be an ad hoc committee that has just been organized to tackle a problem on a six-month or one-year basis.

If such a committee is not currently at work, it may be wise to take a good look at the new recruit before assignment to one of the standing committees. The obvious choice may be the wrong choice. For example, bankers almost inevitably get ticketed for the finance committee. They may belong there eventually, but it is often better to start them out on the academic affairs or student affairs committee where they will get a sense of what the institution is about and receive some new stimulation. Once the committee assignment has been made, the committee chairman and the staff member assigned to the committee should be alerted to see that the new recruit is quickly involved. Generally, some task needs to be done. The staff member should give the new trustee a briefing on the committee's past and current activities so that he or she feels confident to participate in discussions more quickly.

Since private college boards tend to meet less frequently than the boards of public institutions, it is especially important to do something to keep in touch with new trustees. A good idea is for the president or chairman, or both, to talk with each new trustee on the phone or over lunch after a few months. Time should be found to tell the new member what is going on and to listen to questions that he or she has about the institution or the role of trustee. This is also a good time to do a little sounding out. A new trustee should not be pigeonholed on the basis of insufficient information; additional areas of interest may emerge from better acquaintance. If new persons are given a chance to volunteer for something, a pleasant surprise may occur.

Because board members and the chief executive have limited time, capable staff should be enlisted to help cultivate trustees on appropriate policy questions in their areas of responsibility. Once new trustees have become somewhat acclimated, it may be helpful if they complete the trustee audit found in Resource A of this volume.

Solving Special Problems

Finally, let us turn briefly to some special problems in building and maintaining a strong and effective board.

Church-Related Colleges. A church-related institution may have a problem if its board has too few or no lay members. One way to involve more lay persons is through an institutional advisory committee. The president and one or more trustees should work closely with such a committee, so that the members feel that what they are doing will have some impact on policy, even though they have no legal authority. Such an advisory committee can make a real contribution if given a clear purpose, good membership, staff support, and a sense of genuine importance (also see Chapter Five).

On a governing board in which the lay members feel themselves outnumbered by the members of the religious community, they may need some encouragement before they will voice their views. If the president and board chairman help the lay trustees to feel that it is their institution too, the trustees will join more fully in discussions and become more active. When a fixed percentage of religious community trustees is required by policy, it is usually possible to increase the overall size of the board so that enough lay members can be recruited to perform essential tasks, including fund raising and public relations (provided they are meaningfully involved in other areas of board responsibility as well).

Dealing with Weak Trustees. One of the most difficult problems for many boards has been that of weeding out people who have lost their effectiveness or who perhaps never should have been asked to serve in the first place. One solution is to have a chairman who is strong enough to ask such a person to step down. A difficult but necessary conversation may be opened with something like, "Apparently your other interests have kept you from being more involved with the college." Sometimes the result is that an inactive trustee is galvanized into useful activity. Another may welcome the chance to submit a resignation.

Age and term limitations are sometimes easier solutions, though they involve the risk of losing good members. A mandatory retirement age of, say, seventy-two, coupled with a limit of three consecutive three-year terms, can be provided in the bylaws. When particularly effective members come to the end of their final term, they can be told that they will be reelected to the board after a year's absence. Even this creates some risk of losing a good person, since the chairman or nominating committee of another board may "pirate" a trustee on "sabbatical."

Rewarding Outstanding Trustees. Although trustees do not expect recognition for unusual effort on behalf of their institutions, certain courtesies to them are often overlooked. At minimum, a board could be recognized through a well-done brochure that provides a picture and biographical sketch of each trustee, including terms of office and any committee assignments. Reviewed annually, it can also be an effective aid to public relations or development activities.

There is also place for an occasional award, plaque, gavel, or testimonial dinner. These should be provided infrequently, and always from the perspective of recognizing the contribution of the board itself first and of a particular trustee only secondarily. The danger lies in overlooking someone who should not be overlooked; thus the need for a sense of proportion and propriety. Unusual investments of time should be recognized as much as monetary contributions or solicitation.

Recognition in the form of a board resolution may also be appropriate, used sparingly. Outstanding trustees can also be saluted in a dignified way through announcements at institutional functions. An annual award from the board of trustees might be established for the person or persons who meet specified criteria—an administrator, faculty member, student, or trustee who demonstrates unusual initiative. The nominating committee can consider other ideas that are tasteful and timely.

What does one finally look for in a good board member?

Perhaps the most important ingredients are intelligence, good judgment, and the ability to ask the right questions. Persons possessing these qualities, fortified with an effective orientation program, will become useful and productive trustees. Also keep in mind that the more experienced trustees can profit from occasional redeployment of their abilities, interest, and energies through new assignments and participation in special activities outside regular board business. An alert chief executive and board chairman, together with the chairman of the nominating committee in the case of an independent institution, can accomplish a great deal. Good strategy coupled with patience and time will build an effective governing board.

5

Richard T. Ingram

Organizing the Board

The theme of this chapter is that the behavior of a governing board is in large part a function of how it is organized. The manner in which trustees choose to structure themselves for the purpose of meeting their roles and responsibilities is second in importance only to their individual competencies, their awareness of their duties and obligations, and the quality of their relationship with the president or chancellor. Assuming these three elements are firmly in place, what characterizes the internal organization of an effective board?

If boards are to do more than satisfy a legal requirement that called for their invention in the first place, if they are to provide more than what Greenleaf (1974, p. 12) calls "the cover of legitimacy," they should review their organization on a periodic basis. A well-structured board can enhance the use of limited trustee (and administrator) time and energy, help ensure that the board is dealing with the really significant matters confronting the institution, and provide what psychologists call a healthy self-concept. It is a happy observation that in recent years chief executives, together with their trustees, have developed a sense of urgency in their search for ideas to improve the organization of their boards.

Every organization is less a structure than a set of human relationships. It manifests many human qualities, including frustration, benevolence, vindictiveness, competence, pride, defensiveness, aggression, even joy. Although it is subject to the same strengths and frailties as its membership, a board of trustees is more than the sum of its individual parts. It assumes a distinctive character, a personality of its own that can range from resourceful and enterprising to listless or timid.

Moving a cemetery can be easier than moving an organization from one style of conducting business to another. Change can cause insecurity. Nevertheless, handled intelligently and with patience by the chief executive and a few highly respected and influential trustees, a board can come to perform miracles. If a number of the right leaders identify a problem, combine their influence, and decide what should be done, the seeds of a new organization can be planted and cultivated. Some generic principles of board organization are offered in this chapter to serve as a basis for comparing large and small institutions, as well as public and private ones.

Factors Influencing Board Organization

The diversity of institutions of higher education serves to remind us that our origins, customs, and traditions greatly influence what we have become. For example, the governing board of seven or nine trustees that serves a public community college and has a history of meeting at least once each month as a committee of the whole may be hesitant to adopt a committee structure and reduce the frequency of its board meetings even though the college's crucial period of expansion and growth may have passed. The eighty-member board of a large, prominent private university may be reluctant to accept the suggestion that it is too unwieldy to do its job properly and that it has delegated too many powers to a small executive committee. After all, it is difficult to argue with success when money is flowing in. It is difficult to argue with custom and tradition even if the arguments for organizational change are sound or a new set of institutional realities are present.

The size of a board also helps to determine the way it is

organized. Of course, it is not easy to change the size of a public college or university board when a constitutional or statutory provision is involved. But in the private sector there is flexibility for expansion or contraction should a change be considered desirable. Although there may be no such thing as an optimum number of trustees, the size of a board will determine the limits of its ability to improve its organization. More opportunities are present for larger boards of, say, twenty-one to thirty-five trustees than can be expected for boards of seven to nine trustees. To some extent the composition of a board's membership also influences internal structure. A national board means fewer, longer meetings and a greater dependence on an executive committee or other standing committees. A local board will likely meet more often (sometimes too often) and have briefer sessions with less dependence on committees, especially on an executive committee.

The frequency and duration of meetings also affect board structure. A board that meets only four times a year will depend more on a committee structure than will a board that meets once a month. The attitudes of the chief executive and the board chairman can likewise affect structure. A president who has held his or her position for many years will be less apt to recommend or to accept changes, and the same is true of the veteran board chairman. By the same token, these two individuals have great potential to change the shape of the board if they wish to exercise it. Finally, the willingness of individual trustees to assume positions of leadership affects board organization. A committee structure is heavily dependent on persons of competence and dedication who are enthusiastic about assuming chairmanships.

Indicators of Health

The relative health of a board's organizational structure depends on many interdependent factors. The following list can provide the basis for a checkup:

1. *Attendance:* Is it consistently good? What has been the record for the past two years?
2. *Meetings:* Are agendas stimulating, with emphasis kept on

genuine policy issues rather than on reports by administrators? Is routine business handled early and efficiently? Does everyone read the supporting material that accompanies the agenda? Is use of Robert's *Rules of Order* required too often? Are there too many major "surprises"? Do trustees leave the board room with positive feelings of achievement and personal satisfaction?

3. *Quality of Participation:* Does everyone contribute to discussions? Do one or two trustees dominate or consistently prevail in actions taken? Is opinion on issues informed? Are views aired in a spirit of candor, openness, and mutual respect?

4. *Major Decisions:* Are important decisions reserved for the full board rather than a small "inner board"? Do the trustees believe they are often asked to approve decisions already made or implemented by the administration? Is there evidence that all alternatives have been fully considered by both administrators and the appropriate board committee? Are reports and recommendations for action consistently convincing? Does the board have a good record for steering clear of purely administrative matters?

5. *Leadership:* Is there reasonable turnover among the trustees, particularly in officerships and committee chairmanships? Are the best possible trustees asked to lead without unreasonable deference to seniority? Is "automatic" succession avoided?

6. *Committees:* Are standing committees adequately staffed and functioning? Is committee membership occasionally changed to allow trustee exposure to new information and issues? Are charges to each committee explicit? Given the board's size and the array of its responsibilities, are the number and type of committees adequate? Are ad hoc committees given specific charges and deadlines to meet assignments after which time they dissolve?

7. *Bylaws:* When were the bylaws last revised in any significant way? Are they a hodgepodge of amendments? Does the board sometimes violate its own bylaw provisions? Do they contain some of the new provisions urged by attorneys?

Change strictly for change's sake is never desirable. But complacency is equally undesirable. Occasionally there are advantages to altering an organization's structure even when the board and the administration are pleased with their relationship and their ability to cope with institutional business. Even minor restructuring can afford certain opportunities for renewal and growth both for individual trustees and the board as a whole. In any event, the board and the chief executive need to know that their organization is sound. Often the process of review by the board or a board committee can turn out to be as important as any ensuing surgery.

Importance of Bylaws

Few institutional documents are more important and less appreciated than the bylaws of the board of trustees. Because they do not read like a good novel it is easy to neglect them. In substance they range from outstanding to inadequate. Poorly conceived, poorly written bylaws are potentially harmful, and sound but poorly implemented bylaws are not much better. The wise chief executive and board will view this legal document as an opportunity to strengthen the board's organization and performance and use it to correct structural weaknesses, initiate a meaningful process for trustee involvement, and establish a sense of purpose in areas where the trustees are unclear about their role. Significant bylaw revisions usually occur following the installation of a new president or chancellor.

The organization of the board is a highly important function of the bylaws. While the best bylaws are simple and flexible they should be explicit with regard to the responsibilities of the board and the chief executive. Committees also should be given rather explicit definition. Need for additional policy clarification can be covered in a board "policy manual" or separate board document.

Resource C of this book contains a complete set of bylaws for independent colleges developed by the Association of Governing Boards of Universities and Colleges (AGB). Several of its provisions could be useful to tax-supported institutions as well, even though state laws vary widely. These bylaws provide a useful frame of reference for discussion and could be adapted to particular institutional circumstances and needs. Included are suggested provisions pertaining to conflict of interest and disclosure, antidiscrimination, and indemnification. The president is presented as an ex officio, nonvoting member of the board and all its committees except the audit committee. Further, the bylaws require annual review of their provisions.

An additional reference may be useful in clarifying the board's roles and responsibilities at an early stage in the bylaws. The following excerpt is adapted from a recently revised document of Saint Edward's University in Austin, Texas.

Board of Trustees

The Board of Trustees shall have and exercise the corporate powers prescribed by the laws of [this] state. The essential function of the Board shall be policy making, the assurance of sound management, and active participation in the provision of necessary funds. The Board has ultimate responsibility to determine general, educational, financial, and related policies deemed necessary for the administration and development of [the] University in accordance with its stated purposes and goals. The Board shall, but without limitation:

1. Elect a president who shall be the chief executive officer of [the] University and chief staff officer of the Board of Trustees.
2. Consider plans for and participate actively in obtaining funds for budgetary, special program, physical development, maintenance, and endowment purposes.
3. Determine, review, and evaluate the aims, programs, and functions of the University consistent with the spirit and intent of the sponsoring charter.
4. Approve the addition or deletion of a specific degree or degree program and any changes which alter the nature of the basic curriculum design and/or university-wide degree requirements.
5. Approve policies and procedures regarding appointment, promotion, tenure, and dismissal of faculty members and policies related to terms and conditions of employment, salary, and fringe benefit policies and schedules for all staff officers, faculty, staff, and [other] employees.
6. Make the final decision on granting of tenure to a faculty member giving due consideration to the recom-

mendations of the divisional committee, the chief academic officer, and the president.

7. Serve as the court of appeal in the case of dismissal of a tenured faculty member.
8. Authorize the award of all earned degrees upon recommendation of the faculty.
9. Authorize the award of all honorary degrees.
10. Approve policies and procedures related to the instruction, extracurricular activities, [and] campus and residential life of students.
11. Determine and oversee policies and procedures in managing all business affairs of the University.
12. Authorize the acquisition, management, and disposition of all property and physical facilities, having due regard for the corporate purpose, including the construction, renovation, and upkeep of the physical plant.
13. Seek ways and means to become acquainted with all facets of the University and become familiar with forces, issues, and concerns about independent, church-related and private (proprietary and/or nonproprietary) institutions of higher education, whether church related or nonsectarian.
14. Receive gifts or bequests of land, buildings, bonds, stocks, monies, endowments, annuities, and other devices and invest endowment and annuity funds as policies and donor intent determine.
15. Enter into, make, perform, and carry out contracts of every kind for any lawful purpose with any person, firm, association, or corporation in the furtherance of the purposes of the corporation.
16. Appoint auditors and require an independent yearly audit of financial accounts, records, and resources by a certified public accountant and authorize the preparation of an annual report of the same.
17. Delegate any of the above to the Executive Committee, any standing committee, or any ad hoc committee.

Board Committees

Given the range of board responsibilities, there is much to be said for the use of committees. There may be a kind of self-delusion attached even to a small board's reluctance to adopt a committee system that is well defined and adequately staffed. A board's need for information is too specialized to expect all trustees to be experts on all policy issues. There is no perfect committee system. But there is widespread agreement concerning the array of board functions that somehow must be covered. The size of the board will largely dictate what is possible and what is not; a few committees may have to function with one or two subcommittees to get the job done.

The AGB model bylaws in Resource C cover ten separate committees. Even large boards may have difficulty accepting this number, but it should be remembered that all committee members need not be trustees. An efficient committee structure will make room for expertise from outside the board itself, including that of student and faculty leaders. Although trustees should outnumber outsiders on each standing committee, with a trustee as chairman, such committees provide a splendid opportunity to involve carefully selected members of the campus and community in the work of the board and also to identify potential new trustees.

Executive Committee. A few boards that have long practiced a committee system avoid the use of an executive committee either because at one time it had usurped the prerogatives and responsibilities of the full board or because it became useless. Theoretically, this committee holds most of the powers of the board when it is not in session and exercises them in emergencies. In this role it proved valuable for many institutions during the period of student unrest in the 1960s. But the executive committee should now be conceived in new terms: as a sounding device for new or controversial ideas and as an instrument to engage trustees in institutional planning. Many special issues that arise can be better considered by executive than ad hoc committees.

The board chairman should normally serve as chairman of the executive committee, with membership consisting of the other board officers and committee chairmen. It is this bringing together of the most knowledgeable board leaders that gives the executive committee its unique character and potential. As a useful device for the president to test his or her ideas and tentative recommendations, this committee can often make the difference between a chief executive who fails to hold his own with the board and one who is well prepared for the board's likely response to major issues. Both the chief executive and the chairman need to make sure, however, that final decisions of any importance are made by the full board. They should also see to it that the committee does not act on matters that are the primary responsibility of other committees. It is good practice for the whole board to review and approve the minutes of the executive committee meetings. The chief executive should provide staff support and serve as an ex officio member, without vote. Finally, a common function of this committee is annual review of the chief executive's compensation.

Nominating Committee. Some boards have wisely broadened the role and scope of this committee, as reflected in such title variations as "Membership Committee" or "Committee on Trustees." Aside from the need to develop a set of criteria for board membership composition, a profile of present membership (see Figure 1), and a list of first-rate nominees, the nominating committee should be charged with ensuring that new trustees are properly enlisted and oriented to the institution and to their trusteeships, as suggested in Chapter Four. Further, the nominating committee is often asked to oversee formal assessment of individual trustee performance as terms of office expire and renewals are considered and to oversee programs of self-study for the board. It often has the added duty, usually delegated to the committee chairman or the board chairman, of dealing forthrightly with the inactive, incompetent, or troublesome trustee and of commending those who have given exceptional service. Although it is often the most neglected, this committee is second in importance only to the executive committee. More than any other committee, it can help to guarantee the development of an effective board. The president or chancellor should staff it.

Academic Affairs Committee. Few board committees hold more promise for building friendly and cooperative relationships with the faculty than this one. And if properly composed, organized, staffed, and conducted, the academic affairs committee will be personally rewarding for those assigned to it. Its agendas should be the very stuff of the institution: academic mission, purpose, plans, and goals; regular and special programs; student recruitment and admission criteria and policies; academic program budget review; awards and honorary degrees; faculty personnel policies and procedures; and tenure appointments and awards. Some institutions prefer to divide responsibilities between two standing committees: educational affairs and faculty affairs. Others have chosen to use a subcommittee structure to segregate faculty personnel affairs from broader academic program concerns. The size of the board and the import of the educational policy issues confronting the institution will affect committee membership and structure.

The chief academic officer should always staff this committee. He or she, together with its chairman, have unique opportunities to involve the committee's members, indeed the entire board of trustees, with some of the most genuine and challenging policy issues before the institution. One or two faculty and student leaders should be ex officio members, with or without vote. Membership should never be confined only to those who have experience in dealing with educational matters; all that should be required is genuine interest. It is often the banker or the investment counselor who can give and gain the most on such a committee. There is also usually an opportunity to recruit one or two persons from the community at large as full-fledged members. Especially for private institutions, the academic affairs committee provides an exceptional opportunity to identify prospective board members.

The committee's agendas should include short- and long-term planning issues that affect the academic program and the faculty. It should serve as a constant reminder to both trustees and faculty members that boards have a legitimate and helpful role in academic policy development and in review of program quality.

Ongoing, new, and special programs should be brought before the committee (and the board) directly by the faculty members involved. Every meeting should allow time for faculty presentations and for the trustees to ask questions. Committee members should leave every meeting knowing more than when they arrived about at least one aspect of the institution's academic program and about one or more faculty members. Deans and program directors have no monopoly here; the faculty member returning from a particularly valuable sabbatical experience may have much to offer. One or more such presentations in the course of a year should also be brought before the full board. Both successful and problem-ridden programs should be covered on a systematic basis over time.

It has been said that only the board and the chief executive can be expected to maintain a total institutional perspective, free of special interests, consistently mindful of what the college or university is properly about. It is also the board that is best able to interpret the changing tide of society's needs—local, state, and national. Trustees can help the faculty to be certain that its recommendations for establishing new academic programs or discontinuing or modifying existing ones are timely and sound. They can help assess the viability of present and proposed programs by regularly seeing data and interpretation of trends in such areas as teaching load, class size, student-faculty ratios, regular and adjunct faculty ratios, and academic program expenditures.

There are limits to all this, of course. It is a prime responsibility of the academic affairs committee to find a formula of involvement that will be acceptable and meaningful to the faculty and to the board. One observation holds, however: Both faculty members and trustees need to be greater risk takers than their records have shown them to be so far. Too many institutions fail to realize the benefits of a closer working relationship between faculty and trustees and fail to build mutual understanding between the two groups. Trustees can bring planning and management skills—and sometimes their own advanced degrees—to bear on many problems that face the faculty and administration. (Also see Chapter Nine.)

Student Affairs Committee. "To continually assess and appraise the nonacademic areas of student life and to maintain a continuing relationship with student groups" is a phrase commonly found in board bylaws. But translating this into stimulating and useful meeting agendas and other activities that involve students and their leaders (as ex officio members) is sometimes frustrating.

This committee, by itself, cannot be expected to help students to understand the role of the board or to appreciate its contribution to student health and welfare. Where trustees are perceived as persons who pay fleeting visits to the campus to attend perfunctory meetings and enjoy a free meal or two, both student leaders and trustees have a responsibility to reach out and correct the misperception. A solution is possible only when the board as a whole is convinced of the importance of maintaining its image as a diligent and responsive body. At the same time, however, the student affairs committee has a key leadership role to play by demonstrating to the board what is possible through its own example, by arranging opportunities for trustees to meet with students in formal and informal settings, and by insisting that it not be expected to carry the full burden of building effective relationships with students. The administration has a supporting role that may require modifying its natural inclination to look upon student affairs as its own domain.

The committee minimally should be well informed about the range, organization, and quality of student services, have a sense of the priorities for funds within the institution's mission and plan, and review the adequacy of student due process policies and procedures. It should be close to student government activities and programs, and it should be an effective instrument for conflict resolution on the occasions—rare ones, it is hoped—when established administrative channels have been exhausted.

The committee should be creative in the conduct of its business. Among the more customary activities of student affairs committees are receptions with student leaders and honor students, attendance at student government meetings upon invitation, and representation at major campus events. All well and good. But why not ask the editor of the student newspaper to attend a committee meeting and offer a presentation on his or her future plans, or the student manager of the bookstore or co-op to do the same? One liberal arts college provides students with the opportunity to sign up in advance to have lunch with a trustee during each of the board's quarterly meetings. Another has had success with a regular program whereby selected students are asked to address the board on some aspect of their educational experience.

Students are an underdeveloped resource. The student affairs committee is in a good position to identify students who can help in public relations efforts with state legislators or in fund-raising activities with corporations. Perhaps second only to articulate and knowledgeable trustees, students can be effective spokespersons to help interpret the institution to its various publics and to potential supporters. The senior student services officer should staff the committee, provide for stimulating agendas in concert with the committee chairman, and ensure that all meetings are devoted to building closer ties between trustees and students.

Finance Committee. This committee is traditional but too often ineffectual because it fails to relate its oversight responsibilities to institutional mission and purposes. Furthermore, it frequently shirks its oversight role by not working with the president and business officer to develop timely and comprehensible financial reports. In the many institutions that now face declining resources and high inflation, trustees may find their participation on this committee something less than satisfying. Deciding among priorities is never pleasant, but the challenge of interrelating the right data and the information they provide to help the board make the best decisions is a very important responsibility.

Chapter Fifteen provides the framework for new and stimulating agendas for the financial affairs committee. Beginning with an understanding of "fund accounting," this committee may yet realize the full range of its obligations and potential to do worthwhile things. Staffed by the chief business officer, it requires special skills, yet not everyone on the committee need be a banker, investment counselor, accountant, or financial consultant. There is plenty of room for the educator, the scientist, the homemaker, the person unversed in fiscal affairs. Some boards have formed separate subcommittees for investments and audit. Many others, especially larger boards, have seen the wisdom of establishing full standing committees to cover these functions. (See Chapter Fifteen for a discussion of the composition and function of the audit committee and Chapter Sixteen for a discussion of the investment committee.)

Development Committee. The fund-raising responsibilities of the board are usually lodged in this committee, especially in independent colleges and universities. Sometimes the committee is called "resources," sometimes "development and public relations." Its many functions are delineated in Chapter Fourteen, but two matters need to be addressed here.

First, it is far too common for boards to assume incorrectly that the development committee has exclusive responsibility for raising funds. The board as a whole has a duty to function in this area. The board should view the committee as its agent for helping the board itself to meet institutional fund-raising goals.

Second, there is mixed feeling by experts in fund raising about whether public relations and development activities should be centered in a single board committee. Although the concept seems sound, frustration often occurs in trying to conduct both successful fund-raising campaigns and effective programs to upgrade or sustain the institution's public image. Thus some boards have established a subcommittee for the latter function, while others have established two separate standing committees. Whatever the configuration, the two functions should be coordinated.

Other Committees. Some of the more popular additional committees are institutional planning, alumni, buildings and grounds, investments, and mission and purpose. Sometimes there are useful psychological advantages in changing the names of standing committees when they are given new duties. But the real challenge is making whatever committees are in place work properly through effective staff involvement and intelligent agendas that lead to real achievement. Presidential confidence in staff is implicit in this arrangement, but it is incumbent upon staff representatives to keep the president fully informed. It is also important that trustees have the opportunity to change committee assignments from time to time.

Ad hoc committees can be a blessing if they are used sparingly. Too often special committees become living memorials to dead problems if they are not made to conform to two criteria: (1) they should meet a specific charge, clearly agreed upon by all concerned parties; (2) they should have a specific period of existence at the end of which they self-destruct. Perhaps there is a moral in this for other board committees as well; namely, all committees should be required to justify their existence in meeting some institutional need or they, too, should go out of business.

The Board Secretary

A relatively new category of professional leadership in academe deserves mention, namely, the board secretary. Chiefly a functionary of large private and public institutions, the professional staff secretary is still evolving an identity that may one day clear the ambiguity involved in being somewhere between the office of the chief executive and the board itself. There are as many as 250 men and women who serve as full-time staff members responsible to the chief executive and the trustees for a myriad of tasks, from the most professional to the relatively nonessential: planning board and committee meetings and drafting their agendas, writing minutes and maintaining official records of board actions, drafting resolutions, acquiring and interpreting information from departmental offices, orienting new board members, securing football tickets, arranging for trustee housing, and so on.

Typically board secretaries are employed by the chief executive with the approval of the board and serve at the pleasure of both parties. Their primary mission is to help the president or chancellor make sure that board business is transacted properly. They often serve as first point of contact for trustees who ask for information. They assume responsibility for ensuring that committee and board agendas are prepared properly and that all supporting materials are provided board members in ample time before meetings. They keep an eye on the board's bylaws and other legal documents. They sometimes have faculty status (many hold master's or doctor's degrees). Provided that the basic relationship between the chief executive officer and the board is healthy, the professional staff person can be invaluable in helping both parties work as a team.

On the whole, it is not desirable for a board to retain its own professional staff person, since such an arrangement might imply an unsound relationship between board and president or chancellor. The professional board secretary, and any other staff positions that may go with the office, should be part of the chief executive's staff. However, for an opposing point of view, the reader is urged to read Greenleaf's booklet (1974) in which he holds that "trusteeship and administration are very different but complementary roles, and . . . in a large institution, each needs the support of its own capable staff which serves distinctly different purposes from the other" (p. 29). Greenleaf calls for a specialized profession that rests on a unique body of knowledge dedicated to public service and is designed to help trustees to fulfill their function.

While this controversy may grow in the years ahead, it is at present quite commonplace in the vast majority of higher education institutions to find that a person has been designated from within the office of the chief executive to help look after the board and its actions on a part-time basis. Titles vary widely: executive assistant to the president, administrative assistant, executive secretary, secretary of the university or college, or general counsel.

There is a great deal to be said for establishing or strengthening the position of secretary to the board. Although there may not be need for a full-time position, especially in a smaller institution, the person assigned as secretary should be a capable manager who commands respect and understands the institution of trusteeship. The success of an aide to both the president and the board depends in large measure upon the self-confidence of all the parties and their comprehension of one another's functions.

Effective Meetings

Too many board and committee meetings are dreary events not worthy of the investment of time and energy required. Commonsense principles applied by the chief executive, with trustee cooperation, can improve both board and committee meetings. Three questions at the close of a meeting can do wonders: Are we satisfied with how our meeting went today? What could we have done before or during the meeting to make it better? What should we try to do next time? A group of people who are in the right frame of mind and who perhaps have a little advance warning can usually find the solutions necessary to improve future meetings. By definition, a board of trustees *is* a meeting. It is only as a corporate body in formal session that a board can function at all. Improving board meetings means improving trustee performance.

A properly organized and conducted meeting should be a time to weigh and test alternatives; an exercise in creativity where good ideas are made better; a forum calling for candor with grace; an opportunity to demonstrate commitment by all present to the decisions made and the objectives pursued; a time for renewal and rededication to the board's reason for being; a reminder that institutional purpose comes before personal need or ambition. By contrast, an unorganized meeting allows a few personalities to dominate; lacks purpose or focus; provides a platform for ego trips; becomes boring, divisive, and irritating; and, worst of all, is counterproductive to the institution's well-being.

Many boards fall into routine too easily with regard to the *frequency* and *length* of their meetings, two characteristics known to vary inversely as much out of mere habit as out of necessity. Greater flexibility and occasional experimentation are difficult but worthy goals. Earlier assumptions about optimum schedules to satisfy the majority should be tested often. The routines of a "Friday-Saturday" or "second-Tuesday-of-every-month" format, by themselves, can cause boredom in even the most diligent and conscientious trustees, especially if such schedules have persisted for years. Reasonable variation in tune and tempo may cause insecurity in some, but the results overall can be healthy. Occasionally changing the meeting site is an extension of the same idea.

Agendas should determine the length of meetings, not custom or habit. In any event, committee meetings should probably extend no more than three hours at a sitting, preferably on the afternoon or early evening *prior to* the full board meeting. Few persons can sustain their attention at a meeting for more than a few hours, even with stimulating agendas and leadership, unless a significant change of pace or environment is provided. Furthermore, most persons are at their freshest and most creative early in meetings, an argument for placing difficult policy issues high on agendas.

The Executive Session. An increasingly popular, although still underused, practice is the executive session. Where it is not otherwise precluded by unreasonably strict sunshine laws, the adoption of an executive session has important advantages to both chief executives and boards. Consistently scheduled as the last part of every board meeting, the executive session provides time for trustees to privately and candidly ventilate among themselves any lingering concerns, small or large. Sometimes an issue arises during a board meeting that was not aired to everyone's satisfaction. Sometimes the presence of the chief executive discourages board members from fully expressing themselves.

By leaving the board meeting after all official business has been transacted, the president or chancellor acknowledges the trustees' need for a few minutes of solitude. Even in sound marriages the partners occasionally need privacy and time for reflection. In a similar vein, a board should come to terms with occasional frustrations about its responsibilities without being concerned about hurting the president's feelings. Trustees need time to test the validity of their ideas or complaints with peers and to independently review material. Executive sessions can help to assure a president that an additional line of communication exists with the board (through the chairman), that small misunderstandings will not become major problems, and that ideas to further strengthen his or her relationship with the board can emerge. Furthermore, the chairman has an opportunity to receive feedback from the board concerning his or her own leadership role.

Executive sessions ought not to be conducted sporadically or only when there seems to be a problem. Successful achievements by the administration also may invite discussion. In any event, executive session time should always be used for a constructive purpose. No official actions should be taken, since the president is not there, but a "sense of the board" to reflect consensus can help guide the chairman's subsequent conversation with the chief executive. Such conversation should take place immediately following the session or as soon thereafter as possible. It is always good practice for the chairman to sit down with the president to review the meeting.

A board may be reluctant to propose an executive session if the practice has not already been established. Yet because of the value of such sessions, the confident president or chancellor should not hesitate to propose the idea through the chairman and the executive committee (where it exists). For boards that remain skeptical, the chief executive might propose a one-year experiment.

Agendas. Most agendas are faulty because their formats are too brief. Agendas are kept brief partly out of convenience and partly out of misplaced belief that trustees will avoid reading any agenda that exceeds one page. The majority of agenda items should lend themselves to a series of brief but concise statements or questions. Each should be followed by a paragraph of background information or a simple reference to attached supporting materials. The traditional one-page agenda with short, choppy headings (for example, "Review of the Budget for the New Fiscal Year") should be much less the sacred cow than it is. If most of a board's agendas look virtually the same from one meeting to the next, the forgoing shoe surely fits.

There is much to be said for issue-oriented agendas that consistently place the big policy matters to the front. Meetings whose agendas are designed merely for the reading of reports are doomed to mediocrity. Every meeting agenda should contain at least one major issue affecting the institution's future, with clear understanding that a final decision remains perhaps six months or a year ahead. All trustees should suggest agenda items, but it is the chairman who shares the final responsibility with the chief executive for the quality of every agenda.

A familiar rule is that board meetings should deal with policy matters rather than administrative details. Every agenda item should pass what Nelson (1978) calls the harsh test of relevance: Is it a matter of routine validation or ratification of a minor action already taken by the executive committee or staff? Or is it a question of basic policy that calls for careful explication of its importance and for balanced consideration? If the matter falls outside these two categories, it is probably better left to the administration. Along with Nelson's admonition is his helpful definition of policy: "A policy is a general rule or principle, or a statement of intent or direction, that provides guidance to administrators in reaching decisions with respect to the particular matters entrusted to their care" (p. 22).

Some boards could benefit immensely from a quick check of the minutes of their recent meetings against Nelson's suggestions. Honest reflection might yield much enlightenment about how meeting time is budgeted, how careful the president and chairman have been to avoid presentation of purely administrative matters, and how successful the board has been in staying on the right track. With the benefit of hindsight, members can simply ask whether each action taken at three preceding meetings involved (1) routine validation of minor actions already taken, (2) basic policy, or (3) purely administrative detail. Another approach would be to classify each action as primarily involving (1) policy, (2) administration, or (3) some combination of both. Opinions among the members of the board will undoubtedly vary, but a useful picture is likely to develop.

Chairman as Servant. Perhaps the ultimate honor for any trustee is to be asked by his or her peers to serve as chairman, to serve as their spokesperson. It is a singular privilege that requires a wide range of human qualities and leadership skills for its successful exercise, including a certain personal grace and a sense of humor.

In concert with the chief executive, he or she should take the necessary time to ensure that preparation for meetings is adequate, that knowledgeable institutional officials will be on hand when needed, and that advance thought is given to the range and kinds of questions likely to be asked by the trustees. In order to know where the president or chancellor stands on key agenda issues, the chairman should confer with the chief executive about every item on the agenda in advance of its mailing. In doing so, the chairman must think and respond as if he or she were the board itself. The extent of real achievement and group satisfaction is often determined before the meeting takes place; here the chairman and chief executive have almost exclusive responsibility.

Experienced chairmen know that they need not entirely sacrifice their own views on important matters to be good facilitators. But they also know that their advocacy must be used sparingly and timed carefully. It is better for them to give their views later in discussion than too early, better for them to speak on the heels of a trustee who has just expressed a position similar rather than dissimilar to their own. Most of all they know that their relative silence is golden because, when they do choose to speak, the board will be attentive. Self-indulgence, in any event, has no place in the chairman's makeup. The voices of neither the chief executive nor the chairman should be heard more often than those of others around the table.

Minutes. Adequate records of meetings are an important but often neglected matter. Minutes are important not only as a legal necessity but also because they serve as "group memory" and as testimony to achievements of the previous meeting. Minutes are often carelessly written because too many trustees have demonstrated disdain for them. It is a joint responsibility of the chief executive, the board chairman, the board secretary or other signer of the minutes, and the person who actually writes them to see that minutes are not only accurate but written in a way to invite reading.

The substance of discussions should be captured, but it is not necessary to give a verbatim report of "who said what." The major pros and cons on a particular issue are usually sufficient. It is also a good practice to list absentees along with attendees; this helps to focus attention on those who frequently miss meetings. Because written documents outweigh oral testimony in the eyes of the courts, it is important that the minutes be permanently maintained and occasionally reviewed by legal counsel to determine their adequacy.

Open Meetings. Board meetings of virtually all tax-supported institutions are now open to the public, as are some in the private sector. At one time widespread concern was expressed over the prospect of debating issues and making decisions in full public view. Except in a few states where legislatures were overzealous, however, the practice has come to be considered reasonable and workable if not totally acceptable. This has been especially true in the states where public boards can meet privately to discuss real estate acquisitions, sensitive personnel matters, including faculty tenure or dismissal recommendations, and presidential selection. Most boards are also permitted to meet privately for the purposes of self-renewal and assessment, provided they make no decisions directly affecting institutional policy. Eighty-seven percent of 433 community college presidents and 74 percent of their board chairmen agreed that "Sunshine laws on the whole work very well" (Drake, 1977, p. 13).

Yet there is no doubt that it has become more difficult to conduct business with candor and vigor in the public sector, and there are clearly costs as well as benefits to openness. In the earliest days of the great experiment in openness, especially in the case of larger meetings, there was what Cleveland (1975) refers to as the high "ratio of emotion to reason, nonsense to common sense" (p. 8). There were, and still occasionally are, abuses that take their toll on truly reflective thinking and acting. The wheels of open meetings tend to move too fast or too slowly.

On the whole, however, the advantages have been winning out over the problems. The mystery of what boards really do at meetings has largely been dispelled; the role of trustees is better understood, even if not fully appreciated; those most affected by board decisions have the opportunity to hear and to be heard. The key to successful open meetings lies in adherence to guidelines that state who may speak, when, and for how long. These should be kept simple and reasonable and made available to everyone in attendance. Agendas also should be made available in advance of meetings.

Board Officers

There should be a reasonable schedule of rotation for the chairman, other officers, and committee chairmen—a simple extension of the same principle that argues for limitation on the number of terms for all trustees. Some risks are involved. The quality of leadership may fluctuate, and the president may have to adjust a bit to a different personality and set of expectations. An ex-chairman may tend to lose interest. But the advantages have more weight. Trustees who monopolize positions for long periods block others and may cause resentment. There are many occasions when an outgoing chairman or other board officer can be asked to chair an ad hoc project or to assume a special assignment. In any event, it should remain possible to ask a truly exceptional chairman to return to the position for one more turn at bat after a few years' absence.

Life, Emeritus, and Honorary Trustees

Boards of private institutions have wide latitude in deciding for themselves whether to adopt a special category of trusteeship that allows friends of the institution to retain affiliation. Although definitions of the life, emeritus, or honorary trustee vary, common practice is to provide a way for retiring trustees to maintain close ties but without having a vote and without being part of a quorum requirement.

This has not worked universally. Some boards have fallen into the trap of making election to the position of trustee emeritus automatic. The honor should be selectively conferred, and persons who hold it should have a definite role. Trustees who have really earned their life, emeritus, or honorary trusteeships will welcome assignments to committees, opportunities to work on special task forces, and invitations to help with alumni programs and fund raising. Nominating committees always have a diplomatic problem when trustees are up for reelection or for emeritus status. A bylaw provision of a waiting period of one year before nominees are considered can help relieve the inevitable pressure.

Advisory Committees and Councils

Many public and even more private colleges and universities have experimented with enlisting groups of highly visible men and women who could bring to the institution public relations and other skills, as well as access to funds. The record of success of such advisory groups on the institutional level has not been good, even when advance planning has been sound. But efforts continue, because a successful arrangement of this kind can pay dividends.

An advisory committee can provide not only a public relations device and a broadened capacity to meet fund-raising goals but a means of identifying potential members for the board. The ingredients for success are found in four primary areas: an adequate statement of the scope, purpose, and organization of the committee; adequate staffing to ensure stimulating agendas and programs, with the personal involvement of the chief executive and several trustees; careful selection of members; and occasional opportunities for the committee to interact with the board. The more successful ventures seem to require a willingness by the board to delegate or share a few of its functions and to consult regularly with the committee. The latter is probably more feasible for a larger institution.

The attitude of the chief executive toward an advisory committee is perhaps even more important than that of the board. It is he or she who must decide what can or should be shared with such a group. Only genuine issues can provide for an advisory group's sense of purpose and accomplishment; no one is in a more strategic position to identify these issues than the president or chancellor. Such a group can greatly enhance the quality of planning on an institutional and programmatic basis. Although there may seem to be some danger that advisory committees will attempt to become policy makers, this can be minimized by a carefully worded organizing document that is separate from the board's bylaws. An institution that has had a bad experience with such a group in the past might review the reasons for failure and consider a new effort.

Conclusion

The differences among boards in size, composition, and type of institution served, as well as in tradition and custom, preclude the setting forth of an ideal model, but a board of trustees should be organized so that it can fully meet its legal, moral, and social responsibilities. Sound organization practices can facilitate effective operation, but a board should first and foremost be organized in such a way that its members will be fully informed and comfortable.

Reasonable experimentation can be a constructive exercise. Organizations need opportunities for rejuvenation and challenge. Some of the ideas in this chapter can be implemented quite readily; others require careful planning and consensus. But the major objective should be to establish a structure that will enable the majority of trustees to be effectively involved in the board's work; thus the case for a committee system with occasional rotation of trustees, and the caution against an improperly conducted executive committee that places too much authority in the hands of too few trustees. The AGB bylaws for independent colleges, the trustee audit, and the board self-study criteria found in the Resources section of this volume provide additional standards for comparison.

6

Richard T. Ingram

Assuring
Trustee Orientation
and Development

The purpose of this chapter is not to belabor the importance of in-service experiences for trustees but to illustrate some principles of good planning that can make the difference between successful and mediocre events. It is divided into two major sections. The material on *orientation programs* emphasizes development of the new trustee's understanding of the institution as a complex enterprise and of trusteeship as a unique responsibility, while that on *workshops and retreats* emphasizes development of the board as an organization. Each activity requires its own set of planning considerations, staffing arrangements, and agendas, along with its own style of conduct and method of appraisal. Nevertheless, both share some of the same prerequisites.

Basic Program Considerations

Orientation programs and board workshops for new trustees are investments in the future that require expenditure of trustee and staff energy, as well as modest but adequate funds. They need ample planning, strong and effective coordination, patience, sound judgment, some risk—and a little luck. These are obvious needs. But behind them are three other, more elusive decisions that are often overlooked, minimized, or otherwise avoided. Together they determine what will work and what will not.

What are the goals of the program? Decide before beginning. Think in long-range rather than short-range terms. Deal with cures rather than symptoms. The best programs are those that fit into a comprehensive strategy of board education over a two- or three-year period. Objectives should be clearly specified and should provide a rationale for every program feature. Knowing where you hope to finish before you begin is not easy. But by engaging those most directly affected, by discussing needs and opportunities openly, by working together to find the right timing for key activities to meet agreed upon goals, you can make success more likely. Prerequisites include: (1) helping the board to recognize that some need does exist, (2) involving it at key stages of program development, and (3) providing for trustee leadership and program participation.

Who has responsibility for the program? The president, together with a small board committee. Chapters Four and Five argue that the nominating committee should bear the burden and rewards of trustee education in the case of a private institution. On the public side, a small ad hoc committee of thoughtful, highly respected board leaders or elected board officers can provide the necessary leadership. In either case, some instrument of the board is necessary if such programs are to be credible with trustees.

The wise chief executive does not go too far in delegating planning activities to staff. Although many follow-up activities should be delegated, and several key staff may participate in programs, this is too important an area to be left entirely or in substantial part to others. The chief executive should assume the primary responsibility for (1) offering guidance to the committee in its planning function and (2) implementing the program with the help of carefully selected trustees, senior administrative officers, and the chairman. The president should be recognized by the board as the person most responsible for its education and its development as an effective organization. Only through consistent encouragement from the board itself will most presidents or chancellors fulfill this delicate role.

How can trustees be involved in the program? By asking them. Programs dominated by the chief executive or other administrators foreclose real trustee involvement. Administrators have a key planning and staff function in orientation programs, but their profile should be low. Thus, the interest and help of two or three particularly active, dedicated, and highly respected trustees should be secured. They need not be board officers or the most verbal trustees. The participation of board members in planning activities, setting goals, conducting programs, and assessing outcomes is vital. A good chief executive can see the dividends rather than the risks of such an approach and make it work to the institution's advantage. Some ideas for trustee participation are offered later in the chapter.

Orientation Programs

In 1974, a national survey disclosed that about 33 percent of all private and public, four- and two-year colleges and universities had "systematic orientation for new board members, most frequently by the chief executive together with the chairman of the board, occasionally other board members" (Nelson and Turk, 1974, p. 7). The percentage is surely higher now, but it is a safe bet that such efforts vary widely in comprehensiveness and quality.

An unfortunate but common procedure takes the form of the chief executive's asking a secretary to bundle together the college catalogues, bylaws, football schedule, and a few other items and send the package to the new trustee. Besides overwhelming the recipient, such a package fails to make the important distinction between orientation to the institution and orientation to the new board member's trusteeship, two objectives that require separate attention. A sound enlistment process for a prospective board member should make clear that he or she is expected to participate after election. Appointed or elected trustees in the public sector should likewise be asked to participate by the board chairman or chairman of the committee charged with overseeing the program.

Timing the Orientation. One full day is probably the irreducible minimum for orientation. Two days would be better, one and one-half days a golden mean. The temptation to combine orientation with a regular board meeting should be resisted, although it may be wise to allow the new board member to attend at least one board meeting before the orientation. Sometimes two or three new board members can synchronize their schedules to share an orientation.

Content. A comprehensive program should have clearly stated objectives and cover the two basic areas: orientation to the institution and to the trusteeship. Activities should be tailored to the institution, sensitive to any special interests of the new trustee, and flexible. Experimentation based on evaluations from those who have gone through the orientation program will help to perfect the right approach.

No assumption should be made that the trustee knows much of anything about the college or university, and it is best *not* to provide extensive written materials in advance. Such materials, if carefully selected, will be more helpful after the orientation, and their presentation can constitute symbolic "graduation." Material on the institution's history can be valuable for orienting the trustee. All colleges and universities have fascinating stories about their founding, their early trials, their traditions and development. Not all, unfortunately, have a historian who keep the record current and who is knowledgeable about the institution's past history and achievements.

A tour of the campus should be a major part of any orientation program. The main buildings should be visited, at least one of every type or purpose. But the impact of the tour can be lost if the campus is viewed only through the windows of an air-conditioned automobile. Both the pride and physical needs of the institution should be seen from close up.

Resources. There is danger in providing too much in the way of official publications. Bylaws, charter, president's report, minutes of recent board meetings, current budget, auditor's report, lists of board members and senior administrators, organizational charts, faculty and student handbooks—the list goes on and on, and two things are certain: very few persons will read all this material, and none of it tells what is expected of a conscientious board member. A few basic items may be provided immediately following an orientation session, and some of the others later. A good idea, adopted by a few institutions, is to provide a two- or three-page summary of key institutional data.

On the subject of trusteeship there are many good materials written specifically for trustees' consumption. The recommended readings (Resource E) for this and other chapters provide a sampling. But these cannot take the place of the orientation provided by the chief executive, the chairman, one or two knowledgeable trustees, and some top administrative officers. A two-hour open discussion of what a trustee should and should not do, following a brief, formal presentation by one or two persons, can be stimulating and useful. Time also should be set aside for new board members to visit deans, faculty members, and student leaders, with an eye to the vocational or avocational interests of each trustee.

Useful films, slides, and filmstrips may also be available within the institution. Media material used for student recruitment should be considered. A thirteen-minute film available from the Association of Governing Boards of Universities and Colleges (AGB) provides an overview of trustee roles and responsibilities and can help lead into a discussion session. In fact, a variety of possibilities exist to help immerse the trustee in institutional life and to enable him or her to feel comfortable, enthusiastic, and productive more quickly. The following partial list reflects an orientation program that could cover a year or two:

1. Trustee-in-residence. Chapter Four mentions the success some institutions have had by asking all new trustees to spend at least one night in a residence hall sometime during their first year and to take part in scheduled campus activities.
2. Trustee sponsors. Veteran trustees can be assigned as sponsors of new board members.
3. Attendance of classes. If faculty members can benefit from

being startled from time to time, there is no better way to do this than for a new trustee to ask permission to visit a class, perhaps as a guest speaker when appropriate. This kind of trustee participation can be rewarding for all, including the students.

4. Local, regional, and national meetings. It is healthy for trustees to occasionally meet their peers from other institutions to gain new insights and to share ideas and experiences. This can be especially important for the new trustee. The chief executive or board chairman should set an example and personally encourage such participation.

5. Visits to neighboring institutions. Apart from fulfilling the business world's admonition to "know thy competition," such activities can provide fresh perspectives. Some enterprising boards, for instance, have arranged for small delegations to be exchanged.

Program Evaluation. A few questions following a formal orientation activity can lead to improvements: What benefited you the most? What was the least useful part of the program? What should be added or done differently next time? This is also the time to ascertain trustee interests for possible future assignments. Finally, all presentations made to new trustees should be brief and to the point and should allow time for questions. Veteran trustees should also be invited to attend orientations. At private institutions, it may be appropriate to invite prospective nominees.

To make this discussion less abstract, I have adapted the following from a program conducted at Culver-Stockton College in Canton, Missouri. It demonstrates an approach to trustee orientation made in concert with scheduled campus activities.

New Trustee Orientation

Wednesday
6:00 P.M. Informal Reception
        Gladys Crown Student Center, College Lounge
7:00 P.M. Trustees' Dinner
        Gladys Crown Student Center, President's Dining Room
            Dr. Clifford Leece, Chairman, Board of Trustees
            "The College in Perspective"

Dr. Harold C. Doster, President, Culver-Stockton
College
Introductions, Announcements
Dr. Henson Harris, Vice-President for Academic
Affairs

Thursday
7:30 A.M. Trustees' Breakfast
Gladys Crown Student Center
8:30 A.M. Trustee Orientation
Henderson Hall, Board of Trustees Room
"Our Academic Goals and How We Implement
Them"
Mr. Charles Barnum, Board of Trustees
Dr. Henson Harris, Vice-President for Academic
Affairs
10:00 A.M. Coffee
10:30 A.M. Trustee Orientation
Henderson Hall, Board of Trustees Room
"How We Conserve Our Resources and Control the
Budget"
Mr. John Irvin, Board of Trustees
Mr. Glenn Schlager, Vice-President for Business
Affairs
Noon Luncheon
Gladys Crown Student Center, President's Dining Room
Special Guests: Student Organization Presidents
1:30 P.M. Trustee Orientation
Henderson Hall, Board of Trustees Room
"How We Get There from Here"
Mr. Eugene Andereck, Board of Trustees
Mr. Charles Edwards, Vice-President for College
Relations
3:00 P.M. Coffee
Hosted by the Dames Club
3:30 P.M. Trustee Orientation
Henderson Hall, Board of Trustees Room
"How We Recruit and Serve Our Students"

Dr. William Alberts, Board of Trustees

Mr. John Van Dyke, Vice-President for Student Services

5:00 P.M. An Introduction to Trusteeship

Henderson Hall, Board of Trustees Room

"The Measure of the College"

Dr. Harold C. Doster, President, Culver-Stockton College

6:30 P.M. Trustees' Dinner

Gladys Crown Student Center, President's Dining Room

8:30 P.M. "Three-Penny Opera"

Presented by the Culver-Stockton Division of Fine Arts

Friday

Events on this day included meetings with additional members of the administration and faculty, the college's Development Council, and the Parents' Association. A meal in the student cafeteria, a student art exhibition, a residence hall open house, and a Saturday football game rounded out the program.

Workshops and Retreats

A national survey by AGB in 1974 reported that 46 percent of public and private institution boards had, within the preceding two-year period, conducted a retreat with the chief executive officer to discuss in depth the issues bearing on the institution's future. It is hard to believe that a governing board can function well without an occasional opportunity to stand back from its routine business agendas, its immediate preoccupations and concerns.

Too often the *assumption* that trustees are reluctant to set aside additional time for either self-renewal or institutional renewal becomes a convenient excuse for not conducting a retreat—a kind of self-fulfilling prophecy. Trustees will respond to reasonable requests for their time and attention if they have reason to think that they will be rewarded with a first-rate experience.

Defining Objectives. Too many in-service programs fail to reflect comprehensive planning or strategy. Unclear objectives and vague ideas can lead to frustrating results. Here are some *long-term* goals worth considering:

- To improve the board's organization and performance, particularly in problem areas.
- To enable the board to understand (or to improve) its participation in fund raising.
- To encourage inactive board members to live up to their trusteeships or to resign.
- To solicit the board's help in refining a proposed institutional plan.
- To improve relationships between the president and the board.
- To improve relationships between religious and lay trustees (at church-related institutions).
- To reach consensus on a new mission for the institution (or to regain a sense of purpose).
- To achieve greater harmony among the trustees through opportunities for expanded friendships and appreciation for differing viewpoints on issues confronting the institution.

Shorter-term goals can also provide program ideas, but they should clearly tie to broader purposes. Possible goals are:

- To demonstrate how other, similar types of boards are organized and function.
- To present and discuss fund-raising techniques.
- To ask each trustee to review his or her performance (see the trustee audit in Resource A).
- To conduct a self-study program (see Chapter Twenty).
- To tour three buildings on each campus and then to attend a presentation by the director of the physical plant.
- To present and discuss the preliminary recommendations of the ad hoc planning committee concerning future academic programs.
- To present and discuss the president's self-assessment in light of the recently completed board self-study (see Chapter 18).
- To invite a knowledgeable spokesperson to address the issue of

the changing relationships between sponsoring religious bodies and institutions of higher education (at church-related schools).

• To review the proposed statement of the institution's mission subsequent to the receipt of written comments and suggestions for improvement.

Timing. Choose a time that will not be occupied with routine board business. Tacking a program on to the beginning or end of a regularly scheduled board meeting may be expedient, but it is less than ideal. Ample time and attention are key elements. If a two-day event is planned several months in advance and its date is based on the preference of the majority, maximum attendance will be assured. Stay well clear of holidays, ask the chairman to confirm the dates, and send a reminder or two along the way.

Budget. A well-planned and executed function requires adequate funds. For unusual expenses, a local foundation or corporation, a particular board member, or the trustees themselves might be asked to help. Among the items to be considered: speaker or consultant honoraria and expenses, lodging and meals, resource materials, special clerical services, and rental of audiovisual equipment and meeting rooms.

Setting. Choose a meeting place away from the board room and the institution. The added expense (and inconvenience) is usually justified on psychological grounds. The ideal site is one that is comfortable, invites reflection, and provides new stimulation. Flexibility for various meeting configurations is desirable (large and small rooms, dining facilities, U-shaped or open-square table arrangements, audiovisual capabilities). Be certain to attend to logistical details; it is often the seemingly small matters that contribute a great deal to a successful event. Decide in advance if name badges and a list of attendees with brief biographical sketches will be helpful. Should coffee or soft drinks be available or should participants be asked to bring their own canteens?

Other Considerations. There may be great advantage to securing the services of an "outside" facilitator, group leader, or observer. Such a person can help to add objectivity, insight, and information to the proceeding. This may be an experienced trustee from another institution, a former college president, or consultant who has experience in working directly with trustees. Look around for someone who is candid and who can help raise the right questions. It is often the outsider who can raise precisely the point that others would like to emphasize but choose instead to avoid. Keep the number of participants as small as possible. Too many members of the administrative team or too many faculty and student representatives may inhibit some trustees from participating fully.

Consider cochairmen for leadership. Two highly respected individuals who work well together can provide variety in style and help to keep momentum going, especially if the program covers more than half a day. The board chairman is a likely candidate, but the president of the institution should normally be reserved as a resource person.

Encourage some advance trustee preparation. A brief list of questions on the topics scheduled for discussion could be mailed to board members several weeks before the meeting, and the results compiled for presentation and discussion. An advance reading assignment, accompanied by the agenda, could also help to establish common ground for discussion of particular issues.

For large boards, consider dividing participants into two or three preassigned groups toward the latter stages of the workshop. Here is an opportunity to maximize genuine participation, provide closure on key issues, develop an action agenda for follow-up activities, and give more persons a chance to exercise leadership. Each group should be assigned a leader who has the duty of reporting discussion highlights to the full group at its final session. It is also imperative to keep a summary record. Any hope for subsequent action depends on the securing of consensus and hence on an awareness of major points of disagreement. The report should be made available promptly and reviewed by the board at its next meeting.

Be mindful of open meeting laws, but do not use them as an excuse to avoid workshops or retreats. Although New Jersey apparently requires "training sessions" and "workshops" for public college and university boards to be open to the public, most other states do not. Check with local legal counsel or your state attorney general. An agenda in final form that demonstrates that no official actions will be taken, that the purpose of the program is to review how the board is organized and functions, and that no institutional policies or procedures will be decided may help to obtain a favorable decision from the appropriate authority. One public university board in a state with a strict sunshine law found that it could conduct a workshop under the auspices of AGB's Board-Mentor Service, its legal counsel reasoning that such sponsorship did not constitute a board meeting because the final discussion agenda was developed by AGB representatives. The trustees attended on the same basis that they would attend any other conference.

Finally, recognize the importance of a postworkshop evaluation. This is especially important to help plan future programs. A few key questions will usually suffice:

- What did you understand to be the main purposes of the workshop?
- In your judgment, to what extent were these purposes met?
- What was the most valuable part of the program?
- What was the least valuable part of the program?
- What did you learn about the board as a working unit, or about yourself, that will cause you to approach your trusteeship differently?

Consider a combination of objective and open-ended items. Take advantage of the opportunity to ask for ideas for possible follow-up discussions and topics for future workshops or retreats. Consider the need for anonymity to encourage candor. The evaluation form can be distributed at adjournment or a week or two following the event. Include a return, stamped envelope.

Trustee Participation. In addition to trustee involvement in program planning and conduct, all board members should be encouraged to address issues by articulating alternatives and working toward solutions. Windy speeches and lengthy reports can destroy the effect of a good agenda. Along with preworkshop surveys and modest reading assignments, the following techniques and resources may help generate wide participation:

- Committee chairmen can help interpret the issues and discussion as they relate to committee responsibilities; for example, they can lead discussions within their own committees to take advantage of smaller groups to maximize participation.

- Other trustees can be assigned discussion group leadership roles; individuals who have not been active board members should be considered.
- New trustees can be asked to give "first impressions" or to mention areas that need clarification.
- The board member who may recently have attended a relevant educational meeting can be asked to share his or her new ideas.
- The trustee who serves or who has served on the board of another institution can compare the two boards.
- The results of a board self-study or trustee assessment can be presented.
- The most recent institutional plan to assess the extent to which goals are being met.
- A set of questions on key topics for use during the workshop can be provided, particularly if a preworkshop questionnaire is not used.

Shaping the Agenda. The best agendas are issue oriented and include a few key questions, perhaps with a brief background statement for each. The board's size and the availability of resources and time will affect what is desirable and necessary for an agenda. No individual session should exceed two hours without a break, and the breaks should be indicated on the agenda.

Concluding Rules

In-service events for trustees present a unique opportunity but also a challenge. A few well-tested rules are worth setting down:

- *Planning time.* Whatever your estimate of time needed, double it. Then seek more staff help.
- *Budget.* Add 25 to 50 percent to your best estimate.
- *Trustee reading assignments.* Don't assume that more than a minority will actually read the material in advance. Try to make the remainder wish they had.

- *The evaluation.* Positive reaction from half or more of the participants is the mark of a truly successful event.
- *Remember Sorensen's Law.* If things are going better than expected,
  you must have overlooked something.

Effective trusteeship and trustee dedication to the institution often result from experiences and events that take place *outside* regular board meetings. Perhaps some of the suggestions in this chapter will cause more of them to happen.

7

John J. Corson

Participating in
Policy Making
and Management

Fifteen years ago, I found myself embroiled in a public difference of opinion with a distinguished businessman, who was the president of a major insurance company and chairman of the board of a prestigious university. He contended that a university's trustees were fully responsible for and must direct everything that goes on in the institution. Presumptuously perhaps, I contradicted him; boards of trustees, I argued, like Queen Elizabeth, reign but do not rule.

After fifteen years, during which I have served on the boards of four institutions of higher education, the boards of several other nonprofit institutions, and three corporate boards of directors I feel more confident of the judgment boldly asserted then. The gist of what I learned is that while trustees of both private and public colleges and universities are legally responsible

101

for all activities of the institutions they serve, they have lost the ability to fulfill that responsibility. They have lost much power to the faculty and, of late, to state and federal agencies and the courts.

It should not be so. American colleges and universities are larger and socially more important in 1980 than they were two decades ago. Like any other enterprise whose success depends upon the collaborative efforts of a large number of individuals, they need farsighted direction and appraisal from the top. More specifically, there is need for:

- *Trustee participation in goal setting.* Boards must make a continuing effort to ensure that the enterprise knows where it is going and why, that it has clear-cut goals.
- *Trustee review of policy making.* There must be continual revision of plans, rules, and regulations by trustees so that all members of the enterprise will know how they should proceed toward the goals that have been set.
- *Continuing oversight by trustees.* Boards must constantly monitor the institution's functioning to ensure that day-by-day direction is effective and that individuals are motivated to do what is expected of them with reasonable celerity and effectiveness.

The objective assessment of an institution's goals and policies in light of society's needs and the objectives of supporters (that is, contributors to the private institution or the state executive and the legislature for the public institution), as well as the continuous evaluation of its performance, is a task its president and his or her aides cannot perform. Broad-gauged, variously experienced, and detached individuals are needed by each of the many types of institutions of higher education—public, private, and church-related schools, two-year and four-year community colleges, liberal arts colleges, technical and specialized institutions, and comprehensive universities—to perform these tasks.

The boards that serve institutions of these various types differ markedly in size, in the manner in which members are selected, in the time they devote to the institution's affairs, and in the responsibility they accept. The particular needs of individual institutions, and of each institution at different times, will vary. The services required of their boards by private institutions will be different from those expected of the boards of public institutions. Yet in every institution someone must set goals, make policies, and oversee management if faculty members, supporting staffs, students, and others are to collaborate effectively. Whatever its size or however its members are chosen, it is the responsibility of the board to ensure that these basic tasks are performed.

Nature of Academic Organization

The typical college or university appears to be structured clearly and simply enough. The charts, manuals, and catalogues by which these institutions tell others about their organizations describe structures that are much like those of corporations. Take a relatively typical state university in the Midwest. Its chart shows a president underneath a board of trustees. The president's position on the chart suggests that he or she, acting for the board, is responsible for everything. The president's assistants include a provost (or academic vice-president) and four vice-presidents, who are responsible for student services, finance, physical facilities, and external relations. Each reports to the president.

The chart makes it all seem quite straightforward. True, it is a large institution (18,000 students), but the administrative work is divided into five distinguishable sets of activities, each seemingly directed by an individual with authority to see that the work gets done. An organizational chart, however, does not reveal the unique characteristics of a college or university. Nor does it reveal the continuing conflicts that go on within the typical academic organization—conflicts that arise from the complexity of academic organizations. As Baldridge, and others (1978) have effectively pointed out:

- Academic institutions have broad, vague, ambitious goals, such as "to develop Christian gentlemen and leaders," "to develop appreciation of the fine arts," "to equip young men and women for employment," or "to serve the educational needs of the community." It is difficult to bring about agreement as to how such goals will be achieved.

- They are client-serving institutions. The clients, not only students and their parents but powerful constituencies in the community—teachers, nurses, police, firemen, state and local bar associations, alumni, and the general public—attempt to influence what the college or university (particularly the public community college and university) does and how it is done.
- They have no agreed upon, specific technologies for accomplishing what they are about. Thus there are no techniques accepted by all professors and administrators for helping all kinds of individuals learn or for the discovery of new knowledge.
- They have fragmented professional staffs. Faculty members in the various disciplines, for example, physics and sociology, view problems in different ways. Collaboration thus is limited. In a hospital or a law firm most professional staff members are drawn from a single profession.
- They are highly professionalized. Professionals, be they doctors, lawyers, advertising persons, or faculty members, demand work autonomy, have divided loyalties (divided between their professions and their employing institutions) and will accept evaluation only by professional peers.
- They are becoming more and more vulnerable. Academic institutions are being subjected to increasing intervention by outsiders—federal and state officials, powerful constituent groups, the press, and the courts. This intervention lessens the autonomy of the institution and the freedom of the individual faculty member.

Weigh these characteristics and it becomes clear why guidelines are needed if the collaborative efforts of all members of the institution's staff are to be effectively mobilized. Guidelines are needed for the vice-presidents, the deans, the department chairmen, and the administrative officers. They must include goals and policies, as well as the plans, budgets, rules, and procedures by which they are translated into action. These should be developed by the president and his or her staff. The board's responsibility is to approve or disapprove, after studying periodic operating reports, inquiring as to the views of various constituencies (not always accepting the president's version of their views!), considering the programs, practices, and operating costs of comparable institutions, and weighing proposals in the light of the community's as well as the institution's interests. Many of the trustees' efforts then will be reflected in the plans, budgets, rules, and procedures that set forth ends to be achieved and indicate how individuals throughout the college or university should carry on the institution's business.

This output from the trustees of some colleges and universities takes the form of five basic instruments.

Mission Statement. This is a written description of the kind of institution that a given college or university wants to be. It should set forth the goals of the institution in as clear and unambiguous terms as possible. Basically a mission statement is an elaboration of the charter of the private institution or the statute establishing the public institution. Putting in words a fuller statement of what a college or university is charged to do will not ensure accomplishment of its mission. Too much should not be expected of the document that is produced. But the effort is a first-rate exercise for board members, whose minds are probably taken up with other matters during twenty-five or more days of each month.

If the board, in conjunction with the administration and faculty, has not developed such an elaboration of the institution's purpose, it will be well advised to undertake the drafting of one; if such a statement exists, board members should reread it at least once a year and ask themselves: Are we still on the right track?

Annual Academic Plan. This should include a detailed forecast of probable enrollment for the next five years—undergraduate and graduate—by sex, age, part-time versus full-time, school, and discipline. Basic data should be updated each year by the administration. Proposals for new programs should be advanced by the faculty. Then these ingredients of the plan should be carefully weighed by the trustees in conjunction with the administration and the faculty spokespersons for each proposed program. If the plan is truly a partnership effort, it will contribute greatly to the integration of the institution.

Master Plan. The physical plan of the institution will usually be developed for the institution by architects and engineers retained for that purpose. It will provide a picture—in words, sketches, and blueprints—of the campus and each building that already exists, is to be expanded, or is to be built. If done well, the plan will be keyed to and will provide for the physical facilities required to carry out the academic plan and to establish the kind of environment suggested by the mission statement. It will be used as a prospectus for donors who may thereby be induced to contribute to the institution's development.

Annual Budget. This document will provide estimates (1) in the operating budget of the financial resources needed to carry out the academic plan, and (2) in the capital budget of the resources needed for expansion or renovation of the physical facilities, ranging from the construction of new buildings to extension of the power plant or repaving of driveways.

Policy Manuals. These will include: (1) a codification of the board's decisions as to its own organization and operating practices, that is, the committees through which it will operate and the functions of each; (2) the procedures to be followed by the administration, board committees, and the board in considering proposals for new academic programs, for the annual budget, for major capital expenditures, and for other matters of like importance; and (3) regulations on the frequency of meetings, along with an enumeration of those who shall attend them. Other manuals will specify the procedures to be followed by faculty and staff in key areas of administration, that is, personnel, finance, purchasing, and administration of facilities.

The part that trustees play in making policies and monitoring management will depend on the depth to which they explore each of the instruments depicted here and accept, modify, or reject what is proposed by the faculty and/or the administration. Trustees will not fulfill their obligations simply by attending committee and board meetings, voting on each item as it comes up on the agenda, and appearing in academic regalia at commencement exercises and convocations. Trusteeship means more; it involves informing oneself sufficiently to be able to make effective judgments. For example, does a particular educational program submitted for the board's approval conform with the mission statement and the academic plan? Does the gift of a building proposed by a donor fit into the master plan? Are all the expenditures provided for in the annual budget actually required?

For the board of the private institution, trusteeship also includes presenting informed reasons as to why prospective donors should give. For the board of the public institution, analogously, it means presenting informed arguments to legislators whose votes on appropriations are needed, as well as to citizens who question what the institution is doing.

Dependence on the President for Information

To fulfill their responsibilities for the functioning of the institution, trustees need a continuing flow of information from the president. Specifically, they need information concerning:

Educational Program. Presumably the mission statement indicates the relative emphasis to be given to general education versus professional and paraprofessional education, to undergraduate versus graduate education, and to the education of part-time versus full-time students. The continuing flow of information that trustees should seek will reflect its source (for example, the organized teachers), and will include the rationale, the capability of the faculty to provide the level of instruction required, and the relevance to the master plan of each new program (for example, a master's degree program or a department of anthropology) and especially of the doctoral programs it is proposed to offer. (Also see Chapter Ten.)

Quality of the Faculty. Trustees should insist upon being continually informed as to the processes being used (1) to find new appointees, (2) to evaluate their performance, and especially (3) to single out those faculty members who are to be granted tenure. Trustees should keep an eye on the tenure rates in individual departments and schools. Sixty percent or more of the annual operating budget goes for faculty compensation, and in some institutions as much as 70 percent of that total goes for the compensation of tenured professors.

Students. Trustees should regularly see data as to who is admitted—by ethnic group, academic ability, financial status, age, and part-time versus full-time status. With such data trustees can evaluate proposals made to them as to standards of admission, tuition rates, the provision of scholarships, financial aid, and assistance in finding employment. They can also appraise the relevance of counseling programs, entertainment, and publications for the particular mix of part-time and full-time students of various age levels.

Quality of the Institution's Output. The measurement of a college or university's output is difficult, if not impossible. Yet the quality of its graduates is the bottom line of the enterprise for which the trustees are responsible. Thus, trustees should seek such indicators as the success of graduates in gaining admission to graduate, law, and medical schools; the reactions of corporate representatives who interview graduates for prospective employment; and the success of graduates in various occupational fields.

Of course, trustees should regularly see data on (1) the expenditure of funds in relation to the budget that they earlier approved; (2) the status of building projects that they earlier approved, along with the status of efforts to obtain funding for other needed facilities; and (3) the status of external reactions, that is, evidence of both approval and criticism by public officials, the press, peer-group institutions, parents, students, and the public.

To keep abreast of such a flow of information is a substantial task. Whether it becomes an oppressive burden or a manageable duty depends on the president, who of course requires the same information to fulfill his or her responsibility. If it is a public institution, the president needs such information to meet the demands of the state coordinating and budget agencies. A president who is an effective executive will be capable of devising and using a system that produces objective, analyzed, and condensed information on each of the areas mentioned above. If the vice-presidents and the deans are permitted to generate a flood of incidental and subjective reports and reactions, the president will not manage well, and the board will be ill informed. Thus, a major presidential responsibility is the organization and maintenance of an effective information system.

The president serves as executive officer of and principal adviser to the board and simultaneously as presiding officer of the faculty (the title of president flows from that function). He or she is also administrator of the institution's support services: physical plant, publications, food service, dormitories, purchasing, financial administration, and more. For each of these areas the president, as the board's accountable agent, requires the authority to see that all is done that should be done.

The logic of this is obvious. The president is a full-time professional executive; the board is made up of part-time volunteers who are amateurs in educational management. He or she is the one officer within the institution who can view the institution as a whole. Through experience, the president should know the academic staff, their ways, their needs, and their obligations. Finances and support services should be administered in accord with the legitimate needs of the faculty and the students. And the president should be capable of representing the college or university to state and federal governments, as well as to the public, the press, parents, donors, and others.

The key to the relationship between the board and the president is his or her *accountability*. That accountability *cannot* be defined alone by what the board determines the president shall bring to it for decision. It will be defined in practice by the extent to which the president chooses to inform the board and to seek its approval. Many events will take place in the functioning of an institution that part-time board members possessing limited familiarity with academic affairs will not recognize as meriting their consideration. A president's accountability includes the obligation to bring such matters to the board and to permit it to determine whether it shall act or authorize the president to handle such questions in the future.

The Trustees' Role in Policy Making

Conventional wisdom has long held that trustees of four-year colleges and universities are responsible for setting policy but should not be involved in management. In practice most of these boards have been concerned with a narrow range of policy and have tended to involve themselves more deeply in management, but in management of only part of the institution's activities. The practice among community college trustees contrasts markedly. About 60 percent of these boards are elected by popular vote, and their operating style tends to follow that of elected school boards. They often exercise their responsibility for making the policies that govern all the institution's activities and often claim to be partners of the president in management of the institution (Dziuba and Meardy, 1976).

Trustees of four-year and graduate institutions, however, tend to focus their attention on buildings, finances, and public and political relations. They devote little time and attention to student affairs and still less to the educational program and the quality and effectiveness of the faculty. They seldom come in contact with students or faculty members. They make little attempt to assess the educational effectiveness of the institution. (Paltridge, Hurst, and Morgan, 1973). This situation is incongruous, for the business of these institutions is *education*.

Why this misallocation of time and attention? There are three reasons. First, businessmen, lawyers, politicians, and bankers, who make up a large and dominating proportion of most boards, "feel at home" with the consideration of financial matters (budgets, expenditures, investments, accountants' reports); with the construction, maintenance, and operation of buildings; and with the public standing of the institution and its political relationships. They feel less at home with questions of educational program, faculty capabilities, or the desirability of various services offered to students. To repeat, however, the business of the institution is learning and the producing of knowledge. Second, trustees who, if they were to join the board of a shoe company, would feel obligated to acquaint themselves with the company's business—its manufacturing processes, unit costs, the status of its inventories, its markets and margins—tend to assume that education and student affairs are the faculty's province and that they (the trustees) should not trespass on it. This assumption is invalid. Third, the president often—and the faculty more often—tend to discourage any manifestation of interest by trustees. Authority delegated to the faculty decades ago is now regarded as belonging to it by God-given right. That assumption, too, is invalid.

Faculty members are entitled to academic freedom, that is, the right to teach in their classrooms what they believe to be true. They are entitled to academic tenure, which is the assurance that over time they will continue to enjoy academic freedom. But neither academic freedom nor the specialized knowledge of a particular discipline warrants denial of the trustees' right and responsibility to question proposals for educational programs, the nature and quality of student services, and the processes by which faculty members are selected, appointed, evaluated, and promoted.

The illogic of such assumptions becomes apparent when one asks how a trustee can evaluate the institutional budget or proposals for the construction of a new classroom, library, or other building, if he or she is not fully informed as to the educational programs for which the budget is prepared or for which the buildings are designed. If the board is in fact, as in legal theory, to be responsible for all activities of the college or university, its members must concern themselves with the guts of the enterprise, namely, the educational program. It should have a role in determining who shall be taught, who shall teach, and what shall be taught. More community college trustees accept such reasoning than do the trustees of four-year colleges and universities.

That trustees should concern themselves with a broader range of policy making than many boards now do has long been advocated by most observers of institutional governance. The most forthright and reasoned statement of this point of view was made some two decades ago by a businessman who served as a trustee:

> The board of trustees has in fact final responsibility under its charter for the educational program as well as for the property of its institution. Having final authority and responsibility, it has also accountability for a performance it is willing to defend to the state, to the national and local community, to donors of property, to students and parents, to the individual members of the faculty who have committed themselves and their families to an educational and intellectual program as their way of life.
>
> The trustees, therefore, must take back from the faculty *as a body* its present authority over the design and administration of the curriculum [Ruml and Morrison, 1959, p. 13].

I would substitute for Ruml's words "the design and administration of the curriculum," the broader and impliedly less detailed phrase "the determination and periodic review of the administration of all policies governing the educational program, the faculty, and student affairs."

Of course, trustees will also be concerned with annual budgets. By their approval of the operating budget, trustees will fix policies—if they truly study the allocation of funds among the educational program, student affairs activities, and administrative activities. They will also fix policies by their approval of the capital budget, that is, by the priority they attach to the construction of classrooms, laboratories, and libraries versus athletic fields, student unions, dormitories, and landscaping. They will be well advised to develop policies to govern relations with donors, with the press, and with the political forces that be, even though it will be exceedingly difficult to avoid improvisation in dealing with these groups from day to day.

Suggestions that trustees should concern themselves with this range of activities are often met by two objections: first, trustees cannot give sufficient time to consider so many different areas; second, trustees will substitute their amateur judgments on educational matters and student affairs for the expertise of faculty members.

To fulfill the obligations of a trustee requires giving at least enough time for regular monthly committee meetings and for six or eight full board meetings each year. But if the president organizes each meeting and oversees the materials placed before board members relative to each issue that they are asked to decide, the covering of a broad scope will be feasible. And the answer to the second objection is simply that trustees cannot leave all educational policy and curriculum determinations to the faculty and the administration. Faculty members are subject matter specialists—chemists, mathematicians, zoologists. Few will have been trained in curriculum planning or even in such student evaluation processes as examining and grading. They should be free, as previously stated, to determine the content of their courses. They should participate, along with deans and the president or vice-president for academic affairs, in the framing of programs; for example, a program in the study of public policy leading to the bachelor's degree. But trustees should also take part in the framing of such programs and must continually inform themselves about such pragmatic matters as course proliferation and the ratio of faculty members to students.

"The sensible trustee," a wise and experienced trustee of liberal arts colleges has written, "will recognize that there are areas where he can and should ask questions but will customarily defer to the judgment of the person most intimately concerned therewith. This he does every day in his business life" (Bean, 1975, p. 35).

Sensible trustees, following what has been described as "Corson's Law" (Nason, 1975; Dziuba and Meardy, 1976), should keep their noses in every facet of the institution's operations so that they may keep their fingers out. Then if questioning raises doubts in their minds as to the efficacy of proposals presented, the trustees would be well advised to ask the faculty to *reconsider* the proposal and to allow the board to have their reconsidered judgment. A board should not reject a faculty proposal forthwith on the basis of its lay judgment, and it should let stand after reconsideration even those proposals that it still questions if they are clearly based on a specialized competence that board members do not possess.

The Trustees' Role in Management

The trustees' legitimate concern with the management of the institution they serve flows directly from their responsibility for setting policy. Trustees have the added responsibility for seeing to it that policies that have been set are then carried out with reasonable effectiveness. Trustees will also require feedback in order to know whether the decisions they made stood up well when tested in the crucible of day-to-day practice. The feedback they will require will be provided in large part by the channels of information previously described. It should be supplemented by at least quarterly contacts with faculty and student representatives to learn (along with the president) of reactions to issues pending or recently decided. It is not enough to issue ukases from on high and to assume that all respect the wisdom and authority of those who sit around the table in the board room.

It has been argued that trustees have a single management job—to support the president. This statement proposes an avoidance of trustee responsibilities. Trustees have the important managerial responsibility of selecting an able president. Having selected such a person, they have the continuing responsibility of assisting him or her. This means providing introductions throughout the community—local, state, and, in some instances, national; counseling; interceding upon request with interest groups, individuals, or political officials; according presidential proposals the presumption of validity but also persistently questioning such proposals; and monitoring his or her performance.

The president (whether of a corporation or a college or university) "needs to have a group before which he . . . presents his plans, and from which he eventually draws approval; such review does not need to be exceedingly formal, but it needs to be very real. . . . He can lead strongly and at the same time consult freely with his subordinates if he is being supported by them in presenting his plans before a tough tribunal, not if he is being judged (only) by his own subordinates" (Bush, 1961, pp. 507–508).

The board cannot fulfill its responsibility for assuring the effectiveness of management of a college or university only by assisting the president in the several ways suggested thus far. In addition, the information system previously depicted must provide the board with materials by which its members can assure themselves (again by questioning, not ordering) of the effectiveness of four basic activities:

Educational Program. The curriculum is for the college or university what in business is called the product line. It should be characterized, as is the product line of a progressive business, by constant change. Just as new products are added and old products dropped in a business, so it should be in the college or university. To assess the vitality of their products, trustees should review every six months or every year what new programs have been added, especially the programs and courses that have been dropped.

If the faculty regularly and rigorously evaluates the educational product line, programs and courses will be weeded out. It is not for the trustees to determine what courses should be added or which should be weeded out. Rather, it is the trustees' responsibility to ensure that there is a continuing effort, consistent with the institution's mission, to add, reshape, and eliminate programs and courses.

Student Achievement. Even though there are no adequate measures of how well the teaching and learning processes are being carried out, that does not relieve trustees of responsibility for seeking such evidences as can be garnered. They will serve the institution well if they repeatedly ask that information be supplied as to:

1. The quality of students admitted (the proportion, for example, from the top quarter and from the top half of high school graduating classes, their average verbal and mathematical scores on the Scholastic Aptitude Test, and the relative success of enrollees who come directly from high school and those who transfer from other institutions of higher education).
2. The rate of attrition, that is, the number of entrants who drop out for whatever reasons at the conclusion of each semester.
3. The success of graduates in seeking admission to graduate, law, and medical schools.

Personnel Process. The selection, evaluation, promotion, and termination of faculty members are as important in a college or university as in any business or governmental enterprise, and perhaps even more so. Whatever quality a college or university can claim is directly related to the abilities of rigorously selected, well-motivated, progressive faculty members. It fulfills its responsibility when it ensures that well-conceived processes of selection, evaluation, promotion and, termination have been devised and are being used.

Financial Process. Boards of trustees focus much of their attention on this aspect of management. There is little need for urging that they regularly review expenditures. More important is the seeking of comparative data (to supplement any self-serving assertions by the president and the financial vice-president!) as to the institution's revenues by sources (how do its tuition rates and student fees compare with those of similar institutions?) and particularly as to its expenditures by purpose.

A catholic curiosity is the mark of most truly effective individuals, be they bankers, doctors, merchants, industrialists, lawyers, or politicians. It is *the* talent that the most valuable trustees bring to any college or university board. The curious will, at times, make themselves unpopular with the institution's administrators. At other times they will make themselves unpopular with their colleagues when they suggest that the board take the time to look back and assess its own performance—as is eminently desirable. But their questioning will provide an invaluable therapy for ensuring healthier management.

Trustees a Board Can Do Without

Anyone who has observed the functioning of many boards is familiar with certain recurring trustee types. A few are probably inevitable, but unlucky is the board dominated by these five:

1. *The prestige-gratification trustee.* This person attends a substantial proportion of all meetings but does not take an active part. Such a trustee assumes that it is enough to have lent his or her name to the institution.
2. *The old-grad trustee.* Loyalty to the alma mater guides every vote. He or she is especially interested in the athletic program and the architecture of new buildings. This trustee's judgments reflect a belief that the institution should be maintained as it was during his or her student days.
3. *The self-interest trustee.* Despite periodic protestations to the contrary, this trustee is especially interested in those aspects of the operations that are close to his or her pocketbook.
4. *The affirming trustee.* This person says yes to every proposal presented to the board by the president. Proposals are seldom questioned. In being a "yes-man," this trustee serves the president poorly.
5. *The political trustee.* Appointed because he or she is a rising member of the political party in power, this trustee looks upon trusteeship as a step toward higher office. Such a person can be useful for the public institution, but only when good judgment rather than political affiliation guides his or her votes.

Fortunately, there are limited numbers of these several types of trustees. What is needed is more of the wants-to-be-shown category of trustee. Such individuals are characterized by a wide-ranging curiosity. They often and frankly admit to limited understanding of the functioning of an educational institution and ask questions as to why, what, when, and how. But the president and staff come to realize that such trustees want to be supportive and that they must be prepared to answer discerning questions to earn their support. This kind of trustee is "more to be desired than gold" (Davis, 1958). He or she will contribute to the formulation of thoroughly considered policy and will ensure that the management of the institution is alert and effective.

8

John W. Nason

Selecting
the Chief Executive

The average tenure of a college or university president today is eight years. Stated in different terms, 325 to 350 colleges and universities each year are looking for new presidents. Since the president is the central and most influential individual within the life of the institution, 325 to 350 boards of trustees or regents each year face their major responsibility: selection of the man or woman into whose hands they will entrust the future of their institution.

Like other social institutions in a growing and changing society, colleges and universities are more complex than they once were, less single-minded in their goals, more vulnerable to competing demands. No individual can perform equally well in all the roles that presidents are asked to play. There is no such thing as a model college president. The individual who might put on a brilliant performance at one institution could easily be a dismal failure at another. Before deciding *whom* they want, trustees must decide *what* they want.

This is more easily said than done. Vacancies caused by normal retirement, where there is ample time to plan for the succession, are a distinct minority. When a vacancy is caused by the president's decision to accept another position, usually another college or university presidency, the interval between announcement and departure is frequently inadequate for a careful review of institutional needs and a thorough process of search. When the president dies in office, withdraws for family or health reasons, or resigns suddenly under pressure or as the result of some institutional emergency, the college or university faces a crisis for which it has had no time to prepare.

In this last situation the board has little choice other than to appoint an acting or interim president. Someone must be in control of the ship, must keep it in order and afloat while decisions are made respecting its future course and a search is conducted for a new captain. Appointment of an acting president is a holding operation, and those eager to push full steam ahead will be impatient with the delay. But it does provide time where time is needed. The search for and selection of a new president should not be done in a hurry, and it ought to be preceded by an analysis of institutional problems, needs, and goals. Only after such an analysis can the trustees feel confident about the kind of person that the institution will need for the decade ahead.

When an acting president is to be appointed, the academic community tends to favor a senior and respected administrative officer or faculty member. Such a choice has obvious advantages. Its danger, however, is that the natural choice often turns out to be an inside candidate for the permanent job, a situation that is awkward at best and can sometimes be divisive. For this reason trustees are turning more frequently to an outsider—a retired president or dean experienced in the problems of administration and willing to go back into harness for six months or a year. Whether the acting president is internal or external, he or she is serving in a temporary capacity, and the board should provide some guidelines. These will make a difficult job easier and will reduce the danger of erratic or too decisive action by a temporary officer.

The Machinery of Selection

Many boards assume, sometimes hastily and superficially, that they know what they need and want in a president. Some will take the time under the leadership of an acting president to determine this in detail. Others will appoint one or more committees with instructions to decide on the criteria of the new president and then to find one or more individuals who fit those criteria. If the board is small, locally based, and actively involved in the affairs of the institution, as is the case in most community colleges, the board as a whole may undertake the work of search and selection. This may also happen in those institutions where the choice is sharply limited by religious affiliation or where there is widespread agreement on an outstanding inside candidate.

The standard procedure, however, is to appoint one or more committees to engage in search, screening, and recommendations—either a single committee to carry out all three functions; or two committees, one for search and preliminary screening, the other for final screening and recommendation; or a single committee buttressed by one or more advisory committees composed of faculty, students, alumni, and local citizens. Any one of these arrangements will work. The choice among them will depend largely on the degree of involvement desired of or demanded by faculty, students, and others. This in turn will depend on the history of the institution and its political climate.

The single committee working closely with one or more advisory committees emphasizes—quite correctly—the dominant role of the trustees or regents in the selection of the president. Criticism occurs when the advisory committees are treated cavalierly or the members feel that their views are not being seriously considered. In the two-committee pattern, the search group usually consists of faculty, students, and others, along with one or two trustees, whereas the selection group is composed largely or entirely of trustees. This has the advantage of focusing responsibility on the trustees, where it belongs, but it invites attempts to limit or influence the choice of the selection committee by skewing the panel of candidates presented by the search committee.

The present trend, characteristic of the greater involvement of faculty and students in the governance of institutions, is toward a single committee composed of trustees, faculty, and students. In public four-year institutions state education officials and/or officers of multicampus governing systems frequently participate. In community colleges local citizens may be invited to serve. Private and church-related colleges will usually include alumni, and representatives of the parent religious organization will often serve on the latter's committees. The median size of these search and selection committees is ten, and their range is from three to twenty-five (Nason, 1979). The upper range has given rise to frequent criticisms that the committees are too large to function well; and some sensitive critics are convinced that large and heterogeneous committees tend to end up with sound but uninspired choices, being unable to agree on the unusual or unorthodox individual.

A recent survey (Nason, 1979) reveals that over two thirds of the search and selection of committees include faculty, that almost as many include students, and that approximately half have alumni members. Public institutions, both four-year and two-year, are more hospitable to nontrustees than are private colleges and universities. The two great advantages of the single heterogeneous committee are the sense of unity and common purpose generated by the months of working closely together and the assurance that the president-elect will start his or her career with the support of the various constituencies.

Great care should be taken in the selection of committee members, for committees need to reflect diverse points of view and yet be able to cooperate in achieving a common purpose. The board should make quite clear that individuals selected from different constituencies are not representatives of those constituencies in the usual political sense of the term but have been chosen from different backgrounds to provide a variety of perspectives. They should serve because they have the best interests of the institution at heart. Commitment to the institution and its program, tolerance of differing viewpoints, and the willingness to put in long hours of hard work are essential. With members being appointed by different constituencies, it is not easy to get a good mix, but a wise chairman can often turn a dubious beginning into an effective ending.

In establishing the committee or committees, the board should make the mandate clear. Are committee members to establish the criteria for the new president or work within specifications already approved by the board? If the former, should they seek board approval before proceeding? What is the deadline for presenting recommendations? How many names are to be recommended? Are they to be ranked or unranked? How broadly is the committee to look? What special efforts should be made to meet the requirements of equal opportunity and affirmative action? What is to be the budget for the committee's work? Is there leeway for extra expenditures if needed? Is the committee free to employ outside professional consultants? How open or how confidential is the search and selection process to be? Implicit in the board's charge to the committee, and preferably explicit, is the assertion that the final decision regarding the new president is a board responsibility.

Organizing the Committee

One essential factor in virtually all successful presidential selections is complete devotion to the task by at least one individual, usually the committee chairman. It is a demanding job but, as many chairmen will testify, a rewarding one. The chairman must direct and control the committee, set the tone for its deliberations, ease it over awkward moments, cope with emergencies, and also give an example of diligence, humor, and consideration for the views of others. He or she must command respect, know when to be firm and when to bend, and above all be impartial.

Second only to the chairman in importance is the staff. The processing of anywhere from 100 to 500 names is an enormous job. The file of voluminous correspondence on each candidate must be completed and kept in order. Since committee members will be giving large blocs of their time to reading dossiers, interviewing candidates, and debating their merits, they need and deserve someone else to handle the multifarious details. This is usually an administrative secretary or staff officer assigned full- or part-time to the job, though for the sake of convenience or security it is sometimes a private secretary in the office of a member of the committee, usually the chairman. Whoever fills this role should understand its nature thoroughly and be a person of complete discretion.

Presumably the board has given the committee a deadline for making nominations, and one of the first acts of the committee should be to set up a timetable consistent with the deadline. This is particularly important, for committees tend to underestimate the amount of time necessary for each stage of the search and selection process. The Nason (1979) study found wide variations in the length of presidential searches—from one day in the case of a church-related college to twenty-four months for a private junior college. Public institutions take less time than private ones—two to twelve months for four-year public colleges and universities and one to six months for community colleges against four to eighteen months for private four-year colleges and three to twenty-four months for private junior colleges. Median lengths of time ranged from four and one-half months for community colleges to nine months for private universities.

Should the committee make use of outside professional help? This question is being asked more frequently than in the past. Many of the major management firms have expanded their services to include educational as well as commercial clients. A variety of new service agencies, both for-profit and nonprofit, have sprung up in response to educational needs. And in addition there are individual educational consultants—ex-administrators and faculty with backgrounds in educational administration—whose services are available on a *per diem* basis. Approximately 20 percent of the colleges and universities looking for new presidents make use of outside consultants to help define institutional needs and presidential criteria or to develop a roster of candidates. In addition, consultants are sometimes used to screen candidates, conduct interviews, and check background information. Private institutions use such services more frequently than public institutions, two-year colleges more extensively than four-year (Nason, 1979).

Resistance to the use of outside professionals, however, persists in the educational world. It is due in part to the self-centered nature of the academic community and its consequent distrust of the outsider, in part to the conviction that trustees, faculty, and students understand the peculiar character and needs of the institution better than any outsider could, and in part to the additional cost, which in the academic scale of values often seems high, especially if a commercial firm is used.

At the same time, outside professional help, whether rendered by a firm or an individual, can often help a committee avoid serious mistakes and can save its members large amounts of time by doing the necessary legwork. A professional consultant will usually be better at interviewing candidates than will the average committee member and can make on-site investigations with less danger of embarrassment to the candidates. Costs can be negotiated in light of the services desired. If those services result in a better choice or the "right" person, they will be a good investment. The Association of American Colleges (AAC), for example, has long maintained a modest roster of candidates for various administrative posts in higher education. Recently AAC has joined with the Association of Governing Boards (AGB) in establishing a Presidential Search and Consultation Service (PSCS), which for a fee will provide all or some combination of the services that committees of search and selection may need.

And that brings us to the total cost of the search and selection process, a matter to which the committee needs to give its attention at the start. Committee time—a very considerable cost to the members—is free to the institution, which may also carry a staff person for the committee, plus secretarial and clerical assistants, on the regular college or university payroll. Their full- or part-time salaries, however, are a real, even though unassigned, cost, as are the expenses for stationery and postage, file cases, duplication of records, committee and candidate travel, telephone, printing, advertising, and in some cases office rent and fees for consultants. The many hidden expenses make accurate estimates of total costs difficult, but it is hard to see how any sort of genuine search and selection could be completed for less than $2,000 to $3,000, and some institutions have reported $50,000 to $55,000. The one observation that all committees should keep in mind is that the selection of the new president is not the place to skimp. The wrong choice would be far more expensive in the long run than would any investment of money that resulted in finding the right person.

Reference has already been made to the fact that the search

and selection process involves a very considerable amount of detail. Adequate provision needs to be made for this and is part of the cost of conducting the search. Besides correspondence with candidates and references, dossiers must be completed, reports on telephone calls and interviews filed, schedules for meetings and interviews arranged, and records of the number and nature of candidates and of the actions of the committee kept. Federal and state regulations require, for private and public institutions alike, that committees be able to demonstrate, if challenged, their conformity to the regulations governing equal opportunity and affirmative action. Occasionally divisions of opinion on campus will erupt in bitter accusations, or friends of unsuccessful candidates will make charges of favoritism. A complete record is the best defense, and fifty years later, when all the principal characters are dead, it will be a godsend to the college or university historian.

The committee must also decide to what extent the names of candidates are to be kept confidential and how to handle the publicity that surrounds and almost inevitably invades so crucial an operation. Public institutions in states with strict sunshine laws, such as Florida and Minnesota, have no option. The names of all candidates are revealed, and committee deliberations are open to press and public. Some candidates and some committee members profess to like this system, although the latter admit that they lose a number of good candidates, since many individuals will not compete or cannot afford to compete in a public arena. They also note that the process of selection takes longer when conducted publicly, because trustees cannot speak as bluntly as they might in private and thus get on with the business of choice.

Most selection committees, in fact, prefer to conduct their deliberations in private, and most candidates prefer to have their candidacy kept confidential, at least until the final stages. Once candidates are invited to meet with faculty, students, administrative officers, and others on campus, their names will be bruited about, and word will usually get back to their home institutions, although even this can sometimes be avoided.

Frequently premature publicity has led good candidates to withdraw their names and, in some situations, to precipitate undesirable campaigning for particular candidates. Premature publicity, particularly about "leading candidates," can best be avoided by establishing working relations with the student newspaper and local news media at an early stage. They will want to know what is happening, whether the committee is nearing a decision, what problems have arisen. They will maintain that their audiences are deeply interested in, and have a right to know, what is going on. It may prove better to take the media into the committee's confidence than to hold them at arm's length, or at least some committees have found this to be so. Nevertheless, committees should always be on guard in dealing with the media.

Deciding What Is Wanted

Some qualities are essential to the success of any college or university president—an understanding of what education is really about, some capacity for administration (which includes the ability to deal with people), a high degree of physical and emotional stamina, honesty, courage, personal integrity, and leadership. The temptation is to elaborate these and other qualities until the committee appears to be seeking a mythical ideal. What is really needed is a hardheaded analysis of the institution's problems and prospects; from this, one can deduce the particular skills that will be most useful in a president.

This institutional analysis, as was noted earlier, is properly the responsibility of the board: not that the board should make the analysis, but it should insist that a survey be undertaken and should put its seal of approval on the results. All too often, however, committees are set to work without specific blueprints to guide their search. Their first task, then, is to make their own analysis of the present condition and future needs of the college or university.

What should committees look for in an institutional survey? Here are ten questions that should be asked about every college or university:

1. Is the institution at a point in its history where it either wants or needs to change its goals and purposes?
2. What kinds of financial problems will have to be dealt with over the next ten years?

3. Are there pressures, internal or external, to expand certain educational programs? Which ones?
4. Is the need to contract and consolidate educational programs rather than to expand them? Which ones?
5. What changes in the size and composition of the student body are likely to occur? What recruitment programs should be developed?
6. Is the quality of the educational programs right for the institution and the community? Is this problem one of maintaining quality or of improving it?
7. Is the physical plant satisfactory in size and standards for the demands of the next decade?
8. How significant an administrative problem will collective bargaining be in the years ahead?
9. How much attention will need to be given to the institution's extracurricular programs, such as student social life, men's and women's athletics, and counseling?
10. Will the governance of the institution, both internally and externally, need overhauling and improvement?

These questions can be expanded almost indefinitely, particularly in view of the differences between public and private institutions and between two-year and four-year colleges. Public universities face problems of autonomy within statewide systems, of responsiveness to public demands, and of public accountability. Private colleges face serious problems of enrollment, financial support, and maintenance of their independence in the face of growing encroachment of federal and state agencies. Community colleges with their close ties to the local community have governance, support, and growth problems of their own.

The answers to these ten questions, however, will tell the committee what qualifications are most important in the new president—academic leadership, political savvy, fund-raising ability, managerial skills, fiscal competence, public relations skills, understanding of labor relations, ability as a conciliator. No one is equally good in all departments; and for any given college or university looking for a new president, some skills or abilities will be more important than others. As the old saw puts it, "You pays your money and you takes your choice." The wise committee will have decided what it wants and what it will settle for.

Developing a Pool of Candidates

Having reached a decision on what qualities are needed in a president, some committee members grow impatient with elaborate search processes. They favor a quick decision when the first "good" person comes along who meets or approximates the specifications. Long lists are full of unsuitable people, they say, and screening them out is a waste of time and energy. And besides, they argue, the longer the search and selection process, the greater the danger of losing a good candidate who grows unhappy over the delay or who is carried off by another institution.

Most committees, however, seek not just a good candidate, but the best man or woman for their particular situation. To determine who this is, they must canvass the field. In their view, the importance of the president in the life of the institution justifies the extra time and effort involved. Further, in a society that is belatedly opening more and more doors to women and minorities, special efforts must be made to include individuals from those sectors. Although these efforts are mandated by regulations defining equal opportunity and affirmative action, a concern for human justice should itself push most committees in this direction. In a recent survey (Nason, 1979) the number of candidates considered by committees of selection at public institutions ranged from 20 to 400 with a median of 216, that for private universities from 79 to 500 with a median of 217, and that for private colleges from 50 to 500 with a median of 240.

There are several ways of developing a roster of names. The traditional method has been to make the vacancy known through such vehicles as the alumni magazine and parents' news bulletins and to send off letters of inquiry to educators, foundation officers, church officials, selected persons in the state and federal government, prominent local citizens, and friends of the institution. Implicit in this procedure is the belief that individuals should not or would not apply for the position but instead must be nominated by a third party. But the concern to open top administrative positions in postsecondary education to all qualified individuals regardless of race, color, sex, or ethnic origin has in recent years changed the traditional practice. Today it is quite common to advertise openings in the *Chronicle of Higher Education,* the *New York Times* or the *Wall Street Journal,* a local newspaper, and sometimes in one or more educational and religious journals. Those institutions most concerned to include minorities and women among their candidates advertise in the publications specifically designed for professional women and for blacks and will register the vacancy with similar organizations. Finally, there are the professional firms that make it their business to maintain a highly select roster of candidates or to generate such a roster on commission.

The results of advertising are likely to be mixed. Public colleges and universities, and particularly community colleges, have relied more heavily than private institutions on this source, some exclusively so (Nason, 1979). Private colleges and universities, although casting their nets widely, find their top candidates for the most part among those nominated by knowledgeable individuals. In spite of the numbers involved, the recurrent complaint of committees of selection has been that they did not have enough good candidates from whom to choose.

One reason for this is the readiness of committees to accept an individual's response that he or she is not really interested. It is important to understand the phenomenon of the reluctant candidate. Many well-qualified individuals who would make strong candidates are already well placed. They may not have thought seriously of going somewhere else, or they may be reluctant to appear to be jockeying for a job. They need to be courted and to have their interest aroused. A frontal approach may be self-defeating, whereas a request for their advice on what kind of person the committee should be seeking may stimulate their interest. And committees should remember that many a lady who first said no has ended up at the altar.

Screening Candidates

Sorting out candidates according to their attractiveness and suitability is a slow process that will take weeks to complete. Therefore, it is well to begin as soon as names start to come in. The reduction of the long list to a "select list" can best be done in two steps—a preliminary screening that produces somewhere between ten and forty candidates considered worthy of serious investigation and a final screening after which the committee presents one or more names to the board for final decision. The present section is concerned with preliminary screening.

Who sorts the candidates out? Some committees feel that this is a committee responsibility and that every member should vote on each candidate. Some committees divide up into teams to lighten the load, call on advisory committees of faculty and students (where they exist) for the initial sorting, or set up a special task force. Sometimes the chairman or the administrative officer will undertake this assignment. If professional consultants are employed, they frequently perform this function. The choice of method depends on temperament, convenience, available time, and degree of trust among the several constituencies. However the initial screening is done, the committee as a whole should review the preliminary classifications, and significant differences in appraisal should at this point be settled in the candidate's favor.

Sound decisions for or against candidates require adequate information. How extensively and vigorously committees should pursue information about candidates at this stage is a moot point. It is reasonable to request a *curriculum vitae* of any applicant, and some committees have elaborate forms that all candidates must complete. These have the advantage of providing uniform information about all candidates, but they tend to alienate some of the better ones who need to be stalked in subtler fashion. Often the committee staff member can fill in details by consulting standard biographical registries, by sending a letter to an applicant to ask for missing information, and by requesting additional information from those who have proposed individuals. The staff person should probably prepare a standard summary of each candidate, so that committee members can make quick comparisons.

This is the stage for following up references. Those provided by candidates will prove to be of limited value, but it is usually possible to get the names of others who know the candidates and who will be prepared to present more balanced views. There are advantages in using the telephone for such appraisals; inflections and hesitations can be more revealing at times than the words themselves, and most people will speak more freely and openly than they will write. All inquiries of references, whether written, by telephone, or face to face, should be committee approved. At this point, individual initiative will look too much like an end run. Particular care should be taken not to violate a candidate's request for confidentiality.

This is not the time for extensive interviews, but some committees have found it helpful to hold a few interviews as a learning experience for their members and sometimes as a way of showing their interest in a very attractive candidate who might otherwise be lost.

Two cautions are in order. First, it is important to keep in communication with candidates. Applications and nominations should be promptly acknowledged. References should be thanked. Candidates should be informed of where they stand. "We continue to be interested in you, but are having heavy going in working through all the names on our list" is a possible formula to use. Second, it is also important to keep written records of telephone calls, face-to-face conversations, and committee decisions. When hundreds of names are chewed over for months, memories become confused and outlines blurred. What seems like an unnecessary nuisance at the time can settle an important point three months later.

Interviewing Candidates

Once the preliminary screening has yielded a select list of ten to forty names, the committee is ready for the second stage, which focuses on interviewing candidates. The kind of face-to-face impressions that interviews provide are essential. No committee will want to recommend an individual for president sight unseen. Many members find the interview the most revealing and helpful kind of evidence and report that it frequently leads to changes in comparative ratings. But the interview is a risky business. At times it allows the glib and facile candidate to appear much more impressive than the quiet and reserved individual. Effective interviewing is a skill that must be learned. Committees could profit from a little professional instruction and a practice run or two.

The number of candidates interviewed will vary from committee to committee. Both cost and time are often offered as reasons for limiting the number. Neither argument is valid. A wrong choice of president is far more costly in time and money than the investment necessary to find the right individual. More to the point is the danger that interviews will raise hopes on the part of candidates and their friends, with consequent disappointment and sometimes recriminations if the hopes are not realized. This is a risk that must be run. Most committees end up interviewing between five and fifteen candidates. A few will stop with one, if he or she looks really promising; others will try to see between twenty and thirty. (For a more cautious and critical view of the role of the interview in the selection process, see Fouts, 1977.)

Because of their concern for confidentiality, private colleges and universities tend to schedule interviews off campus, frequently in a hotel or motel in a major transportation center or convenient city. Many public institutions follow the same pattern, although on-campus interviews are more common where confidentiality is less important and the convenience of the committee more so. An attractive place for the interviews and for waiting should be provided. The schedule should be so managed that candidates do not stumble across one another, and it should allow ample time for each interview. One hour is too little; two to three hours are much better. This means that four or at most five interviews are all that can be squeezed into one day. Interviewing is tiring work and its quality tends to deteriorate at the end of a long day.

The interviews may be conducted by the committee as a whole, by two or more committee teams, by a single task force, or by an individual member. The time and expense involved decrease as the number of interviewers is reduced; so, unfortunately, do the value and satisfactoriness of the interviews. Interviews by a single individual should be avoided unless the individual happens to be in the candidate's neighborhood. Even so it is unwise to rely on only one person's impressions, unless that person is a professional consultant who is skilled in interviewing and who brings a broad experience of institutions and people to the service of the committee.

Some committees prefer to ask a standard set of questions of all candidates on the grounds that this is the only way of providing a uniform base for comparative judgments. Other committees, however, will follow more flexible lines, deciding in advance what it is they want to know about each candidate and what gaps in the record, what apparent inconsistencies in the reports of references, or what troubling comments in the candidate's papers need clarification. Members should be thoroughly familiar with the candidate's *curriculum vitae*. They should be seeking in the interview, not matters of fact that are on the record but interpretations of the record and anticipations of attitudes and positions that the candidate will take. This is the time to explore the candidate's views on research, teaching, tenure, affirmative action, collective bargaining, graduate study, professional programs, and governance, as well as his or her philosophy of education.

Intelligent and sensitive candidates—the kind the committee is really looking for—will be as full of questions for the committee as the committee is for the candidate. This may be his or her first opportunity to get some impression of trustees and faculty, of the temper of the institution, of its problems and promise. Committee members should be prepared to respond to the candidate's questions as being legitimate and important. Furthermore, the interview provides a golden opportunity to impress the candidate with the quality of the college or university and the commitment of its constituencies. No candidate will come to scoff, but some may arrive in a sceptical mood. The interview will be a great success if the candidate comes to feel a genuine interest in the institution as a result of it.

After the interviews, committee members should record in writing their impressions of the candidates, either by using a standard rating sheet or by making notes for future reference. The committee is now ready to reduce the select list to those candidates worth final consideration. For them a thorough background check is in order and, if nothing adverse turns up, an invitation to the campus. At this point the chairman, or the staff officer acting on behalf of the chairman, should advise all candidates no longer on the select list of their status. Candidates invited to meet with the committee will particularly want to know where they stand. Nothing is so demoralizing as to be left dangling.

Selecting the Final Candidates

Unless thorough background checks have already been made, the committee should now complete its work. What is involved is much more than a few character and professional references. How does the candidate behave in a crisis and under strain? Is he or she liked, admired, respected by colleagues and subordinates? What are the candidate's greatest strengths and most serious weaknesses? Are there episodes in the past that would prove embarrassing given the public status of a president?

Since the search is nearing its climax and time is short, this kind of investigation is better made by telephone or visit than by correspondence, and of the two the visit is likely to be more revealing. It should only be made with the knowledge and consent of the candidate; and while it will clearly be impossible to conduct such inquiries without disclosing the committee's interest, they should be conducted with as much discretion and diplomacy as possible. The outside consultant, experienced in the technique of investigation, can be very helpful at this point.

After eliminating candidates who do not stand up well in this kind of investigation, the committee must decide how to proceed with its handful of top candidates. One school of thought contends that the committee should at this juncture make a single choice and invite that one individual to the campus to meet with faculty, students, and administrative officers. If there is a strong negative reaction to the candidate, the committee should then review its list and come up with someone else. A second school of thought would arrange for two or more candidates to visit the campus and would include faculty, student, and other local reactions in deciding whom to recommend to the board.

Those who favor the first procedure argue that a parade of candidates before the local constituencies turns the final selection into a popularity contest. If all candidates were equal in the eyes of the committee, this procedure might nevertheless be acceptable. In fact, however, committee members, who have lived with the problem for months and who know the candidates' records inside and out, usually have clear priorities that should not be subordinated to local decisions based on first impressions and perhaps influenced too much by "personality."

Nevertheless, faculty, administrative staff, students, alumni, and members of the state educational system (if a public institution is involved) have a strong and legitimate interest in the choice of the new president. They may recognize that the final decision is not theirs but may still feel that they have a right to be consulted. And from the point of view of the candidates it is extremely important that they be acceptable to the local people with whom they will be working. The greater the involvement of the local groups, the better the chances of future cooperation.

Whether one campus visit or several are decided upon, careful plans need to be made. Short exposures are not very satisfactory. At least a day and a half should be scheduled, and many institutions plan three- and four-day programs. Decisions need to be made about the groups to meet the candidate, particularly in universities and large colleges, where not all faculty and students can participate. A schedule of appointments and places must be drawn up, attractive accommodations made available, transportation arranged. Each candidate should have a host who is responsible for seeing that he or she is comfortable, gets to the right places, and is properly introduced and informed. Sometimes the committee will initiate the visit with a luncheon or dinner meeting to describe the "promised land"; sometimes it will meet with the candidate at the end of his or her visit to get the candidate's reactions and to answer questions. Even under the best of circumstances, visiting a campus to be looked over (and to do some looking over as well) is hardly a relaxing experience. Allowance needs to be made for this in the timetable of meetings and appointments, while at the same time it is not inappropriate to observe how the candidate performs under pressure.

Even more than the interview, the campus visit is an opportunity for the candidate to find out what the college or university is really like. Very few candidates will be willing to accept the presidency of an institution they have never seen, and a candidate not imaginative and shrewd enough to insist on learning about its finances, the temper of its faculty and students, its enrollment prospects, and the state of its external and internal relations would not be a good choice. Candidates should be supplied with voluminous information about the institution and the community in advance of the visit. They should be given every opportunity to ask questions of administrative officers, faculty, students, and (in public institutions) representatives of the state educational system about the problems and prospects that they might find themselves facing.

The visit is also one more opportunity—probably the best opportunity—to sell the candidate on the institution. Faculty and students, who sometimes think that anybody would want to be president of their college or university and who accordingly will sometimes be hard-nosed in their approach to the candidate, need to be aware that the candidate is selecting an institution just as much as the institution is selecting a president.

The president's wife was once taken for granted. It was assumed that she would manage the household, bring up their children, attend a wide variety of social functions, entertain distinguished guests, and in all ways aid and abet her husband's career. With the growing trend toward separate careers for wives, the role of the president's spouse needs much greater attention. The family responsibilities, the professional interests, and the institutional obligations of the wife should be taken into account by the committee and the trustees. If she is expected to play an institutional role, this needs to be made clear. Her character and personality will affect the way in which others judge the president's performance. The degree of her interest in the college or university and of her happiness in the new community will in part determine her husband's effectiveness as president.

These considerations are less important in community colleges and in metropolitan universities with a commuter population. But most private colleges and universities and the majority of public colleges and universities will want to see the wife as well as the husband, and she in turn will want to see what she and her husband may be undertaking in the new position. During the campus visit she should have her own tours and her own conversations about the community, its cultural assets, and its schools. At some point the committee or the trustees should have a frank discussion with her on what she will and will not do. Her attitude may be crucial in her husband's decision to accept an invitation if it is offered.

Since committees will be considering women as well as men, thought also needs to be given to the husband's role. What will the appointment of his wife do to his career? Is there a suitable position for him within the institution or in a nearby one? Will he move to the new community or maintain his profession or business where he is? What contribution will the board expect him to make to the social and professional responsibilities of his wife?

At some point in the search and selection process, salary, fringe benefits, and other terms of appointment must be discussed with the candidates. This is better done by the trustee members of the committee or by the chairman of the board. Such discussions sometimes take place at the time of the initial interviews, often at the time of or just after a definite invitation has been issued. Postponement to the very end can be embarrassing if the two parties cannot then agree on terms, and in any event it leaves the candidate uncertain about what he or she may expect. If the reception on campus is favorable, the visit provides a good opportunity for the chairman of the committee or the chairman of the board to outline in general terms what the institution has in mind and to determine what the candidate would need and find satisfactory.

The end of the visit is also a good time—assuming the candidate has survived the ordeal—to find out just how interested the candidate really is. Will he or she accept the job if it is offered? Some candidates resent this approach, arguing with considerable justification that they ought not to be required to make a decision until given a genuine offer. However, the delays, the difficulties, and often the embarrassment that a turndown causes for the institution are such that most committees and boards of trustees will insist on knowing in advance of their final offer whether the candidate will say yes.

Once the visits have been completed, the committee should receive full reports from those who have met and talked with the candidates, should review their own reactions, and finally should make their recommendations to the board—whether a single name, an unranked slate of names, or a list in order of priority. Some boards in their charge to the committee specify that the names of final candidates should be presented in unranked order, but since members know the candidates best, they can hardly avoid rating them in their own minds. Unless committee members cannot agree among themselves, it would seem a serious mistake for the board not to be aware of their preferences; even though not binding on the board, these should carry great weight.

There is much to be said for the single nomination. By the end of its search the selection committee should have a clear picture of the qualities of the various candidates and their "fit" with the institution. That being the case, it would seem to be dereliction of duty not to nominate the best individual. Such a nomination will flatter the candidate and will provide additional inducement for him or her to accept. Furthermore, many committees find that, in spite of efforts to uncover several acceptable candidates, they can identify only one whom they are conscientiously willing to recommend.

A single nomination, however, shifts the responsibility for the choice from the board to the committee. The trustees can, of course, reject the committee's recommendation, but this is rare. Less unlikely, however, is the last-minute withdrawal of the candidate who, flattered and tempted by the new opportunities and the personal attention of the committee, finally decides in a moment of truth against the invitation. This creates an awkward situation. The academic community is poised for an announcement that does not materialize. The committee is summoned into emergency session to review the other candidates. Word leaks out that the institution has been "turned down." Candidates who discover that they were second choices withdraw from the competition. These are reasons why the mark of a good committee is its ability to find several candidates whom it is prepared to recommend.

The choice between presenting one nomination or presenting more than one (on the assumption that the committee has that choice) should probably depend on the nature and climate of the institution. Where a high degree of trust exists and where there is substantial agreement on the kind of president wanted, the committee will be viewed as acting for the board and its informed judgment will be respected. Where the campus is politicized or where strong disagreements exist about the kind of individual who should lead the institution (often reflected in a failure of the committee to agree on its top choice), it is better to leave the final decision in the hands of the board. In public institutions multiple nominations may be mandated. In a recent survey (Nason, 1979) only one fourth of four-year public college and university boards were presented with a single nomination and none of the two-year community colleges. Among private institutions, however, over half of the committees of search and selection ended up with single nominations.

Appointing the President

The committee recommends; the full board confirms or rejects the recommendation if only one name is presented or makes its choice among the nominations. Presumably the president-elect already knows the general terms and conditions of his or her appointment. They should now be spelled out in detail, the more precisely the better, and they should be put in writing. Many community colleges and some other institutions, both private and public, have formal contracts. In the majority of cases, however, letters of appointment suffice. Under no circumstances should the agreement be left in purely oral terms. The terms of appointment should include financial, professional, and administrative aspects and conditions.

The financial terms should include such items as the following: salary, annuity or pension provisions, medical or health insurance, life insurance, moving expenses, housing or housing allowance, household help for entertainment, automobile and expenses, travel expenses, and secretarial help for spouse (if needed). Some institutions provide a president's house, which is often larger and more elaborate than the president's family would normally choose. It should be clear that the institution will provide maintenance and upkeep for such a house as well as domestic help if it is to be used for official entertainment. The extent of such entertainment will also determine whether the president's spouse should have secretarial assistance. Where a house is not provided, the question of a housing allowance should be considered.

With the exception of a few individuals selected from business, law, or the military, presidents come from the ranks of professional educators. Because of the hazards inherent in their position, they need to maintain their professional standing and competence; in order to be of maximum value to their institution, they need to improve and enlarge their professional skills. In addition to the standard month's vacation (which might well be longer if the president works on college or university problems while on holiday), presidents should be encouraged to take time off both to restore their energy and to get a perspective on their work. The practice of granting periodic leaves of absence to presidents is growing. Encouraged by the imaginative programs of the Carnegie Corporation and the Danforth Foundation, as well as by a formal resolution of the Association of American Colleges, boards of trustees are beginning to recognize the need to strengthen and conserve the educational leadership of their institutions or, in slightly different terms, to protect their presidential investments.

In similar fashion it should be clearly understood that the president, subject to institutional demands on his or her time, will be expected to serve on various public and private committees, commissions, and boards, not only as a public service but also as an opportunity for personal growth and for adding to the institution's prestige. To stay alive and alert intellectually and professionally is an important safeguard in a position with relatively limited tenure—a safeguard both for the individual and for the institution.

The administrative terms of the appointment will include starting date, retirement date, length of appointment, conditions of termination, criteria of performance, and provision for review and evaluation. The starting date may require some negotiation if the college or university faces a crisis and if the president-elect has commitments that interfere with an early transition. State law, bylaws, or board regulations may set the retirement age. If not, it should be agreed upon at the time of appointment.

While all presidential appointments should be at the pleasure of the board, there is a current trend in the direction of appointments for a fixed term, such as five years, renewable if both parties so wish. Usually term appointments carry a provision for review and assessment of the president's office and performance before renewal. Since the average length of service of a college or university president is only about eight years, provision needs to be made for the termination of that service. The board has every right to expect that the president will not leave on short notice, and the president is entitled to considerate treatment—reasonable notice, leave of absence with salary, severance allowance, or some combination of these—in the event that he or she is asked to leave.

If the board or the committee has done its job of analyzing the needs of the institution, it should be in a position to say what it wants and expects of the new president and to make clear that he or she will be judged by his or her success in meeting those requirements. Time and again presidents have complained that they were given no clear instructions, no criteria of performance. It is palpably unfair to fault them for failing to do what was never made clear as their responsibility. In the process of appointing presidents, trustees and regents need to give more thought to their expectations of the president and to set these down so that the president and his or her several constituencies (who may have quite different expectations) will know what they are.

Once the appointment has been made and its terms agreed upon, various final details need to be tidied up. A public announcement should be made, but before this takes place the final candidates who were not selected must be notified. Alumni, friends of the institution, those who have proposed candidates, and all the candidates themselves should receive notice of the new appointment as promptly as possible.

The chairman of the committee and its administrative staff member should gather and file the complete record of the committee's activities. This should include a description of the steps that the committee followed, the various documents it used, checklists of issues or of questions for candidates, the roster of potential candidates, schedules of meetings, form letters used, and, unless destroyed at the end of the search and selection process, the dossiers of the unsuccessful candidates. The following set of questions that cover the main issues any committee of search and selection needs to answer might also serve as an outline for the final report.

Presidential Search Checklist

Preconditions of the Search

- Is the institution ready to begin the presidential search process?
- Is there consensus on the kind of person that the institution needs?

The Machinery of Selection

- Will a single search and selection committee or some other procedure be used to conduct the search?
- How will committee members be selected?
- Has the board developed in writing a statement on the committee's authority and responsibilities?

Organizing the Committee

- Which individual is most qualified to serve as chairman?
- What kind of staff will the committee require?
- Has a reasonable timetable been established?
- Should the committee make use of outside professional help?
- Does the committee have an adequate budget to meet the costs of the search?
- Has the committee developed a satisfactory record-keeping system and a program of public information?

Deciding What Is Wanted

- Has an institutional analysis been carried out that will serve as the basis for formulating presidential criteria?
- What questions about the institution must be answered before deciding on the kind of president that is needed?
- Which qualifications are most important in the new president?

Developing a Pool of Candidates

- How wide a net should be cast by the committee for presidential candidates?
- What methods should the committee employ to develop a roster of names?
- Are the requirements of equal opportunity and affirmative action being met?

Screening Candidates

- What is the best way to develop a preferred list of candidates?
- How extensively should committee members pursue information about candidates at this stage?
- How should references be approached?

Interviewing Candidates

- How many candidates should be interviewed?
- Where should interviews be held?
- Who should conduct the interviews?
- What should be asked of the candidates and what kinds of information should be made available to them?
- What steps should the committee take following the interview?

Selecting the Final Candidates

- What kinds of activities should the committee undertake to complete its investigation of candidates' backgrounds? How should this be done and by whom?
- Should final candidates be asked to meet with campus groups?
- If campus visits are arranged for candidates, how should they be conducted?
- Should candidates' spouses be included in the campus visits?
- What steps should be taken after the campus visits have been completed?
- When should terms of appointment be discussed with the candidate?
- Should the committee present more than one nomination to the board?

Appointing the President

- What financial, administrative, and professional matters should be covered in the terms and conditions of the new president's appointment and in what form?
- What criteria for subsequent review of performance should be provided and made clear to the new president?

The Transition

The chairman of the board will need to watch over the transition from the old president to the new. A disappointed inside candidate or that candidate's friends may, consciously or inadvertently, create difficulties for the new president. It is the board chairman who must take firm action in such a situation. The outgoing president will normally postpone as many major decisions as possible in order to allow his or her successor maximum freedom for setting policy and making appointments. This means that the president-elect will have an extra load of important decisions to make at a time when he or she is still learning the intricacies of the new position. Special efforts on the part of the board to assist in the transition can thus be enormously helpful. There are also the outside management training programs of many kinds, one or more of which may be very useful to presidents who lack certain tools of the trade. The chairman should deliberate with the president-elect and encourage whatever steps seem desirable.

The Silver Lining

The selection of a new president is not an easy job, but neither is it an impossible one. It is being done all the time—with varying degrees of success. With a little more thought and care it could usually be done better. One way to ensure a better job is to establish procedures well in advance. When emergency strikes— for example, the sudden death or departure of the president—it is an enormous advantage to have already determined the machinery and steps necessary for picking a successor. Every college and university board should give serious thought to establishing such a procedure. Wrapping up a selection process provides a convenient opportunity to do this. The board members might ask what went right and what wrong, and how they would do it differently next time. But even without this occasion and vivid reminder, the wise board will plan its contingency measures for the inevitable day of reckoning.

In addition to the all-important value of finding the right president, the search and selection process has three other advantages. First, it forces the institution to look critically at itself, its mission, its status, its needs, and its prospects. Second, through their intense cooperation in a common cause, trustees, faculty, students, administrative officers, and others can greatly increase their mutual understanding and trust. And finally, if done well, the choosing of a president can tell the institution's story to a wide audience in a way that will enhance its reputation.

9

Rhoda M. Dorsey

Engaging in
Institutional Planning

All institutions engage in some kind of planning, although the plans produced vary widely in character, candor, and usefulness. At the minimum, a small college has a budget for the coming year; at the maximum, a large university that is part of a state system probably has a detailed five-year plan, filling a good-sized book and covering everything from enrollment and staff size to equipment replacement costs. Some plans are generated entirely within an institution and reflect little except that institution's aspirations. Others, prepared on forms mandated by state educational authorities, are circumscribed in content and form by governmental as well as institutional considerations. Planning in most small institutions is done by faculty or staff who are not planners by training and are temporary planners only by designation; planning in large institutions is usually done by formally trained planners with considerable staff to assist them.

However, the planning is done and whatever the nature of the plan, the members of a board of trustees have a vital part to play in the institutional planning process—a part that goes far beyond putting their signatures to the plan in its final form. They must, of course, approve institutional plans as a proper exercise of their fiduciary responsibility. But they can also help to initiate and improve planning, and they can take an active role in the formulation of a plan. Although the following discussion centers largely on the development of a long-range plan of the five-year variety, its observations about trustee responsibilities and roles are also applicable to shorter-range planning and to the formulation of an annual budget.

The Nature of Planning

Academic planning has some peculiar features of its own, but in its main characteristics does not differ from that done in the corporate world. It is an attempt to define where the institution wants to go, how and when it will arrive there, with whom it will travel, and what the cost of the trip will be. Obviously, in any such effort the farther away the future is, the more uncertain and less detailed the plan can be. It is useful to remember this fact, since the amassing of quantities of numbers, which is a feature of most plans, and the projection of these numbers into a time frame of two to five years often give the illusion that the projections are themselves as solid as the current information and data on which they are based. In fact, the farther plans move from the present, the greater the chance of error. This is why long-range plans rarely reach beyond a five-year span, and why all plans need to be updated annually by careful revision and not simply by moving figures projected earlier into the current-year column. Many a plan has proved useless because, once made, it was left unrevised while the future brought circumstances very different from those envisaged by the original projection.

Planning cannot chart the future, nor is it supposed to. A plan must take account of the future, as far as the wisest persons on the campus and the board can see it, but the plan itself is a means of ensuring that the institution will not only be in a strong position to meet future challenges but will survive them and go on to others. This fact alone makes planning of supreme importance to institutions of higher education today. The future that lies ahead for them is a future of lean years during which demographic patterns, the state of the economy, and an increase in nontraditional means of delivering education—to name only three of many developments—will put a premium on an institution's ability to survive creatively.

But survival of this kind cannot be left to chance. Instead, careful planning must be undertaken—planning that faces the hard questions raised by the necessity to respond to student and societal needs with limited resources and a fairly stable personnel picture. Such planning should not only alert the institution to difficulties that lie ahead but should help it to develop a range of efforts that will keep it strong and alive in the future. By now there are numerous examples of institutions that have followed different paths to survival. Some have attempted to expand their market by offering new professional programs or by going coeducational or by giving credit for life experience. Others have attempted to control expenses by eliminating graduate and undergraduate programs with small enrollments, by recycling space that would once have been replaced, or by increasing the student-faculty ratio. Still others have looked for additional sources of income from rental of their facilities, as well as from capital drives and increased state and federal support. Institutional planning ought to encourage the examination of these and other methods of redeploying resources and revising institutional priorities and thus help an institution to choose its own pattern of response to the challenges of the coming years.

The lean years that loom ahead suggest that for all institutions, large and small, planning will have to be a regular occupation, not something undertaken in a major way once every ten years and then forgotten in between. The plan must set guidelines for all institutional action and, on this ground alone, must be constantly reassessed and altered if necessary. No plan is automatically self-fulfilling, especially when rapidly changing outside conditions can make the best of judgments out of date overnight. Moreover, no plan will be of any help if it is not taken seriously by the institution. Many elaborate plans have been printed up only to be put on a shelf and forgotten. Plans are made to be questioned and revised, but they are also made to be carried out.

Board Responsibilities for Planning

The first responsibility of trustees in relation to institutional planning is to insist that it be done. Leaving aside for the moment the public sector, where planning usually is mandated by legislation, it must be noted that most institutions in the private sector have not routinely and systematically engaged in planning. This is particularly true of the mass of small private institutions. There especially, but not solely, planning has been largely intuitive and reactive, not systematic and predictive. The chief intuition at work during most of the history of these institutions was probably that of their presidents, who were often assisted by a strong board member or members. They operated without much of the information now considered essential to decision making and planning and generally reacted to events, usually crises of one kind or another, instead of trying to anticipate them. The nearest approach most of these institutions made to what we would consider today to be good long-range planning came when they built new facilities, for such efforts necessitated reflection not only on funding possibilities but on questions of academic program, staffing, and student services. Rarely did the planning go beyond achievement of the immediate objective, however, and even in recent years, when planning has become more and more the vogue, major campaigns for funds have been undertaken with only the most inadequate plans to ensure that the funds sought were necessary and sufficient for the long-range benefit of the institution.

Reasons for changing from this posture toward planning are implicit in what has been said above. Perhaps in the past, the world did not in fact change very much or changed so slowly that reactive planning would not doom an institution. Such is no longer the case. It is not only inflation and the shrinking of the traditional college-age group that are going to dramatically change the conditions of higher education within a few years, but other social, economic, and technological factors as well. The appearance of an older age group in the colleges, the growth of what may be called parallel educational programs offered by business and the armed forces, the availability of new ways of learning that may be more effective than the conventional modes employed in most American classrooms, skepticism about the value of education, the new calls to go "back to basics," and the resurgence of the core curriculum—this bundle of changes has already had an impact on higher education, and its impact will continue, often with immediate and critical results. In such conditions, reactive planning postures are both inappropriate and dangerous. Trustees need to be very clear on this point and help their institutions, if they are still frozen in such postures, to break free.

An insistence that planning take place may well meet at first with apathy and inertia, not only in the institution but among board members as well. It is curious that the very corporate board members who are most insistent on planning for their own enterprises seem not to understand that planning is just as important for a college or university. Indeed, one of the first groups that has to be persuaded for the urgencey of the endeavor is commonly the board itself. Content to function in a traditional way and, one may suppose, not anxious for the kinds of decisions that planning necessitates, board members may neglect planning or relegate it to a secondary place in their own schedule of activities. Often it is presidents, approaching the job with more recent training than board members and more acutely aware of the need for institutions to be in a stance of readiness, who have insisted on the initiation of good long-range planning and, in so doing, have contributed to the education of the board. The process of persuasion may take many forms, but until the board asserts its own determination to give planning a major role, effective planning will not be achieved.

The second responsibility of a board in relation to planning is to see that it is done well. This does not mean that the board itself should do the planning; a board by its nature cannot undertake the mass of detailed work that is involved. Board members must, however, make sure that the kind of planning others are doing and that will ultimately be brought to them for inspection, debate, and decision is of high quality. Some of this quality can be guaranteed in a mechanical way—for example, by assigning adequate staff—but much of it will be determined by the attitudes of board members and the kinds of questions they ask about a plan.

A good plan must be based on adequate data and information, and the two are not precisely the same. Data are raw material, frequently (but by no means always in academic planning) numerical in nature. Data that have been interpreted to make them more intelligible and pertinent to considerations at hand become information. In recent years both the generation and use of data within colleges and universities have improved. This has been due in part to projects sponsored by the National Center for Higher Education Management Systems (NCHEMS) and the Western Interstate Commission for Higher Education (WICHE) that produced programs for collection of data, in part to the never-ending requests for information coming from state and federal sources, and in part to the realization by administrators that successful management in hard times requires hard data. The data and information with which trustees are probably most familiar and that they are best able to judge are financial. Financial data are certainly important in planning, but the range of data required to plan for the institution as a whole is much broader. It covers material on output programs such as instruction, research, and public service and on support programs such as student services, administration, plant operation, and auxiliary enterprises, as well as on the budgets on which all these activities are based. Trustworthy data are needed in all these areas, and board members must make certain that such data are available in the institution.

Trustees must also insist that plans be realistic and feasible. If a plan is to be of any help, it must reflect the institution clearly, warts and all. Inflated institutional pride has no place at the planning table, where absolute candor about strengths and weaknesses, triumphs and failures, points of dynamism and points of stagnation is essential. Whether an institution contemplates strengthening a traditional position or moving into a new one, it needs honesty in its appraisal of itself.

Similarly, in an evaluation of conditions in the world outside the institution, whether it is the local community, the surrounding educational community, the nation, or the world as a whole, realism is critical. It is not easy, or course, to come to grips with national trends, especially when they seem to pose dire problems for the institution, but the worst thing a long-range plan can do is to make projections that exempt an institution from such perils as enrollment decline or energy cost increases. When in doubt, it is best to assume that a potential danger will materialize and draw up the plan to help the institution cope with it.

A general responsibility of trustees is to look out for the institution as a whole. This concern translates itself into a third responsibility in planning: to ensure that the plan covers all aspects of the institution. While this does not necessarily mean that action will be required in all areas, it is difficult to think of any academic initiatives these days that do not involve substantial parts of the institution in addition to the academic departments.

Evidence of this institution-wide purview is input received from the nonfaculty, nonstudent constituencies of the institution. The academic plan, given the tradition in most American institutions, will be drawn up largely by the faculty, and students will have a good deal to say about the area of student services. But administrative staff at all levels need to be involved in those segments of the plan that relate to staff operations, and alumni should also have a chance to contribute. Many institutions, especially but not solely community colleges, will find it advisable to provide for input from members of the community to make sure that community needs and interests are integrated into the plan.

As a fourth responsibility, trustees must see to it that when planning is undertaken, for the first time or in its regular cycle, it is done on a schedule that allows for deliberation, consultation, decision making, and revision and will ensure completion of the plan in a manageable period of time. The National Association of College and University Business Officers (NACUBO) has a helpful guide for such scheduling called *A College Planning Cycle* (1975); Parekh's Long-Range Planning (1977) presents a very detailed schedule, but it may also be helpful. In "How Stanford Plans," Miller (1978) reports on the experiences of a large institution that operates on a two-year planning cycle. In any schedule, time for discussion is particularly important because decisions to be reached by means of the plan are frequently not easy ones and the real issues may not emerge until the plan has been worked on for a long time. There is a great temptation, especially the first time around on a plan, for everyone to linger over the initial steps, postponing the moment for final decisions. Trustees must not accept a schedule that allows this to happen, even if the first plan thus turns out to be inadequate. It is better to have gone through the process and produced a spotty plan than never to have finished, provided the process is then reactivated and the second try is better than the first.

If a plan is to be done well, it will cost time and money, and trustees as their fifth responsibility must be prepared to incur such expenses. Planning requires extra work by almost everyone in an institution, from the faculty member examining departmental course offerings to the director of physical plant estimating gas and oil usage, but it is a mistake to try to draw this material together without some additional staffing at the collection point. Large institutions generally have a planning officer with major responsibility for planning; small institutions frequently do not have such an officer and may attempt to plan without additional help. This is poor economy. Quality planning requires someone with a clear, logical mind, an understanding of the institution, and the ability to work with others and inspire them to work. Faculty, with some training and release time, can make excellent part-time planners and may, for a variety of political as well as personnel reasons, be a wise choice for small institutions.

At some point in the planning process, outside consultants may also be used. They are best called in when there is a need for information that is technical in its nature and/or political in its implications. For instance, in small institutions, it requires a degree of expertise not usually present among campus personnel to prepare calculations about mechanical maintenance and replacement or about the installation of equipment to improve energy usage. Outside consultants can do this for the institution. On a campus of any size outside consultants may well be employed, for both technical and political reasons, in planning for improved use of space. It is far easier for faculty or staff with a highly developed sense of territoriality to discuss space needs with a dispassionate outside expert than to fight it out among themselves, and they are far more apt to pay attention to what an outsider says than to the suspect proposals of their peers.

Finally, it goes without saying that if the board is to play an effective part in planning, it must have members who are capable of giving help in developing and evaluating a plan. This does not necessarily mean they must be professional planners, but they should be individuals with expertise in finance, in engineering, in academic and student affairs, and in development. These are hardly extraordinary requirements for board membership, but board nominating committees should remember that their nominees will not only have to make policy for the present but will also have to plan for the future.

Discussion thus far has focused on the general responsibilities of trustees in establishing the circumstances under which planning will be taken seriously and done well in an institution. When the process of planning begins, however, board members have another role to play—a role that will be described in detail below. And when the plan has been completed, it is the responsibility of the board first to accept it and then to help bring it to fulfillment. Acceptance should be more than a *pro forma* acquiescence. Board members must be able to say no to parts of a plan that they find unacceptable and persist until the necessary changes have been made. They must then be sure that the plan is communicated clearly and effectively to all parts of the college community and, in appropriate form, to outside constituencies whose support is being sought. The plan will thus become a guide for the institution as a whole and a picture of the developing institution for those outside it.

As the plan goes into operation, the board should require a schedule for reconsideration and revision of the plan, thus initiating a repetition, smaller in scale but similar in process, of the original plan-making procedure. At the same time, monitoring of the plan should begin in a regular way. Thoughtful monitoring requires close cooperation between board members and the college administration so that there is no infringement on staff functions. Board members are not on the board to run programs but to receive and evaluate information about their operation, especially in relation to the plan.

Monitoring can show where a plan may be faulty. Suppose, for example, that a new academic program is offered according to plan, but enrollment does not materialize. Monitoring the plan will encourage analysis of why the program failed and suggestions for alternate planning. Monitoring also shows whether a plan is being achieved or not. Perhaps targets in the plan for increased student services or building renovation or fund raising are not being met. Board members need to know this fact and then need to know why, especially if the initial plan was sound but has been neglected or disregarded. In addition, board members need to concern themselves, through monitoring, with situations in which a desired part of the plan is rendered irrelevant, as when, for example, a planned community service is made unnecessary by provision of such services by another agency.

In the examples given above, objective statistical data make it reasonably easy to assess whether a goal was achieved or not, whether a program was appropriate or not. But for many of the most central of the board's concerns, such data are lacking and similar judgments will not be as easy. Much headway has been made in recent years in developing tools to measure student perception of the academic and social environment, student attitudes, and student academic achievement. Astin's *Four Critical Years* (1977) is a valuable discussion of longitudinal data gathered over a ten-year period to measure student attitudes, values, behavior patterns, and satisfaction and to attempt to assess how colleges affect these outcomes. Most institutions are just beginning to think in terms of appropriate and systematic studies of outcomes. Board members should realize that in this area there is a good deal of institutional sensitivity and faculty skepticism but should also be aware that more work here is essential for effective monitoring of major parts of any long-range plan.

This discussion of the responsibilities of the board in institutional planning has not attempted to point to a single pattern of organization that will enable boards to meet these responsibilities effectively. In fact, there are many patterns that work, depending on the size, committee organization, and kinds of activity of an individual board. Many boards appoint a special planning committee of their own to work on a continuing basis with planning staff. This committee reviews both the process and substance of the plan as it develops and reports regularly to the board as a whole. Some boards place planning responsibility squarely on their executive committees. Other boards divide it among existing committees, such as those concerned with finances, physical plant, development, academic affairs, and student affairs. This arrangement has the advantage of involving many board members and of utilizing board members with special experience to help plan in the area of their expertise. Such an approach may be used in conjunction with a board planning committee whose job it is to put together the separate parts of the plan received from other board committees and the administration. Recently some boards have appointed planning committees composed not only of board members but of faculty, students, administrators, alumni, and sometimes community members. Although the size of such a committee can make it cumbersome, this approach offers an invaluable forum for the expression of many diverse points of view from the different institutional constituencies—all of whom must be taken into account in making a strong institutional plan.

At the beginning of this discussion it was pointed out that trustees in the private and public sector have different planning responsibilities. In the public sector, growing layers of authority have drastically revised the traditional role of board members in all phases of institutional life and especially in the area of institutional planning. It is not unusual for institutions in the public sector not to have individual boards of their own, but rather to be gathered into segments (such as two-year colleges, four-year colleges, universities) or into geographical groupings (as in the case of the City University of New York) with one board for the whole. Such boards in turn are now increasingly responsible to state-appointed boards of higher education (operating under a variety of different names) whose purpose is the more efficient use of state resources through the coordination of higher educational opportunities with those resources. The existence of such state coordinating boards does limit the determination of institutional direction by trustees. Nowhere can this be better seen than in the development of state master plans for education, which have increased greatly in recent years. Given their number and variety, there is no way to summarize these master plans, but they typically assign different missions to different tiers or institutions within the public sector. The following quotation from the *Maryland Statewide Plan for Postsecondary Education* will give some idea of this development; the quotation comes from a section entitled "Summary of Missions Identified for Public Institutions": "The University of Maryland and Morgan State University will have three major roles: teaching, research, and service. The University of Maryland should emphasize research and service to the State as a whole; Morgan should emphasize research on urban problems and service to Baltimore City and other urban areas. The State colleges and universities and St. Mary's major role is teaching, with secondary research and regional service roles. The community colleges will emphasize teaching as their major role and community services as a secondary role" (Maryland State Board for Higher Education, 1978, p. 29).

As in this instance, these master plans sometimes reflect past institutional missions; at other times they represent a break from the past. The important point, however, is that the existence of such state boards has greatly changed the traditional position of institutional board members, taking out of their hands full determination of institutional mission. This development has left many board members feeling that they have little role to play in institutional planning, and some have become bitter as a result. Although ultimate determination of institutional mission may no longer be in board members' hands, it is not true that board members consequently have no role to play in institutional planning. As state master plans have developed, many board members have shown themselves masters of bureaucratic and political infighting in establishing for their institution or segment the particular mission they think desirable. This new kind of trustee activity in institutional planning has taken place, not in the board room but in the legislature. Nevertheless, the importance of board members' activity for their institution or segment is just as great as it has always been.

Board members in the public sector therefore need not fear that state master plans will remove all their power of determining mission, but they would do well to realize that even under the most favorable circumstances, this power is now circumscribed. Their other responsibilities for institutional planning are not. They must still make sure that planning is done well and realistically, with adequate staff, and that it involves all elements of the college community. They must still examine the plan, endorse it, and work to carry it out. Their work, however, may have to be done not only with the staff of their own institution or segment but also with planning departments both within and outside the state coordinating body and probably also with the legislature itself. The process is complicated, and the precise nature of a board member's role will vary from institution to institution and from state to state, but the role is there to be played, and the institution will be weaker if it is not.

The growth of state coordinating bodies for higher education and the development of state master plans also have implications for the private sector that board members should take into account. State coordinating bodies have authority over the private sector as well, although it is not of the same kind or magnitude as their authority over the public sector. In its study and subsequent closing of weak doctoral programs, the New York State Board of Regents dealt with private as well as public sector programs and closed some in both sectors. The attempt to limit repetitive programs is apparently going to be extended to the private as well as the public sector and perhaps with more devastating effect in view of the size and political weakness of most private institutions. State coordinating bodies and state master plans rarely chart the future for the private sector, but their planning for the public sector may have immediate impact on enrollment and programs in private institutions. It is therefore extremely important that board members be aware of the outlines of state master plans and the activities of state coordinating bodies. At times, their voices, like the voices of public board members, may well be needed to help in discussions that are educational in subject but frequently political in context.

Board Role in the Planning Process

The process of planning and the various patterns that can be used to accomplish this process have been discussed at considerable length in many publications. These discussions will not be repeated or summarized here. This section will instead indicate how board members can play a role during each of the steps that are fairly standard in any process of planning, especially for the long run. It should be emphasized at once that the trustee role throughout is distinct from that of the administration. It is not up to the board member to collect data, to put them together, or to make an initial determination about what they mean or what they suggest for the future of the institution. It is the role of the board member to be assured of the accuracy and adequacy of the data presented and then to react to proposals and projections made by the administration.

All plans rest on assumptions about the future, and one of the first steps in devising a plan is to make these assumptions explicit. Board members can be of particular value in this exercise, bringing perspectives that help to widen the academic aperture. Assumptions should cover both internal matters, including affairs over which the college can exercise some measure of control, and external matters, over which the college may have no control at all. Under the first category come such matters as student enrollment, student attrition, size and remuneration of faculty, teaching load, student housing arrangements, scope of the athletic program, number of community service programs, investment in physical plant, and state of the endowment. Under the second category come factors such as the rate of inflation, national and regional demographic trends, the cost of energy, projected employment rates for both the nation and the region, public attitudes toward higher education, the amount of federal and state support available, and the nature of federal and state policy on higher education.

Assumptions must be made about all these factors and many more with the awareness that there is little certainty about any assumption, especially if it involves a matter that lies beyond the institution's control. It thus becomes tempting to agonize over assumptions and to allow their uncertainty to generate uncertainty about the entire planning process. Neither board members nor administrators have the luxury to do this. Assumptions must be arrived at in a tough-minded way and with full use made of the board members' wide experience.

At their best, assumptions are educated guesses whose quality will vary widely depending on the experience of trustees and administrators. Their part in the planning process is to force everyone to think about fundamental factors that will influence the future of the institution, whether those factors can be controlled or not. Formulating assumptions forces everyone to think not only about the assumptions that they will eventually adopt but also about alternate conditions that might arise. What, for example, would happen to the institution if the inflation rate were not 10 percent but 15 percent? What if day enrollment remained steady but night enrollment increased by 30 percent? What if overall enrollment dropped by 10 percent? What if federal aid to medical schools suddenly stopped? What if faculty became unionized? What if the draft were reinstituted? In larger and more sophisticated institutions, "what if" questions like the above have led to the use of computer programs that make it possible to change assumptions mechanically and have an instant indication of the result. Smaller institutions will have to trust the brains of their administrators and board members in going through the same process.

The first part of the plan proper is a statement of institutional mission. The mission statement should be a brief evocative statement dealing with the institution's particular type of educational mission. Parekh (1977) gives the following as an example: "The ideal of Ardmore University has always been the scholar; its aim, the development of the whole man. The cooperative education (work-study) program attempts to combine academic instruction in the liberal arts and sciences with regular employment experiences, carefully chosen and supervised by the university. Community and university cooperate in providing for Ardmore students an educational experience relevant to the demands of a complex age" (p. 15).

Many writers on institutional mission statements urge that they be made as specific as possible, delineating the institution in a way that is unique or at least distinctive. This is not easy to do. Many of the nation's small colleges are very much alike in program, emphasis, and historical development. In addition, most institutions serve a number of constituencies, and too narrow a statement of institutional mission might operate as an undesirable limiting factor. Obviously, mission statements should not claim that the institution they represent can be all things to all persons. Some qualification of mission is essential as a matter of institutional integrity; moreover, the student as consumer has the right to an accurate statement about an institution's present policies, program offerings, and mission.

At the minimum, the mission statement should designate certain fundamental characteristics of the institution, such as those touched on by the following questions:

1. Is the institution public or independent?
2. Is the institution free standing or linked with another institution or system?
3. What is the nature of the academic program? Is it graduate or undergraduate? Liberal arts, technical, or professional? Comprehensive or specialized?
4. Does the institution have a particular constituency? Women, blacks, a special religious group?
5. Is the institution large or small?
6. Is the institution urban, rural, suburban?
7. Is the mission of the institution a historic one or is it newly adopted?

Closely allied to the mission statement and flowing from it is the statement of institutional goals, usually made in the form of lists of specific goals. Statements of institutional goals tend to be broader than mission statements in that they cover all areas of institutional activity, and more specific in that they attempt to refine the generalized rhetoric that is characteristic of mission statements. Together, mission and goals statements characterize the institution for itself, its students, and the outside world. At their best, they give guidelines for the development of academic and nonacademic institutional programs and a yardstick against which institutional activities may be evaluated. They are, therefore, enormously important to an institution, and trustees must play an important part in their development.

Traditionally, goals statements have focused to a very considerable extent on academic programs and student outcomes. This is natural, because these are the very reason for a college's or university's existence. Board members interested in learning more about the range of goals statements in these areas would do well to read the chapter on "The Institutional Goals Inventory in Contemporary Context" in Peterson and Uhl (1977), which traces the development of a number of different statements of goals. One of the most influential is the Institutional Goals Inventory (IGI), an instrument designed by the Educational Testing Service and first made publicly available in 1972. This is an inventory designed to help faculty and students identify, assess, and reach consensus about institutional goals. The ninety goals that are listed for ranking (how important the goal is, how important it should be) deal largely with educational outcomes, service to the community, and those processes of life and operation on campus that may affect achievement of educational outcomes goals. The following list of the categories of outcomes will give some idea of the scope of the IGI:

Outcome Goals
1. Academic development
2. Intellectual orientation
3. Individual personal development
4. Humanism/altruism
5. Cultural/esthetic awareness
6. Traditional religiousness
7. Vocational preparation
8. Advanced training
9. Research
10. Meeting local needs
11. Public service
12. Social egalitarianism
13. Social criticism/activism

Process Goals
1. Freedom
2. Democratic governance
3. Community
4. Intellectual/esthetic environment
5. Innovation
6. Off-campus learning
7. Accountability/efficiency

The categories of the IGI, broad though they are, do not cover all phases of institutional activity, and it is important in a comprehensive goals statement to go beyond them. Checklists of categories for wider goals are many, and only one is noted here for purposes of illustration. The National Center for Higher Education Management Systems (Collier, 1978) suggests several areas of program classification, including these six: instruction, research, public service, academic support programs, student services, and institutional support programs. These areas are then broken down in the following manner:

Instruction

General academic instruction (degree-related)
Professional career instruction (degree-related)
Vocational/technical instruction (degree-related)
Requisite preparatory/remedial instruction
General studies (nondegree)
Occupation-related instruction (nondegree)
Social roles/interaction instruction (nondegree)
Home and family life instruction (nondegree)
Personal interest and leisure instruction (nondegree)

Research

Institutes and research centers
Individual or project research

Public Service

Direct patient care
Health care supportive services
Community services
Cooperative extension services
Public broadcasting services

Academic Support

Library services
Museums and galleries
Educational media services
Academic computing support
Ancillary support
Academic administration
Course and curriculum development
Academic personnel development

Student Services

Student service administration

Social and cultural development

Counseling and career guidance

Student health/medical services

Student auxiliary services

Intercollegiate athletics

Institutional Support

Executive management

Financial management and operations

General administration and logistical service

Administrative computing support

Physical plant operations

Faculty and staff

Auxiliary services

Public relations/development

Student records

Not all these areas will be needed by all institutions. There are many other ways of looking at and categorizing institutional activity, and many other terminologies. No planner or trustee should feel constrained by a particular pattern. What is important is to recognize that goals need to be drawn up for all the activities of the institution. Planning in the areas of student outcomes, public service, and process will not be adequate if there is not also parallel planning for the academic, student service, and institutional support areas. It is impossible to achieve satisfactory progress in student outcomes without adequate support. Moreover, support services are the most rapidly escalating part of college expenses, and planning for their management, if not their containment, is therefore essential.

Trustees should have an important part to play in developing mission and goals statements, especially in insisting that they be accurate, adequate, and as compelling as possible. This is not to say that the trustees should do the actual writing. Mission and goals statements written by committee tend to lose all spark of individuality, and this is true whether the committee is composed of administrators, faculty, or trustees. Consensus on the import of mission and goals is essential; votes on every term employed to describe them are not. Moreover, from the point of view of the board, any such statement should be able to function as a link that ideologically and programmatically bridges past, present, and future. Most institutions move forward more rapidly if their roots are still in place, even though slightly bent. Mission and goals statements are temporal documents that must reflect and speak to a particular time. But board members should be sure that such statements are also compatible with the long-range purpose and existence of the institution and, in ensuring this, should look back as well as forward.

Missions and goals are substantial subjects for board consideration, but too often they generate little thoughtful response from board members. It is thus important to frame the board's consideration of them in such a way as to encourage maximum deliberation and discussion. At the least, mission and goals statements should be presented to the board while they are still in a reasonably fluid state so that board members' comments can make some difference. Such statements should be sent to board members well in advance of their consideration. At the time of the board meeting, it may be profitable to abandon the usual pattern of a general meeting of all board members and break up into small groups, each led by a trustee. On the assumption that these small groups will have comments to make and questions to raise, their meetings should be followed by a meeting of the whole, during which reports of each of the small meetings would be made and points for consideration listed on a blackboard. Such a procedure may help to ensure that important matters are given serious thought, that trustees who are knowledgeable in particular areas have a chance to share their knowledge, and that communication among board members themselves and between board members and members of the administration in attendance will improve.

Only by working hard with goals and mission statements will trustees come to understand that they are more than pious declarations and they they in fact lay out what an institution is and what it can and cannot do in the future. With such realization the board will cease to be merely a rubber stamp on someone else's plan. Of course, the board should also realize that, at the end of the planning process, decisions about goals and mission may well have to change. It may be conventional wisdom to say that the mission and goals govern the plan, but it is also simplistic; what the planning process reveals may well necessitate another hard look at mission and goals.

It is desirable in all institutions, though easier in smaller ones, to have input on goals and mission from all constituencies. One problem in getting a planning process to run smoothly is determining the times at which different groups should have their say about the plan. This is not simply a scheduling problem, since it frequently involves political considerations, as well as questions of authority and responsibility. The faculty and students, for instance, need to have a say in goals and mission statements at a time when their comments will have some impact. It may in fact be convenient to show a first draft of such statements to them before showing it to the trustees; college calendars do not always allow for the best possible sequence of discussions. However the schedule works, faculty and students need to understand that the final responsibility for adopting a mission and goals statement rests in the private sector with the board of the institution and in the public sector with the board of the institution or segment in conjunction with the state coordinating body.

The next logical step in the planning process is the elaboration of concrete programs designed to attain the stated goals. Actually, institutional planning being what it is, its various stages often run parallel in time and sometimes in reverse order. It is possible to derive a mission statement from programs that are in operation; in fact, many institutions do just this when developing long-range plans. If an institution has been running properly and successfully and the future holds no major surprises, one should be able to move from programs to mission as well as from mission to programs without any disjunction. It is the additional object of program definition, however, to encourage each department—administrative as well as academic—to examine the institution's goals and see how it can help to implement them. As Miller (1978) remarks in his description of the Stanford planning process: from the top come constraints, issues, and goals, and from the bottom come needs and judgments. Responsibility for the development of

concrete program proposals lies with the departments and ultimately with the administration, but some participation in their
elaboration should be possible for the board member.

There are many parts of an institutional plan with which
board members, especially of an independent institution, will and
should feel immediately at home. Finances, facilities, and development are areas where trustees have routinely played a major role,
not only in defining policy but in monitoring operations and helping to achieve objectives. In small colleges the finance committee
will be responsible for receiving all sections of an institutional plan
together with their projected costs. In larger institutions intermediate committees—frequently composed of faculty and students
as well as staff—may receive projected programs and make recommendations to the finance committee of the board. This committee must consider total costs and determine whether there are
resources available to meet them from tuition, endowment income,
state grants, gifts, or unrelated business income.

If the plan cannot be financed, it is the responsibility of the
finance committee to face the fact honestly and either indicate the
need for trimming or attempt to raise more revenue. If additional
revenue cannot be raised, it is the responsibility of the committee to
develop, with the administration, some guidelines for scaling down
programs and then to inform all departments. Stanford University,
recognizing the fact that it is extraordinarily difficult to put projected programs in precise priority order, uses the following
criteria to judge their merit (Miller, 1978):

1. Is the program academically important?
2. Is there now and will there continue to be a student interest?
3. Can we as an institution be outstanding in this program?
4. Can the program be securely funded?

These questions, of course, do not apply to nonacademic programs, but they suggest an approach that may help those who have
to make judgments about the funding of a range of programs.

The buildings and grounds committee, at a time of long-
range planning, must concern itself with an extension of its regular
concerns: the deferred and regular maintenance, the appropriate-

ness of facilities for proposed programs, the need for new facilities or for remodeling old facilities, as well as questions of safety, access for the handicapped, and energy management—and all of these over a long-range period. This committee, too, must operate with utmost candor. It has not been popular in recent years to give much attention in an institutional plan to maintenance, whether for rewiring, replacing plumbing, resurfacing roads, or doing other routine repairs. It was more challenging to build new buildings and more important to meet yawning deficits than to deal with deferred maintenance. However, many campuses have come to a point where deferred maintenance has created hazardous, if not ruinous conditions, and it can no longer be put off. It is the responsibility of the buildings and grounds committee to make this point strongly. Dollars may have to come from other more attractive projects, so forcefulness in this area is very important. The costs will be considerable, but they can no longer be delayed on many campuses.

Finally, the development committee of the board, addressing the plan as it comes from the finance committee, must determine the institution's ability to raise additional support, analyze the gift potential of segments of the plan, and then help to raise the money. It may well be the development and not the finance committee that is most immediately responsible for forcing the alteration of a plan. If it cannot come up with the funds estimated by the finance committee as necessary, there will have to be some revision of programs or even of goals. At the same time, a really good plan may inspire a development committee to new heights.

The role of each of these three trustee committees will of course be different in the public sector. It is the legislative budget analyst rather than a group of trustees who may well have the last word on projected expenditures. It may be a planning department in conjunction with an appropriations committee that will approve proposals for building, rebuilding, or repair on a public campus. And although most state institutions have in recent years established development committees, their work has typically not had the importance for the overall budget that is characteristic of such committees in private institutions. Trustee committees in the areas of finance, buildings and grounds, and development in public institutions do not therefore have the scope of authority and responsibility that private trustees do. As suggested in Chapter One, they may and frequently do have a public policy role to play in ensuring that the interests of their institution or segment are not adversely affected by budget or legislation.

Planning in the areas of academic program and student services is obviously a critical part of institutional planning; it is planning for the fundamental activity of the institution. These are, however, two areas in which trustees in recent years have taken relatively little part. Responsibility for academic program was handed over to the faculty long ago; more recently, with colleges and universities no longer acting *in loco parentis,* student affairs have also generally moved out of the control of the board. With all due respect to the tradition of shared authority that these moves embody, it is at least open to question whether planning in these areas—given the enormous implications they carry for the future of the institution—should be done without some trustee participation. If trustees are expected to carry out, work for, and support a plan, ways must be found for them to take an appropriate part in the planning process for academic and student affairs. To suggest that there is one successful pattern for trustee involvement would be misleading. The mechanics of the process are easier in a smaller institution, where an academic planning committee of faculty, students, and trustees can be established, but it may be easier politically in a bigger institution, where visiting and advisory committees of trustees and outside experts are more common.

Board members who sit on such committees need to observe particular discretion. They must insist that they are only individual committee members and cannot be regarded as the voice, spirit, or power of the board itself, which they are not. They cannot act as all-knowing experts but must, instead, act as outside members, bringing an outside perspective and asking the kinds of questions that lead insiders to explain and understand their own ideas better. Necessary for this kind of task are trustees who know the institution, have sensitivity to faculty and student feelings about self-government, and feel at ease talking with faculty and students. It is usually helpful if one or more are alumni of the institution. If such board members are found, the broad-based planning committees can go to work tackling questions that deal with the shape of the curriculum in the future, the kind of faculty necessary to teach that curriculum, and the support services that will be required. On the student-life side, the planning committees can consider the kind and nature of student services, the facilities they will require, and the staffing they will need to be successful. In this way, trustees will be able to participate in relating mission and goals to programs in the academic and student services.

Board participation in the making of the plan, as suggested above, will require time, study, and thought from board members. There are, however, benefits to be derived from this effort that are worth keeping in mind. Participation brings an increase in knowledge of the institution, and usually increased interest. Participation makes it possible for board members to contribute their special expertise in a way that will be of immediate value to the institution. It involves board members early in the planning process and makes the plan, in a real sense, theirs; this is important, for a board member must feel a commitment to a plan before he or she will work to make it succeed.

Although little has been written specifically on the politics and psychology of long-range planning in an institution, no one who has been through the process can fail to recognize their importance. Institutional planning is now being done for a period that unfortunately combines contraction in student population with continuing high inflation. Planning may be the only way an institution can survive such a period, but it is planning that has a gloomy edge. Planning for contraction or for maintaining a steady state does not bring the elation that planning for expansion does, and it must be done in such a way that it will not cause the college community to lose heart. There is no formula to achieve this result; success depends as much on tone as on process. It may be useful to remember that most faculty now in colleges and universities came out of the era of expansion in the fifties and sixties; the kinds of difficulties that have beset institutions in the seventies and will continue to beleaguer them in the eighties have only slowly penetrated the consciousness of faculty, and they deal with these conditions reluctantly and fearfully. It is therefore critical that within the plan attention be given to faculty development, to faculty salaries, and to faculty recommendations for the alternate use of space as total enrollments fall and enrollment patterns shift. There must be signs that the institution has concern for faculty who are caught in changing circumstances and that it has a forward-looking plan to help them adjust to new conditions. Thus, by displaying both caution and confidence, institutional planners may prevent a sinking-ship syndrome from sweeping over faculty as they survey conditions in the years ahead.

Monitoring the Plan

The final responsibility of the board member in relation to the plan is to help make it work and to use evaluation of its operation as the basis for future planning. Trustee committees should regularly review and revise those sections of the plan they are responsible for. The board itself ought to have an update and forward projection each year. It would help if key sections of the plan could routinely become the subjects for board consideration at meetings. A plan, however, is more than a subject for discussion; it is also a set of guidelines and objectives, and the board needs to be satisfied that, once a plan has been set in motion, its schedule is being met. This means that the board must consider how it will monitor the plan and what kind of information it will require for this task. This should be the subject of agreement among the board, the president, and the planning officer. It is then the responsibility of the president to get the material to the board, indicating how the plan is being fulfilled or, if it is not being fulfilled, why it is not. The last point is important, because if the plan is looked upon as an ironclad set of performance specifications, it will only stifle individual initiative and may well get the institution into great trouble. Any plan needs flexibility, and the board needs to be willing to consider proposals for changing a plan when its own committees, the planners of the institution, or the administration makes a good case for a change. Some change will come routinely with the yearly review of the plan. Consideration of change at other times, however, should always be possible, since conditions now change so rapidly. In summary, the board should be the masters of the plan and not the other way around. The following questions provide a means to test the adequacy of a proposed plan:

1. Is it based on a realistic assessment of the institution and its resources? Are working assumptions made clear?
2. Do the various sections employ adequate data bases? Are key data interpreted to allow for comprehensible implications to be stated?
3. Have all parts of the operation of the institution been covered in the plan?
4. Has the plan taken adequate account of outside forces that may affect costs, enrollment, and the attractiveness of offerings?
5. How does the plan affect resource allocation within the institution? How does it affect fund raising?
6. Have appropriate sections of the college community contributed input to the plan? Are they adequately informed as to its nature and guidelines?
7. Has consideration been given to the ways in which the validity and achievement of parts of the plan can be evaluated?

Special Responsibilities of the Chairman

In any long-range planning process, there are special responsibilities for the chairman of the board. The chairman should be the animating presence of the board, its leader as well as its conductor. There is little hope that a board can be convinced of the importance of planning if the chairman is not. The chairman must always keep the planning responsibilities of the board before himself or herself and the other board members. In those cases where board participation in planning is a new experience, it is the chairman who must help to educate the board as a whole about the aims, process, and results of institutional planning. It will require a good deal of talking, explaining, and perhaps persuading to achieve the kind of board participation that has been presented in this essay as appropriate. But if the chairman takes planning seriously, other board members will too.

The chairman needs also to keep nudging the president to make sure that the planning process is moving ahead according to an agreed upon schedule. As the process continues, the attitude of the chairman should be one of support, understanding, and determination. As a first planning effort gets under way, the chairman must emphasize that, while there will be mistakes and errors in information and judgment, these can be reviewed and rectified as the planning process becomes a continuous one within the institution. Some praise from the chairman for those involved in working on the plan at the trustee, faculty, staff, or student level is always a help. Planning is hard work, and recognition of that fact by the chairman is a very considerable morale booster. It is the chairman, too, who must insist that the extra help needed for the process be provided. The regular communication between the president and the chairman should be the chief vehicle for constant monitoring of the process by the chairman. Finally, a degree of leadership and courage will always be a necessity for the chairman's role. Plans nowadays are apt to cut out more things than they add. Thus, the chairman must be able to move forward while thinking smaller and to sustain the morale of the board and the institution while this is taking place.

10

Martin Meyerson

Overseeing
Academic Programs

At least four functions of the college or university trustee can be cited with little hesitation or ambiguity. Trustees appoint and remove presidents. They hold, invest, and dispose of property. They interpret the institution to, and defend it from, the rest of the world. And they provide financial support from their own resources and by attracting funds from alumni, friends, firms and government.

Conspicuously absent from this unambiguous list is the role of trustees in overseeing academic programs. Academic programs are widely thought to be the province of the faculty to debate, devise, and operate—with a leadership role, to be sure, to be played by presidents, deans, and other officers, and sometimes with involvement by students. According to this conventional wisdom, lay trustees—most of whom are businessmen—are expected to stay at a respectful distance from the academic programs. But here too they have a role to play, even though it is not always clearly defined. After all, colleges and universities exist for little but their academic programs, and most people recognize that American trustees hold supreme authority in the governance of institutions. Trustees tend to be more directly involved in academic programs in schools with strong sectarian missions; with local, teaching faculties rather than more cosmopolitan, research-oriented ones; and during times of unrest rather than times of quiescence. Moderation even in querying educational programs has nonetheless become the norm among trustees.

Trustee restraint in exercising authority over the form and content of the academic programs has not always been the rule. The mid-nineteenth and early twentieth century roots of this restraint were the secularization of American higher education and the replacement of academic dogma with scientific inquiry and greater individuality. These in turn were accompanied by academic freedom for professors and models of faculty self-determination derived from the German universities. By the first decade of this century, President Charles Eliot (1908) of Harvard could write that "trustees should never interfere with matters once consigned to a faculty by statute or custom, unless in the way of inquiry or informal suggestion, or exercise any powers delegated to the faculty" (p. 31). In this century, such forces as the increasing specialization of knowledge, the growth in complexity of many colleges and universities, the rising status of the professoriate, and the emergence of professional associations and faculty unions have encouraged the tendency of trustees to leave most academic matters to faculty and administration.

Since most trustees have been chosen for other characteristics, moreover, they often lack a predilection for academic matters. Some boards have found it advantageous to appoint as trustees a few academics commonly from the faculties of other institutions, to add the perspective of experts. But the norms of trustee restraint in the oversight of academic programs and the delegation of this function to administrators and professors remain strong and largely self-imposed. As Laird Bell (1956), former chairman of the board of trustees at the University of Chicago, wisely said: "the governing board consists largely of men who care about the project but do not overdo the caring. In a word, the board has the power to control the institution but is tolerant in letting the educators for the most part run it" (p. 353).

Trustee Oversight and the Context of Academic Governance

Does this tradition of restraint mean, then, that trustees should restrict themselves to the investment portfolio, fund raising, financial affairs, and the perfunctory approval of new faculty appointments, leaving academic matters to the administration and the faculty? The answer is a qualified no. To do so would be to abdicate responsibility for the very essence of the institution and to ignore the crucial links between academic programs and those other dimensions of the college or university—its financial health, capital needs, fund-raising potential, and overall mission—that are more easily accepted as rightful trustee responsibility. But trustee oversight of academic programs must be exercised cautiously. In particular, it must take into account two dominant characteristics of American higher education. The first is the great diffusion of authority within colleges and universities and the concomitant constraints upon both trustees and chief executive officers. The second, related to the first, is the effect of strong centrifugal forces upon the mission of the institution. Together, these conditions suggest both why trustee oversight of academic programs is difficult and why it is important.

Diffusion of Authority. The responsibility of a governing board, whether of a corporation or a college or most institutions, must be exercised through the chief executive officer and, to a more limited degree, through other officers. But the opportunity for college or university presidents to act unilaterally either on their own or on the trustees' volition is also limited. Higher education is marked by a great diffusion of authority: in large universities, for example, responsibility is delegated to schools, departments, and institutes, as well as to the general faculty. The complex reasons for this situation are beyond the scope of this chapter, but they have to do with the nature of disciplines and professions and the specialization of knowledge, with the professional autonomy widely believed essential to both teaching and research, and with faculty attachment to principles of self-governance. While trustees and administrators are frequently frustrated by this diffusion of authority, most recognize the benefits for which this frustration is a modest price and would have it no other way.

This diffusion of authority has three implications for the proper role of trustees in academic oversight. First, trustees must be prepared to buttress the authority of the president and other officers when necessary; they must be sensitive to the very great vulnerability of a president, provost, dean, or other officer who is not so backed. Second, trustees must recognize that presidents and other officers can weary of the struggle to exercise even their limited powers, and, thus may abdicate too much responsibility to schools and departments. Thus trustees must continue to insist on an accountability from presidents and other officers that they rightfully exercise their central responsibility. Third—a caveat upon the preceding point—trustees must have sufficient understanding of and patience with the canons of collegial governance so that they do not pressure presidents or other officers into needless and potentially destructive confrontations with faculty over questions that involve the fragile balance of academic authority. Aggressive trustee support of a president's or dean's authority may on occasion be necessary (for example, to maintain the financial viability of an institution), but when it becomes merely an exercise of power, such concern will be counterproductive. Furthermore, power, or more likely, influence in an institution is not a zero-sum game; greater responsibility for one group does not necessarily mean less for another.

Centrifugal Forces. The second condition of colleges and universities that underlies both the need for and the challenge to trustee academic oversight is the pressure of strong centrifugal forces upon academic programs. Although these forces are greater in a university than in a college and in a large institution than in a small one, separate schools, departments, and individual faculty members naturally tend to pursue the kinds of work that they know best and can most influence and for which they are primarily rewarded, whether or not their endeavors always fit the mission of the institution or the needs of its students. This is not to say that faculty members, either individually or collectively, are unconcerned about breadth in education, about the proper fit between the academic programs and the kinds of students attending their institution, or about the goals that are or ought to be peculiar to their school. Indeed, most have given thought to these questions, and many are prepared to recommend answers that are both knowledgeable and nonparochial. The faculty are, in fact, the principal source of the answers—often in the form of compromises—to age-old questions of academic content and balance. When consulted, many faculty (and students) understand the importance of viewing the academic program from a detached perspective and, conversely, the danger of tolerating programs that are no more than the sum of many parts, however attractive they may be to given departments, disciplines, or faculty members.

Nonetheless, a broad perspective of this kind does not come into being automatically, and it most certainly is not acted upon unless there is a stimulus to do so. Without questions posed and answers demanded, without constraints and opportunities provided, and without processes established for carrying decisions to execution, the incentives and activities of the college will increasingly reflect the dominant interests of disciplines, departments, and individual members of the faculty. Even when faculty or students seek a wider viewpoint, there is little likelihood that they will speak with anything resembling one voice. At best, they may come up with a range of views, presenting a persuasive case for each. Often the differences can coexist, and the academic program will be the richer. But often, too, coexistence is impossible, and choices have to be made, not by votes or compromises, but by the exercise of central authority.

It is the responsibility of presidents, provosts or academic vice-presidents, and deans, in collaboration with the faculty, to pose questions, set constraints, provide resources, make final decisions where necessary, and implement programs—preserving all the while the balance between the requirements of the institution as a whole and those of its parts. It is the responsibility of trustees to demand of the president and academic officers that the overriding issues are being addressed; that faculty, students, and others are appropriately consulted; that responses come in forms sufficient to guide policy; that key decisions—appointments approved, budgets set, new programs initiated or turned down, or old ones curtailed—are made in ways that reflect the outcome of long-range deliberations.

Oversight as Inquiry: Questions to Ask

Trustee oversight of academic programs is exercised primarily over the president and other officers, that is, over the process of academic decision making. It is an oversight exercised largely by inquiry. A wise trustee learns what should be asked of whom and what should not. He learns what the right questions are, and the circumstances under which good answers are most likely to emerge. Oversight as inquiry suggests the role of gadfly. The questions trustees should ask of the president—or be satisfied that the president is asking of other academic officers and the faculty— should be shrewd and probing, occasionally tendentious, difficult but reasonable, and concerned with the relation of the present to the future. Such questions need not all have direct rejoinders, and they need not always lead to action. Rather, we should keep well in mind the wise counsel of that extraordinary business executive and pioneer in management theory, Chester Barnard (1938), who long ago described the merits of "watchful inaction": "Not to decide questions that are not pertinent at the time is uncommon good sense, though to raise them may be uncommon perspicacity. Not to decide questions prematurely is to refuse commitment of attitude or the development of prejudice. Not to make decisions that cannot be made effective is to refrain from destroying authority. Not to make decisions that others should make is to preserve morale, to develop competence, to fix responsibility, and to preserve authority" (p. 194).

Institutional Mission. No questions are more appropriate for the trustees to ask than those dealing with the mission, character, and ends of the institution. Yet probably no line of inquiry has consumed so much time and energy at so many colleges to so little evident purpose as the attempt to articulate institutional mission. The temptation to cover all bases and be all things to all people is very great. The capacity of an institution to alter its mission is in any case severely constrained: an institution is very much a function of what it has been, what others expect it to be, and what resources can be made available for change. Furthermore, the benefits of a more sharply defined mission—one that must perforce exclude endeavors thought important by some—may not seem worth the inevitable contention and hurt feelings of the excluded. Under these circumstances, trustees, as well as faculty and others, may grow impatient with an inquiry into the mission of an institution. A periodic reexamination of mission, undertaken seriously and courageously, nonetheless prevents academic decisions from being made simply out of caprice or because they involve the least resistance.

In addition to the suggestions offered in Chapters Three and Nine, these questions might be asked in a reexamination of mission:

- What sets the institution apart from others in the area and from other schools elsewhere that are otherwise similar? In particular, what does it choose not to do that these others do well?
- Should it be the mission to be at or near the leading edge of educational innovation, or to be viewed as an anchor and preserver? Should the institution aggressively seek non-traditional students and programs? Indeed, should it seek to change or to reaffirm its mission?
- When it becomes necessary to choose among programs (whether to add, if resources become available, or to conserve, if retrenchment becomes unavoidable), what relative weights should be placed on some of the specific goals of teaching, research, and service?
- How does a formulated mission help to find acceptable answers to the ageless academic questions of breadth versus depth in education, basic versus applied programs, required versus elective courses, and general versus career education? A caution is in order: mission statements ought not to be objects for deification.

Curriculum, Requirements, and Teaching. At the heart of the academic program is a curriculum, a set of requirements for students, and a diversity of teaching styles and abilities that may be as broad as the number of teaching faculty. These are aspects of college and university life that are particularly the province of the faculty. Within the framework of the institution's objectives, faculty members—who are appointed precisely because of their expertise in the areas of knowledge that have been selected as its focus— have the responsibility of developing balanced programs of study. Trustees need to assure themselves that examination of the curriculum and its requirements occurs regularly, rationally, and pointedly and that the quality of teaching receives similar attention. (It often does not.) The president and academic deans should be able to describe the means by which courses, related sequences of courses, major programs, and new means of learning outside the course structure are designed, implemented, evaluated, and— when appropriate—eliminated from the curriculum. Some issues that trustees might aptly raise:

- Have the faculty and administration thoroughly considered specific degree requirements—of breadth, depth, and particular skills—within the last few years? Are the findings of the latest reconsideration accurately reflected in the courses of study offered, as well as in the literature about the institution?
- Are there certain standards that all students must meet, no matter what their concentration? For example, demonstrated proficiency in English, in other languages, in quantitative skills, in certain core subjects? What indeed are the commonalities of educational experience that stand as a hallmark of the institution? By what process have they been selected?
- Do undergraduate major programs have sufficient depth and diversity? Are they neither cram courses for graduate or advanced professional study nor so slight as to deny students a full perspective on the field? What proportion of a typical student program does the major occupy, what courses are required, what comprehensive demonstration of learning is expected, what are the subsequent experiences and responses of graduates? Does the faculty regularly ask and answer such questions to their own satisfaction? To what extent is the curriculum or the faculty under obligation to present alternative intellectual points of view in particular subjects?

- Insofar as American secondary education today poorly prepares students in the oral and written use of their native tongue, how does the institution work to remedy that incapacity? How well have graduates learned to express themselves in written and spoken discourse?
- In large or varied institutions, with many disciplines and perhaps some professional schools, has a dialogue been established that assures full utilization of teaching talents and course offerings and avoids needless duplication? For example, an engineering school's mathematics courses may seem to be luxuries yet can only be eliminated if the mathematics department is willing to accommodate the needs of engineering in its courses. Is undue duplication avoided, freeing faculty time and talent to add new richness and diversity to the curriculum?
- By what means are departmental curricula designed and teaching loads assigned? Are newer, more recently trained faculty given the chance to present their ideas and prepare courses of particular interest? Does the institution provide such continuing education opportunities as its resources permit for residents of the region and for those advanced in their careers who are seeking refresher courses? Is excellence in teaching rewarded by promotions, salary increases, and other means?
- Do students have opportunities for flexibility in their education? Are they allowed to work on two degrees at once, to do interdisciplinary work, to pursue independent programs?

Faculty. The strength of the college or university's academic program depends on its faculty: their intelligence and training, along with their commitment to the aims of the institution. The recruitment and selection of new faculty, along with the review and promotion of existing faculty, are perhaps the most important responsibilities of academic administrators. Undertaken in conjunction with the faculty, these are among the most cherished duties in academic life. There is little role for trustees in evaluating faculty for appointment or promotion, even though in most institutions trustees will be asked formally to approve and legally to bind the institution to these decisions. (In awarding tenure, they may obligate resources and constrain future choices for thirty years or more.) Trustees can and must, however, examine closely the procedures, the criteria, and the rigor of judgment by which these recommendations are brought to them. Trustees must also examine closely the direction, support, and rewards that are given existing faculty to the end of best serving the purposes of the institution. In addition to the discussion of these issues in Chapter Twelve, the following questions may be appropriate:

- What criteria are used in evaluation of a faculty member for appointment or promotion? Are there measures for assessing performance or promise on each of the criteria? How, in particular, is good teaching evaluated? How is an institution's need for a particular post weighed alongside such attributes as intelligence, and scholarship? Are these criteria and procedures widely known, and are they in accord with the stated goals of the institution?

- What proportion of prospective promotions to tenure culminate in the awarding of tenure? Has this proportion changed in response to such factors as an increasing ratio of tenured to nontenured faculty, evidence of overcommitment in certain fields, or a demonstrated surplus of excellent faculty in some fields? Has permanent tenure come to be an expectation in return for merely good performance?

- Is there a long-range plan that describes anticipated faculty staffing levels by department or program? Does this plan yield a total faculty size that is within the conservatively estimated projection of available resources in, say, five years? What departments or programs are judged to be overstaffed and why? What actions are planned in consequence?

- What is the record of the institution in appointing and promoting members of minority groups, women, and those educated abroad? What evidence is there that such diversity is valued by the academic officers and by the faculty? If the recent record is not good, what different procedures are being installed to effect a different outcome in future cycles of appointments and promotions?

- What use is made of nontraditional teachers (for example, artists, business executives, or professionals) in adjunct appointments?

- Are the generally weakest and least productive faculty members (by criteria of scholarship or of teaching) known to the academic officers, and what is being done to help them grow that is, to find new scholarly pursuits and new teaching opportunities? Has a center for pedagogic self-improvement been considered, and do professors sit in on one another's classes and offer helpful criticism?
- What is being done to reward and hold the strongest members of the faculty?

Students. In some contemporary parlance, students are the "consumers" for whose benefit teaching programs are conducted. The tuition and fees that they and their families pay form a large proportion of the financial resources of independent institutions, and such charges increasingly represent significant income for public colleges and universities as well. Today's students will, if all goes well, be tomorrow's alumni—ambassadors for and supporters of the institution's future. For these reasons, quite apart from a natural sense of responsibility for the intellectual integrity of the college or university, trustees will wish to be assured that appropriate academic programs are presented to those students most able to benefit from them and that this is done in an atmosphere consonant with the fullest possible personal and educational development. The effects of students' postsecondary years upon their future lives will preferably meet the college's or university's best hopes but should at least fulfill its explicit assurances. Thus the fit of faculty, students, and programs, though planned and tested on campus, requires trustee review. Some questions and considerations to keep in mind are:

- In presenting what they have to offer to potential students, all institutions naturally wish to describe their distinctive qualities as favorably as they can in literature prepared for that purpose. Yet catalogues are increasingly taken—and properly so—as implicit promises. And if a school attracts students who, from a misunderstanding of its opportunities, cannot gain from the challenges offered, nobody benefits. Thus, is the institution representing itself—its courses of study, its financial aid program, and the like—fairly and accurately in its literature?

- To what extent should grades and scores of prospective students count in the admissions process? What other qualities and experiences ought to be measured in estimating whether each candidate will profit from and contribute to the institution?
- What are the demographic characteristics—sex, race, geographical origin, parental occupation—that current admissions practices have provided in incoming classes over the last five years? Is this mix a sound and considered one? Are there possibilities for improving it?
- How are tuition and other fees set? What is known about the effects of these costs on applicants? What are the policies and procedures for financial aid? Who among both graduate and undergraduate students is funded, in what amounts, from what sources, with what percentage in loans? Are awards limited to need, or are they used to attract desirable applicants?
- What opportunities for academic advice and counsel—in planning students' courses of study and longer-range goals—are generally available to students? To what degree are they utilized?
- Students from isolated rural areas and from impacted inner cities, who in earlier times might not have sought higher education, have enrolled on our campuses in large numbers. Sometimes it is assumed that many of them have been poorly prepared to meet the demands of the college curriculum. What, in fact, has been the institution's experience with such students, as measured by their academic progress, their persistence, or simply by their perceptions of whether or not the institution encourages and supports them? What, if anything, is done to help these students?
- Does every student have an opportunity for learning in a setting that allows him or her to come to know and be known well by professors?
- To what degree and in what ways are faculty involved with students in college life outside the classroom, such as advising student organizations and special-interest groups? What is being done in the matter of such involvement, and what measures have been successful?
- If the institution is residential, do its housing arrangements reinforce an environment of learning, such as providing opportunities for students to meet faculty in informal social and cultural settings or offering small seminars within residential centers?

- All institutions interest themselves in the outcomes of the educational process for their graduates. Courses of study vary in relation to the futures toward which they are directed. Each institution generally recognizes other institutions with which it can reasonably compare itself in as many categories as it has programs. In comparison to similar programs, both career-oriented and in the liberal arts and sciences, what jobs do graduates hold several years after commencement? Which graduates are pursuing advanced studies, of what type and where? How do these data affect program planning?
- How is student opinion brought to the attention of the administration? To the attention of the faculty? Do the students feel that they are sufficiently heard? Do the student leaders know at least a few trustees?
- What aspects of the college or university would various students change if given the opportunity? Are some administrators and faculty aware of these views? How is this information received from students and conveyed to others?

New Programs. Trustees are often called upon to approve new academic programs. By the time approval is sought, it is usually too late to ask fundamental questions, and trustees are usually not in a position to evaluate the answers. Trustees should therefore insist on a set of questions that the president, provost, key administrators, and faculty ought to ask throughout the process of devising and approving new academic programs. The questions might include:

- What is the rationale for the proposed new program? Does the proposal respond to changing interests or needs of students (and do those same changes thereby make other programs candidates for elimination)? Does it take advantage of existing special talents or special interests of certain faculty? What would those faculty otherwise do? Does the proposed program complement another program; if so, what will happen to that other program if the proposal is not successful?
- Has the proposal widespread support, or does it merely lack active opposition? Would those who profess support for it be willing to forgo something else to support it?

- What evidence is presented to back assertions of need, student demand, or interest by donors? What corroborating evidence would be collected early in evaluations if the proposal is adopted?
- What, if any, are the new resources needed for the proposed program? Will the proposal attract resources beyond its real costs, and what will be done with the surplus? Are the benefits worth the costs? Are library, computer, and other facilities and services adequate for the program? What would be the consequences if the proposed new program were to be mandated but no new funds were provided—in other words, if funds were provided not by addition but by substitution or reallocation?

Such questions are only the beginning of oversight by inquiry. More could doubtless be added. The role of the trustees in such an inquiry is not so much to demand answers as to ensure that the questions are asked and that the answers are taken seriously. Asked by trustees of the president, the chief academic officer, and others, such questions can do much to establish the expectation of academic health.

Oversight as Watchfulness: Academic Warning Signals

Trustee oversight of academic programs should also include vigilance for signals of academic difficulty. Of course, nearly every college and university these days shows some indications of trouble, and trustees must be careful not to overreact. With the decline in the size of the traditional college-going cohort, the new skepticism about the value of a college degree, the taxpayer revolt, and rampant inflation, warning signals are sounding everywhere, and one or two indications may mean little. Nevertheless, trustees should be alert to signals that might indicate serious problems. Among the relatively accessible signals, several of which together could suggest the need for thorough assessment, are:

- A drop in numbers of either applicants or matriculants greater than the decline in the national or appropriate regional pool of prospective applicants.

- A significant falling off in yield—that is, the percentage of accepted applicants who actually matriculate.
- A significant and unplanned decline in test scores, class ranks, or other traditional measures of academic selectivity.
- For private institutions, an increasing percentage of students who need institutionally provided financial aid—that is, aid beyond that provided by federal, state, or other external sources.
- A significant increase in student attrition—that is, a loss of upper-division enrollments.
- A decline in the success of graduating seniors who apply to competitive graduate and advanced professional schools.
- A loss of valued faculty that goes beyond the occasional bittersweet loss of a star faculty member to a more prestigious institution.
- A reluctance by faculty and others to allocate resources to such nondepartmental areas as the library, computer center, and academic advising office or to cultural events and other academic support activities.
- For graduate institutions, a decline in the number and quality of their graduate students in comparison with similar institutions.
- A drop in sponsored research activity.

Summary Observations

Oversight of academic programs is an important responsibility of college or university trusteeship. The difficulty of measuring the success or performance of academic programs, coupled with concern on the part of faculty about outside monitoring of academic endeavors, requires that this oversight be exercised with subtlety and balance. A few summary observations may provide some guidance to trustees entering this fascinating thicket.

The tradition of trustee restraint in academic matters has served higher education well. By and large, we have in America some of the most vibrant campuses and some of the most firmly rooted principles of academic freedom to be found anywhere. The lay board of trustees, which combines supreme authority with self-imposed restraint, is a key element in this achievement. At the same time, trustees must not shy away from asking difficult questions about academic programs and the processes by which they have come into being. Trustees cannot automatically assume that academic programs have been carefully examined by administrators and faculty in relation to institutional mission, how well they complement other programs, or their costs.

Colleges and universities provide an ambiance in which criticism, debate, intrigue, testing, and candor all flourish. Trustees ought not be alarmed by a level of internal static probably far greater than would be found in a business corporation or public agency. Especially is this so in times of financial duress. But a certain level of dissatisfaction about the academic programs is only a signal that the faculty and students are alive and independent. Trustees must be alert to potential problems but should take care not to overreact to the occasional amplification of the normal noise in academic life.

Trustees should understand the process of academic decision making and appreciate the reasons why it seems so cumbersome to those more accustomed to the faster pace of business or professional decisions. It is natural for trustees to expect a somewhat more expeditious process than is likely, in the end, to be possible. But they should be careful lest they present the president with unattainable expectations and thus damage the fragile balance between efficiency and collegiality, even though trustees must at times share the burden of unpopular but necessary decisions with the administration and the faculty.

Acting as a trustee should be, above all, a rewarding experience. A significant share of this reward should come from oversight of that which is the college or university's central reason for being: its academic programs. But in pursuing this particular charge of questioning administrators and faculty, trustees should remember that valued axiom: "Noses in, fingers out."

11

John D. Millett

Working with
Faculty and Students

The authority and responsibility for governance of a college or university in the United States are vested by state constitutional prescription, by law, or by charter almost universally in a governing board of lay trustees. In many states this governing board oversees a multicampus system of public colleges and universities. As a rule, the governing board for an independent college or university is responsible for only a single campus.

There is a great deal of difference between the scope of work for the governing board of a multicampus system and that for the governing board of a single campus. The multicampus governing board must serve as the ultimate governing authority for each individual campus within a system, preserving and protecting the unique attributes of the various institutions. At the same time the multicampus governing board must give appropriate attention to those interinstitutional concerns that require some degree of common information, planning, budgeting, and coordination. The governing board of the single campus is spared the need for attention to interinstitutional uniformities.

189

These differences between a multicampus governing board and a single-campus governing board undoubtedly affect faculty and student relationships. An impetus to faculty collective bargaining is more likely to arise in a multicampus system, simply because the governing board is perceived as somewhat remote from campus interests and issues. Students are more apt to organize on an interinstitutional and even a statewide basis in a multicampus structure in order to have some impact upon the decision-making process. Presidents tend to be delegated greater authority to manage institutional affairs in a multicampus than in a single-campus arrangement, and more issues are likely to be labeled issues of management rather than issues of governance simply because of the time constraints experienced by the multicampus board.

Discussions of campus governance have for the past twenty years identified various so-called constituencies within the academic community. These separate groups are ordinarily described as the administration, the faculty, the student body, and the alumni. The labels suggest that each of these groups has a common interest and a common point of view, but this in fact is seldom the case.

Students, particularly in the traditional college-age group (eighteen to twenty-two years of age) and in full-time residence on a campus, have their unique intellectual, social, and individual concerns. Some have substantial intellectual abilities, others have lesser abilities. Some evidence a high motivation to learn, others are content to get by. Some possess a considerable ability to understand and to respect other persons, while others display egocentric ruthlessness or become withdrawn. It is true that students tend to be peer conscious, resentful of or hostile to authority, and suspicious of "the establishment." Yet students have such different intellectual, social, and personal objectives that they tend to fall into various groups rather than form a single cohesive association. As an organizational enterprise and as a geographical entity, a campus learns to encourage, guide, and accommodate students.

Faculty members are engaged in the most highly individualized, competitive, exacting, frustrating, and anxiety-prone profession in America. Each faculty member is expected to be a scholar of highly specialized and profound knowledge, an innovative and imaginative explorer of the unknown or the far reaches of creative expression, an effective communicator of knowledge and values, a stimulator of intellectual and social maturity for students, and a person who is skilled in the practical use of knowledge or in the esthetic appreciation of the arts. Only a few faculty members ever evidence the full range of abilities to which they aspire, ever experience the satisfaction in work performance that they seek, or ever obtain the external recognition that they consider their just due. The academic way of life is demanding and seldom as fulfilling as anticipated. Some quickly give up their impossible dream, others never.

Whatever the characteristics of students and faculty members on any particular campus, the college or university exists to provide a learning environment in which they can interact. At the same time, however, administrators, professional staff members, and the operating staff are essential participants in the college or university enterprise whose job is to facilitate the learning process, assist student-faculty interaction, and ensure achievement of the intended learning outcomes.

Over the campus as a learning environment, over the enterprise as an educational process that produces various outputs, the lay governing board presides as a kind of balance wheel. On the one hand, a kind of internal balance needs to be maintained among students, faculty, and the enterprise as a whole. On the other hand, balance must also be maintained between the aspirations of students and faculty and the expectations of society, including the willingness of society to support the enterprise. An academic institution is also a unit of economic enterprise, requiring income and capital plant and expending limited resources to sustain the learning endeavor.

The governing board of a private or independent college or university is a trustee of the public interest in the enterprise, a conservator of assets, a governor of income and expense, and a reminder to the academic community of its social dependence. The governing board of a public college or university in effect represents the executive, legislative, and judicial branches of state government in the performance of an essential public service. As such, it helps insulate the institution from partisan and ill-considered politics. But it also provides advocacy for the needs of public higher education, including the need for political support. In both the independent and the public sectors, the governing board must formulate and enunciate an enlighted public interest in the performance of higher education.

An essential factor in the decision-making power of the governing board is often overlooked. The governing board in the public sector has no taxing authority; publicly sponsored colleges and universities must depend upon state and local governments to provide appropriate income from the general revenue fund. But the governing board in the private sector can, if it wishes, charge students and clients. Tradition decrees that student instructional charges be less than cost and that the gap be filled by philanthropic support. The governing board must then seek this philanthropic support or cause it to be sought.

In the discharge of its authority and responsibility, the governing board needs help. This help is ordinarily, and properly, provided by the president, who serves at the pleasure of the governing board and who is the professional leader of the academic community. The president is generally one who has served in academic roles—faculty member, department chairman, dean, or vice-president for academic affairs—and one equipped by temperament and ability to meet the multiple demands of the presidential role. In his or her leadership role the president must have general assistants in planning and budgeting, personnel, and public affairs. In his or her managerial role the president must have specialized assistants for academic affairs, student affairs, administrative affairs, and financial affairs. These assistants collectively constitute "the administration" that faculty and students too often think of as "the enemy" in the academic community.

This organizational sketch provides essential background for understanding the concept of constituent groups within a campus structure. Nothing has been mentioned here about the alumni and wealthy friends or about such external constituencies as local communities, local and state governments, the federal government, church bodies, private foundations, corporations and professions, voluntary associations, labor unions, accrediting bodies, the media, higher education associations, and the other interested "publics" of higher education. These external constituencies, which are very real and very powerful, must be catered to in varying ways whether faculty members and students like it or not. But our focus here is on internal rather than external constituencies because the former are responsible for the internal complications that have arisen in the structure and process of college and university governance.

Faculty Role in Institutional Government

Several years ago, Jencks and Riesman (1968) wrote about the "academic revolution" that occurred in the United States after the Second World War. Actually, however, this academic revolution began with the professionalization of scholarship in the last third of the nineteenth century. This radical change was simply accelerated by the events of the Second World War and its aftermath.

The academic revolution has had several aspects: the specialization and accumulation of knowledge, the development of increasingly sophisticated and expensive methods of advancing knowledge (research), the increasing utilization of knowledge in the service of people through professional, technological, and economic applications. In the very center of this academic revolution has stood the scholar-researcher and the scholar-teacher, that is, the faculty member of the American college or university. Furthermore, the Second World War completed the transfer of the intellectual base of Western culture from Western Europe to the United States.

The academic revolution has had its price: the fragmentation of knowledge, the emergence of the academic department as the basic organizational unit of a college or university, the concentration upon empirical and symbolic knowledge with a corresponding sacrifice of other kinds of knowledge (synoptic, experiential, esthetic, and ethical), the dispersion of intellectual leadership, and the loss of a sense of community within the academic community. The problems of knowledge, and the uses of knowledge, have become too complex to be dealt with by lay intelligence except in a superficial way. And lay persons today include not only members of governing boards but also members of the administration and members of the faculty outside their own fields of expertise.

The academic revolution has also increased the concern of faculty members with the structure and process of governance within the college or university where they practice their profession of scholarship. The early charters and bylaws of American colleges and universities had usually delegated authority from the lay governing board to a faculty senate for the determination of course offerings, the establishment of course and grade requirements for award of a degree, the arrangement of the academic calendar, and the promulgation of student conduct regulations. Sometimes admission standards and almost always admission decisions were added to the scope of faculty authority, although such delegation was on occasion made subject to governing board review. The individual faculty member was left to determine course content and instructional methods and to evaluate student academic achievement.

With time and growing academic specialization, faculty members acquired additional authority: the authority to decide who should be appointed as a faculty member, what should be the rank and tenure status of each faculty member, and the desirable compensation of faculty members. These decisions were made at the level of the academic department, with such review by deans, the administration, and the governing board as might be provided by ordinance or by institutional bylaws. Intervention in faculty personnel affairs by the administration and the governing board was exercised only on rare occasions, usually when some unfavorable public notice had been attracted by a particular faculty member or possible appointee. The one matter over which faculty members could not exercise unfettered discretion was that of faculty compensation. The constraints of institutional budget balancing had to take precedence over faculty expectations.

The extensive role of faculty members—individually, departmentally, and collectively—in resolving issues of academic (instructional) affairs and of faculty (personnel) affairs led Corson (1960) to assert that American colleges and universities presented "a unique dualism of organizational structure" (p. 43). There was one organizational structure and process for deciding academic and faculty issues, and another organizational structure and process for deciding institutional issues. The difficulty with this model of organizational behavior was in deciding just what questions were academic and faculty issues and what questions were institutional issues.

Nor did the concept of organizational dualism go unchallenged. In my book, *The Academic Community* (Millett, 1962), I argued that the constituent groups of a campus have a common interest in institutional welfare and that, by a process of consensus building, these groups (faculty, students, and administration) undertake to determine issues of mission, program, supporting effort, and resource allocation. Baldridge (1971) presented a different interpretation, declaring that the competing constituencies of the academic community engage in a political process that includes interest formulation, power struggles, and compromise in order to arrive at institutional decision making.

In 1966 the AAUP joined the American Council on Education and the Association of Governing Boards in issuing a joint statement on the government of higher educational institutions. This joint statement called for mutual understanding of the requirements of college and university government (American Association of University Professors, 1966). It endorsed the need for participation of faculty members, administrative officers, and governing boards in determining general education policy. The statement proposed that long-range planning, preparing plans for physical facilities, budgeting, selecting a president, appointing other academic officers, and conducting external relations be joint endeavors. The statement set forth certain general duties of a governing board, emphasized the role of the president as an institutional leader, and declared that the faculty has "primary" responsibility for the curriculum, methods of instruction, research, faculty status, degree requirements, and those aspects of student life related to the educational process. The statement also recognized a possible student interest in institutional governance and urged students "to participate responsibly" in such governance when they wished to do so.

Other documents of similar importance might be cited: a report by a task force of the American Association for Higher Education (1967) and a report from the Assembly on University Goals and Governance (1971) sponsored by the American Academy

of Arts and Sciences. In addition, the prestigious Carnegie Commission on Higher Education issued a report on *Governance of Higher
Education* (1973). The commission identified six "priority problems": (1) adequate provision for institutional autonomy, (2) the
role of boards of trustees and of presidents, (3) collective bargaining by faculty members, (4) rules and practices governing faculty
tenure, (5) student influence on campus, and (6) the handling of
campus emergencies. (The recommendations of the commission
concerning faculty and student participation in governance will be
discussed later.)

It is clear that the general thrust of the documents just mentioned is for substantial participation of faculty members in campus
governance. The problem then becomes the practical one of how to
structure such faculty participation. Various arrangements have
been advocated and attempted, but no arrangement has yet proved
entirely satisfactory.

Faculty Participation in Academic and Faculty Affairs

It is generally agreed that the faculty of a college or university should exercise a primary role in deciding academic and faculty
issues. But there does remain some controversy about the level of
such decision making—should it be departmental, college, or
campus-wide?— and about the extent of the veto power to be
exercised by presidents, deans, vice-presidents for academic affairs, and governing boards. My own experience as a faculty
member, as a state university president, and as a trustee of an
independent college provides certain conclusions.

In a college or university, it is desirable to have a faculty
committee within each instructional unit as an advisory and consul-
tative body for the dean. The faculty members should be elected
from each department but should not include department chairmen, who should instead serve on the dean's management council.
This faculty committee should be consulted about policies and procedures of college-wide concern in curriculum construction and
degree requirements, admission, enrollment, financial assistance,
instructional methods, student evaluation, research activities, and
public service activities. In addition, it should be consulted about

college-wide policies and procedures for faculty workloads, staffing patterns, personnel actions, tenure decisions, compensation, standards of professional performance, and evaluation.

Similarly, it is desirable for a comprehensive or research university to have a faculty senate of elected representatives from the constituent colleges. The presiding officer of this senate should be the president of the university, with the vice-president for academic affairs serving as the president's alter ego when necessary. This faculty senate should be consulted about policies and procedures of university-wide applicability that have to do with the same range of academic and faculty matters as those enumerated above for college committees. I am assuming that there will also be a council of deans that meets periodically with the academic vice-president or the president.

Some disagreement may arise over this pattern of consultation when one asks whether consultation means discussion and an exchange of viewpoints or whether it means the authority to decide. My own judgment is that a dean should have the authority to disagree with any formal action of a faculty committee and to take such an issue to the vice-president for academic affairs for further consideration. Also, if a vice-president for academic affairs disagrees with any formal action of the faculty senate, he or she should have the authority to take the matter to the president for review and decision by the governing board. I would expect deans and faculty committees to be in agreement under most circumstances and I would expect the same for vice-presidents and faculty senates. But I would fear absolute power vested in faculties just as much as I would fear absolute power vested in presidents.

In addition to academic policies and procedures, there are also individual actions to be considered—actions involving individual appointments, terminations, promotions, granting of tenure, evaluation, compensation. Some form of committee consultation is highly desirable in all such individual actions in addition to the recommendation or decision of chairmen, deans, vice-presidents, and presidents. Some kind of formalized grievance machinery is also essential for reviewing actions considered by any individual faculty member to be undeserved or discriminatory. Again, in unusual circumstances an appeal for review of an individual grievance may come to the governing board, and governing boards should thus have the authority to accept or reject such appeals.

On occasion there may be some difficulty in determining whether a particular issue actually involves academic and faculty affairs. The question of student admission standards is more than just an academic matter; in fact, it raises profound issues of social policy. Should access to the institution, for example, be based exclusively on meritocratic considerations? The recommendations of the faculty on admission standards are certainly to be given great weight, but they should not necessarily be controlling. There may be other issues of similar importance: What is acceptable political behavior off campus by faculty members and administrative officers? What is acceptable personal behavior on campus in advocating dissent or protest of institutional decisions? To what extent shall the campus be a forum or stage for social protest? To what extent shall the institution adopt standards of acceptable individual behavior in the classroom, in research, and in public service activities that may differ from those prevailing in the general community? These questions are not simple to answer and may well require resolution by a governing board.

Faculty members consider the appointment of department chairmen, college deans, vice-presidents for academic affairs, and presidents as a matter of major faculty concern. As a consequence, faculty usually insist on participating in a formalized process of selection. Such faculty participation is desirable and should be provided for. But it needs to be understood that the role of a selection committee is advisory to the appointing authority, and that for good and sufficient reasons the recommendations of a selection committee can be rejected.

Faculty Participation in Institutional Affairs

Some difficulty arises when one turns from academic/faculty affairs to institutional affairs. Let us grant for the moment that there is a definable, even if sometimes uncertain, distinction between academic and institutional affairs. To what degree should the faculty participate in institutional affairs? The answers given in various commentaries range from no participation to complete faculty determination. Both extremes are unacceptable, but someplace in between is a workable middle ground.

One solution is to have one or more faculty members elected to serve on the governing board. A few institutions, such as Cornell University, have tried this approach, and a few state governments —California is one example—have provided by law for such an arrangement. A number of both public and private institutions are required by law or by their bylaws to include a faculty representative on the governing board. A study by Gomberg and Atelsek (1977) indicated that some 3 percent of all governing board members came from the faculty: 2.5 percent for single-campus public governing boards; 2 percent for multicampus public governing boards; and 3.5 percent for single-campus private governing boards.

Most faculty trustees, however, do not serve on the boards of their own institutions; in its report on governance, the Carnegie Commission on Higher Education (1973) recommended that faculty members from within the institution not be elected to serve as trustees. Such membership is undesirable for several reasons. First, faculty membership tends to dilute the board's role as an intermediary between institutional interest (including faculty interest) and the public interest. Secondly, faculty membership may tend to encourage extensive board consideration of academic affairs and faculty affairs that are better resolved short of decision by the governing board. Indeed, faculty membership on a governing board may tend to distort rather than to clarify the faculty role in institutional governance.

At the same time, it is highly desirable in my judgment for a governing board to include in its membership one or more faculty members from *another* college or university. I have found in my experience as a president that such membership on a governing board can be very useful. Board members who are corporate executives, professional practitioners, labor leaders, and community workers can be very helpful in relating the academic community to society. But these board members usually lack an understanding of the intricacies of the academic community, of the special professional status of faculty members, and of the college's or university's unique organizational structure, with its precarious balance between faculty interests and other interests. A faculty member from another institution provides a special point of view when a governing board must decide how the institutional interest is different from the faculty interest.

In addition, there are workable ways of interrelating the faculty point of view and that of the governing board short of faculty representation on the governing board itself. One such arrangement is to include one or more faculty representatives as either voting or nonvoting members of an academic and faculty affairs committee of the governing board. Such representation can assist the president or academic vice-president in presenting policy recommendations for consideration by the governing board or can assist in clarifying differences between faculty advice and presidential recommendation. Another arrangement is to invite the chairman of a faculty senate to attend meetings of the governing board with the privilege of speaking but without the authority of voting.

In the internal governance structure of a college or university, it may be useful to have a college or university council in addition to a faculty senate. This council should include representatives of the faculty senate, the student senate, and the staff senate (if one exists), as well as representatives of the administration, and it should be headed by the president. The agenda should be determined by the president in consultation with an executive committee and should consist primarily of advisory proposals from one constituency that the president believes would be of interest to other constituencies. The role of the college or university council would be to give advice to the president on college- or university-wide matters prior to the president's decision about recommendations to be submitted to the governing board.

The definition of issues to be resolved by a governing board should be fairly simple to formulate. Apart from personnel actions that are usually considered on a routine basis and apart from budget matters, which are always of major importance, a governing board should assist a president in maintaining some degree of appropriate balance among faculty interests, student interests, and institutional interests. When a president must reject advice from a faculty or student senate, there is one reason and only one reason for such action: the president believes that the advice does not sufficiently take into account the institution's relation to and financial dependence upon an external society. Whenever there is a disagreement between the president and the faculty senate, or the president and the student senate, that disagreement automatically transforms the point at issue into a matter of institutional interest; the disagreement must then be resolved by the governing board in a way that preserves and increases the effectiveness of the organization as an economic enterprise.

This author recently completed a study on "new structures of campus power" (Millett, 1978b). The study was based upon case reports of experience in developing and operating instruments of campus-wide governance in the decade from 1967 to 1976. In undertaking this study I examined eight areas of institutional concern:

1. The clarification or reformulation of institutional mission.
2. The specification of program objectives.
3. The allocation of resources.
4. The development of new or expanded income.
5. The improvement of management practices.
6. The determination of degree requirements.
7. The determination of appropriate standards of faculty, student, and staff behavior.
8. The evaluation of program accomplishment.

In general, this study found that faculty participation in a college or university council had been productive in helping to clarify institutional mission, in determining degree requirements, and in establishing appropriate standards of campus behavior. But the study also found that faculty participation at the institution-wide level had been only partially effective in specifying the objectives to be accomplished by programs of instruction, research, public service, and student financial aid and had done little to assist in determining the work objectives of support programs (academic support, student services, plant operation, and institutional administration). Finally, faculty participation had made almost no contribution to the allocation of resources among programs, to the development of new or expanded sources of income, to the improvement of management processes, or to the evaluation of program accomplishment.

In my experience as a trustee I have found that faculty members are generally concerned about two or three matters. First of all, faculty members want to be sure that their vital roles of instruction, research, and public service are fully understood and appreciated by the governing board. Secondly, faculty members want the institution to obtain more income but are reluctant to face up to the issue of the desirable relationship among tuition, government subsidy, and philanthropy in providing that income. Thirdly, faculty members want to be insulated from the world outside the walls of the academic community without forgoing support from that world.

As a trustee I have yet to hear a carefully formulated faculty position on the intellectual, personal, and social objectives of a degree program; on the relevance and effectiveness of the curriculum in achieving these objectives; on the growing gap between the available models of rationality and the real behavior of individuals and institutions in society; and on the reconciliation of intellectual quality with personal equality in society. Trustees are not provided with such disquisitions because faculty members tend to be deeply divided among themselves on these issues and tend to resolve their differences through individual rather than collective decision making. (It is also true that the agenda of a governing board is often crowded with the trivia of institutional needs rather than with the vital issues of institutional performance.)

Nonetheless, governing boards must always keep in mind that the work of the faculty is what a college or university is all about. A college or university acquires prestige through the competence and the performance of its faculty. The president is administrative leader of a learning environment and an economic enterprise. The president can encourage intellectual achievement but he or she cannot direct its realization. Since an institution of higher education could not exist without a faculty, it must find the ways and means to incorporate the faculty into the ongoing life of the college or university as both an intellectual and economic enterprise.

Student Role in Institutional Government

The student enrolled in higher education is more than a customer or a client; he or she is an active participant in the learning process. Under the guidance, encouragement, and prodding of faculty members, the student undertakes to advance his or her own ability to learn, to increase his or her own stock of knowledge, and to develop his or her own skill in the use of knowledge or in the performance of the creative arts. At the same time, the learning environment may directly or indirectly assist the student in the development of emotional maturity, appreciation of the creative arts, the understanding of interpersonal relationships, and the clarification of a personal structure of values.

Students are quite diverse in their abilities, interests, socioeconomic backgrounds, and the objectives they bring to the learning endeavor. As a consequence, the performance and achievement of students vary a great deal. Some students of limited abilities may become relatively high achievers, while some students of substantial ability may become relatively low achievers for various personal reasons. A college or university can encourage learning, but it cannot guarantee learning.

In general, students have two reasons for seeking higher education: self-development and preparation for employment. The objective of self-development may or may not be very clearly defined in a student's thinking and performance; it may, in fact, mean little more than an opportunity to get away from home and family or to associate more fully with peers. The objective of preparation for employment may be highly developed, or it may be only partially formulated. Some students choose higher education as a means of finding a useful career; others are certain about their career goals from the start.

Students are of various kinds. One important group of students is composed of individuals of the traditional college age (eighteen to twenty-four years) who enroll full time and pursue a definite degree program. Another important group of students is composed of individuals who enroll only part time, who have jobs to support themselves or family work to perform, and who seek degrees in order to improve their employability or to find new personal interests. This second group of students tends to be older than the first, to be little interested in the campus as a place to live, and to be more mature in outlook and expectation. There tend also to be important distinctions between undergraduate students and graduate students, between students in the social sciences and the humanities and those in the biological and physical sciences, between students in the arts and sciences and students in professional fields of study. Important distinctions also exist between the student in a highly selective learning environment and the student in a nonselective one.

The point in these obvious reminders is simply that there is no such person in higher education as a typical student. Some colleges and universities do have a predominance of students who evidence a particular set of characteristics. Such institutions tend to be residential campuses that enroll mostly students of traditional college age; some of these institutions are located in communities of relatively small population, and some are selective in their admission of students. But other colleges and universities are located in large urban centers, offer many kinds of degree programs, and enroll a wide variety of students in terms of abilities, age, and interests.

The student role within a college or university depends in large measure upon the nature of the student body. Part-time, commuting, and older students have a particular set of interests that they expect the institution to accommodate to some extent. Full-time, residential, and selected students of traditional college age have a different set of interests that they expect the institution to satisfy, particularly if the institution is located in a small community with limited off-campus attractions.

Various studies suggest that student concern about participation in institutional governance is most evident in the college or university that enrolls full-time, residential, and selected students. These students have a dual set of concerns: intellectual and residential. Ideally, the residential interests should undergird and reinforce the intellectual ones. In practice, however, the student who attends classes and laboratories an average of four hours a day for five days a week but who lives on campus twenty-four hours a day for seven days a week, is likely to be considerably more preoccupied with the conditions of residential life than with intellectual concerns.

Much of the so-called student revolution of the 1960s was aimed at conditions of residential life. Residential colleges and universities had tended to take seriously their obligation to act *in loco parentis.* The trend toward more permissive family life and the changing social standards of acceptable moral behavior were sometimes less perceived on college campuses than elsewhere. Student revolt resulted, and—more rapidly in some institutions than in others—the old restrictions upon student residential life and social behavior were relaxed or even abandoned. The movement for change was still going on in some places throughout the 1970s.

The student movement in the 1960s also focused upon certain social issues beyond the campus: the Vietnam War, poverty, racial discrimination, urban deterioration, and environmental pollution. The interest of some students in these concerns raised in an acute form the whole question of the relationship of higher education to American society—a question neither governing boards, presidents, nor faculty members as a group were prepared to answer. The question was not answered in the 1970s, but somehow the urgency of providing an answer disappeared when selective military service came to an end, when the war in Vietnam was terminated, when economic recession and a crisis in energy resources occurred at the end of 1973, and when the boom employment market for college graduates vanished.

Perhaps the single most important common student interest to arise at the end of the 1970s was the issue of the cost of higher education. Higher energy costs, inflation, mounting governmental regulations, demands for increased salaries and wages—higher education is a labor-intensive industry with a very high proportion of current operating expense going into compensation for personal services—all these forces brought about an escalation in expenditures that was not adequately offset by either governmental subsidies or philanthropic contributions. As a result, tuition, as well as room and board charges, mounted year by year. Students began to express increased concern about this trend and to protest the constantly rising charges of colleges and universities.

In the summer of 1977 representatives of statewide student

associations in twenty-two states met in Columbia, Missouri, and at the end of four days issued the so-called *Missouri Statement*. Put together by students who in the main were undergraduates from state universities, this statement criticized inadequate public funding of student financial aid, rising tuition charges, misleading "consumer" information about higher education, and racial and sexual discrimination. The *Missouri Statement* expressed concern about rising unemployment among youth, demanded that governing boards divest themselves of investments in corporations "doing business in South Africa where they comply with apartheid laws," and advocated effective steps to promote reduced energy consumption on college campuses. The *Missouri Statement* declared: "It is imperative that students be placed on governing boards of colleges and universities with equal standing and all rights and responsibilities of other governing board members, including the right to vote. As the consumer of higher education, students have a right to active participation in governance at the highest level and at each major level of policy making, including, but not limited to, administration, curriculum, and collective bargaining" (pp. 8–9).

While *Missouri Statement* may be taken as the agenda of student activists at the end of the 1970s, various kinds of student organizations and various forms of student government have been characteristic of American colleges and universities for many years. In the American college of the nineteenth century, student clubs and fraternities were often discouraged or even outlawed as activities that distracted students from learning. In the early years of this century, however, colleges and universities learned to accommodate many different kinds of student social groups: fraternities, sororities, living and eating clubs, honor societies, student newspapers, other student publications, and various student activities (intramural sports, student health services, recreational facilities and events, cultural efforts). Student and university centers began to appear. Special fees were introduced as a form of student tax to help pay for student service programs and activities.

Colleges and universities experienced considerable difficulty in devising a satisfactory form of campus-wide or overall student "government." One problem was that of authority. On some campuses all students automatically became members of a campus-wide student association and were then expected to select student body officers and members of a student senate. On other campuses student representation was based upon educational units, living units, or some other constituent group whose members were presumed to have a common interest. In terms of authority, a student senate might recommend policies concerned with student organizations, student services, residential life, and academic requirements, but the decision-making power remained vested in faculty bodies, in administrative officers, and in governing boards.

In the 1960s students came to see governing boards in particular as the holders of power, and amid various protests about the use (and to some students the abuse) of this power came demands for student membership on such boards. It was evidently assumed that the concerns of students would automatically be satisfied if students had access to power. Or at least it was assumed that the older generations represented by governing board members would better understand student concerns if they heard them directly.

In several states some action was taken to require that there be a student member on the governing boards for public colleges and universities. Laws to this effect were enacted in Connecticut, Florida, Illinois, Indiana, Kentucky, Louisiana, Massachusetts, Montana, New Hampshire, New York, North Carolina, Oregon, Pennsylvania, and Washington. A student member to serve without vote was added by executive order to the boards in Alabama. In a few instances, as in Rhode Island, a state board has invited student membership, and in other instances, as in California, boards have been authorized to invite student membership. A poll of governing boards at land-grant institutions indicated that in 1975 some 29 percent had students as full-voting trustees. Over 50 percent had some form of student participation through committees of the governing boards. Another study published in 1977 found that 1 percent of public single-campus trustees and 4 percent of public multicampus trustees were students. For private colleges and universities 1 percent of all trustees were students.

No doubt governors and state legislators have been influenced by the fact that the Twenty-Sixth Amendment requires states not to deny the privilege of voting to citizens who are eighteen years of age or older. Political leaders have seen numerous advantages and few, if any, disadvantages in adding student membership to governing boards. However, the Carnegie Commission (1973) on Higher Education, in its report on governance, recommended against such membership. It did urge that board membership be broadened to include some recent graduates and that student members be added to certain board committees, especially to board committees on student affairs. In addition, the commission said that some opportunity should be provided for student presentation of student concerns directly to governing boards, and some such arrangements do seem eminently desirable.

There can be no doubt that in the past twenty years faculties, administrative officers, and governing boards have given increased attention to student interests, points of view, and concerns. On occasion the student voice expressed by some student activists has been strident, intemperate, impolite, and insulting. But students have been heard, changes in student conduct regulations have been made, and student grievances have received more careful attention than in the past.

There are two major checks on student influence. The faculty of a college or university remains the final arbiter of what a student is expected to learn and of how well the student has met those expectations. A few institutions have experimented with a student learning contract formally entered into between a student and a faculty member. In most instances, however, the learning contract is implicit rather than explicit. Faculties continue to determine the courses to be offered to students and the quality of student learning. The second major check on students is the continued predominance of external governmental and philanthropic support of student learning. The student can scarcely reject the existing social structure and then ask society to provide him or her with increased financial support. In fact, the likelihood of a favorable response always depends in large part upon how the request is made and upon the behavior of students when making the request.

Governing boards have the essential task of reconciling students and society. It is not a simple task. Virtue, however defined, in not always evident in the behavior of students or in the behavior of society. A governing board strives to interpret social values and processes to students, and student values and processes to society. The effort is sometimes thankless, but it is at all times indispensable.

Conclusion

It is constantly necessary for governing boards to remind themselves, and others, that a college or university is not a political association or a self-governing community. As a productive enterprise, a college or university is in the business of obtaining economic resources that will be used to render service to individuals and to produce useful outputs for society.

The primary need of a college or university is management: work planning and work performance. The task of governance must advance the job of management, the job of work output. Leadership must provide the necessary linkage among decisions about desirable work output, income available from prices and other sources, and essential expenditures. Both governance and leadership within a college or university operate within the context of work to be planned and work to be accomplished. The work comes first, before governance and leadership.

Faculty and student participation is necessary in the governance process of a college or university. But this process serves a social, as well as a faculty and a student, interest, since higher education is an institution of society. Nevertheless, higher education is a unique social endeavor in that it serves society and at the same time seeks to make society better. So unique an endeavor requires careful nurture, and governing boards are above all else the conscience and the trust of that nurture. And for nearly 350 years, from colonial times to the present, governing boards in America have pursued that task with considerable distinction.

12

Richard Chait

Setting Tenure
and Personnel Policies

Colleges and universities offer students academic programs staffed by faculty. The academic programs largely define the institution's mission, and the faculty largely determines how well that mission is fulfilled. When we list the great universities or the strongest departments, our judgments are inevitably assessments of the caliber of the faculty. Thus, although administrators, architects, athletic directors, and even trustees sometimes like to think otherwise, the quality of the faculty and the quality of the university are very nearly synonymous.

The faculty's direct relationship to an institution's reputation might be reason enough to carefully consider policies and practices that affect academic personnel. There is, however, an equally powerful economic argument. Faculty compensation and related instructional expenses consume the lion's share of an institution's budget. In any year, instructional expenditures may represent as much as 60 percent of the operating budget. Over the long term, the compensation package (salary and benefits) for a faculty member tenured at age thirty-five could reach $680,000 in the equivalent of today's dollars by the time the professor retires at sixty-five. Were retirement delayed until age seventy, the costs could exceed $800,000. In that context, faculty are expensive and tenure decisions are costly. A decision to tenure five faculty members, for example, could represent a $4 million decision or, otherwise stated, a $4 million capital outlay. Colleges and universities need to be as attentive to tenure decisions as to construction decisions. Indeed, it may be easier to refurbish an outmoded facility than to rejuvenate an outdated faculty member.

In the current environment, marked by proceduralization and no growth, both academic and economic arguments to manage faculty resources prudently assume added force. Sometime in the late 1960s American higher education entered an era of proceduralization, a period when a spate of externally imposed rules and regulations started to prescribe and proscribe the behavior of academic institutions. Examples are plentiful: legislation for the handicapped, the Family Educational Rights and Privacy Act (Buckley Amendment), even decisions by the Environmental Protection Agency that, for instance, dictate the mix of fuels a college may burn.

While many kinds of regulations have thus had an impact on colleges and universities, the most dramatic effects can be observed in the area of personnel administration. In 1968 President Johnson signed Executive Order 11246, which together with Titles VI and VII of the 1964 Civil Rights Act and Title IX of the 1972 Education Amendments Act, provides the basis for affirmative action. Other prominent examples of such regulation include the Equal Pay/Equal Work Act and the Occupational Safety and Health Act. These statutes and orders govern the recruitment, appointment, promotion, and compensation of faculty, as well as the entry and advancement phases of employment. Other externally generated procedures affect the exit process. In 1972 the *Roth* and *Sinderman* decisions of the United States Supreme Court set standards for procedural due process as a protection against dismissal. In 1978 the Age Discrimination in Employment Act was amended to extend mandatory retirement to age seventy.

Taken together, these rules, laws, goals, timetables, underutilization analyses, regulations, orders, policies, and procedures have narrowed the traditional prerogatives of faculty, administrators, and trustees to control the lifeblood of the university—namely, the flow of faculty into, up, through, and out of the institution.

If legislation has not proceduralized all of academic life, unionization will probably fill the gaps. The scope of bargaining grows wider and wider. Salaries, workloads, evaluations, retrenchment, and leaves have all become matters of one contract or another. At a college in rural New Hampshire, the faculty contract even specifies how much firewood faculty can chop on campus and cart home.

What does proceduralization portend? We are likely to have more fairness but less freedom. The rules will ensure uniformity at the expense of flexibility. Members of the academic community will enjoy more protection and fewer prerogatives. The red tape may require that better personnel records be kept and more formal personnel procedures be followed; whether better personnel decisions will result seems less certain. Administrators and trustees may be tempted or required to rule by the book and to cite chapter, verse, and clause. After all, the failure to follow procedures or adhere to the letter of the law may spawn grievances and lawsuits. Whereas college personnel administration was once notoriously casual and slipsod, now the other extreme may result: an automated, impersonal, inflexible system.

In the midst of proceduralization, student enrollments have held steady or actually declined, and financial resources have become scarce and likely to grow more scarce. For faculty, the ramifications of this steady state that has come in the aftermath of a period of spectacular expansion are quite clear. Faculty mobility has slowed to a near standstill. Interinstitutional job changes by faculty dropped 60 percent from 1968 to 1972. Voluntary attrition among faculty with the doctorate declined from 8 percent in the mid 1960s to about 1.5 percent currently. In the mid 1960s mobility and growth created circumstances where, on the average, 20 percent of a faculty was new to the campus each year. Rampant expansion yielded a younger faculty whose median age today is forty-two, with only 15 percent of the professoriate over age fifty. Since demand exceeded supply, appointment standards were relaxed. Fewer than one of every four new faculty members hired in 1968 held a doctorate. Thus, we entered the present no-growth period with a relatively young, inexperienced, less credentialed, and largely immobile faculty. And for the most part these faculty are here to stay. Cartter (1976, p. 172) predicts that, by 1990, 87.5 percent of all faculty will be over age thirty-five.

In an era of equilibrium personnel decisions will be more critical and mistakes more costly than they were previously. The academy can no longer rely on growth to cover over mistakes. There will be far less maneuverability to change people and hence programs exactly at a time when the ability to respond to change should command a top priority. The importance of the link between people and programs in higher education cannot be overstated. In higher education, product changes almost always require personnel changes. Unlike auto assembly line workers, who can turn with relative ease from production of one model to production of another, few classicists could shift from a course on Plato to a course on pollution. In other words, since there will be so few opportunities in the coming years to change people and thus programs, each personnel decision will assume added significance and each mistake will be magnified. Now, perhaps more than ever before, human resources must be managed effectively.

Managing Human Resources

Most colleges and universities recognize the need to manage their physical and fiscal resources. Capital and operating budgets are developed routinely, and five- and ten-year fiscal projections are hardly uncommon. Although the management of human resources also requires planning and monitoring over the short and long terms, many institutions fail to carry out these tasks.

Nearly all boards receive on an annual basis a balance sheet and a statement of changes in fund balances. The balance sheet presents a financial picture at a particular moment, and the statement of changes helps a board to compare current circumstances with conditions twelve months ago. Typically, these documents are presented to the board on a routine basis. But how many boards receive similar information about personnel generally and faculty in particular? Planning for the management of human resources might begin with an inventory of current staff. With faculty, for example, the data might be arrayed by (1) department or school, (2) age, (3) sex, (4) race, (5) salary, (6) workload, (7) tenure status, (8) degree attainment, and (9) retirement date.

There are a number of computer-based programs that allow such data to be entered, stored and, retrieved. Programs have been developed by Robert Linnell at the University of Southern California, George Lamson at Carleton College, Carl Patton at the University of Illinois at Urbana, and Vernon Miller at the University of Chicago, to name only a few. Each model enables the user to conduct statistical analyses that may inform, for instance, salary equity studies or affirmative action plans. Far more importantly, the models permit and facilitate simulation exercises based upon various policy assumptions made by the institution. One can manipulate the several policy variables that affect faculty flow, such as rates of promotion and tenure, length of probationary periods, retrenchment plans, and voluntary attrition.

One well-managed college had a faculty-flow update on the president's desk less than a week after amendment of the Age Discrimination in Employment Act to bar mandatory retirement before age seventy. In other words, through the application of these models a college and its board can ascertain the current characteristics of the faculty and the likely effects of contemplated policy or environmental changes. Above all else, the models compel the college to collect data that the college should collect in any case. (For faculty-flow models not dependent on electronic data-processing systems, see Luecke, 1974; American Association of University Professors, 1973.)

With or without the assistance of a computer, some fundamental analyses can be undertaken with regard to workload, salary scales, and tenure ratios. In concert with the president, the board should establish a system that furnishes such data on a regular timetable. There should be both retrospective analyses and prospective forecasts—data that suggest where the college has been, where it is, and where it is going.

Placing a particular college within a larger context can be accomplished without much difficulty. The American Association of University Professors (AAUP) makes available annually a compendium of salary levels and tenure ratios. The National Center for Education Statistics publishes yearly a very valuable statistical summary of *The Condition of Education* and periodically the center issues data-rich reports such as *Salaries, Tenure, and Fringe Benefits of Full-Time Instructional Faculty* . . . (1977). Likewise, the College and University Personnel Association conducts surveys on administrative salaries. An institution can select some appropriate counterparts and make comparisons. If some data are not available to the institution, it can initiate an information exchange with a group of similar institutions.

With respect to the faculty and the curriculum, trustees worry most—and occasionally too much—about institutional flexibility. But despite all the expressed concerns, very few colleges attempt to measure or gauge flexibility, except to monitor one index, namely, the tenure ratio. Tenure ratios may communicate something about flexibility *if* the bases for the calculation are sound. In one actual case, the tenure ratio could be made to vary from 29.5 percent to 73.8 percent, depending on who was included or excluded from the base. For example, should research assistants, teaching assistants, staff, and librarians be counted or only full-time, tenure-track faculty? (Simpson, 1975)

There are some other useful measures of flexibility that might be applied. West (1974) recommends that colleges calculate the percentage of instructional salary dollars committed to tenured and untenured faculty respectively. This would give some sense of the financial flexibility necessary to achieve institutional or curricular flexibility. In a financial shorthand, tenured faculty under multiyear contracts might be viewed as relatively liquid short-term notes, and vacancies might be viewed as cash on hand. How these assets are managed will largely determine the efficacy of faculty flow.

There are two other measures to consider: faculty turnover and course turnover. For most institutions, infusion of new blood will result from turnover, not from growth. A properly footnoted computation to determine what proportion of the faculty is new to the campus each year should include adjuncts and visitors as well as new full-timers. What is the average employment period for all faculty? For tenured faculty? For untenured faculty? How do these

figures compare with those of five years ago? How do they compare with those of similarly situated colleges? As enrollments
stabilize, more program changes and innovations may have to be
generated from within. In that light, one might ask how often
courses are substantially revised, replaced, or simply abandoned.
Some guidelines could perhaps be developed to standardize the
definition of a new or revised course.

Armed with all the data on institutional flexibility, trustees
must still be cautious. There are no magic formulas for achieving
and maintaining flexibility. In 1978, at the Harvard Law School,
fifty-three of fifty-nine ladder-rank faculty held tenure. Would the
school, generally acknowledged to be among the nation's foremost
schools of law, somehow be better if the tenure ratio were only 50
percent? Would a low tenure ratio be a mark of success if all the
"wrong" faculty were denied long-term commitments? Would
there be cause for celebration if a school's tenure density dropped
because the best faculty departed for other institutions with better
conditions and brighter futures?

To summarize, the effective management of human resources requires that (1) a personnel data base be maintained; that
(2) appropriate data be regularly presented to the board; and that
(3) the board analyze the data retrospectively and prospectively,
mindful of both local and national conditions. With this information at hand, a board will be better prepared to contemplate policy
changes.

Contemplating Changes in Personnel Policy

Before considering changes in personnel policy, the board
should ask at least two questions: Does the problem derive from an
inadequate policy or from the ineffective administration of a sound
policy? And does the weakness lie with the policy or with the persons charged to administer the policy? Obviously, the board should
not change policies when it should change people or, conversely,
change people when it should change policy. Sometimes both may
need to be changed.

A simple factual illustration may suffice. In an eastern state,
College A and College B, both public four-year colleges, opened in
1971. Both schools are subject to the same state statutes on tenure
and are governed by the same collective bargaining agreement. As

of September 1979, the faculty of college A was 38 percent tenured and that of College B 81 percent tenured. There may be some very defensible reasons for College B's higher tenure ratio. But if the board of trustees at College B suddenly became disturbed by the school's tenure density, should tenure policy be the focal point of criticism? Obviously, administrative practice and not tenure policy accounts for the difference. The same principle applies more broadly. Not every college is tenured-in—many have tenure ratios of less than 60 percent. But their tenure policies are not necessarily different from those with high tenure rates.

With affirmative action, however, there seem to be genuine problems with policy. Some college and university policies are simply weak, others are unclear. At the federal level, policies on jurisdiction, enforcement, and sanctions confuse and confound even the most well-intentioned persons. Policy revision could go far to improve the effectiveness of affirmative action programs.

If a policy change seems well advised, the president and the board, as noted above, need as much hard data as possible to supplement the ever-present opinions, impressions, and intuitions. Moreover, the board should identify the "problem" that a change is meant to resolve and then devise some means to monitor and evaluate the effectiveness of the change once it has been adopted. Rather regularly, colleges and universities adopt "solutions" unrelated to their "problems" (Cohen and March, 1974). The problem may be a faculty that produces little in the way of research. A more generous sabbatical policy emerges as the solution. But will sabbaticals make heretofore unproductive scholars any more scholarly? At least one study (Boswell, 1970) suggests not.

There are many other erroneous hand-me-down shibboleths that prevail in higher education and guide policy decisions. Some examples of widely accepted propositions that have been disproved by research are:

- Faculty research productivity declines after receipt of tenure (Blackburn, 1972).
- Active faculty researchers teach far less than inactive researchers (Fulton and Trow, 1974).
- Class size significantly influences faculty work time (Yuker, 1976).

Despite research to the contrary, such folklore persists; myths are not easy to dispel. But this is all the more reason to make sure that policy changes are based on more than conventional wisdom.

Where policy changes will affect the faculty, the faculty should be consulted for two reasons. First, consultation may yield some valuable ideas. Second, consultation improves the likelihood that the change will be effectively implemented, especially in those instances, such as new criteria and standards for tenure, where the faculty will actually be called upon to apply the new policy.

When the moment arrives to write the final version of a new policy, the college should always select language appropriate to the institution. Policies should not be borrowed wholesale from other schools. So many of the problems that beset Bloomfield College in New Jersey emanated from a decision (made by many other colleges as well) to adopt AAUP language on retrenchment word for word. In litigation, the court repeatedly made reference to policies that the college had voluntarily adopted but that prohibited the very actions the college wished to take. Whatever one's views of Bloomfield's proposed policy solutions, the college had clearly constrained itself by incorporating into its handbook the language of another organization with a different set of objectives and concerns.

While policies are enormously important, deeds, in the last analysis, speak louder than words, and personnel actions speak louder than personnel policies. To whom a board awards tenure communicates far more about institutional standards than does tenure policy. To whom a board awards a promotion, a merit increment, or a sabbatical communicates far more about institutional values than do policy pronouncements. In that sense, personnel decisions are clear signals widely broadcast. The board's actions should closely fit the intended message.

Understanding Academic Tenure

Among personnel policies and actions none looms larger than academic tenure. As noted earlier, tenure decisions represent substantial economic and contractual commitments to individuals and to programs. In effect, to tenure a classicist is to tenure classics.

Despite tenure's central importance, however, many academicians and trustees alike are confused about the provisions and purposes of tenure policy. This confusion, in turn, adds to the larger controversy over the value and wisdom of a tenure system.

Some definitions may help to minimize the confusion. Traditionally, the academic community has regarded the 1940 AAUP Statement on Academic Freedom and Tenure as the definitive exposition. In part, that statement declares: "Tenure is a means to certain ends—specifically, (1) freedom of teaching and research and of extramural activities and (2) a sufficient degree of economic security to make the profession attractive to men and women of ability. Freedom and economic security—hence, tenure—are indispensable to the success of an institution in fulfilling its obligations to its students and to society" (American Association of University Professors, 1977, p.2).

As much a characterization as a definition, the AAUP statement might be compared to a more operational definition offered by the Commission on Academic Tenure—the so-called Keast Commission—cosponsored by the AAUP and the Association of American Colleges (1973). The commission defined tenure as "an arrangement under which faculty appointments in an institution of higher education are continued until retirement for age or physical disability, subject to dismissal for adequate cause or unavoidable termination on account of financial exigency or change of institutional program" (p. 256).

Taken together, these statements provide a useful, albeit general, definition of academic tenure. However, the reader must remember that general definitions by associations and commissions do not supplant or supersede the specific policy provisions adopted by a board of trustees, enacted by a legislature, or negotiated by a faculty union. Academic tenure will be neither more nor less than what official institutional policy stipulates; in the absence of official policy, common past practices at the school are likely to be the controlling factors. With that caveat in mind, we can speak broadly of the primary purposes of academic tenure.

As the 1940 AAUP statement suggests, tenure aims to safeguard academic freedom and ensure a measure of economic security. Like academic tenure, the term *academic freedom* enjoys no common definition. To critics the term suggests a license to speak irresponsibly on any issue. To defenders, academic freedom represents a hallowed doctrine and a prerequisite to the practice of the profession. In fact, academic freedom has three essential components:

1. The freedom to conduct and publish research.
2. The freedom to teach and discuss issues pertinent to the course or subjects without introducing into the classroom irrelevant matters.
3. The freedom to speak or write as a citizen without expressly speaking or writing on behalf of the institution unless authorized to do so.

In short, academic freedom is meant to provide an atmosphere conducive to the open and unfettered pursuit and exchange of knowledge. Tenure safeguards academic freedom, it is argued, because the award of tenure formally and explicitly confers the three privileges mentioned above. Tenured personnel are thereby assured that their research and teaching can be guided by their best professional judgments, not by outside pressures or forces or by concerns for continued employment.

Unlike academic freedom, economic security is a well-established and easily understood concept. By carefully specifying the grounds and procedures whereby tenured personnel may be dismissed, tenure protects against arbitrary and capricious personnel actions, thus providing significant job security. Indeed, some people argue that this greater measure of employment security offsets, at least in part, the higher salaries purportedly available in other sections of the economy.

As originally conceived, tenure was meant to benefit the institution as well as the individual, and many proponents of tenure argue that then benefits are indeed mutual. Traditionally, it has been held that tenure creates an environment that encourages faculty to undertake long-term and, perhaps, high-risk projects. Second, the presence of a tenured faculty helps develop a coterie of professionals loyal to the college yet sufficiently secure to act as constructive critics. Finally, and perhaps most importantly, the very nature of a tenure decision presumably forces the institution to assess each candidate carefully and thus to exercise quality control. Needless to say, intent and actuality are not one and the same, whether it is a question of the extent to which tenure protects faculty or the degree to which it benefits the institution. It is important, nevertheless, to understand the espoused goals and objectives of tenure policies. Only then can one examine tenure practices fruitfully.

Within the history of American higher education, formalized academic tenure is a product of this century. Although various forerunners such as indefinite and "undated" terms of appointment were available to some faculty in the 1800s, academic tenure as a systematic policy was not well established until the early twentieth century when univerisites such as Harvard and Johns Hopkins adopted the policy. It was not generally accepted as a fundamental tenet of the profession until the 1915 Declaration of Principles by the then newly formed AAUP.

Today, however, academic tenure operates on almost all college campuses. About 85 percent of all colleges and universities have a tenure system, and these institutions employ about 95 percent of all full-time faculty. All universities, nearly all four-year colleges, and some two thirds of all two-year colleges have a tenure system.

While nearly all institutions have tenure systems, obviously not all faculty have tenure. Nationwide, about 63.5 percent of all full-time faculty hold tenure. A comprehensive survey published in 1979 by the National Center for Education Statistics revealed the tenured population to be as follows (note that M = male, F = female):

All Institutions			*Public Institutions*			*Private Institutions*		
M and F	*M*	*F*	*M and F*	*M*	*F*	*M and F*	*M*	*F*
63.5%	68.5%	48.7%	66.4%	71.1%	52.5%	56.2%	62.0%	38.1%

An earlier study by the American Council on Education (Furniss, 1973) examined tenure ratios and the rate of tenure rewards. In 1974, almost six of every ten colleges had faculties that were 50 percent or more tenured. While the percentage of faculty with tenure has increased, the percentage of eligible faculty actually awarded tenure has declined. In 1972, 72 percent of those colleges with tenure systems awarded tenure to at least six of every ten eligible faculty members. By 1974, the percentage of colleges awarding tenure at that rate dropped to 65 percent. Regrettably, there has not been a more recent comprehensive survey. But the fragmentary data available would suggest that the trends toward more densely tenured faculty and less frequent award of tenure have both continued. Proportionally, fewer faculty gain tenure and fewer faculty leave the tenured ranks, the latter phenomenon being in large part a reflection of an overcrowded marketplace.

In a word, a good many faculty hold tenure—a reasonable estimate might be about 251,000 of the some 457,000 full-time faculty employed by the approximately 3,000 American colleges and universities. Although those figures represent a large number of faculty members from many different colleges and although criteria and procedures for the award of tenure differ from college to college (and often from school to school within a university), there are enough commonalities to construct a generalized description of the bases and processes that govern tenure decisions.

How do tenure decisions arise? Normally, a faculty member automatically stands for tenure at a fixed time, generally one year prior to the expiration of the probationary period. Denial of tenure almost always means that the unsuccessful candidate *must* leave the institution after a terminal year's contract. Such provisions are referred to as the "up or out" rule. In other cases, a candidate may be considered a year or two earlier through self-nomination. Less frequently, an exceptionally strong candidate outside the university may be extended an offer of tenure concomitant with appointment to the faculty.

Tenure decisions typically reflect assessments of performance and judgments about potential. Minimum eligibility requirements usually include:

Service in a probationary period. Normally three to seven years—although exceptions exist at both ends of this range—the probationary period offers the faculty member an opportunity to develop and refine the skills necessary for the position, and it offers the institution a chance to observe and evaluate the faculty member's work. Service elsewhere may be counted toward fulfillment of the probationary period, although credit for prior service usually may not exceed half the total probationary period. Satisfactory completion of the probationary period represents one measure of professional experience.

Attainment of appropriate academic credentials. This would usually mean attaining the highest degree, such as a Ph.D. or D.B.A., normally awarded in one's field or discipline. In the current marketplace, many institutions hire only faculty who already possess a terminal degree; appointment to tenure without the terminal degree has become more and more the exception.

Appointment to an appropriate academic rank. Most commonly, faculty must hold or be qualified to hold the rank of assistant or associate professor. Some universities tie tenure to appointment to the professorial rank; in a few instances, instructors are eligible for tenure. It is commonplace, but by no means required, to link the tenure decision to promotion in rank.

Successful past performance. This is normally assessed in three broad areas: teaching, scholarship (or research), and community service. Of course, depending upon the institution or even the department, these criteria are weighted differently. While some institutions require excellence in all three areas, more often institutions require excellence in one or two with solid performance in the other(s).

Growth potential. An individual's capacity and ability to continue to develop as a teacher and scholar are also considered. Most often, these forecasts are based upon past performance and the value attached by students and colleagues to work done thus far by the faculty member.

Although tenure decisions are ultimately, like most personnel decisions, subjective in nature, a body of evidence is usually assembled to inform the deliberations. A typical portfolio or personnel folder might include letters of recommendation, some solicited, other not; letters from outside references (usually in the same or an allied field) that address the quality of the candidate's scholarship; the candidate's publications and scholarly reviews of these works; student evaluations of teaching; course syllabi; and, with increasing frequency, a self-evaluation that includes the candidate's goals and objectives for the future. Not all institutions collect all these materials; obviously, each institution will assess the evidence differently.

As a matter of procedure, the review process typically entails a sequence of deliberations and recommendations, often beginning at the departmental or program level. In many universities and some liberal arts colleges, the recommendations of the department and department chairman carry great weight. Beyond the department, the process moves to the dean, a school- or college-wide committee, the academic vice-president, and the president. At some major research universities, ad hoc committees of eminent scholars from outside the university evaluate the candidate and report directly to the president. In nearly all cases, the president eventually places a recommendation for action before the board of trustees.

Establishing Tenure Policy

With respect to academic tenure, a governing board may be engaged at two levels: matters of tenure policy and matters of tenure decisions. Before embarking upon a consideration of tenure policies, a board should first recognize that these policies must be set within the larger context of the institution. More concretely, the board must achieve a working knowledge of the following six items and how they interrelate: (1) existing bylaws, rules, regulations, and relevant statutes; (2) contracts and negotiated agreements, especially those that directly affect staffing patterns; (3) the institution's affirmative action plan; (4) the institution's budget; (5) the institution's priorities, mission statement, or long-range plan; and (6) a profile of the institution's faculty as described earlier.

Tenure policies and practices are unusually sensitive issues for faculty. Therefore, the need to be clear on policy objectives and to consult widely with faculty is acute. Moreover, certain aspects of tenure policy involve contractual obligations between the institution as employer and the professor as employee. Changes in policy may require that some faculty be "grandfathered" (that is, excluded). For example, an institution may elect to no longer award tenure, and thereby abolish it, but the institution cannot rescind the tenure of those faculty who already have it. Legal counsel should be close at hand whenever a board considers tenure policy.

What tenure-related policies should a governing board establish? There are basically two aspects to tenure policy: the *criteria* upon which tenure decisions are based and the *process* employed to reach these decisions. Since trustees bear ultimate as well as legal responsibility for the adequacy and equity of the process, the board should determine that the procedures are fair, reasonable, manageable, comprehensive, and structurally appropriate to the institution. On many campuses, these procedures are established with approval of the board. For some public campuses, they may be settled at the state level. At still other institutions, they may be part of a collectively bargained agreement. Whatever the mechanism or location for these decisions on procedure, a board should attempt to exercise maximum influence and leverage.

The same proposition applies to the establishment of the criteria upon which tenure decisions are based. With appropriate and substantial participation by the college community, a board—unless restricted by other agreements or agencies—ought to set policies governing the probationary period, credential or degree requirements, and rank requirements for tenure. On the advice and recommendation of the faculty and academic staff, the board should also set general guidelines on the relative importance of teaching, scholarship, and service. Criteria affecting judgments of past performance and forecasts of future contributions are best determined by faculty peers and academic administrators, although the board would be well advised to insist that such criteria be clearly stated and clearly supportive of the institution's mission.

Making Tenure Decisions

Individual tenure decisions, at one level, require considerable familiarity with an individual's qualifications. The decision requires a sophisticated assessment of the candidate's professional expertise—an assessment best rendered by other experts. Yet, at another level, a tenure decision requires familiarity with institutional needs and priorities. In general, trustees are more likely to be acquainted with the institution's needs than with the individual's strengths. A governing board should consider the "fit" between individual merit, as judged by academic professionals, and institutional needs, as judged by the board in consultation with the academic administration. Such a role implies that, compared to the faculty and to a lesser extent to the administration, the board will ask a somewhat different set of questions and will require a somewhat different set of materials to make an informed decision.

With a perspective focused on institutional needs, a board may ask questions such as:

1. Do we have the financial resources to support these tenured appointments?
2. Are these permanent appointments consistent with the school's long-term objectives, curricular needs, and affirmative action plans?
3. Will these decisions unwisely constrain institutional flexibility or unduly bind a particular department?
4. Do enrollment and placement patterns warrant a permanent appointment?
5. Will these decisions foreclose even more attractive appointments to tenure within the foreseeable future?
6. If tenure were denied, where would the dollars "saved" be allocated—to the same position, another program, a different department?

These questions start to suggest the kind of data that a board requires to participate effectively in tenure decisions and, for that matter, to review tenure policies. All too often, administrators furnish to boards the very same information provided to faculty and deans even though trustees have (or should have) a different set of concerns. If trustees receive only information about the individual merit of a candidate, how can the board help but dwell on that aspect of the decision? If the board receives information on enrollments, placements, finances, faculty flow, tenure levels, and affirmative action, however, a very different discussion might ensue.

The division between individual merit and institutional need can be too sharply drawn. Surely, faculty deliberations on merit should be made within the context of institutional needs and, conversely, trustees should have an acquaintance with the qualification of tenure candidates. In general, however, the board should concentrate on the extent to which individuals with strong credentials for tenure meet institutional needs.

As a rule, if the board feels assured that the prescribed process has been followed and the appropriate criteria applied, it should rarely have cause to review tenure recommendations for individual merit. (A fair question might be whether a president or a board *can* determine the academic quality of highly specialized experts working in so many diverse fields.) The board may receive these assurances formally or informally from the president or from its normal review of faculty portfolios. On occasion, the board or one of its committees may elect to review a tenure recommendation more meticulously than usual solely to ensure that the prescribed process has been followed, the proper documentation collected, and the appropriate criteria applied. Carefully limited to questions of procedure and discreetly conducted, such a spot check would probably not be seen either as an intrusion on faculty prerogative or as lack of support for the president.

So far, we have identified two reasons why a board should review recommendations for tenure: (1) to determine the "fit" between the individual and the institution and (2) to ensure procedural regularity. Other circumstances that *may* warrant an indepth review by the board are widely disparate evaluations of the same candidate or a conspicuously disproportionate number of either positive or negative recommendations.

While a board may be tempted to investigate the merits of recommendations from the president that generate an uproar on campus, care should be exercised to review only in cases where the board has considerable reason to believe that established policy has been violated. In other words, unless state policy or a labor contract requires otherwise, a board should not serve as a court of last resort for faculty members considered talented by some but found wanting by others when established policies and procedures have been equitably applied. The risks associated with a review on merit by the board are substantial. Very likely the board's action will be perceived by faculty as an intrusion on their autonomy. Morale may sink as tension heightens. The president, too, may regard the review as an inappropriate intrusion on his or her authority or as a vote of no confidence. Thus, such reviews should be conducted only rarely and then with great care.

In certain cases, institutional bylaws, state policy, or a labor contract may *require* that upon petition the board review a tenure decision or hear a grievance. Boards should have guidelines that anticipate and address these circumstances—guidelines that include:

1. Assertion of the board's authority to render a final decision.
2. Establishment of a review procedure that assures due process and respects confidentiality.
3. Assignment of the responsibility for review to an appropriate board unit, such as the education or faculty affairs committee.
4. Prescription of the range of sanctions and remedies that can be applied.
5. Description of the general circumstances, such as a charge of unlawful discrimination, under which the board might consider questions of individual merit. (In such cases, the board would be wise to consult outside experts.)

More generally, boards should, prior to undertaking a review, consider the advisability of legal counsel to assist them in such matters as due process, need for transcripts, sources and uses of evidence, and personal liability.

Revoking Tenure

As difficult and unpleasant as a decision to deny tenure may be, an attempt to revoke tenure will prove doubly so. Of course, tenure policies are quite deliberately designed to guard against capricious and arbitrary dismissals. Thus, dismissal proceedings are typically cumbersome and weighted to favor the tenured faculty member. In general, tenured faculty can be dismissed for three reasons: (1) adequate cause, (2) financial exigency, and (3) program discontinuation. In all three cases, the burden of proof rests with the institution, and due process must be provided.

Dismissal for *adequate cause* traditionally encompasses professional incompetence, acts of moral turpitude, neglect of duty, insubordination, and dishonesty in teaching or research. Dismissals for cause are rare not so much because colleges and universities have no incompetent faculty but rather because few administrations systematically evaluate faculty and document inadequacy. After twenty years of "benign neglect," a university cannot suddenly decide to remove a tenured faculty member. How long has the professor been incompetent? What efforts at remediation were undertaken? What evidence supports the decision to dismiss? An examination of the personnel folder reveals evaluative data from the tenure decision twenty years earlier and copies of notices about changes in the university's health coverage and life insurance. Suddenly the case seems weak, and the impulse to initiate dismissal proceedings vanishes. Usually, the problem is not with the policy per se—most schools have reasonable statements about adequate cause—but with policy execution. The poor records that most schools maintain reflect a laissez-faire approach to supervision and evaluation.

Until the 1970s and the onset of a no-growth era, policy statements about dismissal due to *financial exigency* were little more than boiler plate buried deep within the faculty handbook. Few academicians—faculty or staff—ever anticipated that there would be occasion or need to act on the basis of that policy. More and more, however, colleges and universities have been compelled by financial stringencies to exhume and apply the policy. As a rule, tenure policy permits the dismissal of permanent faculty when fiscal conditions are so severe that institutional survival requires the release of these persons. In most but not all instances, the dismissal of untenured faculty within a program or department precedes the release of tenured personnel.

There have been numerous court cases on the issue of retrenchment generally and the dismissal of tenured faculty more particularly. On the whole, these cases suggest that the administration and board of trustees enjoy considerable authority to determine whether or not a true exigency exists and considerable latitude to determine the most prudent means of reducing expenses. Decisions to dismiss tenured faculty due to financial exigency were upheld, for example, in *Johnson* v. *Board of Regents of the University of Wisconsin System* (1974), *Lumpert* v. *University of Dubuque* (1977), and *Levitt* v. *Board of Trustees of Nebraska State Colleges* (1974). In the absence of violations of contractual provisions in bylaws or a negotiated agreement or of evidence of malintent (see *AAUP* v. *Bloomfield College,* 1974), the courts have afforded universities broad discretion, as these excerpts from the judges' opinions suggest:

> I can see good reason to afford all tenured teachers an opportunity to be heard at this penultimate stage before the decisions are taken and perhaps an opportunity to participate in making the decision. But I am not persuaded that the Fourteenth Amendment requires that a tenured teacher be afforded the opportunity to express the opinion that the college of letters and science or the history department should bear a greater or lesser share in the fiscal sacrifice [*Johnson* v. *Board of Regents* . . . , 1974, p. 238].
>
> Perhaps the next question is whether the federal constitution requires that the selection be made on one specific basis or another: in inverse order of seniority within a department, for example; or in order of seniority; or in terms of record of performance; or in inverse order of seniority, but with exceptions for the necessity to retain teachers in the department with specific skills or funds of knowledge. I believe that the federal constitution is silent on these questions and that the identity of the decision maker and the choice of a basis for selection lie within the discretion of state government [*Johnson* v. *Board of Regents* . . . , 1974, p. 238].
>
> The question whether a financial exigency existed is primarily a matter of subjective judgment to be exercised by the university officials charged with the responsibility of operating the university. We do not believe it is a question of fact to be determined by a jury. Moreover, we do not believe it is a matter for the substitution of the court's judgment or the juror's judgment for that of an administrative body [*Lumpert* v. *University of Dubuque,* 1977, p. 10].

Tenured faculty may also be dismissed when an institution elects to discontinue or curtail a particular program or department. Very often, dismissals due to *program discontinuation* relate closely to financial considerations. (See *Browzin* v. *Catholic University of America*, 1975, and *Scheur* v. *Creighton University*, 1977.) However, the decision may be motivated solely by redefinition of mission or qualitative considerations.

From all the court cases on retrenchment and layoff one extraordinarily important principle emerges, a principle that simply cannot be overemphasized: "Each case is subject to its own contractual provisions" (*Lumpert* v. *University of Dubuque*, 1977, p. 10). There is no universal list of rights or wrongs or do's and don'ts. What a college can or cannot do depends almost exclusively on what the controlling institutional policy or document allows. Likewise, an institution's obligations to dismissed faculty depend largely upon the obligations the institution assumes as a matter of policy and practice. In a period of stability or decline, it is, therefore, imperative that colleges fashion policies that are fair to the employees without unduly constraining the institution and that are, above all else, clearly stated.

These policies may or may not take the form of the Recommended Institutional Regulations proferred by the AAUP. From an institutional standpoint, the AAUP's policies on retrenchment have significant weaknesses. In an incisive summary of these drawbacks, Furniss (1976) notes that AAUP policy (1) artificially and imprudently separates matters of financial exigency and program discontinuation; (2) affords faculty too many separate and individual hearings on institution-wide issues that could be more expeditiously heard and decided in one hearing; and (3) unwisely requires "extraordinary circumstances" to justify new appointments concomitant with layoffs. More generally, Furniss advises institutions to employ terms other than financial exigency to describe the various gradations of fiscal difficulty or strain that may require cutbacks of varying magnitude. In that same vein, an institution might consider gradations of personnel actions. Terminations are not the only alternative. One could consider, for example, across-the-board pay cuts, work sharing, temporary layoffs, hiring freezes, part-time assignments, and early retirement. In another equally excellent essay, Furniss (1978) questions and challenges the legal and professional status of *all* AAUP policies. Furniss also urges institutions not to mindlessly adopt AAUP policy word for word or to assume that AAUP policy recommendations must control institutional thinking.

Whatever the retrenchment policies of an institution, they ought to be adopted in advance of the need to use them. The moment of crisis is not a particularly opportune time to formulate policy, least of all retrenchment policy. Moreover, as a matter of sound practice, academic personnel and programs should be evaluated periodically. Such evaluations will help identify problems early, establish a history and habit of review, and provide valuable data to inform retrenchment decisions should cutbacks some day be deemed necessary.

Considering Modifications and Alternatives

Although a well-established concept and a widespread practice, academic tenure has always been subject to criticism, most especially in the last decade or so. Briefly stated, these criticisms are:

Tenure reduces accountability. Critics argue that tenure is a one-sided contract binding the institution to the teacher, but not the teacher to the institution. With a "lifetime contract," a tenured faculty member is effectively removed from accountability and the performance incentive implicit in periodically having to seek contract renewal.

Tenure constrains flexibility. Each time an institution confers tenure, it makes a long-term financial and program commitment. Since these commitments are not easily withdrawn, the institution becomes that much more rigid and less capable of making commitments to other individuals and programs.

Tenure impedes affirmative action. Tenure removes positions from the job market for extended periods of time. The larger the percentage of positions filled with tenured personnel, the fewer the vacancies. Consequently, the institution must await retrenchment, death, or dismissal for cause before it can hire affirmatively in a given position.

Tenure establishes a class system. Tenure policies largely confine academic freedom and academic privileges to the tenured faculty. If academic freedom is essential to the profession and tenure is essential to academic freedom, how can untenured faculty successfully practice the profession?

Tenure duplicates other protections. Critics of tenure maintain that state and federal law and numerous court decisions afford faculty all the freedom needed to teach, conduct research, and speak out. Furthermore, in the opinion of some observers, collective bargaining agreements render tenure superfluous since these contracts provide due process, employment security, and academic freedom.

As the demographic forecasts and economic realities for higher education have worsened, criticisms of tenure have intensified. To many, a heavily tenured faculty appears to be an almost insurmountable obstacle to change. Thus, colleges tenured-in are searching for a way out and colleges not yet tenured to capacity are looking for strategies and policies that will enable them to stay that way. From these efforts, some alternatives have emerged that either introduce modifications into a tenure system or replace tenure with a contract system.

The simplest, although not always most desirable, modification is a tenure quota, that is, the establishment of a ceiling on the percentage of faculty who may hold tenure at any given time. The only options are to waive the quota or wave farewell. About 12 percent of all colleges and universities—Vassar, Colgate, and the New Jersey State Colleges, to name a few—have tenure guidelines or quotas, with maximums that range from 50 to 80 percent.

Tenure quotas or guidelines do ensure some flexibility and the introduction of new blood. They also force hard choices, since the fixed number of tenure slots available means that only so many among those eligible can be accommodated. However, because only untenured faculty are adversely affected in a direct manner by tenure quotas, the burden of resolving an institutional problem falls unevenly on one constituency. Moreover, junior faculty, faced with bleak prospects for tenure, start to think more of enhancing their mobility than of serving the campus community. Finally, a tenure quota may shift the discussion to numbers, and quantitative considerations may overtake qualitative ones in a way that, ironically, places a self-imposed limitation on managerial discretion.

More and more institutions have elected to *extend the probationary period*, normally three to seven years, that faculty must serve to qualify for tenure. Extended probation affords a longer time to observe and evaluate faculty; and since more faculty will leave, for whatever reasons, over a longer time period, the lengthened probationary period increases the mathematical probability that a cohort member will ultimately achieve tenure. Of course, the longer an untenured faculty member remains at an institution, the more likely that his or her anxiety will increase and the more difficult the decision to terminate the faculty member will become. While the AAUP sets seven years as a standard, institutions such as the Harvard Business School, the University of Georgia, and the University of Rochester have policies that permit a probationary period to extend to eleven years; at the University of Tulsa a thirteen-year period is possible. None of these schools has been censured by the AAUP for lengthening its probationary period.

A modification related to extended probationary periods is a waiver of the "up or out" rule. Colleges such as Union (in New York), Albion, and Hartwick no longer require faculty to either earn tenure or leave the institution at the conclusion of the probationary period. Instead, faculty may be retained without tenure on renewable multiyear appointments. These so-called tenurable faculty may be considered for tenure at some future date should a tenure slot open. While relaxation of the "up or out" rule may allow a college to retain talented faculty without tenure, the policy invites de facto tenure at one extreme and the gradual erosion of tenure at the other extreme. To allay faculty fears about an end to tenure, Union established a *minimum* tenure quota of 33 percent. If less than one third of the faculty holds tenure, "tenurable" faculty would automatically be granted permanent status until the tenure ratio reached at least 33 percent.

While retaining the essence of traditional tenure policy, the modifications discussed thus far do alter the notion of tenure as originally conceived. The periodic evaluation of tenured faculty, however, is not inconsistent with conventional policy. The AAUP does not object to periodic evaluation so long as the first negative evaluation does not result in immediate termination. The AAUP recommends that adequate time for remediation be provided and that the cases on dismissal for cause be heard by a faculty board. The system adopted by St. Lawrence University in 1976 mandates a performance review at least every four years. If there appears to be "reason for concern," the dean discusses the problem with the faculty member, negotiates a timetable for improvement, and provides a written summation of the discussions. If no improvements result within the prescribed time frame, the dean may request that the university's Committee on Professional Standards initiate a peer review to guide further action or, alternatively, the dean may initiate termination proceedings. At Coe College the periodic evaluations are based on individual ten-year plans (reevaluated every five years) developed by each faculty member. An initial ten-year plan must accompany any request or recommendation for tenure.

Lastly, as a means to accelerate faculty flow and break the logjam, many institutions have turned to early retirement plans. For the most part, these were developed prior to passage of the new retirement legislation that raised the earliest mandatory retirement to age seventy. In that context, "early" retirement may occur later, perhaps now at sixty-six or sixty-eight. Should, as some policy analysts predict, mandatory retirement as a legal notion be altogether abandoned, then the question of early retirement programs may be largely moot. Moreover, recent studies have suggested that, with the exception of community college faculty, senior professors are not particularly eager to leave the active work force (Patton, 1979). An imaginative alternative might involve a gradual transition from full-time to part-time status and then to full retirement. Dartmouth College offers such an option.

For colleges that wish to abandon rather than modify conventional tenure policies, term contracts represent the only alternative. Although contract systems operate on relatively few campuses within only certain sectors of higher education, most notably two-year colleges, policies vary considerably among these schools. Each system has a different name and at least one different wrinkle. There are, for example, growth or learning contracts (Hampshire College and Evergreen State College), rolling contracts (Franklin Pierce College), and variable length contracts (Austin, Texas, Community College and the Virginia Community College System). Despite the different catchwords, all these systems share a common element: an appointment for a specific and limited time period with no assurance (or proscription) of continued employment beyond the expiration date of the contract.

In most cases, initial contracts are for a relatively brief

period, that is, one to three years. As a contract term draws to an end, the college evaluates the candidate's performance to date, and the candidate presents a prospectus or statement of goals for the next contract period, which might be three to five years, certainly no more than seven years. Under the rolling contract system, the faculty member's contract extends or rolls to three years at the end of each year as long as favorable evaluations continue. Should there be a negative evaluation, the faculty member has a year to remedy deficiencies. If weaknesses are overcome, the contract again rolls for three years; if weaknesses persist, the third year of the contract becomes the terminal year.

In theory, contracts offer opportunities to exercise discretion, cut losses, minimize long-term commitments, maximize institutional flexibility, and make personnel changes. Equally clearly, not many institutions exercise these opportunities. Almost all institutions renew nearly all their contracts. For the academic year 1973–74, 93 percent of the schools with contract systems renewed at least 9 of every 10 contracts. (By contrast, in that same year only one of every two colleges with a tenure system awarded tenure to at least 8 of every 10 candidates.) At Hampshire College 125 of 140 contract reappointment decisions between 1970 and 78 have been favorable; at Evergreen State College only 8 of 123 decisions have resulted in terminations.

The reasons for the high rate of renewal are many. On some campuses open files reduce the likelihood of strong criticism and heighten fears of retribution for negative comments. In other instances, the inclination to say yes to one more contract cannot be resisted and, eventually, "one more contract" becomes "years of loyal service." Unlike tenure decisions, contract renewals do not present long-term or sizable risks and thus are readily granted. The very nature of a renewal decision invites renewal, especially in today's environment when nonreappointment may mean unemployment. Finally, contract reviews require close and frequent scrutiny. At a large institution with three-year term appointments there could be several hundred reviews annually. How much attention can be allocated to each prospectus and each evaluation? In sum, contracts *could* promote turnover and change; empirical data suggests that they do not.

Thus far we have considered some modifications *of* tenure and some alternatives *to* tenure. Another option would be some combination of modifications and alternatives. In some ways, the "peaceful coexistence" of tenure and nontenure systems hardly represents an innovation. Nearly all institutions have had part-time and adjunct faculty in nontenure positions working side by side with tenured and tenure-track faculty. What is new is the presence of full-time faculty in positions expressly designated as outside the tenure track. Coe College has authorized a maximum of 10 percent of the total faculty lines for so-called off-track positions. Chatham College employs "limited-term appointments," typically three-year contracts, where service does not apply toward fulfillment of the probationary period.

Limited-term, off-track positions do ensure some turnover. Although the same turnover could be achieved by nonreappointment of a probationary faculty member, the off-track policy does not raise false hopes of tenure and does not leave any ambiguity about long-term prospects. Not, that is, until the first person crosses over to the tenure track. Then, of course, everyone starts to anticipate similar treatment, and a key advantage of the policy disappears.

Perhaps the most imaginative combination of tenure and nontenure track systems has been installed at Webster College in Missouri. Mindful of the risk/reward principle common to the investment world, Webster offers somewhat greater rewards, namely, more frequent sabbaticals, to faculty willing to take a greater risk, namely eschewal of tenure. Faculty who waive the right to be considered for tenure are eligible after three one-year contracts for a one-semester leave at half pay. After five one-year contracts without sabbatical, faculty are eligible for a combined semester and summer leave at full pay. In this fashion, the faculty at risk presumably remain current, fresh, and marketable, and the institution minimizes long-term commitments. There may be some danger, however, that the most dollars will be spent on the faculty least likely to remain at the college over the long run.

To summarize, there are numerous modifications and alternatives to tenure (Chait and Ford, forthcoming). Each entails some trade-offs that need to be assessed within a specific institutional context. In all cases, changes in tenure policy should be approached carefully and investigated thoroughly. No other issue touches so many nerves and spawns so much controversy. Legal, administrative, and organizational questions are at the heart of the matter. Most institutions that contemplate changes in tenure practices fail to articulate clearly the problem at hand, the policy objectives to be achieved by a change, or the system that will be used to monitor the effectiveness of that change. With respect to all personnel policies, but especially academic tenure, answers must be given to these questions before changes are instituted.

Administering Tenure Policy Effectively

Among all the alternatives to tenure, the most obvious option is often easily overlooked: to administer current policy more effectively. As noted earlier, many colleges are able to make discriminating and discerning judgments and thereby hold tenure ratios to a reasonable level, perhaps between 50 and 66 percent. While one cannot generalize too broadly, colleges and universities that do exercise selectivity share certain common policies and practices.

First, these institutions approach faculty excellence as a matter to be judged, not measured. While some aspects of performance can be quantified, most cannot. Therefore, parties to the tenure process collect and review evidence appropriate to the decision at hand. Something of a judicial model applies with the first level of review by a "jury of peers": opinions may differ; dissents may be filed; decisions may be overturned. Ultimately, though, informed professionals reach a decision and render a judgment.

Second, the judgments are based on clear criteria that are spelled out to the faculty at the time of appointment. Again, clear criteria do not necessarily mean specifically measurable criteria. At some universities, faculty can elect, within institutionally established parameters, to concentrate more on one activity than another—more on research than on teaching, for example. In such a case, the evaluation might be weighted: 50 percent research,

40 percent teaching, 10 percent community service. While criteria must be consonant with an institution's mission and purpose, the criteria listed beiow may serve as illustrations:

Teaching	*Scholarship*
Thorough class preparation	Books, monographs, articles
Effective class presentation	Participation in professional
Cross-disciplinary work	organizations
Application of new knowledge	Critical recognition by peers
Thoroughness of student	of one's work
evaluation	Fellowships
Effective student advising	Receipt of grants
Thoughtful evaluation of	Development of innovative
student work	educational materials
Maintenance of appropriate	
academic standards	

Whatever the particular criteria applied, they do not change from the moment of appointment to the time of the tenure decision. Standards of performance may change—the institution may expect more from a full professor than from an assistant professor — but the bases of judgment remain relatively constant.

Third, the criteria are not limited to individual merit; institutional priorities are also considered. As suggested earlier, college presidents and boards of trustees must make tenure decisions against a backdrop of institutional needs. Thus, at St. Olaf College, where 64 percent of the faculty is tenured, each department prepares a long-range plan complete with curricular objectives and manpower needs under various assumptions about enrollment patterns.

Fourth, there are usually interim evaluations, more frequent at the earlier stages of a candidate's progress. Many colleges, either formally or informally, employ a threshold or breakpoint evaluation at or near the halfway point to tenure. These more comprehensive evaluations are clearly understood by all to be a significant hurdle en route to tenure. At this juncture, the department head and/or dean releases the weakest faculty and encourages and assists the strongest faculty to develop greater and additional strengths—a process colloquially referred to as "weeding out."

Fifth, nearly all institutions with well-managed tenure practices require multilevel reviews at the time of the tenure decision. Each level introduces a somewhat different perspective, a somewhat different set of concerns. To maintain institutional quality, a department (or initiating unit) must be made answerable to a larger constituency, for example, colleagues at the same institution but in allied fields, peers in the same field but at other institutions, or perhaps both. Divisional or college-wide committees can actually serve to protect strong departments against weak departments with lesser standards.

Finally, these institutions employ someone at or near the top able to say no on close votes if institutional priorities so dictate. To retain the confidence and goodwill of faculty party to the decision and to ensure the integrity of the process, however, the president or provost shares his or her thinking with the college-wide committee, the dean, and the department head.

These policies and practices are by no means surefire solutions to the tenure problem. Much depends on the institutional context, local tradition, and individual leadership. But any steps taken to administer tenure policies more effectively are likely to have a more immediate, positive, and pragmatic effect than are rhetorical assaults against the concept.

Practicing Affirmative Action

With the exception of academic tenure and faculty unionism, probably no personnel policy has generated more controversy or more position papers than affirmative action. Briefly, affirmative action seeks to ensure that colleges and universities (among other organizations) take positive actions to overcome the effects of previous exclusion of and discrimination against racial and ethnic minorities and women. It is more than mere nondiscrimination and less than so-called reverse discrimination.

The legal bases for affirmative action rest with various statutes and orders. The most significant documents at the federal level have already been noted: Titles VI and VII of the 1964 Civil

Rights Act, Executive Order 11246 as amended, Title IX of the Education Amendments Act of 1972, and the Equal Pay/Equal Work Act. All institutions, public and private, that employ at least fifty persons and receive $50,000 or more in federal contract funds must develop and implement a written affirmative action plan. Should institutions violate federal provisions, the government may cancel current contracts and prohibit application for or receipt of future federal funds, although such sanctions have not been applied to date. Many states have also enacted affirmative action legislation.

But what does affirmative action require? As a first step, institutions must maintain a basic data file that classifies employees by race, sex, age, ethnicity, salary, job category, and job title. After the basic data have been aggregated, the institution must analyze the data to determine whether minorities and women are "underutilized." Underutilization means that the institution "has fewer women or minorities in a particular job than would be reasonably expected by their availability" (Carnegie Council on Policy Studies in Higher Education, 1975, p. 119). Availability can be determined through an analysis of the appropriate labor market, perhaps locally for clerical and plant staff and nationally for academic and administrative staff.

Where underutilization exists, the institution must establish specific numerical goals and timetables. Goals are projected levels of achievement based upon current deficiencies, available remedies, ambitious recruitment, expected turnover, and the pool of potentially available qualified women and minorities. Goals are thus estimates and targets, not rigid quotas. Where clear and strong evidence of good faith exists, penalties and sanctions will not be applied even if the stated goals are not achieved.

To overcome underutilization requires that colleges move well beyond traditional patterns and sources of recruitment. It no longer suffices to rely on word-of-mouth referrals and narrow distribution of vacancy notices. The recruitment net must be cast as widely as possible, with special attention to avenues of communication most likely to reach women and minorities. The college must also establish an internal audit and reporting system that is sufficiently organized to provide a ready indication of successes and shortfalls. Policies, practices, goals, and timetables can then be reviewed, and, as necessary, revised.

As with academic tenure, there exists no model plan for affirmative action. Nevertheless, a report of the Carnegie Council on Policy Studies in Higher Education (1975) has recommended that the elements listed below be part of an affirmative action program:

1. A widely disseminated statement of nondiscrimination and a pledge of compliance acted upon by the board of trustees.
2. A clear statement that a senior-level campus official, such as the president or chancellor, bears overall responsibility for affirmative action.
3. Clear delegation by the president or chancellor of responsibility for affirmative action to a top-level line officer.
4. Provision of adequate staff to meet the responsibility. On larger campuses, a full-time affirmative action officer with support staff should be available, whereas on smaller campuses an administrator may assume these responsibilities on a part-time basis.
5. Provision for an affirmative action committee, representatively comprised, to assist with policy formulation, performance reviews, and corrective actions.
6. Wide dissemination of the plan and careful collection and analysis of necessary data.
7. Determination of appropriate and realistic goals and timetables.
8. Development of "wide-net" recruitment procedures, along with affirmative action reviews of each search process and each recommendation for appointment, promotion, or tenure and periodic analyses of salary equity.
9. Provision for adequate grievance procedures on matters related to affirmative action.

Happily, the Carnegie Council report translates each of these general recommendations into operational terms.

Since the council's report, however, a new controversy has arisen as a result of conflicts between the principle of affirmative action and the principle of seniority. The tension has been captured by the phrase "last hired, first fired." As relative newcomers to faculty (and administrative) positions, women and minorities face the prospect of being among the first persons released when cutbacks occur. These individuals suffer directly, and affirmative action programs suffer more generally.

For the most part, courts faced with this dilemma have upheld the validity of seniority systems that are neutral on the face, even where the layoffs disproportionately affected or even eliminated the entire minority work force (*Waters* v. *Wisconsin Steelworkers*, 1974; *Watkins* v. *U.S. Steelworkers of America, Local 2369*, 1975; *Jersey Central Power & Light Company* v. *Local Union 237 of International Brotherhood of Electrical Workers*, 1975). Southeastern Massachusetts University and the faculty union there have agreed upon an affirmative retrenchment plan that permits layoffs of faculty hired subsequent to the signing of the contract to be conducted in such a manner as to maintain the proportion of women and minorities on the faculty. But a similar plan proposed for school principals by the New York City Board of Education has been declared unlawful (*Chance* v. *Board of Examiners*, 1976).

In an "industry" on the decline, the conflict between affirmative action and seniority raises an especially troublesome question. Fundamentally, it is a problem of competing equities. However, the difficulty of the dilemma does not excuse any college or university from trying to fashion reasonable solutions. The issues and principles at stake are too important to ignore.

Summary

Personnel policies extend well beyond tenure and affirmative action. There are, for example, the questions of salaries, promotions, workloads, benefits, and leaves. Not all of these issues can be addressed in a single chapter, perhaps not even in a single volume. Yet, policy formulations on all these issues can be approached in a similar manner. Above all else, there should be a clear understanding of the purposes to be served and the goals to be attained by a particular policy or practice. Against that backdrop, policies should be formulated in concert with the faculty, not in isolation from them. The discussions should be informed by both quantitative data and qualitative judgments: both are essential. And, finally, the effectiveness of a policy—the degree to which it attains the stated objectives—should be monitored, and changes should be made as deemed necessary.

Sound personnel policies and procedures are neither a panacea nor a substitute for talented faculty and adequate resources. However, poor policies or ineffective policy execution can reduce motivation, provoke dissatisfaction, and waste human as well as fiscal resources. By contrast, well-reasoned and well-administered policies can help to create an overall environment that is conducive to bringing out the best in people. And is that not another way of stating the principal goal of education?

George W. Angell
Edward P. Kelley, Jr.

Responding
to Unionism

Social movements and critical events of the past two decades have had a profound impact on the decision-making and governance processes within institutions of higher learning. The student demonstrations of the 1960s and early 1970s, the increased activism of minorities and women, the cutbacks in federal and state funding, the determination of legislatures to control expenditures and expansion of higher education, and the explosive growth of faculty unionism and collective negotiations have all left their mark on postsecondary education. Faculty unionism in particular has introduced new variables into institutional management.

    An activity once considered wholly outside the province of higher education, academic unionism has emerged as a dynamic force on both public and private campuses throughout the country. Unlike the slow and turmoil-marred growth of the noneducational labor movement, unionism in higher education has, in general, gained widespread acceptance in a relatively short period of time without suffering the often disastrous effects of strikes, work stoppages, and property destruction that appeared to be endemic to collective bargaining in the industrial sector. During a twelve-year period the number of unionized institutions increased from fewer than 10 in 1966 to more than 361 institutions with 645 campuses employing over 120,000 faculty members by the close of the 1977–78 academic year (Kelley, 1978). A recent study (Ladd and Lipset, 1973) suggests that the growth of faculty unionism will continue. According to this survey, over two thirds of all faculty in public and private postsecondary institutions endorse the principle of collective bargaining. In addition, 72 percent of those questioned said they would vote for a faculty agent if a collective bargaining election were held at their respective campuses.

Although there are numerous theories to explain the phenomenal growth of faculty unionism, the most important factor appears to have been the enactment by twenty-four states of legislation enabling college and university faculties to organize for the purpose of bargaining. The growth of bargaining at private colleges was advanced by the 1970 decision of the National Labor Relations Board (NLRB) in the *Cornell University* case (1970), wherein the NLRB reversed a twenty-year practice of refusing to assert jurisdiction over institutions of higher education. Since the *Cornell* decision, faculties at more than seventy private institutions have been unionized. In some states, most notably Illinois and Ohio, where no enabling legislation exists, trustees have passed policies making it possible for faculties to organize and bargain. These trustee policies differ widely; some resemble legislation and speak to almost every critical issue, others are skeletal. This new trustee response to faculty demands will be discussed later in this chapter.

Since enabling legislation is evidently a paramount factor in the growth of faculty unionism and since such legislation often changes the role and responsibility of trustees, trustees themselves must become involved in the legislative process whenever such a bill is being considered. One example of the negative effects of such legislation on trustees may be seen in New York State. In 1967 the legislature passed the Taylor Law without consulting educators or trustees, who were totally ignorant of its import for public higher education. This law granted faculties the right of "organiza-

tion and representation" and required public employers "to negotiate with and to enter into written agreements with employee organizations" (New York Civil Service Laws, Sections 200–214).
More importantly, it established the governor as the employer at
the state university rather than the trustees. The governor established an Office of Employee Relations (OER) empowered to bargain with faculty representatives. From that point forward, the
Office of Employee Relations determined salaries, fringe benefits,
and all other working conditions for faculty members. In addition,
OER was designated as the organization to which faculty members
could appeal their grievances, as often as they wished, over the
head of the chancellor of the university. Faculties in the community
colleges bargained with and became responsible to county governments rather than to trustees. In other words, much of the management of colleges and universities was abruptly and unilaterally
removed from the uninformed and unsuspecting trustees.

Trustees of private universities and colleges may reasonably
expect a spin-off effect; that is, as more faculties in public institutions organize and sign contracts and as the national faculty organizations grow in membership and political experience, they will
spend more of their time, effort, and dollars on organizing private
institutions and strengthening federal legislation. As an example,
the National Education Association has in recent years doubled
and tripled its expenditures on collective bargaining in higher education. As a result, more nonunionized faculty members are dis-
covering the benefits that have been gained by many of their
unionized colleagues and may soon seek some type of bargaining.

The second most important factor contributing to faculty
unionization falls within the broad category of employer-employee
relations. *Poorly managed institutions and those with histories of little or
no effective faculty participation in campus governance are prime targets
for unions.* Lack of an effective grievance procedure for settling
promotion and tenure issues is particularly likely to attract the
attention of unions. Unilateral decisions to terminate unproductive
programs and to initiate new ones also make collective bargaining
look appealing. Lowering the percentage of university funds assigned to salaries and salary increases is always perceived by faculties as being unwarranted and as inexcusably bad judgment. These

are the weather vanes about which trustees must keep informed if they wish to successfully discharge their public trust for excellence in education.

Effects of Faculty Unionization

With the number of faculty represented by exclusive bargaining agents having increased from fewer than 60,000 in 1974 to more than 120,000 by the end of 1978, some effects on the campus and its constituencies may be observed.

Overall Effects on Campus

1. Some presidents, vice-presidents, and deans resign within the first two years after the emergence of collective bargaining on their campuses, often assuming that collective bargaining is incompatible with their concept of good administration.
2. Students may become less effective in bringing about campus change (that is, collective bargaining takes the place of traditional governance).
3. There is a general upward movement of decision-making authority in the administrative hierarchy (increased centralization).
4. Department chairmen, where included in the faculty bargaining unit, are often reduced to providing liaison between their departments and the dean. They may come to be considered "first among equals" or may become "mouthpieces" for faculty.
5. Third parties (mediators, labor boards, arbitrators, and the courts) begin to play a greater role in institutional management through the grievance process.
6. Decision making throughout the institution becomes more formalized.
7. Generally a reorganization of administrative personnel takes place.
8. There is greater polarization of administration, faculty, and student leadership.
9. There is a tendency toward increased bureaucratization of authority in personnel and business offices.

10. Innovation and institutional experimentation slow down.
11. The institution is forced to plan more carefully; that is, closer review of existing academic programs becomes necessary, and budgeting becomes more stringent, complex, and closely scrutinized by several parties.
12. Evidence of past discrimination in employment practices will be sought and reviewed.

Effects on Trustees

1. Trustees in four-year institutions often lose personal touch with and responsibility for academic and fiscal policy because it is assumed by administrative agents and government officials. (In some two-year institutions trustees become more involved by actively negotiating and administering contracts. This is not recommended.)
2. Trustees usually are forced to delegate more authority to presidents, who must interpret and administer contracts daily.
3. The institution frequently employs a special assistant (for example, a vice-president for personnel or university affairs) for labor relations, thus creating another layer of administration.

Effects on the Presidency

1. The president can no longer deal with the faculty senate regarding terms and conditions of employment other than in the bargaining process.
2. The president (through his bargaining team) must negotiate with the faculty union on developing issues that may have an impact on terms and conditions of employment and/or contract interpretation.
3. The president must spend much more time communicating with the legal employer (usually the state government for public colleges, trustees for private institutions) and with faculty union leaders before, during, and after negotiations.
4. Communication usually becomes more regulated and formalized. "Meet and discuss sessions" between institutional and union leaders are often negotiated into the contract, and more faculty-wide meetings are held separately by the administration and by the union to explain changes in administrative policy.

5. The president must negotiate the "impact" of any decision (for example, a program change) that may affect the terms and conditions of employment negotiated under the contract.
6. The president can no longer deal individually with faculty members relative to their wages, hours, and terms and conditions of employment.

Wide variations in the impact of unionization on each institution, the current growth status of faculty unions, and the possibility of negative effects of faculty unionism require that trustees carefully review their current institutional role and their relationship to the faculty. Trustees may wish to reorganize their responsibilities and assume a new and more active role as policy makers.

Responsibilities of Trustees Prior to Faculty Unionization

The effects of faculty bargaining are much too serious to be left to chance. Trustees must know the causes and consequences of faculty unionization and their own responsibilities for planning and shaping the institutional policies that will adequately respond to collective bargaining and direct it toward institutional excellence. There are at least four critical issues upon which trustees must act intelligently prior to a faculty election for union representation.

Monitoring and Shaping State and Federal Legislation. Trustees, through their state and national organizations, should be constantly aware of pending labor legislation and how it may affect the operations of the university. Since trustees usually meet only once a month in the public sector, and even less often in the private sector, it is essential that they receive regular reports that will keep them informed on critical bills before the legislature or Congress. The chief executive officer should assign to an appropriate person, usually the university attorney or the director of personnel relations, the responsibility for preparing a concise monthly report on labor legislation to answer such questions as:

1. Does higher education have an active consortium of agencies in Washington, D.C., working effectively to defend the interests of

higher education in the area of labor legislation? If so, who is in charge of it? What has it done? How can universities help?

2. Are congressional committees considering bills that would extend coverage of the National Labor Relations Act to part-time faculty? To students? To graduate assistants? To state and municipal employees? If so, how will these bills affect the welfare of the university? What specific issues should be reviewed and influenced by representatives of higher education?

3. Is the state legislature considering legislation that will affect faculty-administrative relations? If so, who is sponsoring the bill and for what purposes? In what ways are the state colleges and universities being represented in legislative hearings? How can trustees help?

A trustee must constantly be aware of the special problems that poorly conceived labor laws can create for universities. Here is a checklist of objectives that a labor bill should accomplish for the institution:

- Designate the board of trustees as the legal employer.
- Protect institutional autonomy from encroachment by state officials.
- Protect institutional autonomy from encroachment by a labor board.
- Reaffirm institutional management responsibilities as prescribed by education laws.
- Limit the scope of bargaining to employee salaries and working conditions.
- Affirm collegial governance over academic matters.
- Provide a single-ballot, two-step election procedure.
- Provide legal limitations to negotiated contracts (they are not to exceed appropriated funds, not to supercede education or civil service laws, and so forth).
- State a clear, achievable purpose for collective bargaining.
- Provide a research service for evaluating the effectiveness of the law.
- Prohibit strikes and lockouts and provide adequate safeguards for resolving crises.

- Provide means of resolving impasses.
- Establish an educational labor board with appropriate qualifications for members.
- Provide for faculty members the right to join or not join a union.
- Protect the university's responsibility for long-range planning.
- Provide qualifications for unit membership.
- Provide for unfair labor practices by management.
- Provide for unfair labor practices by unions.
- Provide a method for resolving unfair labor charges.
- Provide a role for students where appropriate.

Monitoring and Analyzing Union Activities on Campus. Whether or not there is a law that permits faculty members on a particular campus to unionize, it is vital for trustees to request that the president keep the trustees informed as to the nature of current faculty-administrative relationships. The best index of these relationships may be the extent of faculty union activity on campus. National faculty unions are eager to extend their services, especially to campuses where faculty members are unhappy about their working conditions. Trustees should know which national unions have local chapters, the estimated number of members in each, the purposes of each organization, and its general attitude of cooperation with or opposition to the administration. The president's report should also include a copy of each union's latest "newsletter," often the best source of information about union activity and intent. It is of critical importance that the trustees realize that this is a particularly difficult report for the chief executive to make because it is really a report about his or her relationships with the faculty. Nevertheless, the trustees must know how the faculty members feel about their working relationships with the president and the executive staff. Do faculty leaders think that the institution's salaries are "competitive?" That too much money is being spent on salaries for too many administrators? That the president is spending too much time and money on academic ventures not central to the university's mission (institutes, centers, special programs, and so forth)? That the president is not listening to the pleas of faculty for more research support, secretarial assistance, and student assistants? That the president generally accepts the recommendations of the faculty relative to appointments, promotions, and tenure? That when faculty recommendations are not accepted reasonable explanations and alternatives are provided? That there is an acceptable appeals procedure to resolve complaints and grievances?

Few presidents have enough valid information to answer these questions, although every effort should be made to find whatever information is available. Too often administrators downgrade or even overlook national or local unions and their efforts to unionize the faculty. Interviews with trustees, presidents, and faculty members at unionized campuses indicate that a common attitude among trustees and administrators prior to a union election was that "our faculty will never vote for a union. Only a small vocal minority want to unionize." No president should depend on his or her particular contacts with faculty members as a basis for judging the temper of faculty. Nor should the trustees. A better source of information on such questions might be a committee appointed by the faculty senate that could act independently and confidentially in preparing and submitting a report to the president and trustees for review and response. Such reports can help the trustees and president remain aloof from day-to-day administrative detail yet still perform their unifying function.

Leadership requires not only the establishment of goals and organization but the mobilization and motivation of all the people who are asked to share in achieving educational excellence. Overall motivation often depends on the extent to which faculty members and administrators share decisions about available resources. The key element in sustaining broad support is fair and equal treatment of each and every faculty member. This means equal opportunity for promotion, salary increases, tenure, and other benefits. And no matter who makes the decisions or what procedures are used, there will always arise charges of unequal treatment. Prejudicial or cavalier treatment of grievances by administrators or uneven distribution of funds are common causes of low faculty morale and can easily lead to unionization. Reports to trustees must focus on these targets, and new policy should be directed at alleviating apparent as well as real injustices. Too many trustees are so impressed by a highly intelligent, well-mannered chief executive that they believe every faculty member must think that he or she is fortunate to work with such a person. At times, nothing could be farther from the truth. It is often the most creative, well-meaning, and brilliant president who stirs faculty unrest by constantly initiating new projects and new expenses before the projects begun last month have had faculty review and approval.

Reviewing Institutional Organization. Trustees and administrators should, of course, constantly review university organization to improve its effectiveness. But when union activity begins to appear on campus there is a special reason for review: to preempt decisions that may later be made by a labor board and may be unfavorable to the university from the trustees' point of view. When there is no faculty union, most campuses operate in a relatively informal atmosphere that permits the tides of human feeling and attitudes to supply decisive power in matters of the moment. Collective bargaining, however, operates in a much more formalized atmosphere in which past practices and legalistic interpretations of the contract become the bases of decision. It is the "past practices" aspect of collegial life that trustees and administrators must shake down before a labor board takes jurisdiction. Following are some areas that trustees should be concerned about:

Department chairmen. Are they to be considered essential members of the administrative team or should they have the right to join the faculty union? The labor board will decide this question on the basis of past and current practice. In other words, if the trustees want department chairmen to be designated as management rather than as union members, chairmen must be assigned administrative duties and *required* to perform those duties in a reasonably uniform manner from department to department. Unless this practice can be proven to the labor board, chairmen are likely to be designated as members of the faculty unit rather than as members of the administration.

Part-time faculty members. Most institutions do not expect the labor board to assign part-timers to faculty union status. Yet, if they are employed year after year, permitted to vote in faculty senate elections, and given promotions they will probably be placed in the bargaining unit and will enjoy all the benefits of the union contract, including salary increases and retrenchment procedures. Part-timers can become a rather large, inflexible, and important part of the budget when they are included in a faculty bargaining unit, especially where there is a sufficient number to affect union politics.

Faculty participation in administrative matters. Faculty members are often called upon to help in a variety of administrative affairs. They help to evaluate current administrators and select new ones, they sit on budget committees, and some are invited to meet with trustees on a regular basis. There are cases on record where a faculty after unionization has demanded the continuation of such past practices based on their legal rights under labor law. But such participation by faculty can greatly complicate the administration's bargaining with faculty.

Faculty as administrators. There is one case on record, *National Labor Relations Board and Yeshiva University Faculty Association* v. *Yeshiva University* (1978), where faculty members shared so widely in managerial decisions that the courts ruled that they could not be considered as "employees" within the meaning of the National Labor Relations Act and, therefore, had no right to form a union for purposes of bargaining. It is conceivable that some institutions may prefer to vest more authority in its faculty in order to improve faculty morale and to discourage unionization.

Responding to a Faculty Demand for the Right to Bargain Under Trustee Resolution. Only half the states have legislation that permits faculties of public universities to unionize. Yet faculties of public institutions are beginning to unionize in states without such laws. They do it by persuading the trustees to allow an election to be held and to bargain with a faculty union should one be elected. Usually trustees and presidents try to avoid responding to such pressures in the hope that delay will somehow provide time for self-correction of factors motivating such "unseemly" faculty behavior. A few institutions have deterred the faculty by providing substantial salary increases or by adjusting highly criticized administrative procedures and personnel. Nevertheless, some of the most effective faculty bargaining is now taking place under trustee resolution without benefit of or hindrance by a state or federal law. And preliminary reports indicate that there may be many advantages and few disadvantages in bargaining under the egis of trustees' policy as compared to bargaining under law. In any case, trustees cannot sit back and assume that faculty bargaining cannot happen at their institution simply because there is no state enabling legislation or because there is no union presence in the state. Should faculty members demand the right to bargain, trustees will be facing their sternest test of leadership. The faculty will demand a response even if it takes ten years as it did in the case of the Board of Governors in Illinois. In the absence of a state or federal controlling law or of resort to the NLRB, a faculty demand to bargain places the *total* responsibility for shaping the conditions and nature of faculty bargaining upon the trustees.

The board of trustees must make a reasoned decision as to whether or not it will permit the faculty to bargain with the administration (except in Texas, North Carolina, and Virginia, where state laws prohibit even voluntary bargaining with public employees). If the answer is affirmative, then regulations must be established to govern every aspect of bargaining; for example, unit membership, (identification of those faculty members who will be eligible to vote in an election), election procedures, the scope of bargaining, unfair labor practices, methods of resolving impasses and unfair labor charges, right to strike, and all the other issues listed earlier in this chapter. This is a challenging but not impossible task. Good examples now exist and there are consultants qualified to prepare models and explanations as a basis for hearings. The important message is that trustees, far from being sheltered by the absence of legislation, actually have greater flexibility and therefore more responsibility than when enabling laws exist (Angell and Kelley, 1979).

Role of Trustees in Faculty Bargaining

The role of a trustee in a particular matter will vary with his or her knowledge and interest, the type of institution, and the degree of encouragement offered by the chief executive. Yet it is a fact that no individual trustee has executive authority unless specifically granted this authority by total board action. A trustee's authority is ordinarily limited by law or by charter to legislative action taken in concert with other trustees. There is, however, another equally significant role for each trustee, and this is to act, as time and expertise allow, as a confidant and personal adviser to the chief executive. No individual has all the knowledge and insight needed to be the chief executive of a university, and competent, thoughtful advice is almost always welcomed.

Yet policy making is not a passive role. It requires considerable study and knowledge of a subject to be able to visualize not only the parts and the sum total of policy but the probable effects of alternative policies in moving the institution toward its stated goal of excellence. The following discussion will therefore attempt to provide a breakdown of the policies that will be needed two years prior to a faculty union election and for the ongoing activities of negotiating and administering a contract. The policies and actions suggested here are drawn from first-hand experience and from interviews with several hundred trustees, presidents, and institutional negotiators.

The Bargaining Unit. "Unit" refers to a group of people (faculty, in this case) who are to decide whether or not to unionize and bargain. The first union-related action of the board is to approve and publish a chart of administrative officials *with their duties stated on the chart.* A chart of this kind should clearly show where responsibility lies for making "effective" recommendations and final decisions relative to employment and working conditions for faculty members. It is essential, as suggested earlier, that the chart establish past and current practice prior to review by a labor board. The trustees should ask the administration to prepare and present amended personnel policies to make it clear who are to be considered members of the faculty (full-time faculty, part-time faculty, athletic coaches, librarians, graduate assistants) at any time, now or in the future, should the "faculty" want to vote on unionization.

For a large multipurpose university the question of unit size should be analyzed and acted upon early. For example, if the trustees want the college of law to be a separate unit, the law faculty should be given enough flexibility in salary and working conditions to show that it does not share a "community of interest" with other faculties. Should the institution want a single large unit that includes all university faculty members, it will have to prove that all faculty members, regardless of program or location, share common salary scales, similar criteria for promotion, comparable teaching loads, and membership in a common faculty senate. The intent here, of course, is to bring current administrative practices into line with the kind of faculty union the institution would prefer to bargain with sometime in the future should the faculty ever elect to bargain.

Institutional Posture Toward Labor Unions. The institution serves all sectors of society, including labor unions and their members. For this, if for no other reason, the institution cannot afford to take action or permit its administrators to take action that may be interpreted as "anti-union." This is especially true during the campaign period of an election, when all actions of trustees and administrators are scrutinized for evidence of unfair labor practices. An antiunion attitude does not in itself constitute unfair practice. But threats, coercion, and punitive action against faculty who engage in prounion activities do constitute unfair practice. Once an administrator or trustee has been publicly tabbed as antiunion, it is difficult to prove that denial of promotion or tenure for a faculty union organizer was not punitive and coercive. More by advice and discussion than by formal resolution, the trustees should request the administration to take whatever steps are necessary to advise and educate subadministrators at all levels as to the proper attitude and actions to take during the months preceding an election.

Education Programs for Trustees. Trustees commonly make one or the other of the following serious mistakes when considering faculty labor relations:

1. They feel they lack expertise with the issues and decide to stay out of the discussion rather than making a special effort to become informed and so be able to influence policy.
2. They refuse to admit that they know very little and take strong positions in the discussions.
3. They feel that their experience in industrial relations provides the essential knowledge, and they take action (and often assume leadership) on the basis of their industrial experience.

The evidence points to the need for everyone on the board to become at least moderately well informed. Industrial experience does have valuable carry-over relative to the *technical* aspects of bargaining (for example, unfair labor practices) but sheds almost no light on such special aspects of faculty bargaining as the scope of bargaining (governance issues), the impact on organizational and administrative patterns, the psychology of faculty-administrative relationships, the impact on student and alumni relations, the reorganization of administrative resources and authority, and the new governmental and political relationships. Faculty bargaining establishes new relationships based on legal authority external to education law. Trustees facing this change should ask for carefully planned educational programs for themselves, the chief executive, and the administrative staff. The programs should be coordinated.

A Comprehensive Policy for All Major Aspects of Faculty Labor Relations. The most common error made by boards is to establish no policy at all. This, of course, permits the chief executive considerable flexibility, but it also provides no guidance or protection. In the absence of policy, a "strong" trustee (often the chairman) may step in and push the chief executive aside, thus creating the type of friction that weakens both the administration and the academic community. The board should delegate the execution of program and policy to the chief executive by formal action. It may wish to provide a three-person trustee committee for advice and support. Should the chief executive be uncertain or feel ill prepared, the recommendation may be to provide funds to employ counsel or a new chief personnel administrator *experienced in faculty negotiations.* Ordinarily trustees are not assigned to operational functions because they must remain objective enough to evaluate the effectiveness of programs; that is, a trustee can hardly move into the operational arena on one day and then join the rest of the trustees in evaluating his or her work the next. It inevitably creates divisiveness on the board whenever the "administrative work" of one trustee is open to criticism by the others. Even more important is the fact that direct trustee participation in labor relations creates a channel between trustees and faculty members that bypasses and weakens the entire administrative staff, a situation in which the chief executive cannot be held responsible for one of his or her major functions: personnel administration.

The evidence calls for a policy that will restrain trustees from the executive function and will delegate full authority to the chief executive, along with sufficient resources and guidance. This general policy should be clarified by the following actions relative to essential elements of a labor program:

Appointment of a chief negotiator is a key decision and requires advice, considerable thought, and a realistic examination of the qualifications of existing staff. The advice of the chief executive is crucial. Only the president can reasonably determine whether some of the current staff members are qualified in the field of labor relations, or what effect an outside professional negotiator may have on faculty attitudes and their negotiating team. Some experience suggests employing a professional negotiator with known success in bargaining with *faculty unions,* but only when the chief executive recommends that an outsider be employed. If that is the case, the chief executive should be authorized to employ a negotiator who will report directly to him or her for all operational decisions. The chief executive and negotiator should have authority to select the other bargaining team members.

Presidents and management negotiators point out that a serious mistake is often made by "giving away" too much in the first negotiations. But there is also another serious error: limiting the scope of bargaining so rigidly as to tie the hands of the chief executive and the chief negotiator. This creates unnecessary bargaining tension and may result in an impasse. It is essential that the board help the chief executive by establishing the minimal management rights that are to be protected and by providing counsel as to other subjects of bargaining. In addition, the trustees should establish maximum costs for a financial package, giving the chief executive flexibility in determining details.

The question often arises whether the trustees themselves should attempt to be the final arbiter of faculty grievances or whether binding arbitration by a neutral outside party is legal or preferable. It is clear that trustees can become embroiled in a number of problems when they attempt to arbitrate grievances. Grievances not only are complicated by academic traditions and personal emotions but can also involve highly technical and legalistic questions. One of the conditions of due process is the right of appeal to a neutral adjudicator. When this right is not supplied by the contract in the form of arbitration, nothing can prevent grievances from being taken to court by unions, whose responsibility it is to protect the rights of unit members. Arbitration is relatively inexpensive and becoming more widely accepted (Weisberger, 1979); it is highly recommended, but its conditions should be carefully bargained to protect the rights of both management and faculty. In addition to the grievance procedures designed to clarify and protect the integrity of the contract, ordinary collegial procedures for noncontract grievances may be retained where they have operated effectively.

Trustees should establish a policy that assures their continuing understanding of campus labor relations. Usually a policy that requires an informal report from the chief executive at each board meeting will suffice. (During periods of crisis, however, daily reports may be needed.) The chief executive should report at least four types of information: the progress of negotiations (during negotiating periods); the relative status of salaries and benefits as compared to those in similar institutions; new contracts as they are completed at other institutions; and grievances in progress. From time to time the chief executive will also want to report on relevant legislative, as well as court and labor board, actions.

It is essential that trustees help to control the flow of confidential information necessary for management effectiveness in labor relations. At least a three-point policy is needed to protect the flow of confidential information: (1) a declaration that all discussions in executive sessions of the board or its committees relative to labor relations activities are confidential in nature; (2) a recognition that the unauthorized disclosure of such information may be highly detrimental to the institution and therefore may be an appropriate basis for censure or other disciplinary procedure; and (3) the appointment of a university spokesperson responsible for all public announcements relative to labor relations. In states with sunshine laws that require public bodies to hold open meetings, trustees have special problems relative to confidentiality. Usually the law permits executive sessions to be held in private. If not, the trustees may wish to delegate more responsibility to committees or to administrators in order to provide for the employer the same opportunity for confidentiality as that available to the union. Successful bargaining assumes for each party relatively equal restraints and freedom.

As a matter of common sense and practical planning, trustees, prior to the first negotiations, should develop a viable strike policy and a plan of operations during attempted strikes. The policy should include as a minimum: (1) that the institution will attempt to settle all disputes peacefully through good faith negotiations but at the same time will not sacrifice in any way the character and future of the institution; (2) that should a union decide to strike, the trustees and administration will invoke a carefully prepared strike plan to keep the institution in full operation; (3) that the institution will carry out the full intent of government as prescribed by law or the intent of parties as prescribed by a no-strike and no-lockout contract clause (antistrike penalties, injunctions, conciliation, and so on); and (4) that it will invoke every legally available means to overcome the impact of the strike. The policy should reaffirm the principle that good faith bargaining, including conciliation services rather than force, is the way to settle differences. The plan for operations during a strike should be carefully structured by the chief executive with advice from professionals who have been through a strike at another campus.

At some public colleges, government officials have created serious problems in faculty labor relations by insisting on exercising their authority to bargain directly with public employees. While this may make little difference to classified employees, it can create havoc when politicians intervene between trustees and faculty. State education law gives trustees the authority to establish personnel and educational policy. Faculty bargaining has a serious impact on both areas. Since trustees cannot be accountable for policy and programs over which they have little control, they should pass a resolution as early as possible and apply whatever political pressure is necessary to see that they remain in charge of the institution as a whole and in charge of faculty bargaining in particular. Where government officials control bargaining, trustees slowly become little more than an historical appendage shorn of any final authority, and college presidents tend to become little more than branch managers of a government agency. These conditions can destroy any hope of professional excellence achieved through a self-governing community of scholars.

A New Trustee Role?

Only trustees can prevent the search for truth and enlightenment from being stifled by the intrusion of powerful self-interests. Collective bargaining by its very nature brings the university into new political relationships. In at least three public, four-year institutions, faculty and trustee representatives have negotiated contracts that authorize a delegation of some trustee authority to faculty-administrative committees. In addition, governments and donors are increasingly influencing college policy. And so are students and alumni. The university cannot hope to escape the onslaught of new political and economic realities. And trustees cannot avoid the two choices they face: to fashion a viable role in a new academic world reshaped daily by massive public forces or slowly to become a relic of social progression. Some faculty members are attempting to meet the challenge through union organization. Students are organizing for local and state political action. Governments are passing more and more laws governing higher education, and government agencies are becoming more diligent in "reviewing" the actions of colleges.

Do trustees have a new role? Only they can answer this question for themselves, and that answer must be couched in terms of positive initiative. In most instances, trustees have far more authority and influence than they are willing to exercise. But unexercised authority creates a vacuum that may be interpreted as negligence and perhaps as irresponsibility.

14

Michael Radock
Harvey K. Jacobson

Securing Resources

The trustee truly involved in fund raising feels a
part of the plan, a part of a group pulling together. . . . This
can be the greatest pleasure, in my judgment, that trustees
can have in their trusteeship [William B. Dunseth, vice-
president for development, Pomona College, 1978,
pp. 24–25].

People who volunteer fill a gap in their lives. To
be a volunteer is to be part of a full life. It is rewarding to
improve a community, to grow as a person, to make a difference to somebody else ["Monitor Spotlights Harriet
Naylor," 1978].

I was fortunate in getting financial assistance
throughout my entire undergraduate and graduate college
career. Because I benefited from the generosity of others,
I am continuing the process [Letter from a university
alumnus].

He who obtains has little. He who scatters has much
[Chinese proverb].

These comments reflect the joy and personal satisfaction that can
be derived from giving and, in particular, from devoting time,

264

talent, and money to improving the assets of a college or university. At the institutional level, this process goes by rather detached names such as "obtaining resources." At the operational level, however, the process can be an extremely personal enterprise, filled with a human dimension that is both absorbing and gratifying. Trustees may well find that this is one of the most exciting dimensions of their social stewardship.

Trustees are in a better position than any other group to preserve and improve the financial health of the institution. Sufficiently distant from its daily operations, they possess a valuable perspective, and they can experience the unique satisfaction of "putting it all together" for the institution. They are often the key link in the exchange that allows a source of funding to accomplish a goal highly desired by the source and of great benefit to the college or university.

The trustee can be an advocate, a linkage agent, and a broker for constructive change. A trustee has the opportunity to weave together his or her personal interests and contacts with those of the institution and to facilitate the achievement of the institution's goals. The results: institutions are more in tune with their constituencies; cases for support are made more convincing; fellow trustees, as well as volunteers and major donors, become more committed and involved; and the team that works together to obtain resources sees more clearly the natural thread that binds together public relations and fund raising as a comprehensive force to advance the institution.

Obtaining resources is a basic responsibility of board members. Never was this assignment more important than it is today. Leveling enrollments and financial stringencies dictate that practically all institutions, public and private, that wish to survive with excellence must maintain a comprehensive program for raising funds.

Higher education obtains its income from governments; tuition, fees, and other charges; and philanthropy. If increases in tuition and fees are undesirable, the other two sources of income must be increased or institutions of higher education will have to learn to live with less income or with only minor income growth. If more income is desired, colleges and universities must utilize a systematic approach to obtaining it. Many things can be done. In general, the assignment calls for the academic community as a whole to work together to demonstrate its needs and to present a convincing case that higher education more than ever is essential to serving and preserving the public interest. It means in particular that the American college or university must seek more support from the private sector.

This chapter will consider the trustee's role in both the general and specific areas just mentioned but will place strong emphasis on voluntary support. The sober fact facing us is that the college or university, public or private, that cannot rely on substantial voluntary support from alumni, corporations, foundations, or friends in the next decade is destined for mediocrity or something worse.

Private colleges and universities have always relied on the private donor as a major source of revenue. However, it is now generally accepted that tax support for the public institution is less than adequate to meet rising costs. Leveling enrollment patterns have resulted in a decrease in revenue. Thus, as the financial situation tightens, public institutions have sought and obtained more private dollars, and private institutions have pursued and received more tax dollars.

Voluntary support will go to those institutions with well-conceived and well-planned strategies for shaping their fiscal destinies. Hence, institutions are now doing their best to obtain a clearer look at the general picture of philanthropy. In early 1979, *Forbes* magazine ran an article pointing out that philanthropy in the United States is a remarkable demonstration of what private initiative can accomplish when nurtured by a free society. In 1978 private philanthropy generated $35 billion, a large sum indeed. However, the same article noted that the figure represented only about 2.25 percent of disposable income, or about the amount Americans spent on cosmetics, movies, and liquor. Private money is available, but the competition for it is intense and will get even more so.

Exactly what is the role of board members in fund raising? How can they become better at this task?

Guidelines for Obtaining Resources

Here are some guidelines designed to help board members increase their effectiveness. Board members should:

- Legitimize the program for obtaining resources.
- Understand the basic patterns and trends in the financial support of the institution.
- Avoid the major misconceptions about fund raising.
- Make sure the institution states clearly its concept of development and institutional advancement.
- Insist that the institution organize a systematic program based on the concept.
- Clarify the role of the trustee in the division of labor for members of the institutional team.
- Accept specific responsibilities and tasks as individual trustees involved in obtaining resources.
- Learn the basics of fund raising.
- Rely on the "case statement" for articulating the case for support.
- Agree on the role of the capital campaign.
- Know when to use counsel.
- Build a reporting system.
- Encourage and support fund raising research and analysis.
- Determine the role of the college or institutional foundation.
- Maintain relationships with assorted publics.
- Participate in the institution's governmental relations plan.
- Evaluate the fund-raising effort.
- Be prepared for the major issues.

Legitimizing the Program. The cornerstone of a successful program for obtaining resources is its legitimacy. The program must be recognized as a significant and integral component of the institution. Legitimacy begins with the governing board. It is the responsibility of the chief executive officer not only to gain the endorsement of the board for the program but also to educate the board about the purpose, function, and operation of this component of the university. Ignorant of purpose, board members may be insensitive to start-up costs and other necessary expenditures. Ignorant of function, board members may be unappreciative of budget requirements, staff needs, and project diversity essential to the success of the office responsible for obtaining resources. Without knowledge of the total operation, board members will be inclined to misunderstand their own role in the program as a whole. Further, misunderstandings will abound when large sums of external funds are requested and granted, if the board is not involved in the process (Ottley, 1978).

Steps must be taken to ensure a total institutional commitment to create the best circumstances for a flourishing fund-raising program. On some campuses, legitimization takes the form of board bylaws. At the University of Michigan, section 2.08 of the Regental Bylaws states that the vice-president for university relations and development "shall perform such duties with respect to matters pertaining to the relations between the University, its alumni, and people and institutions of the State of Michigan and elsewhere as shall be assigned to him from time to time by the President. . . . He shall act as public relations and development counsel to the Board, the President, and policy-making bodies of the University and shall be responsible for the administration of public relations and fund-raising programs."

Understanding Basic Patterns and Trends in the Financial Support of the Institution. Where does the money come from? Where will it come from in the future? What amount of time and money must be expended to secure this support?

There are six general revenue sources on which most institutions rely in varying degrees: federal government appropriations, state government appropriations, local government appropriations, student tuition and fees, institutional sales and services, and private philanthropy. Although each institution's money sources vary, it is useful to compare the facts for any given campus with some national averages. Statistics for 1975–76 and selected comparison years are presented in Table 1 and Figure 1. Out of the estimated $39.7 billion income reported by all institutions of higher education in 1975–76, a total of 30.9 percent came from state governments, 21.6 percent from institutional sales and services (including auxiliary enterprises and hospitals), 20.6 percent from student

Table 1. U.S. Higher Education Proportions of Total Revenue Support, 1939–1976 (current funds)

	1939–40		1949–50		1959–60		1969–70		1975–76	
	$	%	$	%	$	%	$	%	$	%
Federal government	.05	5.4	.5	22.1	1.1	18.3	3.8	17.6	6.5	16.3
State governments	.1	21.2	.5	20.7	1.4	23.8	5.9	27.3	12.2	30.9
Local governments	.05	3.4	.1	2.6	.1	2.6	.8	3.6	1.6	4.1
Student (tuition and fees)	.2	28.1	.4	16.6	1.1	20.0	4.4	20.5	8.2	20.6
Institutional (sales, services, other)	.2	26.3	.7	28.9	1.4	23.9	5.0	23.3	8.6	21.6
Private philanthropy	.1	15.6	.2	9.1	.6	11.4	1.6	7.7	2.6	6.5
	.7	100.0	2.4	100.0	5.7	100.0	21.5	100.0	39.7	100.0

Note: Total dollar amounts in billions.
Source: Table and figure prepared by Jerry A. May, Office of State and Community Relations, the University of Michigan.
Data Sources: National Center for Education Statistics, *Financial Statistics of Institutions of Higher Education; Digest of Education Statistics, 1977–78.*

tuition and fees, 16.3 percent from the federal government, 6.5 percent from private philanthropy, and 4.1 percent from local governments. Proportions will vary, of course, for different institutions, but the aggregate data provide a starting point for making decisions about current and future funding.

It should be noted that 51.3 percent of all college and university income was obtained from government appropriations—federal, state, and local. No doubt about it, higher education depends significantly upon the patronage of government and its systems of taxation, the funding decisions of chief executives, legislators, and congressmen, and the attitudes of taxpayers who influence the governmental process.

Adding together student charges and institutional sales and services, one gets a total of 42.2 percent of income from internal sources. Of the 57.8 percent from external sources, 6.5 percent comes from philanthropic giving. Various trends can be detected in Table 1, but primary attention shall be given here to private giving. Between 1939–1940 and 1975–1976 private philanthropy in colleges and universities increased from $.1 billion to $2.6 billion. Both private and public universities have increased their efforts over the past three decades to attract private funds. During this era, however, such income fell from 15.6 percent to 6.5 percent of total income (see Figure 1).

General trends in charitable giving in America were presented in the 1977 report of the American Association of Fund-Raising Counsel. Giving totaled some $35.2 billion in 1977, an impressive increase from the $29.42 billion reported in 1976. Americans contributed an estimated $4.66 billion to education in 1977, an increase of almost 15 percent over the previous year. Substantial increases were recorded for business corporations, foundations, alumni, and nonalumni. However, several institutions, especially public colleges and universities, fell short of their potential in contributions from friends and in bequest and other deferred giving categories.

The six traditional sources of voluntary support for higher education have remained fairly constant through the years, according to the Council for Financial Aid to Education (see Table 2). The

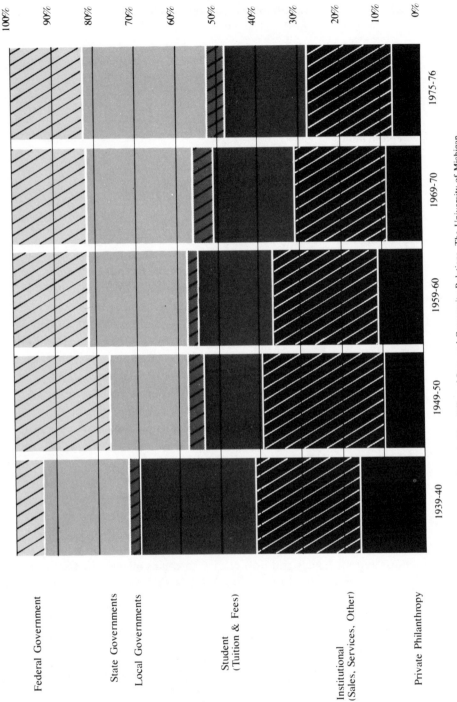

100%
90%
80%
70%
60%
50%
40%
30%
20%
10%
0%

1975-76

1969-70

1959-60

1949-50

1939-40

Federal Government

State Governments

Local Governments

Student
(Tuition & Fees)

Institutional
(Sales, Services, Other)

Private Philanthropy

Chart prepared by Jerry A. May, Office of State and Community Relations, The University of Michigan.
Data Sources: U.S. Department of Health, Education, and Welfare, National Center for Educational Statistics. *Financial Statistics of Institutions of Higher Education; Digest of Educational Statistics,* 1977-78.

Table 2. Percent of Total Private Support by Source
and Total Dollars Received from All Sources

Source of Support	1970-71	1973-74	1976-77
Nonalumni individuals	26.6	24.8	24.2
Alumni	24.6	22.7	23.9
Foundations	22.5	23.9	20.9
Business corporations	13.9	15.8	16.7
Religious denominations	5.6	5.2	5.1
Other	6.8	7.6	9.2
Total percentage	100.0	100.0	100.0
Total dollars (billions)	$1.86	$2.24	$2.67

Source: Council for Financial Aid to Education (1972, 1975, 1978).

Council's report put its charts in perspective by looking back: "Despite the large gains in voluntary support in 1975-76 and 1976-77 [a two-year increase of 23.6 percent], the growth in total voluntary support since 1965-66 has been inadequate in terms of past performance and, more importantly, in terms of the needs of higher education. The rate of growth since 1965-66 has averaged 5.8 percent annually, which compares with a rate of 11.9 percent per year for the preceding sixteen years and 6.0 percent per year for the forty years prior to 1949-50. . . . Prior to 1965-66, total support averaged about 12 percent of total college and university expenditures (current plus capital); since 1965-66, voluntary support decreased in relative importance, and in each of the last three years it has averaged less than 6 percent of total expenditures. . . . Total voluntary support has not, since 1970-71, kept pace with inflation" (Council for Financial Aid to Education, 1978, pp. 5-6).

The deeper one digs into the statistics, the more one catches the view of challenging horizons. For example, 60 to 80 percent of most alumni bodies still do not give to their colleges. In fact, nonalumni support of higher education is slightly ahead of alumni giving.

Avoiding the Major Misconceptions About Fund Raising. Fund raising, like politics, is full of mythology. Here are four major misconceptions:

1. *You can "get rich quick."* All a college has to do is hire a fund raiser at a high salary, provide fancy offices, elaborate electronic sys-

tems, a generous expense allowance, and its cash needs are
solved! (Alas, not so.)

2. *Fund raising is one big hodgepodge.* It's called different things, but
   whether you call it public relations, publicity, public affairs, development, advancement, it's all the same thing. (Not true. Each
   of these elements has identifiable components that play a special
   role in the total institutional effort.)

3. *Fund raising is a one-shot deal, a "campaign."* (This view limits
   one's horizons considerably; it makes much more sense to think
   beyond short-term fund-raising campaigns to long-term fund-
   raising *programs.*)

4. *Fund raising is basically a one-way street.* You simply go to the
   source and get some money. (False, of course. Fund raising
   is an interactive process; concerns of both the giver and the receiver are important. Many appeals to funding sources fail because they are too much *producer* centered, too little *consumer*
   oriented.)

*Stating Clearly the Concept of Development and Institutional Ad-
vancement.* Fund raising cannot be conducted as an isolated activity.
It must be viewed as an integral part of the total life of the institution. The responsibilities for obtaining funds should therefore be
clarified by the administration. The trustee should be able to obtain
from the institution a written statement of the concepts that govern
its fund-raising philosophy. Especially deserving of examination
are the following elements: its breadth, its acknowledgment of the
academic goals of the institution, and its stance on team effort.

   The advantages of a broad and comprehensive concept of
development have been outlined by one consulting firm as follows:
"Those colleges and universities which have made the greatest
strides in development are those which understand the development concept. Development is an effort on the part of the entire
institution to analyze its educational philosophy and activities, to
crystalize its objectives, to project them into the future, and to make
sure that its highest destiny is realized by taking the necessary steps
to reach its established goals. As a concept, development is institution-wide. It includes academic planning which charts the
kind of support and resources required by the college in meeting

future goals. It is based on an academic blueprint, evolved by the faculty and administration and approved by the trustees. It involves the business operations of the institution—the wise conservation of resources and the accountability to those who invest in it" (Stuhr, 1977, p. 82).

Organizing a Systematic Program. Fund raising or development should be viewed within the context of what is now known as "institutional advancement." American colleges and universities have long recognized the importance of being responsive to the people they serve. In higher education's infancy, presidents personally assumed the responsibility for exercising this function—the pursuit and maintenance of public understanding and support. Through the years presidents have delegated more and more of this assignment to other staff members. Today it rates as one of four major functional areas of administration in higher education, the other three being academic affairs, business management, and student affairs.

The structure and organization needed for institutional advancement shall not be belabored here, but it is extremely important to note the emergence of the coordination of a wide gamut of public relations, development, and alumni activities into a major centralized function (Rowland, 1977; Shea, 1977). The chances for success are increased if an institution has a dedicated professional who directs a carefully conceived function rather than if it has various individuals working at cross-purposes. Centralization can increase professional coordination and efficiency of staff, improve the identification and monitoring of program expenditures, and enhance the objectivity and comprehensiveness of a data base for planning and decision making.

Institutions of higher education differ widely in purpose, size, and scope. Thus, no one model of organization for the institutional advancement function can be cited as the most effective for all institutions. However, to persons unfamiliar with the detail of this dimension of university administration, an organizational prototype may serve to demonstrate that many aspects of a program can be pulled together to improve coordination (see Table 3). A prototype of this kind reminds us that fund raising should be planned in conjunction with public relations and alumni programs

Table 3. Programs Associated with Institutional Advancement

Development	Public Relations	Alumni Relations	Service-Management
Annual fund	Government relations	Alumni clubs	Special events
Deferred giving	News bureau (media relations)	Alumni publications	Printing plant
Capital campaign	Publications (design service)	Alumni camps	Marketing
Special gifts	Catalogues	Alumni—branch campuses	Placement services
Estate planning	Community and neighborhood relations	Records	Institutional research
Wills and bequests	Advertising	Undergraduate alumni relations	Planning and evaluation
Government grants and contracts	Public relations staff—branch campuses	Secondary school recruiting	Student affairs
Foundation relations	Internal communications	Alumni education	Intercollegiate athletics
Faculty fund raising	Sports information		Labor relations
Corporate relations	Student publications		Budget office
	Press (publishing house)		Information systems
	Speakers Bureau		Summer Programs
	Public relations staff—hospital and medical school		Security
	Motion picture service		Summer music festival
	United Way		
	Photographic service		

Source: Adapted from a 1976 survey of twenty-three colleges and universities conducted by James M. Shea, Temple University.

and that it can also benefit from association with assorted "service-management" programs.

Clarifying the Role of the Trustee on the Institutional Team. If the development effort is a team effort, what is the responsibility of the various members of the team? What is the division of labor?

The president is the key link between the campus and the board. The president and the board must believe firmly in the value of institutional advancement activities or even the best devised organization will fail. The president's outlook will probably be reflected in the organizational chart, showing the level of responsibility that he or she assigns to this function.

The vice-president, director, or other person serving as coordinating officer serves as an extension of the president in managing the advancement program. Personnel in the development office initiate activities on and off the campus. They help faculty and staff in developing their own prospects, and their office acts as a repository and dispenser of information and opportunities. As catalysts and advisers, they encourage faculty members to develop projects. Several development officers feel that their responsibilities also include assistance to student groups and individual students in their quest for external funds. Through volunteers or directly, development personnel solicit funds from foundations, corporations, and individuals.

What is the board's responsibility? Board members establish the climate for giving. They do this by approving policies that provide an atmosphere in which understanding and support flourish. If this atmosphere does not exist, the case for financial support cannot be made successfully. Essential policy questions that board members must deal with are:

- Does the institution have a good development program?
- Is the development budget adequate for an effective program?
- What are the educational priorities in the fund-raising effort?

The board's policy role is extremely important, but beyond this trustees should take an active part in a wide range of activities that will help to build a sense of public trust and confidence in the institution. As a living symbol of faith in the institution, the board

member sets an example for others. He or she does this by understanding and supporting the resource acquisition function and by
making a personal contribution of time, talent, and money. All
these contributions should be made within the means of the individual board members; each board member has something special
to give.

The Need for Trustee Participation

*Accepting Specific Responsibilities and Tasks as Individual Trustees
Involved in Resource Acquisition.* Board members must give not only
philosophical but also practical support. Since they are busy people,
they obviously are not expected to be full-time fund raisers. What
tasks should board members undertake? How can they best use
their time? Specifically, the board member can engage in (1) public
relations activity and (2) fund-raising activity, including personal
gifts of money and cultivation of potential donors.

Public Relations Activity. To be successful in attracting funds
the institution must be known; that is, it must be recognized for its
contribution to society, for its fulfillment of goals and objectives,
and for its potential for growth and greater service. Board members should make an effort to explain the value of the college or
university to the community. Before doing this, of course, board
members should have asked questions, sought answers, and, it is
hoped, become convinced that the institution is genuinely worth
supporting. Trustees can enhance public understanding by building a bridge between the campus and its clientele. They can interpret the needs of the campus to the clientele and those of the
clientele to the campus. Nason (1975) expressed it well when he
said trustees can persuade the hostile, disarm the critical, spike rumors, correct misunderstandings, refute misstatements, explain the
problems of the college, and interpret its premises and principles.

Fund Raising Activity. Board members can persuade alumni,
corporations, foundations, and friends to contribute money if they
work steadily on the cultivation of these potential donors. The basic
formula is simple: (1) *Identify* those individuals or groups who might
make a contribution; (2) Stimulate their *interest;* (3) *Involve* them in the
life of the institution; and (4) Move them to *invest* in it.

When it comes to obtaining major gifts, for example, the trustee can play a significant role by agreeing to accept a certain number of major gift prospects for cultivation and solicitation, by submitting names of potential donors and of candidates for positions on advisory committees and the board itself, by expressing appreciation to donors, and by suggesting ways and means to give them institutional recognition. Trustees should encourage friends of the institution to give through wills, bequests, insurance policies, trust funds, annuities, and other forms of estate planning. Trustees who accept this role of leadership by example not only give strong evidence of their interest in the institution but also increase the confidence of others in it.

The trustee should not limit his or her involvement to the major gifts program. The annual giving program is also important. After all, most major individual gifts—and corporate and foundation gifts—are based on long histories of involvement with an institution and on established habits of giving smaller gifts on a regular basis. Moreover, corporations and foundations with no assumed allegiance to the institution frequently consider the health of the annual giving program as a gauge of its worthiness. The annual giving program nurtures new donors with initially small contributions capabilities. From this group come in time the replacements for the current generation of mature, major givers who will eventually pass from the scene.

What can the trustee do to assist the annual giving program? The trustee can volunteer to serve as chairman or honorary chairman of the annual campaign, enlist others as chairmen or volunteers, be present at campaign kickoffs, represent the institution at regional campaign meetings, sign letters of appeal or published endorsements of the campaign, and reply or help draft answers to complaints by alumni prospects who question institutional policy.

Board members should personally give financial support. A trustee at two colleges in Minnesota has noted: "I . . . find annoying the argument that the contribution of time is the equivalent of money, and that this justifies the person of substantial income and means contributing few dollars. We need money as well as time, and money has to come from those who have it" (Bean, 1973, p. 9). Board members can greatly influence the giving of others by giving themselves. Furthermore, in keeping with their leadership role, they should give early. Not all board members can give the same amount. Some can and should give large sums; each should give to the best of his or her ability; and, very importantly, *all* should give. This exerts a highly positive force on the success of a fund-raising effort. Perhaps there should be annual reports to the board of aggregate trustee gifts, including the percentage or numbers of trustees who gave, average gift, and total amount given for at least the preceding year.

An excellent illustration of the ripple effect is the "trustee nucleus fund" for capital campaigns. Such a fund is typically obtained in the form of nucleus pledges by board members. These pledges, which are made in proportion to the trustees' means and are payable as they stipulate, can account for a substantial percentage of the fund goal. The nucleus pledges typically are announced at a very early stage to give the total effort impetus and momentum. The University of Chicago, under the leadership of its board chairman, Edward L. Ryerson, pioneered this plan in the early 1950s. It has been employed with success by many other institutions. David Ketchum, chairman of the board of a national professional fund-raising counseling firm, reports (correspondence to Radock, 1979) that the percentage of capital campaign objectives contributed by members of boards of trustees is:

	Weighted Average
Private colleges and universities	32.7%
Public universities	19.4%

What should the trustee's time commitment be? A national survey of 5,180 board members conducted in the late 1960s (Hartnett, 1969; Rauh, 1969) found that trustees were giving less than two hours per week to their positions on the board, devoting this time largely to board and committee meetings. The survey also shed some light on board involvement in giving or generating money. The large majority (78 percent) of the trustees spent twenty hours or less per year in fund raising. Only at the private universities did more than 5 percent of the trustees devote eighty hours or more per year to fund raising. And even at these institutions almost

70 percent of trustees spent only twenty hours or less, although 75 percent made a try at fund raising. Again, even at private universities and other selective institutions, less than 30 percent of the trustees felt that their efforts had generated more than $20,000 per year over the previous five years. It should be noted, however, that data for this survey were collected a decade ago, and it is generally believed that trustee participation in fund raising has increased considerably.

How much do trustees give? Rauh (1969) asked how much the trustees themselves had contributed over a five-year period: "Except for the private universities and the selective private institutions, the large majority of trustees contributed less than $2,000 per year" (p. 178). The survey noted that, while one might not be surprised to learn that trustees of public institutions had not contributed funds, findings indicated that trustee giving patterns at private colleges and public universities were not remarkably different. However, it is extremely important to note that in those fortunate institutions in which trustees do contribute, the impact can be impressive. For example, 2.8 percent of the trustees at private colleges and 3.6 percent at selective private colleges contributed over $1 million in five years (Rauh, 1969). But taken as a whole, the findings of the national survey indicated that, while a few trustees may make significant contributions of funds, most trustees do not participate to the degree usually thought.

Fund Raising

Learning the Basics of Fund Raising. One of the most important principles to accept is that fund raising is a long-term process. Fund raising has been compared to house painting: "Most of the work and some of the greatest challenges are in *preparing* to do the job, rather than the job itself" (Schneiter, 1978, p. 33). The institution that hopes to attract large gifts, especially from individuals, should keep in mind that substantial advanced planning and months, even years, of cultivation are often necessary. Prospects are not inclined to give until they are positive that a given cause is a sound philanthropic investment. This knowledge can only be secured in a long-term relationship.

Here are some commonly accepted truisms among college fund raisers:

1. Effective fund raising in any institution requires long-range planning, solid institutional commitment, and adequate budget, talented leadership, enthusiastic volunteers, skillful management, and teamwork.

2. Educational fund raising must begin at home. Trustee contributions set an example for potential donors. The best solicitor is one who has already contributed. Thus, the best way to obtain a large donation is to place the solicitation in the hands of persons who have already made large gifts themselves.

3. The most effective technique is to approach a potential donor one on one, "eyeball to eyeball."

4. Many people (alumni, foundations, corporations) do not give simply because they are not asked.

5. When in doubt about priorities, focus on the large gift. Most institutions have many "large gift" prospects. In fact, *90 percent of the money donated to higher education comes from 10 percent of the donors.* This all-important segment, the large-gift prospects, must be identified, cultivated, and approached. The approach, of course, must be made with a proper knowledge of timing and strategy. The approach must fit both the individual and the overall fund-raising program. Board members can help the president and the development staff by accompanying them on calls and by making unaccompanied calls on their acquaintances and business associates.

6. The secret of success in any fund-raising program is an urgent need that is well understood and effectively communicated.

7. A college or university must have visibility with its constituencies. As mentioned earlier, the institution must obtain understanding before it can win support.

8. Donors respond to urgent needs and are less likely to give to those projects or facilities that are in the category of "It would be nice to have a _____ (fill in the blank)."

9. The strongest appeal to motivate alumni is pride in the institution.

10. The most neglected constituency of many colleges is the so-

called friends category, which includes neighbors, parents of students, and others who have benefited from the college's programs.

Articulating the Case for Support. Why is money needed? What are the institution's problems? The "case statement" is the institution's statement of need, its argument for support, its plan of action, its source of inspiration. The most quoted person in the fund-raising field, Harold J. Seymour, author of *Designs for Fund Raising* (1966), recommends that the case for fund raising "should aim high, provide perspective, arouse a sense of history and continuity, convey a feeling of importance, relevance, and urgency, and have whatever stuff is needed to warm the heart and stir the mind" (p. 43).

Veteran fund raiser David M. Church offered this advice about the building of the case statement (Radock, 1978). First, state the problem. Then answer these questions:

1. What is being done about the problem?
2. What needs to be done about it?
3. What does your case statement propose to do about it?
4. How is your case statement fitted to attack the problem?
5. What are the costs of your program?
6. What can your audience do about it?

It is essential in preparing the institutional case statement to seek the counsel and assistance of other members of the community—administrators, faculty members, students, alumni, and friends. Those who will be involved in the campaign also need to be involved in determining the definition and design of the case for support. Case statements are essential elements of the development process because writing and drafting helps hone ideas. Both readers and framers of the statement obtain a better understanding of what the program is, why it should be supported, and by whom. Persons who prepare campaign case statements and proposals will find Kohr's *Checklist of Institutional Data* (1977b) helpful. It includes a list of institutional data that should be kept current.

Agreeing on the Role of the Capital Campaign. Capital campaigns are a "hot item" in American higher education today. The *Chronicle of Higher Education* recently listed more than 100 campaigns for $10 million or more that were under way in American colleges and universities ("Fund Raising . . . ," 1978). Many of them are succeeding. More than $700 million was contributed in 1977 in campaigns for $10 million or more. Yet some institutions set their goals too high. In 1978 at least two major universities with giant-sized goals ended their capital campaigns considerably short of the mark. The decision to engage in a campaign obviously must be made with care.

What can the intensive capital campaign do? It is only one tool in a well-balanced development program, but it provides some opportunities that simply do not exist in the ongoing program. Trustees should heed the well-known axiom that an organized, efficient capital campaign is the very best fund-raising method because it produces money fast and at a relatively low cost. For one thing, donors will often give extra funds to a capital campaign. For another, volunteer leaders will often accept assignments with preestablished time limits whereas they may shy away from permanent assignments. Deadlines and a predetermined schedule force a sense of urgency that serves to motivate action. Furthermore, the capital campaign can buttress other forms of fund raising. Almost invariably it increases the flow of annual support and uncovers new possibilities for deferred giving. The well-conceived capital campaign creates opportunities for participation and engenders community enthusiasm and support. A successful campaign usually establishes a new, higher plateau of voluntary support.

A capital campaign is like an all-campus x ray, revealing weaknesses in the organization of the institution but, one hopes, confirming the strength of its basic structure. A capital campaign is attention getting, like a giant spotlight focused on the university. The institution is on stage, the moment has come for it to do its thing, and everyone will know whether it succeeds or fails.

It is highly desirable to have certain conditions present when conducting a capital campaign:

- The institution must have valid needs that will stand up to examination and scrutiny.

- The institution must have a dedicated and committed group of leaders, especially trustees, who will contribute both prestige and funds to the institution.
- The institution must have an informed and cultivated constituency.
- The institution must have a reasonably good reputation among its potential donors, including alumni.
- The general economy must be reasonably sound whenever such funds are to be sought.

A feasibility study is often essential to the success of a capital campaign. Such a study can determine whether a community is ready to support a campaign. A careful, objective study by a consulting firm can reveal reactions, attitudes, and intentions of potential contributors. In-depth interviews within selected constituencies can result in incisive, valuable recommendations about awareness, interests, timing, potential pitfalls, leadership availability, and realistic financial goals.

Knowing When To Use Counsel. When are outside professionals needed? What do they do? How are they paid? What criteria should be used in choosing a firm? Seymour (1966) offers this advice:

- The function of the professional firm is not to raise the money but to help the institution raise it.
- One of the most important characteristics to look for in choosing a firm is candor, and assurance that the firm will be straightforward in its advice.
- Better firms are more likely to help train the institution's own personnel and to leave behind them a sound and workable blueprint for the future.
- All firms worth obtaining services from are paid a fee, never a percentage. Their charges are based on the number of personnel assigned, the duration of the service, and the out-of-pocket expenses involved.

Most consultants are employed for a given time period at a flat annual retainer, plus traveling expenses. Three to five years is the normal period for a contract. "In most cases, the cost to the institution is about that of the salary of one full professor. . . . Expenses for reputable campaigns, including retainer fees, and varying with institutional types, constituencies, and goals, are known to range from about 3 percent to 17 percent. The average cost will be around 5 or 6 percent" (Bremer, 1965, p. 32).

Where do you look for counsel? The annual directory issued by the Council for Advancement and Support of Education includes in its list of associate members the names of a number of firms. Firms that are members of the American Association of Fund-Raising Counsel (AAFRC) are usually reliable organizations because they had to meet ethical and business standards to gain membership. Lists of AAFRC member firms may be obtained from the organization's New York office.

Building a Reporting System. Trustees cannot be effective members of the fund-raising team if they do not receive regular reports of progress. Trustees should insist that a systematic reporting system be set up to show various members of the team how their particular tasks fit into the big picture and how the work of other team members affects their own. Trustees should regularly feed data into the system as well as receive information from it.

Information needed by board members for obtaining resources is mainly conveyed through oral messages, routine documents, responses to inquiries, analyses, and other forms that collectively may be called reports. Typically, trustees will keep their eyes on the long-range perspective. Board members usually prefer summaries that highlight key items (such as ratios, cost variances, trends). There will always be a need for reports triggered by specific events, but the chief advancement officer or other specified person should be expected to provide a systematic flow of reports throughout the year.

Careful thought should be given to the nature, content, and frequency of reports. If the reporting system is left to chance, it will produce a flood of data in some areas and a dearth of information in others. Key tasks are the production of reports on a scheduled basis and the assignment of responsibility for aggregation and synthesis of data especially appropriate for trustees. At a minimum the chief institutional advancement officer should submit monthly status reports. Graphic reports are helpful because they condense significant trends.

At the University of Michigan one technique employed for periodic updates is the "pyramid of giving" (see Figure 2). In use since 1974, the pyramid shows how a broad base of participants is essential to building a pinnacle of benefactors at the $1 million level

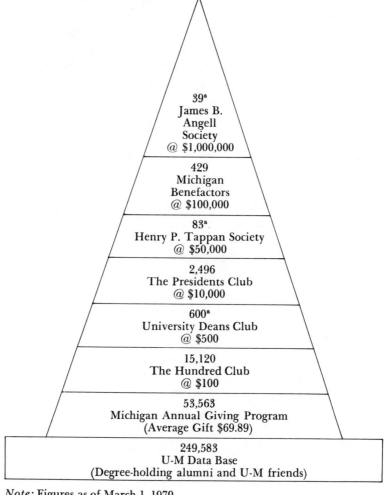

39[a]
James B.
Angell
Society
@ $1,000,000

429
Michigan
Benefactors
@ $100,000

83[a]
Henry P. Tappan Society
@ $50,000

2,496
The Presidents Club
@ $10,000

600[a]
University Deans Club
@ $500

15,120
The Hundred Club
@ $100

53,563
Michigan Annual Giving Program
(Average Gift $69.89)

249,583
U-M Data Base
(Degree-holding alumni and U-M friends)

Note: Figures as of March 1, 1979.
[a]Programs established in 1978.

Figure 2. The University of Michigan Fund-Raising Pyramid

and also illustrates the value of a system of upgrading donor contributions by an incentive and recognition program.

Encouraging Fund-Raising Research and Analysis. People making decisions about the future of resource procurement should elevate the priority of, and the dollar commitment to, research and analysis. Trustees and administrators must know more about their potential revenue-generating publics. Thus, research and analysis, from marketing studies to demographic analyses, can be viewed as a wise investment in protecting present revenue sources, developing new sources, and incorporating change and improvement in a systematic manner.

It is absolutely essential to assemble information to help evaluate the giving patterns of individuals, foundations, and corporations and to relate them to the cause of the institution. One of the main assignments for development offices is identifying "targets of opportunity." As mentioned earlier, 90 percent of the money in a fund-raising effort typically comes from 10 percent of the prospects. *About 85 percent of the "10 percent" group are individuals, as opposed to foundations and corporations.* Thus, one sees the extreme importance of carefully identifying, evaluating, and studying the characteristics and interests of major-level individual prospects. Research can make the difference between a $100 gift and a $100,000 gift.

One of our greatest needs is systematic research on motivation for giving. In order to complete a successful philanthropic exchange, the institution has to give something in return to the donor. This something can be appreciation, recognition, or the naming of a building, laboratory, or other facility after the donor. The fund raiser must become acquainted with the donor's needs if he or she is to help the donor achieve self-fulfillment through supporting institutional programs and projects that will also serve the needs of society. The trustee can help colleges and universities use resources to arrange a more meaningful, more profitable philanthropic exchange: dollars for good works.

Research findings can challenge old assumptions. For example, it is not safe to assume that taxes are a major consideration in giving. A nationwide study by the Survey Research Center at the University of Michigan (Morgan, Dye, and Hybels, 1977) showed that only at the $100,000-plus level do more than 50 percent of the donors cite taxes as a major factor. Only one taxpayer in five knows, even roughly, how much in taxes each added dollar of deductions will save. Only twelve times in thousands of interviews did people offer tax reasons for changing their giving patterns. However, many respondents felt deductions were important to others. The Fund-Raising Institute reports that donors rate tax considerations as tenth or lower in priority (Schneiter, 1978).

Findings from the Survey Research Center study of American giving behavior and attitudes have numerous implications for fund-raising strategies:

- The level of giving goes up with the level of education; a college graduate gives four times as much as someone with only a grade school education.
- People with higher incomes give proportionately more money.
- Age also affects giving behavior. Younger persons (under thirty-five) tend to give less money than older persons with similar incomes. Average annual giving for those between eighteen and twenty-four was $60 compared to $742 for persons seventy-five or older.
- Persons fifty-five and older give substantially more than the average for their income level (about one third more).
- Americans aged seventy-five and older are the most active givers, contributing 87 percent more money for religious, charitable, and educational institutions than younger persons with similar incomes.

Determining the Role of the Foundation. College or university foundations are not an uncommon component of the advancement program. A foundation is defined as a nongovernmental, nonprofit organization having a principal fund of its own, managed by its own trustees or directors, and established to maintain or aid social, educational, charitable, religious, or other activities serving the common welfare. In some cases state regulations have specifically prohibited public institutions from soliciting or keeping private gifts. Thus, these institutions have turned to the foundation as a means of avoiding such restraints or being required to forward gift funds to the state treasury. In other instances the foundation was set up to raise money for special purposes, such as athletics or specialized institutes and centers, or to conduct real estate or other business enterprises.

Why establish a foundation? Alumni and friends are often suspicious of fund intermingling. They also fear that public agencies may be inclined to reduce public fund appropriations if private funds have been received. Some foundations exist as "flow-through" devices for the receipt, managing, and reporting of funds. In this situation, promotion and staff are elements of the institutional budget, but the foundation serves as a separate accounting system (Frantzreb, 1977, p. 138).

Careful examination of the foundation concept is a key element in its later failure or success. As Ottley (1978) explains:

> The prospect of establishing a foundation must first receive the endorsement of the trustees and the faculty. Trustees and faculty, therefore, need to be "educated" about the purpose and use of a college-related foundation. The sole purpose for the existence of a college-related foundation is for the benefit of that college. There is no other purpose. College trustees, therefore, have at least two responsibilities: to create it, and to dissolve it, should it no longer fulfill its purpose. College trustees must create the foundation with complete confidence and sanction; therefore, foundation directors must be selected with care since, once created, the board of directors of the foundation will act independently of the board of trustees of the college. Trustees, therefore, should have another responsibility: to ratify new additions to the board of directors. In this way, some assurance is provided to the college board that the foundation board will not become self-serving. Thus, the board of trustees has three responsibilities or controls over the board of directors of the foundation: to create it, to ratify new and additional members to the board, and to dissolve it (all, not part) should it no longer fulfill its purpose. [pp. VI-2].

Relating to the Institution's Publics

Maintaining Relationships With Assorted Publics. Key publics deserving board attention have been identified by Louis H. Heil-

bron (1973), former chairman of the board of the California State
College Trustees:

1. *General public.* Trustees should encourage faculty to bring leaders of business, professions, labor, and government to the institution at appropriate times in order to develop a better understanding between campus and community.
2. *Mass media.* Trustees should encourage the media to present a
   balanced view of higher education; they can suggest that media
   personnel go beyond the bizarre and dramatic event and report
   research and other undertakings in perspective. The cardinal
   rule is "Honesty is the best policy." Incomplete disclosure will
   make it difficult to build personal and institutional credibility.
3. *Alumni.* Trustees should seek to strengthen the ties of alumni to
   the institution. To this end the institution should keep the alumni
   informed of current achievements, research projects, student
   life, and problems on campus and should periodically bring the
   alumni back to the campus. Publications should be frank about
   unsolved problems (affirmative action, finances, enrollment,
   drugs) and indicate how the administration is dealing with
   them.
4. *Parents.* Trustees should encourage the orientation of parents to
   the campus. Campus contact should help parents obtain a clear
   idea of the institution's objectives and its impact on their sons
   and daughters.
5. *Federal government.* Trustees should seek from the federal government reasonably stable, long-term policies of financial aid to
   assure educational opportunity to students and to ease the financial burden of their institution.
6. *Legislators, public officials.* An important function of boards of
   public institutions is requesting funds from the budget office,
   the governor, and the legislature. Trustees should work closely
   with the president in these activities. Once the institution's needs
   have been determined, the board should fight for them. Trustees should maintain continuing liaison with legislative and public officials.

Governmental Relations

Participating in the Institution's Governmental Relations Plan.
Since more than half of the funds obtained by the nation's institutions of higher learning come from federal, state, and local government, the trustee needs to keep in touch with developments in government. The need for trustees to monitor and influence policies at the federal level is examined in Chapter One; state and local considerations will be the focus here.

Political structures and processes differ substantially from state to state. Variations exist in higher education systems, legislative makeup, and state constitutional and statutory provisions that affect lobbying. Thus, one must exercise caution in discussing legislative relations across states. In general, however, it is clear that although most colleges and universities long have regarded political involvement as uncomfortable and inappropriate, they can no longer afford the luxury of standing aloof from the political arena. No longer does higher education find itself in a favored role in competition for the scarce state tax dollar. Governors, legislatures, and taxpayers are demanding greater accountability, forcing institutions to reexamine and improve their programs to achieve understanding and support. Determining effective strategies demands careful thought. Which representatives of the institution are most effective in informing and influencing which people and which methods work best?

"Reaching the legislature" may be a simple phrase but it is a complex assignment. Determine target persons and groups—the governor, the governor's staff, state budget offices, state coordinating and governing boards, state-level education interest groups, and local governing bodies. Legislators can be divided into significant classifications, such as: (1) legislators representing the geographical area within which the institution is located, (2) those who are alumni, (3) legislators representing the area served by the institution in terms of student enrollment and public services, (4) those interested in education in general and in higher education in particular, (5) legislators who serve on appropriations, finance, and education committees, (6) those with sons, daughters, or other close relatives currently enrolled, and (7) newly-elected legislators. Legislative turnover each election ranges between 25 and 50 per cent in most states, offering recurring challenges to keep up with the changing interplay of personalities, issues, and influences.

In a number of states, governing boards have held conferences in advance of legislative sessions to call attention to the needs and achievements of higher education. Although sometimes an institution finds it necessary to "go it alone," most observers advocate a unified approach among institutions of like interest. Trustees can be of immeasurable assistance in promoting such unity of purpose.

Grass roots campaigns, involving wide-ranging interactions with alumni, the general public, community leaders, and others, have been carried out successfully in various states. Examples of interinstitutional cooperation are the award-winning programs in Alabama, Florida, and North Dakota. The unified effort by Auburn University and the University of Alabama in 1963 helped obtain an increase of 21.6 per cent in state appropriations (American College Public Relations Association, 1964). Florida's state universities and public junior colleges combined to generate broad public support through the Higher Education Legislative Program (HELP) (American College Public Relations Association, 1965). Nine state-assisted institutions in North Dakota employed a wide variety of mass media and interpersonal communication in a legislative relations campaign, Working In Support of Education (WISE) (Jacobson, 1967). In an effort to counter shrinking state appropriations for higher education, the University of Michigan launched the Michigan Awareness Program in 1978 (Yoder and May, forthcoming). Citizen testimony at public budget hearings has been a key element in the "direct-to-the-people program," developing interest in and support for the community college budget of Montgomery College in Maryland (Froeschle, 1972).

How can the trustee be effective in governmental relations? A university official experienced in the legislative process offers the following tips to trustees in working with state legislatures (Crawford, 1975):

1. Besides stocking up on general information about the institution's operations, needs and accomplishments, acquaint your-

self with its philosophy of education. A specific mission may require special data. Be well informed.

2. Identify contacts that best serve the purpose of the effort. Often the focus will be a personal acquaintance or legislative leader, such as the heads of selected committees.

3. Refrain from efforts that are not part of a coordinated program directed by the president of the institution. Once having accepted the responsibility of trusteeship, it is vital that the individual trustee support the policy approved by the entire board.

4. Think carefully about the setting (home district or the capital) and the time (in session, recess) for making contact. Relationships built over a long period of time before the legislature meets are extremely valuable. One must keep working at legislative relations year after year. Legislators have more time available when not in session.

5. Know how government works. Many trustees are out of touch with political reality.

6. Develop an awareness of the written and unwritten rules of the legislature, its crosscurrents and realities, its moods and prospects.

7. Emphasize person-to-person communication. Subtle personal contacts contribute to a valuable network of mutual trust and respect.

8. Beware of impugning the men and women involved in politics as basely motivated, opportunistic, or intellectually inferior. Recognize that allocative decisions are difficult and that America's political process requires pragmatic accommodation among competing interests and objectives.

9. Do not bristle when higher education is referred to as a "special interest" or you are called a "lobbyist." Many people consider education a special interest. Lobbying is an essential function in dealing with government.

10. Do not hesitate to extend your efforts to other groups that may contribute light and weight to the legislative process. Examples are the legislator's constituents, editors, and broadcasters.

11. Remember the simple but important grace of saying "thank you" when the mission is accomplished.

One more rule: Keep in mind that it is ill-advised and counterproductive to denigrate other institutions.

The trustee who desires to increase his or her effectiveness in governmental relations needs to keep abreast of the changing nature of state legislatures. "Reapportionment has brought to the Capitol more urban legislators, younger and better educated, but because they have somewhat higher turnover, they tend to occupy fewer leadership positions. . . . Most legislatures meet annually now, and committees are much more active, holding hearings and considering legislation on a year-around basis. Legislators, too, have expanded the staff serving them. Indeed, the whole operation has become more formal, more professional" (Folger, 1976, p. 159).

Many observers feel that the legislative process increasingly relies on analysis rather than rhetoric. The age of accountability, accompanied by the growth of complex problems and legislative staffs, means that the silvery tongues of college presidents have lost some of their effectiveness in legislative halls. U.S. Congressman John Brademas of Indiana has observed (1971), "What we need from the higher education community is more information and less persuasion." Peter Magrath, president of the University of Minnesota, said recently, "I really think our case depends on reason and facts. A lot of higher education issues aren't partisan issues. We need to have friends on both sides of the aisle" (Fields, 1979).

What is the outlook for the years ahead? As competition for resources becomes more severe, higher education representatives are likely to adopt a more and more assertive, if not downright aggressive, political role. "Although associations of institutions are not as prominent in the state lobbying arena as in Washington, they are becoming more active and effective in state capitals. . . . Private colleges have formed state organizations that in many cases have lobbied extensively and successfully for years. Their primary purpose is to gain state financial support for their member colleges, preferably in the form of direct grant assistance" (Gove and Carpenter, 1977, p. 369). Its official legal status and large number of member institutions help make the Commission on Independent Colleges and Universities an influential force in New York. When it comes to legislative advocacy, the Illinois Community College Trust-

ees Association is unique. Since at least one community college
district is included within the boundaries of every legislative district
in the state, and several legislative districts contain parts of more
than one community college district, these Illinois colleges can call
upon every legislator's obligation to represent the people and institutions in his or her district. "Effective contact can be made by
the local trustees across the state in a pattern coordinated by the
association's central office in Springfield" (Gove and Carpenter,
1977, p. 370).

Governing boards will be watching closely for infringements
on institutional policy-making territory. Future actions of not only
legislatures but student lobbies, faculty unions, and the courts can
leave a considerable mark upon governance. Thus, the conscientious trustee not only needs to help build understanding and consensus for the institution's interests but also to monitor government
trends. One trend meriting attention is the wave of state laws reg-
ulating charitable contributions. The American Association of
Fund-Raising Counsel (AAFRC) reported in 1978 that 35 states
had enacted legislation governing charitable solicitations and administration, compared to only 15 states with such laws a few years
earlier. In a two-year period AAFRC looked at more than 530 state
bills which proposed to regulate charities in one way or another.

The trustee can also perform a beneficial service by simply
listening carefully to what people are saying. A Maryland legislator
offered the gentle reminder that "The response you get from legislators will be conditioned by the attitude you bring to the relationship. . . . Remember that legislators are people. They will respond
to helpful, knowledgeable assistance. . . . Failure to keep in mind
the objectives and needs of your legislators will only damage your
relationship with them" (Blount, 1976, p. 17). Legislators hear all
kinds of witnesses in endless hours of testimony. They appreciate
people who can supply facts in support of a position, who condense
information in meaningful fashion, and who respect the time constraints of busy lawmakers. Sometimes administrators on the campus are too involved in the details of daily activity to perceive significant trends. A survey of gubernatorial opinion of higher education
in 1977 found "little reason to believe that the governors and state
legislators will lift the austerity imposed by recent years of reces-

sion" (Budig, 1977, p. 373). Significantly, only eight of the thirty-five governors thought that public higher education in the United States has been unfairly treated in respect to financial support. More than one third of the governors believed that public colleges and universities are overbuilt in academic programs and capital outlay. Only eight governors indicated that public higher education could expect significant increases in state support. Trustees can be of immeasurable value to campus leaders by examining social and economic conditions and then determining the appropriate aspiration level for the institution's resource procurement.

Evaluating the Fund-Raising Program

One of the obligations of the board is to evaluate the quality of the institution's administration and the degree of progress toward goals in the many areas of teaching, research, and service. Evaluators have long lamented the difficulty in measuring intellectual accomplishment and academic endeavor. However, the fund-raising area is perhaps more measureable in terms of production and performance than are many other spheres of university activity. It is true that the measurement of cost effectiveness, cost benefit, and performance in educational fund raising and institutional advancement is still not highly sophisticated, but progress is being made in improving this shortage of procedures and instruments.

A model for financial reporting of fund-raising activities has been advanced by the Institute for Continuing Education of the National Society of Fund Raisers (Smallwood and Levis, 1977). Twenty-five colleges and universities, located primarily in the Northeast, compared private gift support profiles, capital campaign experiences, and annual fund results through a survey known as "the COFHE study," with COFHE standing for Consortium on Financing Higher Education (Ramsden, 1977). Varied approaches to program evaluation in development, public relations, and alumni affairs are being used at colleges and universities across the nation (Jacobson, 1978–79).

The many variables that feed into fund raising make evaluation difficult. One way to proceed is to contrast one institution's performance against that of other, similar institutions. This is usually difficult, since standardized bases of comparability are not easy to achieve. But while work on such standardization is moving forward, the individual institution can compare its current performance with its own track record in previous years. Here are examples of indicators proposed by the Fund-Raising Institute and the Council for Advancement and Support of Education:

- Dollars of gift income received each year.
- Dollars raised for each dollar expended for institutional advancement.
- Dollars raised per staff development officer.
- Institutional advancement costs as a portion of the institution's budget.
- Dollars raised as a portion of the institution's budget.
- Total number of donors for each of the past five years.
- The average size of gifts received over the past five years.
- Number of volunteers working in the development program each year.
- Number of prospects visited.
- Number of decisions made about a gift, and the percentage saying yes.
- Independent appraisal of the quality of supporting materials prepared for workers and prospects.
- Analysis of gifts by type of donor, in terms of total dollars and quantity.
- Analysis of gifts in terms of number of dollars and type of donor.

One of the most difficult areas to assess is the "acquisition stage," that is, precommitment activities such as list building and constituency building. Acquisition efforts are investments intended to create "assets" that will produce net revenue in the future. The purpose of these activities is *donor* raising or *friend* raising rather than *fund* raising. "If revenues exceed expenses, the net revenue is almost incidental to the acquisition of new friends who will provide increasing financial support year after year" (Smallwood and Levis, 1977, p. 15).

The trustee who wishes to examine funding trends and compare levels and categories of voluntary support for hundreds of institutions will find detailed information in reports published annually by the Council for Financial Aid to Education. Trustees wishing to monitor patterns of state tax funds devoted to higher education will find annual analyses in the *Chronicle of Higher Education* (for example, Coughlin, 1978), based primarily on data compiled by M. M. Chambers, a professor at Illinois State University. Other bases of comparison for resource procurement efforts are "rules of thumb" or best professional judgments offered by seasoned leaders in the field. Some examples:

1. Reasonable costs refer to the generally accepted figures for various fund-raising activities: "Acquisition of annual fund donors may cost one dollar or somewhat more per dollar raised; annual donor renewal through direct mail and personal solicitation usually costs about twenty cents per dollar; fund raising for special events, fifty cents per dollar; capital campaigns, life income (deferred giving) and bequest programs, ten cents per dollar" (Smallwood, 1979, p. 18).

2. "Fund raisers sometimes puzzle over how much to spend on thank-you activities [for private gifts]. National practice suggests 1.5 percent to 3 percent of the contribution. For example, a $10,000 gift would suggest a $150 to $350 expenditure" (Schneiter, 1978, p. 109). Thank-you activities can range from a recognition dinner for a major donor to plaques or personal visits for donors at lower levels.

3. "Direct mail is the least effective fund-raising solicitation technique. In fact, if five percent of the prospects you solicit by direct mail respond with a contribution, you're doing exceptionally well" (Schneiter, 1978, p. 66).

4. A rule of thumb for quotas in capital campaigns is the so-called rule of three: "About one third of the money has to come from the top ten gifts, another third from the next 100 gifts, and the last third from all other gifts" (Seymour, 1966, p. 50).

One of the most valuable services board members can perform is to take a reading of the current situation at their particular institution. Diagnostic information can be obtained by the use of two checklists. The first is a personal checklist, which alerts board members to their responsibilities in resource acquisition and points to potential problems in the organization of the campaign team.

The Fund-Raising Audit: A Personal Checklist for Trustees

1. Do you have a written statement that defines your personal role in the fund-raising effort?
2. Are you convinced that the institution does indeed need private dollars?
3. Do you give your support to providing the budget necessary for a good fund-raising program?
4. Are you "on the lookout" for possible sources of private support?
5. If the institution has a major campaign, are you willing to give leadership in the effort?
6. Are you willing to make a gift commensurate with your ability?
7. Are you positive in your own mind that the cause merits your support and the support of others?
8. Are you willing to use your influence to establish priorities for the institution?
9. Are you willing to support the president and/or executive officers when certain policies are needed to ensure the smooth operation of fund raising (for example, guidelines for fund-raising and capital campaigns)?
10. Are you prepared to authorize or assist in feasibility and planning studies?
11. Are you willing to discuss openly with institutional leaders points of difference or misunderstandings?
12. Do you assist in enlisting top volunteer leadership for your institution's development program?

The second is an institutional checklist. It comes into play after the board member has obtained a clear picture of his or her personal commitment. The second checklist provides questions that help define the college or university in the board member's mind, clarifying both the need for funds and the strategies for raising them. Individual institutions will benefit by adapting both lists to their circumstances.

The Fund-Raising Audit: An Institutional Checklist

1. Does your institution have a procedure for devising institutional priorities?

2. Has your institution determined the placement of fund raising among its priorities?

3. Has your institution made a commitment to "big dollar" fund raising rather than "nickel and dime" fund raising?

4. Has your institution made an analysis of the programs and projects that possess greatest potential for attracting funds?

5. Does your institution have a long-range plan spelling out purpose and direction for the next five or ten years?

6. Is your institution able to supply documentation, project descriptions, approximate costs, and other background on specific programs and projects?

7. Does your institution have an estimate of the total amount of money needed and a breakdown of proposed sources (foundations, corporations, and so forth)?

8. Does your institution have a coordinated approach to public relations and development?

9. Does your institution provide adequate funding for the conduct of public relations and development programs and activities?

10. Does your institution have a plan for interpreting the fund-raising process to the institutional family, whose understanding and cooperation are essential?

11. Does your institution keep trustees advised and informed through news reports, informational materials, and a public relations program?

12. Does your institution maintain adequate and up-to-date alumni and gift records?

13. Has your institution incorporated meaningful personal touches in the acknowledgment of gifts?

14. Does your institution periodically compare itself with peer institutions in the scope and effectiveness of its fund-raising efforts?

Preparing for the Major Issues. Provision of relevant information as a preliminary to decision making is a sound policy, even though difficult to achieve. In order to make intelligent decisions, the board member must keep informed not only about the purposes and accomplishments of the institution but also about its needs and future projections. The long-range plan should consider sociological, economic, political, and technological trends that contribute to the fund-raising environment, as well as estimates of sources for future income. Issues to be faced include:

Government Intervention. At the federal level, there is the entire domain of tax incentives and attitude toward philanthropy. At the state and city level, an array of confusing restrictions shows that the lifeblood of private donor prospecting and growth can be legislated away.

Diversified Board. Claims have been made that the obtaining of resources will suffer from efforts to develop boards with representation from nontraditional segments of the community served. Such claims do not always seem justified. The appointment of women, minorities, and others who have rarely or never held positions as trustees generates a new mix of skills, talents, and contacts that provides opportunities for broad representation and involvement, as has been demonstrated by government, corporations, and such nonprofit organizations as art museums and health agencies. The substantial promise of diversity is that it adds a valuable dimension of depth and experience.

Legislative "Offset." For public institutions, there is the danger of legislative offset. If there is no clear legislative policy supporting the principle of special private funding for public institutions, the legislature may tend to count the income, if not the principal, of private funding as a resource to be deducted in arriving at net appropriations. Such a situation makes solicitation efforts self-defeating. Public institutions that think voluntary support may result in "offset" or "deduct" in the legislative appropriations process may wish to consider a course similar to that taken in North Carolina. A state law concerning endowment funds for constituent institutions of the University of North Carolina states that "it is not the intent . . . that the proceeds from any endowment fund shall take the place of State appropriations or any part thereof, but . . . shall supplement the State appropriations to the end that the institution may improve and increase its functions, may enlarge its areas of service, and may become more useful to a greater number of people" (North Carolina General Statutes, sec. 116–36[b], p. 520).

Ethics of Obtaining Funds. Calling attention to problems inherent in a college's search for money, the *Christian Science Monitor* examined the topic in "Academia for Sale" (Parsons, 1979). The analysis raised the questions: Is the giver or the receiver "getting" the most? Are gifts sometimes tied to admissions? Does acceptance of funds from a foreign government to endow a professorship threaten academic integrity? Which gifts should be refused?

Stock divestiture has also grown as an issue. In the spring of 1977 nearly 300 students were arrested at Stanford University during a sit-in protesting the institution's holdings in companies that do business in South Africa. Since that time student activists have repeatedly confronted trustees over similar questions. Divestiture issues and related "strings attached" allegations are likely to continue to pose moral conundrums with financial and political repercussions.

Financial transactions of institutions and individual board members will no doubt come under increased scrutiny. Reminders of situations to be avoided are presented in a study of new college presidents by Kauffman (1977). The study, which found presidents keenly disappointed in board members' lack of knowledge and candor about the financial conditions of their institutions, reported at least one instance in which a president felt she had been misled by the board. She was bitter because the board "misrepresented a $7 million fund-raising campaign" and because she felt "many trustees use the college to lower their taxes by giving gifts-in-kind" as tax write-offs that burdened the college rather than helping it (pp. 148–149).

Lack of Professionalism. Some people decry the lack of professionalism in educational fund raising. In a recent survey of college fund raisers and consultants, one respondent said: "To put it bluntly, I doubt that more than 25 percent of the 'development officers' in higher education, or indeed in all the rest of philanthropic services, are really qualified for the positions they hold" (Radock, 1978). Others deplore the proliferation of would-be fund raisers and moonlighters, the high staff turnover, the lack of continuity, and the dearth of programs to encourage participation by more women and minorities. Effective deployment of resources presupposes an able and professional staff. The immaturity of the profession is distressing to many. Too many fund raisers rely disproportionately upon emotional allegiances, and far too few approach their work systematically, analytically, creatively, and according to high professional standards.

Think Big. Good advice to the board member is to "think big." The trustee possesses enormous influence as an activist for excellence. The trustee's twofold responsibility as both "custodian" and "builder" is extremely important. The first role calls for holding in trust the properties and good name of the institution, the second for helping to build a better educational institution. The trustee must try to be a "seer" as well as an "overseer."

The trustee should avoid preoccupation with the exercise of control, refrain from intervention in institutional affairs, and concentrate on more far-reaching endeavors. An oft-repeated phrase in the fund-raising field is "Encourage toward boldness." Although this quotation was first used in a Northwestern University campaign in 1923 and has been used by many other institutions since then, it has rarely if ever been surpassed. To be an educational statesman, one must have the courage to dream the impossible dream and to think the unthinkable idea. Optimism must be tempered with realism, but unexplored horizons beckon the trustee who accepts the invitation to think creatively about obtaining resources for higher education.

15

John W. Pocock

Reporting Finances

It is no news to any trustee or regent of an institution of higher education in America that the dollar seems to be at the root of most problems—or, at least, that it exerts a considerable influence on how problems are resolved. Nor would it surprise a trustee to learn that the governing board is seen by the constituencies of the institution and the public at large as the central body responsible for the acquisition, custody, and expenditure of dollars for the enhancement of the institution's programs. And, indeed, the board of trustees does carry ultimate financial responsibility, and there is simply no way for it to shirk this duty. So it has been ever since the first Harvard board gathered on the banks of the Charles River to plot the future of the fledgling college.

To the outburst of the provoked and frustrated trustee, "But dollars aren't everything," the only answer is, "Of course, dollars aren't everything, but. . . ." But, they do make possible those things that are embodied in the essential program of a college or university; wise expenditure can enhance the quality of the educational experience offered; prudent investment can assure the survival of the institution. The frustration of many trustees is that the window through which they must view the financial operations of their institution is often obscured and sometimes even distorted. That window is the series of reports on the financial affairs of the institution, and it is often obscured both by the accounting technicalities of the presentation and by the omission of indicators as to program relevance and priority. This matter of visibility is of critical importance to the individual trustee or regent and to the board as a whole.

There is a difference between reporting on finances and financial reporting on a program or programs. The family bankbook is a report on finances, and the household budget relates these finances to family needs and priorities. While the bankbook is a necessary item, this chapter for the most part looks beyond the bankbook to the health and progress of the programs it supports.

In all of this the dollar is the necessary common denominator and indicator. It is, first of all, an indicator of the basic financial health, the progress, and the future prospects of the institution. But since these dollars must be usefully employed to the advantage of the institution, their application can also provide an indicator as to the status of programs—the priorities, the achievements, the weaknesses, and the gaps. Better faculties tend to follow better salaries, but high average salaries may also indicate an aging teaching staff. More efficient buildings tend to require fewer maintenance dollars, but fewer maintenance dollars may also indicate poorly maintained buildings. Lower tuition dollars may attract more students but decrease the dollars available for unfunded scholarships for needy students. In such cases the dollar is by no means an absolute indicator of the direction that the institution is taking. But it is a clear indicator of an issue and so helps sharpen the trustee's questions.

Let it be noted that, in approaching decisions with financial implications, the trustee or regent is not the owner of the college or university (except in the narrow legal sense of many private institutions) but the steward overseeing the affairs of the institution on behalf of the benefiting constituencies and the public at large. The owner can accept self-penalizing errors in the use of his financial resources. The steward is not granted this luxury as readily by those he or she serves. And each trustee or regent, as a steward, carries this individual fiduciary responsibility.

How, then, shall the individual trustee or regent exercise his or her responsibility in an intelligent fashion and contribute to the group decisions of the board on financial matters? It seems clear, as a first requirement, that the system of financial reporting to the board—the window through which the trustee views the flow and use of dollars—must be adapted to the unique needs of the trustees. Among other things, this means developing reports that accommodate the financial aptitude and experience of individual trustees. The professional administrators and accountants charged with the detailed conduct of the institution's financial affairs have given too little consideration to this. True, there have been a number of attempts in recent years by individual institutions and by the accounting profession to simplify and improve the reporting apparatus. But these suggestions, which have generally moved in the right direction, have come from the professional side of the issue, and a considerable gap remains between the needs of the trustee and what he or she is actually receiving. Trustees and regents haven't helped much in trying to improve the situation. The recently issued monograph, *Financial Responsibilities of Governing Boards of Colleges and Universities* (1979), from a joint project of the Association of Governing Boards of Universities and Colleges (AGB) and the National Association of College and University Business Officers (NACUBO), is the first broad attack on the problem from the trustee's side.

One reason for the confusion is that board members are drawn from many walks of life to provide the variety of experience and concern necessary to group stewardship. With this diversity of background comes a wide range of financial understanding and appreciation. In addition, the part-time involvement of trustees means that the individual may not have enough time to delve into the technical intricacies of institutional accounting and so develop a capability to extract the information required for intelligent decision. This problem is not limited to those who have had little previous exposure to operating statements and balance sheets. The corporation comptroller, newly arrived on the board, may also be confused by the strange patterns of institutional accounting. Board members have often expressed to the author a sense of embarrassment in having to ask questions about financial practices that they do not understand. As a result of all this, many trustees simply defer to the apparent wisdom of a few financially astute fellow trustees and, in effect, give them their proxies in rendering financial decisions. But this is a distortion of stewardship. Group stewardship is based upon the individual responsibility of each trustee to participate meaningfully in the group decision. And the financial reporting system must be so designed that the intelligent but financially inexperienced trustee may confidently participate in group discussion and decision.

Problems in Understanding Financial Information

As an opening proposition, it should be stated that professional administrators, finance officers, and accountants have generally done a creditable job in setting up and maintaining financial and accounting systems. These systems are often complex and must serve a variety of clients, only one of whom is the trustee. The trick is to identify within the established sytem the information required by the board and to extract it without unduly disturbing the basic system. Excessive tampering with the basic system and overdevelopment of elegant subsystems to meet every whim of the board can inflate system costs with little tangible benefit to board decisions. Rest assured, the information desired is probably in the present system somewhere, and the financial officer can find a way of extracting it if the board will tell him or her what they want and why.

In a survey conducted in 1978, as a preliminary to the preparation of *Financial Responsibilities of Governing Boards of Colleges and Universities,* trustees and regents expressed their views on the shortcomings of current financial reporting to their boards. The respondents repeatedly identified four problem areas that obscured full understanding of financial matters and their impact on the programs of the institution.

First was the problem of consistency of content and figures in the various reports presented to boards. Often the reports had been prepared for other purposes or had been prepared without reconciling terminology and figures with companion reports. A typical example was a "report on current operations" that included under "revenue" the line item, "gifts to current operations," with a figure of $850,000. A companion report, submitted by the development office, also included a line item, "gifts to current operations," but the figure was $970,000. It was explained to trustees that the "report on current operations" was as of the close of December 31 and included only cash gifts. The "development report" included both cash and pledges, closed as of January 15, and a large cash gift had been received in the interim. The explanation was both logical and complete, but at what cost in trustee confusion and in implanting doubts as to the validity of information placed before them.

This was by no means an isolated occurrence, as similar stories testified. The lesson is that whatever financial reports are presented should be consistent in terminology and dollar figures. The information flow should move clearly and simply from one report to the next. A systems expert would call this a "coherent" system. The board should require the establishment of such a system to enable the trustees to quickly and easily absorb the basic financial picture without wasting time in explanation, correction, and interpretation.

The second problem identified by respondents has to do with the amount of information presented in reports to trustees. It was always too little or too much. There is no easy answer to this problem except to say that the amount of information needed by each board will be unique to that board's interests, problems, and legal requirements. Generally speaking, the trustee's or regent's needs for information are different from those of day-to-day administration. Simply passing on selected reports prepared for administrative purposes will rarely suffice. And what one board needs in great detail another board will gladly do without. The board of a small private college may require detailed information about the sources, restrictions, and timing of gifts. The board of a public community college may need details on purchases and contracts prior to giving approval. Only the board can say what financial information it needs and why. If these needs are not spelled out by the board, the odds are that the required information will not be forthcoming—at least not in the form desired. The board must first understand just what financial information it needs in order to have an adequate grasp of the big picture.

The third problem area cited by trustees and regents can be best summarized by noting that data are not necessarily information. As a personal aside, there are few things that irk the author more than opening a package containing three six-foot lengths of computer printout and a note saying, "This is the information you asked for." It is not information—it is data from which information must be extracted. If such questions as "what are our current scholarship costs, who gets the scholarships, what trends are visible, and what is our projection of scholarship obligations" are posed, the answers will not be found in the computer listing of all students on scholarship during the last three years with amount and source of funds, although the needed information can be derived from these data. Financial officers and administrators know this, but the offering of raw data in quantity is often the only way they have of responding to imprecise requests for information. Again, it is up to the board to be sufficiently precise in requests for information so that the administrator can carry on with the task of extraction, analysis, and interpretation and thus provide information.

The fourth problem area has to do with the presentation of reports. If the objective of a report is to enable the trustee to quickly grasp the significance of the figures and the story they tell, many institutions have a bit of tidying up to do. At any rate, the trustee should look for the following characteristics:

- *Summarization*—the elimination of unimportant details and the use of aggregation to focus attention on the significant figures that really tell the story.
- *Comparison*—historical actuals (last year's figures, average of last three years), what was expected to happen (budget, cash flow plan), and what is now expected (projection based upon current trends and outlook).
- *Coherency*—consistent linkage of terms and figures between one report and parallel or supporting reports.
- *Explanatory notes*—short statements as to reason for significant variances or comments on probable upcoming shifts not yet apparent in the current figures.

Whatever the inadequacies of presentation as perceived by the board, it is up to the board to so advise the administrators and work jointly to correct the situation. If this is not done, trustee understanding and grasp of financial matters will continue to face an unnecessary impediment.

Fiduciary Versus Management Reporting

To the new trustee or regent, and indeed to many who are more experienced, there is no more formidable obstacle to the understanding of the institution's financial affairs than the practice of "fund accounting." Yet every trustee should have some insight into the basic tenets of fund accounting if he or she is not to be repeatedly diverted by some of the seeming idiosyncrasies in financial reports. The concepts of fund accounting are relatively simple. The procedural mechanics are more complex but can be left to the accountant.

The concepts of fund accounting stem directly from the stewardship or fiduciary role of trustees; that is, from their responsibility to hold in trust for the benefit of others those funds and assets that come to the institution. Donors and legislatures specify the uses to which their funds are to be put, and it is the obligation of the trustee to see that these directions (restrictions) are honored. Incoming funds are, therefore, aggregated into classifications according to purpose. These aggregations include the plant fund, the loan fund, the endowment fund, and the annuity fund, as well as the current fund, which, along with those funds designated for current operations, also receives all funds to which no restrictions are attached. Each fund receives its own uniquely designated funds and holds and expends them for their stated purposes. Through this structure of funds the board is able to watch over and control the use of funds for the specified purposes and to certify their stewardship. The annual audit report, prepared by outside auditors, is largely devoted to such stewardship certification.

At least three other matters pertinent to fund accounting are of interest to trustees. First, the board can make transfers between funds as long as legal obligations and restrictions are observed. Excess dollars not required for current operations, for instance, can be transferred from the current fund to the plant fund to provide for future repairs and major improvements, to the endowment fund as a trustee-designated endowment, or to other funds for appropriate use. Likewise, the board can reverse the flow and, for example, return the trustee-designated endowment from the endowment fund to the current fund in time of need. All such board-designated transfers should be reviewed as to purpose and financial and program impact and should be formally approved by the board.

Second, fund accounting distinguishes between unrestricted and restricted funds. Restricted funds are those that carry a clear legal donor restriction or a legislative designation—that is, an externally imposed restriction as opposed to internal designation by the board. Both restricted and unrestricted funds can be found in any of the primary funds. The current funds may include gifts restricted to scholarships as well as unrestricted tuition. The plant fund may include board-designated improvement reserves as well as funds restricted by the donor to the construction of, say, a music building. In aggregate, unrestricted funds, located in whatever primary fund, represent the board's financial flexibility since it can redesignate these unrestricted funds to higher-priority needs as circumstances change. The board should follow the status of both unrestricted and restricted funds.

Third, fund accounting identifies expendable and nonexpendable funds in terms of current availability. Unrestricted funds are generally currently expendable. But restricted funds may vary in terms of current expendability. A gift restricted to scholarships may be totally expendable during the current year. But a restricted foundation grant for faculty development over a four-year period may be only partially expendable during the current year. Thus, the expendability of funds is a further measure of financial flexibility, and a periodic report on the status of expendable funds can be most useful to the board.

Notwithstanding the value and necessity for fund accounting, the board, as overseer of management, has need for additional financial reports, distinct from those required to support its fiduciary role. Fund accounting is a financial inventory device that tells how many assets are in each bin and what comes in and goes out of each bin. For operating purposes a more dynamic reporting mechanism is required that will enable the trustee to follow clearly the flow of all incoming resources through allocation and expenditure in the ongoing programs of the institution and to preserve whatever resources remain. For want of a better term, this may be called "management accounting."

Essentially we are talking about preparation of something akin to the corporate operating statement or profit and loss statement. Some accountants might point out that this same information can be derived from the fund presentations and that the current fund statement gives much of this management information. This is true, but such information can be interpreted only by the trustee well versed in and at home with the mechanics of fund accounting and willing to take the time to make the conversions required. Management accounting and fund accounting use the same input data and should be completely reconcilable. But they differ in their manner of aggregation and presentation of figures.

The traditional objection continues to be raised (although less often in these days of financial stringencies) that the college or university is not a profit-making institution and that a profit and loss statement is not in keeping with its mission. Philosophically, this is an interesting argument, but to most trustees and regents it is at least of moderate importance to see that the money spent is in reasonable balance with the money received. There is a bottom line, call it what you will. Nevertheless, management accounting reports have been slow to develop in institutions of higher learning, and this omission has considerably inhibited trustee understanding of the financial dynamics of their institutions. It has been left to the trustees and regents, supported by a small but stalwart band of professional accountants and finance officers, to put this concept into action.

Again, the basic concept is simple. It is the flow-of-funds concept that in one way or another is present in the mind of every businessperson, homemaker, or ten-year-old on allowance: How much money am I taking in, how much am I spending, and why and how should I save what is left over? In translating this simple concept to the trustee's reporting needs, four steps are involved:

- Establishing the path of the flow of funds through the institution—from acquisition through expenditure to preservation.

- Relating the flow to specific functions and programs of the institution.
- Identifying the control or information points along the path of flow at which reports will be generated for trustee information.
- Providing means for trustees to inject policy decisions on allocations or priorities to correct or improve use of the flowing funds.

To state that such a reporting structure also benefits the administrator and the financial officer is to state the obvious. Some administrators have already begun to provide this type of financial report to their boards. Finance officers participating in the AGB/NACUBO project mentioned earlier were highly supportive of the model reporting system developed. It is up to trustees and regents to further speed the adoption of these concepts.

Acquiring Funds

The board is basically a policy-making body; thus, financial reports to the board should focus on information pertinent to policy issues. But policy has its financial outcomes, and certain financial outcomes may force a change in policy. The generation of income, as well as the underlying policy implications of this process, is an area often given far less attention by boards than is the spending of income. Yet financial health starts with acquisition of adequate funds to support the programs of the institution.

Colleges and universities rely on many sources for their financial support: students, government, private donors, investment income, and sale of services. Each source has its unique opportunities and limitations. This diversity of sources requires a continuing understanding by the board of the mix, trends, and causative factors at work, so that financial strategies and policies can be developed.

Student Tuition and Fees. These are the most important sources of income for most private institutions and are of growing importance to many public institutions. Torn between the desire to keep the tuition down and the need to balance the budget, the board must set the tuition figure. But there is more to establishing the tuition rate than simply making an intuitive stab at a figure somewhere between the two conflicting requirements. Historical precedents, political feasibility, competitive status with other institutions, and general economic conditions are all matters deserving consideration. While trends in these areas are not specifically part of a financial reporting structure, some understanding of them is useful to trustees before they make the financial decision implicit in setting tuition. It is highly advisable to have the administration prepare pertinent background material for board consideration as it prepares to take action. Beyond this there is specific, internal information that is highly relevant to the basic tuition figure—information on student aid and student retention.

Student Aid. This includes scholarships, grants, loans, and employment. Each has its unique financial implications. To simply agree that an increase in tuition will probably require some sort of parallel increase in student aid is not a real decision and can leave the board open to later, unpleasant surprises. The financial interactions between the basic tuition rate and the various forms of student aid that impact upon the net tuition income are not well understood by many trustees. To oversimplify: one group of students pays full tuition, while a second group receives a "discount" (in the form of a scholarship, grant, or other financial aid) that is provided by external sources, such as private donors or government, and so is not a cost to the institution; a third group (usually overlapping the second) receives a discount coming out of the institution's own funds—usually termed "unfunded scholarships." Clearly, the relative number of students in each of these three groups and the size of the tuition discounts are key factors in determining the net additional income resulting from a tuition increase. Furthermore, the student loan fund may have to be increased, and these dollars must come from somewhere. And if work credits are to be increased, the added dollars must show up on a payroll somewhere and are an added cost to the institution.

An important report for all trustees is the student aid report. This should include the number of students receiving financial aid and the type of aid, the source of such aid, and the impact of any change in student aid patterns on the financial requirements elsewhere in the institution. Increases in unfunded scholarships, the student loan fund, and student payroll frequently offset a larger share of tuition increases than is realized by many trustees. In any event, consideration of student aid policy and practice is a critically important factor in setting tuition, and trustees should have the necessary financial information to deal intelligently with the problem.

Information about student admissions and retention has less obvious financial relevance. The flow of students from application through admission to matriculation is followed by most boards, and past "yield" ratios are available for comparison. Financial implications may not be so well developed in the minds of trustees. If applications and admissions appear to be lagging behind the rate anticipated, the board may wish to consider an increase in student aid or an easing of admissions standards—both at a cost to the institution that may be more acceptable than lower enrollments. Student retention rates are important not only because of potential loss of expected income but also because lower retention means higher costs in the admissions department to replace the departing students with more incoming students. As part of the income information presented to the board, there should be a report on the status of admissions and retention, together with an etimate of the financial variances to be expected if planned rates are not achieved. The income penalties can be substantial, and the board should be alerted to the size and potential financial impact as early as possible so that it can consider potential avenues for corrective action.

Government Sources. These are dominant sources of funds for almost all public institutions. The nature of the financial reporting to the board in this area is often conditioned by the requirements of the appropriating source (federal government, state legislatures, and local governing bodies) and varies widely enough to make it difficult to generalize about specific financial reporting needs. Several of the administrators and financial officers who participated in the AGB/NACUBO project observed that the financial reporting concepts developed in that project should be helpful in more clearly presenting the institution's financial needs to those from whom the funds must come. Legislators, like trustees and regents, can gain an enhanced understanding through simplified operating reports.

Grants and contracts are usually for specific purposes and often have specific reporting requirements attached to them that are seldom of much interest to trustees. A number of larger institutions, public and private, derive considerable income from these sources. Mot individual grants and contracts are of relatively short duration, and the aggregate income can fluctuate significantly from year to year. As the institution's income from these sources increases, so also does its financial vulnerability to such fluctuation. If income from these sources is significant, the board should receive a regular report on the status of such grants and contracts in summary form. The report should include as a minimum:

• The amount of such income.
• The expected duration of income from the backlog of projects on the books.
• Concentrations of grants and contracts with individual principal investigators or within departments that may make the institution vulnerable to personnel failure (or departure) or to departmental overloads.
• An estimate of the contingent financial liability due to failure to live up to the conditions of grants and contracts.

Private Donor Sources. These have always been a most important source of funds for private colleges and universities and have become increasingly so for public institutions. The gift report is one of the presentations most eagerly awaited by trustees. The typical gift report covers the source of the commitment (alumni, trustee, foundation, corporation), its general intent (current or capital operations), and whether the gift is cash or its equivalent or is a deferred commitment. However presented, it is the total that catches the eyes of trustees and brings joy or sorrow. But without discounting their sincere appreciation, of every donation, there is a certain financial utility attached to each gift that is of critical importance. There is a vast difference in utility between the estate note for $500,000 executed by a healthy person of age fifty and the certified check for $250,000 handed to the president by a local merchant. A cash gift for endowment of scholarships has much of its impact extended into future years. Annuities have actuarial implications. Real estate gifts can bring with them substantial problems of conversion to resources useful to the institution.

The complete gift report should give the trustee information about three interlocking areas. First is the reporting of all incoming commitments during the period of the report, whether cash or its equivalent or a deferred commitment, and the restrictions on the gifts. This report identifies the rate of acquisition of assets and is a raw measure of the efficiency of the development progam. Next is the reporting of funds becoming available during the period of the report for current use, with applicable restrictions, including not only current cash and equivalents but also proceeds from conversion or previous deferred commitments. This is the available cash income for operating, plant, and investment purposes. Third is the reporting of remaining outstanding commitments; this report should include a schedule of estimated future time of availability based on fixed payment schedules or actuarial projections. Without getting into arguments about whether these outstanding commitments should be shown on the balance sheet as unrealized future income, the board should have some notion of future conversion expectancies for financial planning purposes.

Investment Income. The endowment fund, including trustee- designated endowment, produces investment income. Boards have long played the major role in this area. The traditional reports are those common to all investment enterprises and, whether the performance has been good or bad, the reports themselves are readily understood by most trustees. Information should include the portfolio values and mix, current yields and appreciation, changes in the portfolio, and some comparison with the performance of the general markets and of other similar funds. Restricted investment funds such as those for scholarships, student aid, and annuities carry similar reporting requirements, although investment criteria may differ. Most trustees report little difficulty in grasping these typical reports.

Not so well understood is the opportunity for investment income from other liquid assets. The current fund often has cash available that is not required immediately for operations. The plant fund may have funds awaiting the start of construction projects or included in reserves for major repairs and improvements. These funds should also be put to work. Investment will probably be for the short- or mid-term; but whatever the criteria and policy, it is up to the board to give guidance here, and regular reports on performance should be available.

Income from Auxiliary Enterprises. Residence halls, food services, bookstores, athletics, hospital services, and agricultural extension activities generate income for the institution and have associated costs. Usually each is operated as a separate business, and the trustee is well advised not to become involved in the financial details unless problems are clearly indicated. Summary reports should be available to the board as to the net gain or loss to the institution from each activity. Sometimes a profit may be sought in one enterprise as a matter of policy and so contribute to other programs of the institution. More often, the policy is to balance income (pricing) against actual costs incurred. Some costs may be deemed worthy of subsidy funding by the institution. Whatever the policies, it is up to the board to make or approve them, and regular financial reports should be available to keep trustees up to date.

To return to and repeat the opening theme: the board and the individual trustees or regents should understand the unique characteristics and forces at work with each source of income. Even more importantly, they should be continually aware of the interplay among the sources of income, the visible and expected trends, and the changing mix of sources in order to intelligently develop their short- and long-term financial strategy.

Spending Funds

Expenditure reports usually view (or should view) the outgoing dollars from three different vantage points that in turn should help answer three simple questions: For what was the money spent? For what were the things it bought used? Who was responsible for buying them?

The breakdown and presentation of expenditures by *object* class answers the question, "For what was the money spent?" Thus, expenses are identified as being for faculty or staff compensation, for laboratory supplies, for fuel, for books, or for pencils and paper clips. The trustee can draw two pieces of wisdom from object-class presentation. First, it gives a clear picture of the relative magnitude and, thus, the relative importance of the various types of things purchased. It focuses attention on the spots where trustee policy decisions will make the greatest difference. Faculty salaries are a far more important expense than are office supplies. So, the areas for cost attention are targeted. Second, object-class presentation increases the trustee's understanding of overall expense trends and the underlying causes of these trends. Different classes of expenditures have different trends and volatilities. Costs for fuel and utilities may be moving well beyond the general inflation rate. Interest charges fluctuate with economic conditions. Only by blending the different cost expectancies of the various object classes can a valid projection of the overall cost trends be derived. There is little reason for the board to be presented with a report covering all object line items down to the smallest detail. Aggregation into ten or a dozen major classes will give the needed quick grasp of the overall picture and of the trends therein.

Higher education, being a labor-intensive enterprise, always has compensation as a major expense. A subreport on the breakdown of compensation expense is highly useful to board decision making. A common breakdown presents faculty compensation by faculty rank, including number in each rank, total and average salaries, pension contributions, and other benefits such as children's tuition and leave credits. Information should also be available on trends in faculty compensation over the last several years and on comparisons with both national averages and averages of similar institutions. The same breakdown should be available for administrative positions.

Each board will want to indicate those major object classes for which they wish a further breakdown, depending upon the perceived significance of the expenditure. Public institutions may require a report on purchases and contracts that exceed a specific amount. If fuel and utility costs are a problem, a brief report may be desirable. Some of the subreports may be useful over only a short period of time, such as a period of planned acceleration of library acquisition. Such reports should be discontinued when the need no longer exists. But knowing what things the money is spent for is only part of the answer as to how resources are being applied.

The breakdown by *function* answers the question, "For what are the services and items purchased being used?" Expenses, regardless of whether for faculty compensation, books, or supplies, can be arrayed by functional purpose—for example, instruction,

research, student services, scholarships, or operation and maintenance of the plant. Again, such a presentation focuses the attention
of the trustee on the significant expenditures for identifiable components of the institution's operating program. Of course, different functions consume different mixes of services and things. Instruction has a dominant faculty compensation component, while
the plant maintenance function may be dominated by hourly labor
and supply costs. It should be possible for the financial officer to
develop reports showing the object-class composition of the various
functional categories, but such reports take time and money to
prepare, are rarely of continuing interest to the trustee, and should
be required only on an exceptional basis. The board should know
that the basic data are available as required and only request such
cross-analysis reporting in specific instances when financial problems seem to be seated in a particular, significant function. The
main purpose of the report of expenditures is to give the trustee an
overview of the mix and balance of the use of funds as they are
applied to institutional functions.

The presentation of expenditures by *organization* component
answers the question, "Who is responsible for buying the things
used in these functions?" Most trustees find this report to be the
most useful for their management overview purposes when
coupled with the two previously discussed reports. Often the organization expenditure report includes the object-class expenditures incurred by each organizational component—college, department, president's office—to give visibility as to the type of
expense incurred. The reason for the popularity of the report on
expenditures by organization is clear. It brings the management
structure into the picture with its individually assigned duties and
parallel cost-control responsibilities. Cost problems are discussed
with, and answers are given by, people in charge, not by object
classes and functions. Budgetary control starts with people, and the
trustee feels comfortable in dealing with the financial report built
around people. The report indicates at once the people who are
accountable for the expenditure of the dollars and where the dominant dollar flows are, and it thus sets priorities for board attention.

A word of caution is in order concerning the overextended
use of this report for cost-control purposes by the trustee. The

report is simple but its interpretation can be complex. The quick scan tells who is spending the money and for what. It does not tell what value is being received by the institution as a result of these expenditures. The input costs are tangible and easily measured. The output values are less tangible, are often subjective in measurement, and must be assessed on the basis of their contribution to the total program of the institution. Cost-conscious boards have been known to damage the total program of an institution irreparably by overquick reaction to apparent out-of-balance input costs in a department or office without understanding the true output values.

The input costs per credit hour of a physics department, for example, are greater than the input costs per credit hour of a philosophy department because of laboratory expense and equipment maintenance costs. Even if two departments are equally good, there is no reason to expect equivalent input costs. In a liberal arts college, it is important to expose the student to the world of physics through laboratory experience. Physics department expenses, however, can be cut to a presumably "equitable" level only at the cost of a diminished educational exposure and damage to the greater objective of a balanced liberal arts education. This is the cost-benefit assessment, and trustees ignore the implications at their own and the institution's peril.

However the expenditures for operations are broken down, and whatever the procedures for cross-analysis among the several breakdowns presented in the reports to the board, the totals are the same and, combined with the reports on current revenue, bring the board to the bottom line.

The Bottom Line. Revenues and the appended restrictions are generally explicit figures accounted for and presented in a straightforward fashion with little room for financial maneuver. Expenditures, on the other hand, offer a somewhat greater latitude in their legitimate accounting treatment. For example, an extraordinarily large expenditure for a major plant rehabilitation that threatens to throw the bottom line into the red for the current year may, with justification, be amortized over two or three years. This lowers the current year's reported charges at the cost of increased charges during the immediately following years. Start-up costs for a major fund-raising campaign may, likewise, under justifying circumstances, be spread over the period of the campaign. There are often good and proper reasons for such treatment, but trustees should be fully aware of such deferred charges and their future implications for the bottom line. The potential danger is that the soothing reassurance of a bottom line in the black today may beguile trustees into forgetting the later impact of a deferred charge.

An even greater temptation may be the postponement or temporary suspension at budget-making time of actions that will clearly throw the bottom line into the red. Necessary building maintenance may be put off "for a year or two." A vitally needed new program of instruction may be deferred. In such cases it may be that the essential health of the institution is being sacrificed to the apparent health of the bottom line. Too often, in such cases, the board is refusing to recognize the real ongoing costs of the institution and its programs. Since these ongoing costs must be met by revenue over the years, it is better that the board fully recognize that these costs, intermittent though they be, will continue to rise and that it must get to work on increasing the revenue to accommodate them. Postponing the cost only postpones the misery. And it requires a self-imposed, long-term financial discipline on the board's part to come to grips with this type of problem.

Assuming that the board has attempted to account for all true costs, the single most important report to the individual trustee is the "statement of current funds, revenues, expenditures, and transfers" (to use a common title) and which a nonaccountant author prefers to call the "operating statement" in order to emphasize its primary purpose. The summarized "operating statement," which can be prepared in a variety of acceptable formats, should include:

- Revenue by source.
- Operating expenditures by function, with, if useful, a functional breakdown by major organization responsibilities.
- Charges for interest and debt retirement.
- Provisions for specified reserves.
- The resulting operating excess or deficit.
- Allocations of excess fund or transfers of funds to accommodate deficit.

The statement suggested by the AGB/NACUBO project can be found in *Financial Responsibilities of Governing Boards of Colleges and Universities* (1979, p. 94).

Cash Flow Monitoring. While it should be assumed that the financial officer will exercise supervision over the cash flow, investing short-term excesses and borrowing to cover short-term needs—both according to board-established policy—the board should be kept aware of the situation that is actually evolving as compared with projections. The board need not receive detailed information, but a simple summary of actual versus projected cash requirements should be available. The first indication of impending financial problems may be an excessive variance from the projected cash flow.

Preserving and Enhancing the Capital Assets

To this point the discussion has centered on the flow of funds into the institution and the expenditure of a portion of these funds in support of institutional operations. The financial transactions thus far described have mainly involved the current fund, and the operating bottom line has indicated what surpluses are available for other uses or what deficits must be accommodated from other sources. The accumulated operating surpluses may be left in the current fund as a general operating reserve or may, by action of the board, be designated in all or part for transfer to other funds for other uses. Whether or not these current fund surpluses are transferred, they are part of the capital assets of the institution and must be managed, preserved, and, one hopes, enhanced under board policy guidelines.

The other funds contain most of the capital assets of the institution. These funds receive inputs directly from external sources in the form of restricted gifts, grants, and investment income, as well as by transfer from the current fund through trustee designation and some mandatory transfers. In a sense, each of these funds may be considered a separate economic unit, and the board will require reports concerning the status and flow of funds through each. This information is traditionally presented in a "Statement of Changes and Fund Balances" and in subsidiary reports. Each fund has its own unique characteristics. The plant fund usually has as its dominant dollar figure the recorded investment in land, buildings, and associated equipment. The trustee need not dwell too long on this frequently impressive dollar amount since it has little meaning in active management. The figure represents the original cost, or value at the time of acquisition, of the fixed assets and has little relevance to current value or replacement cost. It is simply a convenient carrying figure. Acquisitions are entered as they occur; deletions come only with sale, destruction, or demolition. Since values are as of the time of acquisition and depreciation is not taken, the plant investment figure is little more than a record of past application of funds.

The other components of the plant fund are where the action is and should receive continuing board attention. There are generally three:

- Reserves for major plant rehabilitation or repair may be established by transfer from operating surpluses (in the current fund) by board action.
- Reserves for retirement of plant debt may be set aside by the board and included in the plant fund.
- Funds, usually from restricted gifts or grants, may be awaiting expenditure for building construction or equipment purchase.

These three components of the plant fund are usually relatively liquid; they require board attention in at least two ways. First, the board should see to it that the amounts are adequate for the purposes intended. If not, additional funds may have to be sought externally or transferred internally from some unrestricted funds being held for lower-priority purposes. If the plant funds are excessive, the board should consider redesignation of those funds that are unrestricted to a higher-priority need. Second, the board should watch the changing mix of the components of the plant fund and understand the implications of these changes for future financial flexibility. For example, the plant fund total may show an increase of $500,000 for the period reported, but within the fund the monies available and awaiting construction may have dropped $1.5 million as dollars were converted to bricks and mortar. Though total plant funds have increased, financial flexibility has been sharply reduced.

Endowment Funds. These are composed of two major groupings—restricted and board-designated endowment—each of which has its subcomponents. Restricted endowment, where the donor has specified that the resources so contributed be held forever (or for a given period) in the endowment, with the income to be used for general institutional purposes or with the further restriction that the income be used for specified purposes such as scholarships or support of a professorship or a specific educational program. Board-designated endowment (often called quasi-endowment), where the board has set aside otherwise unrestricted funds for endowment purposes. This portion of the endowment fund can be retrieved by the board if required for higher-priority use.

More important than the question of generation of optimum return on investment is the question of the adequacy of the endowment itself. At no other point is the board's requirement to balance present and future obligations brought more clearly into focus. The greater the endowment, the greater the future stability, viability, and independence of the institution. Yet, inadequate support of today's programs can also undermine the future health and prospects of the institution. Should endowment appreciation and income be reinvested at least to the extent that the purchasing power of the endowment not be diminished? Or should all income and permissible appreciation be applied to current needs in the expectation that future donors will provide endowment growth? The answer is never clear-cut, and different boards will have different priorities according to the size and mix of endowment funds and future institutional aspirations.

Nevertheless, the board should set some guiding policy. As an aid to this policy judgment, the following information should be presented periodically:

- Comparisons with endowments of similar institutions.
- Comparisons of endowment per student with national trends and with the ratio of similar institutions.
- Decay or improvement in actual purchasing power of the endowment.
- Impact of endowment growth or decrease upon student tuition and fees—the availability of endowment "subsidy."

Judgment is still the major and final input of the board, but informed judgment is to be preferred over ignorant compromise.

Loan Funds. These are established to provide loans to students and, occasionally, to faculty. The activity is really a separate business and should be so treated. Inputs to loan funds may come from restricted donations, government sources, and board designation of unrestricted funds, as well as from interest earned on loans. These are revolving funds, and the availability of loans for future students depends on repayment of loans by present recipients. For this reason, the board should receive periodic reports concerning the aging of student receivables, delinquency rates, collection procedures, and defaults and write-offs. While the detailed activities of the management of loan funds are not the concern of the board, the board must establish the policies governing the activity and seek and preserve loan resources for the benefit of both students and institution.

Annuity and Life Income Funds. These are deferred gifts to the institution that are invested to provide income, either in actual or in specified fixed amounts, to the donor or to donor-designated beneficiaries. Upon death of the donor (or at the termination of a stipulated period), the principal becomes available to the institution. Management of such funds, together with the reporting requirements to donors and beneficiaries, requires considerable professional expertise, and the board should be sure that such expertise is available and used. Stripped of detail, the board's major interests should be the rate of incoming commitments, the rate of conversion to institutional availability, the inventory of commitments for future conversion, and the degree to which fixed income payouts are supported by income actually realized.

Statement of Changes in Fund Balances. This is highly important to the trustee in that it gives a summary picture of financial activity across the entire institution. The publication *Financial Responsibilities of Governing Boards of Colleges and Universities* (Association of Governing Boards . . . , 1979, pp. 84–85) illustrates a common format for presentation. The column, "total all funds," is not universally accepted because it obscures the presence of both restricted and unrestricted funds in the total. While appreciating this accounting nicety, the author finds in this column the answer to the central question, "Did we end the year ahead or behind on an overall financial basis?" In other words, this column is the ultimate gain or loss statement.

The summarized "Balance Sheet" of *Financial Responsibilities of Governing Boards of Colleges and Universities* (p. 83) presents in traditional format the assets and liabilities of the institution. Again, it is usually presented with each fund noted separately and with the "total all funds" column giving the all-inclusive summary. If the business-oriented trustee will simply read "total balance all funds" as "net worth," the essential mental conversion will have been made.

Timing Reports

If all of the reports suggested in the forgoing pages were to be prepared monthly, financial officers would recoil at the workload and trustees would be smothered in paper—with no appreciable increase in wisdom and understanding. Different reports have different urgencies. Different boards have differing needs and priorities. The "operating report" may be called for monthly by the executive committee or finance committee of the board, while the remaining trustees might receive it only quarterly or immediately prior to a board meeting. The "statement of changes in fund balances" may be required only once a year in conjunction with the annual audit report. Various subsidiary reports, such as a report on the status of student loans, may be required more frequently during a problem period and then relax in frequency as the problem comes under control.

It is useful to both trustees and administrators to establish a reporting schedule that meets the unique information requirements of the specific board. Such a simple schedule should include:

- The list of reports in a manner that indicates the interlocking of principal reports and subsidiary reports.
- The office or person responsible for preparation of each report.
- The schedule for publication of each report.
- The recipients of each report.

Not only does such a schedule permit the administration to plan workloads more effectively, but it also serves to establish a regular reporting rhythm in board agendas throughout the year.

The Audit Committee

It is a responsibility of the board to see that the financial activities of the institution are subject to regular audit as to the validity of the procedures, their compliance with applicable donor restrictions, as well as with laws and regulations, and their conformance with board policies. Some larger institutions may have established internal audit staffs, while smaller institutions may combine the function with other responsibilities. The external audit may be performed by public accounting firms or by state and federal auditors. Since boards must be concerned with both the internal and external audits, they are increasingly establishing audit committees to give focus to the audit responsibility. A committee of three to five is generally deemed adequate; some boards appoint alternates to assure proper representation at meetings with auditors and management. The chairman of the board should not be a member, nor should financial officers or administrators. Responsibilities of the audit committee generally include:

- Meetings with internal auditors to discuss the scope of internal audit activities, procedures used, findings, and recommendations.
- Meeting with the representatives of the appointed public accounting firm, prior to the audit, to confirm the general scope and procedures of the audit and to discuss areas where the board may desire specific emphasis.
- Detailed review of the audit report and direct discussion with the auditors, unattended by management, concerning audit findings and recommendations.
- Discussion with management concerning any corrective action to be taken as a result of the audit and seeing that such corrective action is undertaken promptly.
- Recommendation to the board for the appointment or reappointment of the accounting firm to undertake the subsequent year's audit.

The central thrust of this chapter has been that all—not just some—of the members of the board must participate in financial decision making. To accomplish full participation requires a financial reporting structure, along with individual reports, geared to the specific information needs of the board as perceived by its members and understandable to the less financially experienced trustee. It is the board's job to see that such reports are available. When all is said and done, here as elsewhere, responsibility falls on the board.

16

Charles A. Nelson

Managing Resources

When trustees turn their attention to managing money and the physical plant, those with business backgrounds at last seem to find themselves on familiar ground. The academic program, the departmental structure, the faculty senate, and other such matters may be foreign and arcane, but money and buildings are as familiar as Chevrolets and apple pie. However, I want to open this chapter on a cautionary note: this seemingly familiar ground often turns out to be less familiar as the special character and needs of the educational institution emerge. The business executive whose only thought is to "run the university like a business" has very little to offer the university, because the university is not a business. It could run at a "profit" and do its "business"—education and research—abominably. It could be scratching for funds and still be educating superbly: Yale and the University of Chicago are not coining money.

Yet trustees drawn from outside the institution provide a highly useful perspective. Indeed, perspective may be the most significant contribution of the trustee. The business executives on the board do understand that a string of deficits leads to dissolution—and many faculty members don't seem to understand that at all. Lay trustees, or at least those with broad experience, also have a realistic sense of possibilities and threats: they have seen other organizations rise and fall; they know that the past is no sure guarantee of the future; and they may have developed antennae for detecting the signs of weakness or folly beneath a smooth executive facade.

But trustees will not provide the perspective that the institution needs just by being outsiders. An uninformed trustee is like an American baseball fan who watches a game of cricket in the British Isles, knowing neither the object nor the rules of the game. The outsider as such is simply outside. The useful perspective derives from a combination of the outside view with sufficient knowledge of the particular characteristics of the institution being observed to understand how that perspective may be applied.

There is, of course, always the risk that executives serving on a board will substitute their administrative judgment for that of the chief executive they have hired. In so doing they abdicate their role as trustees. Colleges and universities hire full-time professionals for day-to-day management of resources. The task of trustees is to provide appropriate guidance for those who have such responsibilities. In this chapter, therefore, attention is focused on those policies and procedures that will effectively provide such guidance.

The Four Resources of the Institution

The resources of a college or university—whether it is large or small, private or public—can be organized, for conceptual convenience, into four categories: (1) funds; (2) land, facilities, equipment, and supplies; (3) support staff; and (4) faculty.

The funds, that is, the necessary financial resources, typically include current funds (restricted and unrestricted), loan funds, endowment and similar funds, annuity and life income funds, plant funds and agency funds. The term *budget* usually refers to an estimate, for this year or next year, of current fund revenues and expenditures (including mandatory transfers).

The second category—land, facilities, equipment, and supplies—includes all the inanimate objects that are necessary for the operation of the institution: the campus grounds; classrooms and laboratories; dormitories; faculty housing; pencils, paper, and chalk; computers; test tubes and microscopes; trucks and lawnmowers.

By support staff is meant everyone who works for the institution except the faculty. That includes the grounds keepers, the clerks in the business office, the librarians and, yes, the president. They are all support staff because—whether cutting grass, keeping accounts, answering reference questions in the library, or acting as chief executive—the sole justification for their existence is to help provide the conditions under which teaching and learning can best take place.

The fourth category is faculty. Although mentioned last, it is of course the most important resource, for the faculty is of the essence of the institution. Some members of the faculty may not like to think of themselves as a resource, because that is not *all* that they are. But it would hardly make sense, in any discussion of resources, to leave out the most crucial element.

Funds, then, are not the *sole* resource of a college or university, although such a notion might arise from observing the nearly exclusive attention given to money matters by many boards of trustees. And because money is, after all, a medium of exchange, it may appear at first that other resources can readily be converted to funds. But consider the following examples:

- A university built a dormitory complex at a cost of $3.5 million in 1968. The dormitory complex is no longer needed, and it is not readily convertible to another use—at least not without major additional expenditure, and it already carries a heavy load of debt. Who will pay the university $3.5 million *now* to take this structure off its hands?
- A college has a tenured professor who is no longer very productive. His teaching is uninspired, and he does not produce anything particularly admired by his colleagues when he turns to writing. His salary is $24,000 and he has twelve years to go to retirement. The dean and the chairman of the department would gladly trade him in for two young instructors at $12,000 each. But it can't be done since he is tenured.

• An institution accepted a restricted gift of $500,000, the income of which—currently about $25,000 per year—is to be used solely for the support of its Oriental museum. The museum requires a great deal more than $25,000 a year to operate, and the president doesn't see how the university can afford to keep it going. The donor, who is still living, is not prepared to add to his gift and is also adamant about maintaining the restriction. At the moment, the matter has reached an impasse; it looks as if the institution will either have to continue to use its own funds to help support the museum or forgo the use of the restricted gift income.

There is no need to labor the point. Certain resources are not readily translatable into dollars; and even within the fund category, restrictions may limit the options of management. It follows that if trustees are to give attention to resources, they must not limit their scrutiny to the current operating budget. This chapter, however, discusses only two resource categories—funds and physical plant. For discussions of trustee policy guidance with respect to faculty and staff see Chapters Eleven, Twelve, and Thirteen.

Management of Funds

The management of funds in a college or university calls for a substantially different approach from that which would normally be employed in a business enterprise. The difference is reflected in the basic principles of "fund accounting," as described in Chapter Fifteen. Some aspects of fund accounting are so technical that most members of a lay board will probably not understand them, yet they are of sufficient importance that the reputation and credibility of the institution can be placed in jeopardy if they are ignored. So it is crucial that a well-briefed finance committee give careful attention to these matters. It may also be possible to rotate a portion of the membership of the committee as a means of developing a broadened understanding of financial matters among board members generally. For maximum expertise, a small, virtually permanent committee would be desirable; for maximum education of the trustees, a large, rapidly rotating membership would be best. What I would suggest is a core of seasoned members, always including the chairman, and a smaller number of positions that would rotate every two or three years. This would combine the advantages of both arrangements.

The trustees' fiduciary responsibilities run in two directions: (1) to the institution (trustees must see to it that funds are employed in the furtherance of its purposes) and (2) to the providers of funds (trustees must ensure that any restrictions placed on the use of funds by those providers are strictly adhered to). Fund accounting is the formal mechanism by which funds are segregated so that administrators and trustees will not unwittingly apply funds for a purpose contrary to that specified by the provider, whether that provider be a government agency, a student, or a donor with a particular benefaction in mind. For these reasons the members of the finance committee at least, and preferably some additional members of the board as well, must know the differences between restricted and unrestricted funds, between current funds and endowment funds, between restricted and designated funds, and so forth.

In the management of funds, there are three distinct functions to be performed by the trustees: budget review, managing the endowment, and audit review. They all require committee effort, which can be performed either by a single finance committee—with three subcommittees or subfunctions—or by three separate committees. The structure will depend in part on the size of the board itself, the size and complexity of the institution's funds, and the availability of the appropriate talent on the board. In a large board, with twenty or more members, a good solution is creation of three separate committees, each having three to five members. On the smaller boards, such as are common with public institutions, there may not be a sufficient number of trustees with requisite background to make up three separate committees. But the distinct functions are equally important (unless there are no significant sums to invest), and each function deserves separate treatment.

Budget Review. This involves review of the process by which the budget has been developed, review of the revenue and expenditure estimates prepared by the administration and incorporated in the budget document, and preparation of a recommendation to the board regarding adoption of the budget. Each of these topics is taken up in order in the following pages; it will be useful, however, to provide a brief introduction to budget presentation techniques and formats, since this is one respect in which colleges and universities differ markedly from other enterprises with which trustees may be familiar.

A variety of budgeting techniques and formats is employed in colleges and universities depending upon their form of control (public or private), complexity, and level of sophistication. The most common of these are incremental budgeting, program budgeting, and formula budgeting.

The *incremental budget* is traditional and widely used, though less popular than it once was. This budget begins from the basis of the previous year; it contains the unexpressed assumption that the pattern of expenditures and revenues for the previous year and the current year can serve as a sound guide for the next year. Attention is focused on the marginal differences in expenditures and on the proposed increments or decrements. Usually this presentation is organized under broad functional categories (for example, instruction and research) and by object of expenditure (salaries, equipment, supplies, heat and light), and thus the attention of the budget reviewer tends to focus on increments in salaries, increments in fuel costs, and so on. The decline in the acceptance of this traditional approach stems from two major weaknesses: it prevents up to 90 percent of the expenditures from being examined with care, since it is the marginal changes that are highlighted; and it does not make it possible to determine what the expenditures are meant to accomplish. The administrator or trustee who would like to know how much of the resources are devoted to a particular program will not find the answer in such a budget presentation; hence, a poorly conceived basic allocation of resources may be perpetuated. Perhaps the chief advantage of this traditional method is the ease with which expenditure *control* can be monitored since the objects of expenditure in the budget are the same as those by which the accounts of the institution are organized.

Some form of *program budget* is the growing alternative to traditional budgeting methods. The program budget focuses the attention of the reviewer on the costs of carrying out activities or programs and only secondarily on the objects of expenditures themselves. It also tends to invite attention to the allocation of total resources among programs, not just to the marginal differences from the current or preceding year. The more complex the institution—and hence the more programs or activities that are competing for resources—the more important it is that some form of program budgeting be adopted. However, there appear to be two chief obstacles to the successful installation of a program budget. One is the difficulty of coming to agreement on program definitions. The process of resolving this difficulty is in itself worthwhile, however, since it usually requires clarification of the mission and objectives of the institution. The second obstacle involves a technical complication; that is, the presentation of actual expenditures in comparison with budgeted expenditures requires extra coding and reformatting in the accounting office, not readily accomplished without the aid of a computer.

Formula budgeting applies almost exclusively to publicly supported institutions (but not to all of them). The term usually refers to the revenue side of the budget—in this case, the process by which available public funds are allocated among publicly controlled colleges and universities. The specific elements of the formula vary widely from state to state: some are simple and clear, others are very complicated. Usually, however, their key variable is enrollment, and their common object is to provide an equitable distribution of funds that is relatively free of changing political pressures. There is a tendency for legislators and state coordinating councils to go beyond basic revenue allocation to determination of the ways in which the funds should be spent. Trustees should be alert to this tendency since, if carried very far, it weakens their authority as a governing board. Administrators on the campus are likely to be more effective in efforts to preserve the autonomy of the institution if their trustees exert appropriate leadership in that effort. Where formula budgeting is essentially a revenue allocation technique, it can coexist comfortably with a program budget for expenditures that is developed by the college administration and reviewed by its board.

Whatever budgeting technique is used, the budget committee (or the finance committee performing this role) should be concerned with the process by which the budget document is prepared as well as with the content of the document itself. There should be an established budget preparation process and calendar. The budget committee should determine whether the prescribed process and calendar have been followed, for lack of adherence may indicate haste (and therefore the likelihood of carelessness in the outcome) or lack of consultation with an important department or officer (and therefore the possibility of an undisclosed disagreement or an expense not provided for). Clearly the budget committee should not *conduct* the budget process—that is an administrative responsibility. But checking to see whether procedures have been carried out is an appropriate—and often revealing—responsibility of the trustee committee. From time to time (not every year) the committee should examine the process itself, to determine whether it is the best possible one for producing a budget suited to the needs and resources of the institution. The committee should of course make certain that the part of the process involving the trustees provides sufficient time for committee review and for subsequent board action prior to the commencement of the budget year. When necessary, the committee should bring to the board for action major changes in the budget-making process.

The heart of the budget review is, of course, the examination of the revenue and expenditure estimates. Only experience in reviewing the budget of the particular institution can provide knowledge of the unexpected pitfalls that may lie hidden away, but certain criteria can be usefully applied in almost every case.

First, is the budget consonant with long-range plans? Does it bring the school one year closer to the objectives it has set for itself? A budget document examined without a sense of where the school is headed can hardly be examined at all. If the institution has no long-range plans, then the budget committee should voice its concern to the full board and recommend that work begin on such planning (see Chapter Nine). Budget committee members will bear in mind that by the time the budget comes before them (typically in the spring of the year, about three or four months before the beginning of the budget year) commitments have already been made for 80 to 90 percent of the expenditure items (including virtually all personnel expenses based on existing patterns of appointment and notice requirements for faculty and on contractual commitments to organized personnel). Unless those commitments have been made in accordance with a plan previously approved by the board, the budget committee can do little more than observe as bystanders the chain of events already set in motion. However, if a long-range plan exists, the committee can perform the very crucial function of determining whether the proposed budget will bring the objectives set forth in that plan closer to fulfillment.

Second, does the proposed budget provide for the corrective actions seen to be necessary as the result of operations during the current year? If fuel costs have risen unexpectedly, does the new budget take that adequately into account? If enrollment in the current year is not following the pattern earlier predicted, what corrective measures have been taken with respect to revenue projections, student aid requirements, and faculty staffing needs? The committee should bear in mind that expenditures in excess of budget are frequently due to weak financial controls rather than to poor budgeting. In looking at financial results, trustees will frequently find that there is no adequate explanation for cost overruns except that they were incurred unknowingly or were simply allowed to happen. It still occurs with disturbing frequency that the chief business officer predicts a break-even operation a month before year-end and that the audit shortly thereafter reveals a substantial deficit. In such cases the remedy is obviously not in the budget-making or budget review process, but in financial controls and timely periodic financial reporting.

Third, how realistic are the projections? If past projections have consistently erred on the side of optimism, does the new budget reflect a more sober view? If past projections have proved to be too conservative, does the new budget reflect an appropriate adjustment? And does the budget include a contingency provision so that the institution can quickly put to work any unexpected extra revenues or, conversely, reduce its commitments if revenues fall short?

Fourth, how adequate is the justification for the key revenue and expenditure items in the budget. Is the documentation convincing? Does the reasoning stand up to close scrutiny? In a word, has the staff done its homework?

Once its review is completed, the budget committee has the responsibility to present a recommended budget for adoption by the full board. The committee must have resolved with the chief executive prior to this time any differences between his or her and its recommendations. It is crucial that the committee not shrink from its responsibilities, even in the face of opposition from the president and staff, since the board must rely on the committee as its best source of opinion on the soundness of the budget. Once the board acts, inexorable forces are set in motion for a twelve-month period. Frequently the long-term health, and sometimes the very existence, of the institution are at stake.

The forgoing discussion of budget review relates to the *operating* budget. A *capital* budget is also required. The capital budget should reveal the estimated completion date and the estimated total cost for each construction project, the actual cash outflow to the beginning of the current fiscal year, and the estimated cash outflow for the current year and for the budget year. The sources of funds should be listed for the same periods, and a cumulative net cash flow thus derived. Such budgets should be prepared not only for proposed projects but for those underway as well.

For most institutions the irregular seasonal flow of revenues, together with a relatively constant outlay of expenditures, makes a close watch on cash flow of critical importance. Even when the annual operating budget shows a surplus, vigilance is required to ensure that bank borrowings can be anticipated and short-term cash surpluses can be effectively invested. The preparation of the capital budget is thus an essential precondition to the cash flow projection, since cash requirements of both the operating and the capital budgets are necessary ingredients of the projection. In institutions in precarious financial condition, the cash flow report should be reviewed carefully by the finance committee every month. A quarterly review will be sufficient in most other cases.

Managing the Endowment. Most observers readily acknowledge that for private institutions at least, endowment funds are a major responsibility of the trustees. In recent years a number of public institutions, especially major state universities, have been recipients of significant private funds, and endowment management has also become a major concern for them. While pains have been taken in this chapter and elsewhere in this volume to stress the range of concerns that trustees must address, it remains true that the management of the endowment is one of their heaviest responsibilities.

There has become available in the last few years a significant body of research on educational endowments. One result of this is that members of investment committees can obtain answers to many questions that were formerly subjects of uninformed speculation. Another result, paradoxically, is that the task has, in one sense, become more complex: since a useful body of knowledge is now available, it is no longer sufficient for a member of the budget or investment committee to generalize from personal investment experience or general knowledge of economic conditions and the stock or bond market. Nor are these difficulties entirely resolved by turning to professional investment advisers, for it remains the responsibility of the trustees to provide the policy guidance for such outside counsel and also to evaluate the performance of such advisers.

Recent research has served in part to confirm commonly held opinions. One is not surprised to find, for example, that long-term studies of market prices show that common stocks are inherently riskier than bonds. But the same studies have also produced results that are more illuminating. These results are both conceptual (that is, they may change the way one looks at endowment policy) and factual (they show that what actually happens with endowment funds is different from what one might expect).

Conceptually, the most significant contribution is the distinction between endowment income and the "spending rate." While trustees have always been able to spend at a rate lower than the endowment yield, it was not until 1972 that various states began to legalize the spending of some portion of the appreciated value of the endowment principal. Given the sharp fluctuations in market value to which virtually any portfolio may be subject from year to year, it would be difficult for an institution to work with a budget in which the revenue to be drawn from endowment would be determined only at the end of the year for which the budget is prepared; that is, only after all the results are in, including the stock and bond prices on the last day of the school's fiscal year. But it would also be foolish to assume that last year's interest and dividends, plus a fixed percentage of last year's appreciation, would be a sure indication of this year's results. Thus, a spending rate designed to smooth out these fluctuations serves the need of the institution for stability in budgeting. If properly designed, the rate also serves to balance current needs for revenue with future requirements, and it should enable the investment policy to be guided by long-term objectives. Constant changes in the portfolio would not be needed in order to achieve a return required for the current year.

These considerations led to the concept of "total return" (interest plus dividends plus capital gains) and the notion of stabilizing spending by adopting a spending rule governed by an average of market values calculated over several years.

As George F. Keane, executive director of the Common Fund, has said: "The severe stock market declines of 1973 and 1974 created widespread concern over the wisdom of spending more than current income yield" (Ennis and Williamson, 1976, p.viii). As a result the Common Fund, which provides—especially for institutions with small endowments—the benefits of a pooled investment fund with multiple managers, sponsored studies of the effects of various spending rules, employing simulation models to test a wide range of hypothetical conditions. The results, reported by Ennis and Williamson in *Spending Policy for Educational Endowments* (1976), will be of interest to all trustees who are members of college or university investment committees. Some findings are surprising, and one or two go contrary to one's intuitive expectations. Among the results reported are these:

- When the rule is adopted that a fixed small fraction (the "spending fraction") of the endowment be spent annually, it follows that the rate of endowment growth is equal to the rate of growth in spending.
- Under the same conditions, the *level* of current spending is inversely related to the rate of endowment growth.
- The more spending is stabilized (by adopting a moving average

over a period of years, for example), the more uncertainty is introduced into the future value of the endowment. As Ennis and Williamson (1976) explain: "When no attempt is made to stabilize spending, . . . spending fluctuates just as the endowment fluctuates. If spending is stabilized, however, a small proportion of the endowment is expended when the fund has risen in value, and a larger proportion is expended when the endowment is depressed. Therefore stabilizing spending causes a greater decline in the value of the endowment during a period of falling investment values and a greater increase in the value of the fund during a rising investment market than would be the case if spending were not stabilized" (p. 34).

- It follows that spending should be stabilized no more than is necessary for budgetary purposes. If moving averages are calculated for a period of five years or less, the increase in uncertainty of the future value of the fund is negligible.
- Nothing is gained in stability by calculating average market values weekly or monthly over three years rather than by calculating them annually over the same period.
- The broader the diversification of the portfolio, the more stable the market value of the endowment fund over time.
- Diversification as such has no adverse effect on investment performance.

These excerpts from a single study are not offered as a summary of *all* the available knowledge on endowment investing and spending. I provide them as examples of the findings that are available and to support the argument that trustees responsible for educational endowments must be well-enough informed to adopt wise spending rules and to distinguish spending from endowment income.

The investment committee, then, has a number of important responsibilities. It should select professional management for the investment portfolio, and it should regularly assess the performance of such managers and replace them if they are not performing adequately. It must make certain that the institution's treasurer or other financial officer has properly classified funds received according to the terms of the gift; the committee must also satisfy itself that the principal of true endowment funds is not invaded. It must establish an investment policy as a guide for its professional managers, and it should see to it that such a policy is formally adopted by the board of trustees. It should determine the spending rate from endowment fund earnings; further, if the committee wishes to adopt the policy of total return, it should obtain opinion of legal counsel that such policy conforms to state law. Such a spending rate should also be adopted formally by the board on recommendation of the committee. The committee should obtain regular performance reports from its portfolio managers, and it should forward these reports at least in summary fashion to the full board. The committee should also see to it that an annual report of its stewardship is publicly released.

Audit Review. The third fiscal management responsibility of the trustees, after budget review and the overseeing of investments, is audit review. The audit committee and its responsibilities are described in Chapter Fifteen.

Social Policy and Investment

In recent years social conditions in the Republic of South Africa have prompted many concerned citizens, and especially students, to question whether colleges and universities should retain investment in companies operating through affiliates in that country. Clearly, broader issues are involved, since any investment policy applicable to South Africa is likely to have ready application in other parts of that continent and in parts of South America, Asia, and Europe as well. The argument for divestiture might even be extended to the operation of companies in the United States.

Trustees of most institutions sooner or later will have to make up their minds on this issue. Policy will have to be developed for the guidance of the investment committee. I will not attempt here to prove that one particular policy is the best overall, but I will instead set forth briefly the apparent alternatives and then suggest ways in which the issue might be dealt with. At least four positions are distinguishable among institutions that have faced the issue thus far.

One view is that the fiduciary duty of the trustees is to preserve the principal of the endowment and to maximize the return to the extent consistent with preservation of that principal. Any other considerations will only serve to dilute that objective, and it is therefore irresponsible to take them into account.

A second and quite different view is that, by maintaining investments in corporations operating in countries with policies like those of South Africa, the college implicitly supports racial inequality, denial of political freedom, and other oppressive practices. The only morally acceptable position is divestiture. Other investments can be found that will be free of such heavy moral taint and yet adequate for the institution's financial objectives and fiduciary responsibilities.

A third position is that adoption of a policy of divestiture based on disapproval of the national policies of another country is essentially a political act. The university must not take political positions, domestic or foreign; it has no method for determining the political will of the faculty, students, and staff. Even if it did have such a method, it would still be inappropriate for it to take a political position, since this would be inconsistent with the fostering of complete freedom of opinion—and thus of dissent—so essential to the operation of a free university.

The fourth position is more complicated. It argues that divestiture is likely to have little, if any, effect on company policy; that it is better to shoulder one's responsibility as a shareholder; that the social policies of a corporation will have a significant effect upon its economic performance in the long run; and that, while investment performance is the first criterion for the portfolio, other criteria (including the social performance of the company) may properly be introduced. Those who take the fourth position frequently ask whether a corporation has adopted the "Sullivan Principles." These principles, formulated by Leon Sullivan, a director of General Motors, call for companies operating through affiliates in the Republic of South Africa to provide nonsegregation of facilities and equal employment opportunities and practices within the company and to seek to improve the quality of life for employees outside the work environment as well.

How should a board of trustees resolve such an issue? First, it should not leave the matter in the hands of the investment committee or the portfolio manager. Just as the portfolio manager must look to the investment committee for policy guidance on investment objectives, so the investment committee must look to the full board for guidance on an issue in which investment performance is linked with much broader questions. I suggest that the trustees invite and obtain broadly representative opinions from faculty, students, and staff, as well as from their own membership. The matter should be carefully studied, and copies of policy statements adopted by other institutions should be reviewed and debated. The board should not be overly influenced by conditions in one country or by the behavior of a single corporation. It should adopt a policy that is broadly applicable and that it can reasonably expect its investment committee to implement—in other words, a policy consistent with its obligations to provide earnings from investments to support the operations of the institution.

Overseeing the Physical Plant

The trustees are responsible for ensuring that the physical plant is adequate to support the program of the institution and that it is properly maintained. They also have the responsibility to see that a campus master plan is developed and kept current and to make sure that new structures are provided and old structures removed in accordance with that plan. Beyond those important duties they must control the growth of plant debt and set conditions for the acceptance of gifts and grants for new construction.

A committee should be established with responsibility for dealing with these matters and for bringing recommendations to the board with respect to them. This committee—variously known as the building and grounds, campus development, physical plant, or maintenance committee—should also establish liaison with the finance committee because of their interrelated concerns over debt levels, investments, and maintenance expenditures. One trustee, for example, could serve on both.

Frequently a campus committee of faculty and administrators is established with parallel concerns. This is a useful device; frequently those who make daily use of campus facilities will have an appreciation for a range of problems—adequacy of parking, temperature levels in buildings, esthetic concerns, problems of distance and communications—that will not be evident to the occasional visitor or to one looking over maps and blueprints. Periodic joint meetings of the campus committee and the trustee committee are advisable.

The physical plant committee is concerned with land, facilities, and equipment. These concerns encompass not only the efficient operation and attractive appearance of the plant but also the plans for acquisition of land and major equipment and for the construction of new buildings. In a large institution, or one rapidly growing, adequate attention to both concerns may call for two subcommittees.

When an institution becomes financially hard pressed—as now frequently happens—the physical plant is usually allowed to deteriorate, and very high future costs are thus incurred. This deferred maintenance is a large and sometimes hidden liability (it usually does not show up on financial statements) in many institutions. The first responsibility of the trustees here is to find out the extent to which maintenance has been neglected; then they can better balance other demands for available funds against those needs. One of the responsibilities of the physical plant committee is to make sure that the needs for plant maintenance are adequately considered when the budget is under review by the trustees. Another of its responsibilities is to ensure that appropriate planned maintenance programs are in place and are systematically followed.

An especially heavy responsibility falls on the trustees when new construction is under consideration. An ugly or inefficient or badly sited building is likely to plague the campus for a hundred years or more. Beyond that, there is the problem of unnecessary building; the "edifice complex" is as common an affliction of college presidents as hoarding books is among librarians. A substantial number of institutions are in financial difficulty today because of overbuilding in the sixties; if these institutions had simply maintained the plant existing in the previous decade, they would have sufficient space for current enrollment and would not be burdened with debt service on buildings now discovered to be unnecessary.

When debt is to be incurred, trustees must always ask: How is it to be serviced? When the structure is revenue generating, as in the case of a dormitory, the answer is clear, provided that no mistake has been made in estimating future demand for rooms. If it is not revenue generating, then what sources of funds are to be tapped to meet debt service? Tuition charges, special student fees, income on endowment, or what? That question should be answered satisfactorily before the building contract is approved.

Caution must also be exercised in the acceptance of gifts or grants for new structures. Frequently the funds offered are not adequate to meet the full cost of construction; rarely do they provide continuing support for maintenance of the building. As energy and personnel costs rise, it becomes more and more evident that there are some gifts an institution simply cannot afford to accept.

Resources: For What and for Whom?

It is not sufficient to say that resource management in the university involves the four categories mentioned at the outset and that trustees must devote equal attention to all four. The trustee must consider what the resources are to be organized to achieve and how well they are managed to meet those purposes. It follows that, in addition to the four resource categories, two other considerations must be introduced: programs and students. The task of managing a college or university may be described as organizing and allocating *resources*—funds; land, facilities, equipment, and supplies; support staff; and faculty—among *programs* for the benefit of *students*.

This is, of course, a simplification. If the purpose of the institution is to impart knowledge, skills, and understanding through teaching, then the degree to which students learn is the final test. Where the institution has a major commitment to research (the discovery and verification of new knowledge) or public service (the utilization of knowledge in society at large), there are other and more complex factors to be taken into account. I have chosen the simpler case because instruction is the major function of the vast majority of American institutions of higher education.

Programs and students are inextricably tied together. Hence, academic programs ought not to be devised without consideration of the capabilities, interests, and attainments of the students who are to benefit from the programs. Conversely, the process of selecting students for admission ought to assure that those who are accepted are prepared to benefit from the programs available.

Our main concern here is to emphasize that resources cannot be managed, whether by the administration or the trustees, except by reference to a purpose or set of purposes—and these purposes are embodied in programs and students. Thus if trustees are to be concerned with the management of resources, they must inevitably become involved in such vital matters as student selection and academic standards. So this simple analysis carries a very long way: Trustees cannot limit their attention to the budget, the investment of funds, and the management of the physical plant. Such scrutiny will be an uninformed exercise in the absence of an understanding of the programs that the budget and the facilities support and of the students for whom the programs exist.

17

David M. Lascell
Alfred M. Hallenbeck

Contending with Conflicts of Interest and Liability

It is commonly known that a college or university trustee is a fiduciary who must exercise special care and loyalty in managing the institution's affairs. Equally recognized is the fact that the fiduciary duties of care and loyalty prohibit a trustee from influencing an institution's affairs so that he or she benefits personally at the expense of the institution. Conflict-of-interest problems go well beyond such premeditated self-dealing, however. A conflict may arise whenever a college or university trustee has or represents interests that could compete with the interests of the institution that the trustee serves. And, although charges of conflict of interest most commonly arise when trustees are accused of obtaining personal enrichment from their management of an institution's financial assets, a conflict may exist even though the trustee involved cannot possibly receive any direct or indirect financial benefit. For example, a trustee who serves on the boards of two colleges that are located in the same area and are competing for the same students may face difficult potential conflicts involving curricular or program development.

The legal implications of failing to recognize and eliminate potential conflicts, or at least neutralize their effect on the institution, are now more serious than ever. Recent court decisions have more clearly defined standards of conduct for trustees and other fiduciaries. In addition, public attention is focusing more closely on what many perceive to be questionable relationships between colleges and universities and businesses whose directors, officers, or major stockholders sit on the boards of those educational institutions.

Unfortunately, in the face of this increasingly complex legal and public scrutiny of conflict situations, many institutions—especially smaller institutions not located in major cities—will find that many people who are willing and able to devote the talents necessary to trusteeship are also associated with or interested in other organizations that may have conflicting or competing interests. For most colleges and universities, potential conflicts of interest for some of their trustees seem inevitable. Accordingly, this chapter will define a trustee's fiduciary responsibilities, outline which aspects of those duties are absolutely incompatible with conflicts of interest, and suggest the minimum standards of conduct necessary to safeguard both the institution and its trustees.

Fiduciary Duties

As a fiduciary to a college or university, a trustee owes special duties of care and loyalty to the institution *as a whole* rather than to its individual constituencies, such as faculty, alumni, or students, even though they may have been responsible for the trustee's appointment or election to the governing board. The duty of care essentially requires that a trustee be well-enough informed to set policy for the institution and to make honest, good faith business decisions about the conduct of its affairs. The duty of loyalty, however, involves greater possibilities of conflicts of interest, since it requires more than simple honesty. The duty of loyalty means that a trustee acting on behalf of a college or university must keep the institution's interests paramount to *all* others. Furthermore, the trustees must subordinate not only their own personal interests but also the interests of their "affiliates" to those of the institution. Affiliates may include a trustee's spouse, children, or other family members, as well as businesses or nonprofit organizations of which the trustee is a director, trustee, officer, partner, shareholder, or key employee.

How does a trustee eliminate conflicting personal interests or interests of affiliates from his or her decision making? How may the nonprofit institution assist its trustees either to avoid or minimize potential conflicts of interest? Is it sufficient for the trustee to ignore competing interests and to try to manage the institution's affairs in good faith, as if the potential conflicts did not exist? Apparently not. A recent court decision directed that both trustees and the institutions they represent cannot simply ignore potential conflicts but must directly face them and attempt to minimize their effects. A failure on the part of trustees and their institutions to take such action could leave trustees individually liable for breaching their fiduciary duties. In the decision *Stern* v. *Lucy Webb Hayes National Training School for Deaconesses and Missionaries, et al.* (1974), a federal court in the District of Columbia established minimum standards of conduct for trustees who have business interests that may compete or conflict with the business interests of the institution they serve as trustees.

The *Sibley Hospital* case, as it has come to be called, involved a suit by the parents of children who had been patients in Sibley Hospital against several defendants, including nine of the hospital's trustees. The parents claimed that the cost of the hospital care given their children would have been far less if the trustees had properly managed the hospital's assets. Among the allegations of improper trustee action was the claim that the trustees had sought to enrich themselves by placing the hospital's cash in accounts in banks in which the trustees were principal stockholders, officers, or directors. Another allegation of mismanagement involved the hospital's use of a trustee's brokerage firm as its investment adviser.

After a lengthy trial, the court found that none of the trustees derived personal financial benefit from the suspect transactions. It also determined that the "favored" transactions were not detrimental to the hospital. Nevertheless, the court sharply criticized the trustees for allowing the hospital to deal with institutions with which they were affiliated:

> It must be made absolutely clear that board membership carries no right to preferential treatment in the placement or handling of the hospital's investments and business accounts.
>   [An institution such as Sibley Hospital] would be well advised to restrict membership on its board to the representatives of financial [organizations] which have no substantial business relationships with the [institution]. The best way to avoid potential conflicts of interest and to be assured of objective advice is to avoid the possibility of such conflicts at the time new trustees are selected [*Stern* v. *Lucy Webb Hayes.* . . , p. 1019].

Although the court's suggestion may be the best formula for completely avoiding conflicts of interest, it offers little practical help to institutions and their trustees, given the relationships that often inevitably exist between colleges or universities and the business interests of many of their trustees. Recognizing this difficulty, the court in *Sibley Hospital* ordered the auditors of that institution to incorporate within each of their audit reports for the next five years a summary of all business conducted with any financial institution with which any hospital trustee was affiliated. This requirement is consistent with certain state laws, such as New York's, that permit transactions between an institution and a business in which a trustee has a substantial financial interest, as long as the trustee's interest in the transaction is disclosed to the board and the board approves the transaction without the vote of the interested trustee.

Disclosure and Nonparticipation

The court in *Sibley Hospital* also suggested two procedures that are essential in avoiding or neutralizing all conflict situations, not simply those involving the financial management of the institution. The two procedures involve *disclosure* of potential conflicts and *nonparticipation* by members of governing boards in certain actions of the board. To ensure that those precautions are carefully followed, each governing board should consider implementing a four-step process:

First, the board and principal administrators of a college or university should establish a written policy that sets forth the trustees' duty of loyalty and the need to avoid self-dealing or other conflicts of interest. The policy should also set forth a mechanism (such as that described below) for reporting and reviewing conflicts. A sample conflict-of-interest policy has been developed by the Association of Governing Boards of Universities and Colleges (AGB) and is included in Resource D of this book.

Second, a reporting system should be established that requires all trustees and key administrators to submit at least annual written reports disclosing their personal business interests and relationships, as well as their relationships with other nonprofit corporations. Many of the country's major accounting firm already have developed material to assist institutions to set up these systems. Two sample disclosure forms are included in Resource D.

Third, a senior administrator of the university—in small institutions, a trustee—should be charged with evaluation of the individual reports by trustees and administrators as well as with monitoring all institutional transactions with trustees and their business and nonbusiness affiliates. That administrator or trustee should summarize this data and report at least annually to an appropriate board committee or to the full board.

Finally, the committee or full board should review all transactions involving the interests of trustees or their affiliates and should either reject or ratify those transactions. Trustees whose interests are involved should abstain from voting.

Although sanctioned by the *Sibley Hospital* court and many state statutes, such disclosure processes will not always be enough to insulate trustees from charges of conflict of interest and in certain situations from being held personally liable. Disclosure systems are a good start for governing boards to make; but as the examples that follow indicate, they do not provide a panacea.

It was noted at the outset that trustees owe a high duty of care and loyalty to the colleges or universities they serve. Hence, whenever the outside interests of trustees or their affiliates in any way impinge on the interests of the institutions, a potential conflict of interest exists. Although such conflicts most commonly arise out of the financial management of the college or university, they may also occur in areas such as curricular or program development and recruitment policy. Furthermore, a conflict may exist even though a trustee's outside interests will not result in any financial or other enrichment to that trustee.

The court in the *Sibley Hospital* case enunciated specific situations in which conflicts are inherent and are for the most part be easily avoidable: (1) deposit of an institution's funds in banks in which trustees are officers, directors, or key employees, and (2) use of a trustee's brokerage firm as the institution's investment adviser. Other conflicts arise from the trustees' responsibility for what can be loosely described as an institution's "financial" concerns—endowment, fund raising, management of a stock portfolio, and so on. Still others arise from gifts of securities, land, or valuable objects, such as works of art or library collections. Conflicts can also be related to trustee fund-raising efforts or to the school's contracts with trustee-related businesses for services or goods. The remainder of this chapter will consider common conflicts of interest, together with suggestions about procedures that help insulate trustees and the institutions they serve from liability arising from those conflicts.

Conflicts Involving the Donation or
Management of Securities

An institution's endowment may include securities in a corporation in which a trustee is an officer, director, major shareholder, or key employee. Such a situation creates several problems in portfolio management. When a trustee has stock in the same company as the institution does, his or her holdings may be affected (positively or adversely) if the institution buys or sells a large block of that stock. Accordingly, federal securities laws, as well as those of many states, prohibit use of "inside information" in buying or selling stock and other investment instruments regulated in the same way as securities. Inside information is information available to officers, directors, or key employees of a corporation, but not publicly available. Securities laws prohibit its use to prevent financial harm to outsiders who must trade their securities without the benefit of such information. Unfortunately, the restrictions of the securities laws and the disclosure requirements of the *Sibley Hospital* decision can create something of a "Catch-22" situation for trustees involved in the financial management of a college or university.

Consider the case of a trustee who serves on an institution's finance committee but is also an "insider" of a corporation whose stock is included in the endowment portfolio of the institution. Since the stock has consistently performed well, the institution's finance committee is considering increasing the institution's holdings in it. However, as an "insider" of the business corporation, the trustee already knows that certain problems suffered by the business in the past year are likely to cause the value of the stock to drop. But until that inside information becomes public, the trustee is prohibited by the securities laws from counseling the finance committee to unload the stock rather than acquire more. Nevertheless, the fiduciary obligation of the trustee imposes a duty to provide the finance committee with significant information affecting any contemplated stock transaction.

One of the ways to attempt to avoid such a problem is for the governing board to erect a so-called Chinese wall between trustees who might possess inside information and those who make investment decisions for the institution. This wall consists of barriers that prevent inside information from reaching other members of the group charged with investment decisions. To build this kind of wall, institutions have used separate outside managers who are not usual participants in board decisions; they have used inside managers who report to the president rather than the board; and they have adopted rules that require the trustee to absent himself or herself when his or her company is considered or even discussed as a possible investment position. Obviously, the best "Chinese wall" would be created through use of an outside independent manager who would report to a committee of the board whose membership included no officers or directors of business corporations. Unfortunately, the governing board would then lose the investment acumen it needs and seeks in board members.

In sum, potential conflict in the area of securities management cannot be entirely avoided, only minimized. And while disclosure of such potential conflict is therefore a necessity, avoidance of the "Catch-22" position of the trustee who is also an "insider" may still be impossible.

Gifts of Securities by Trustees

Some trustees prefer to donate securities rather than cash to institutions on whose boards they sit, obtaining income tax benefits if those securities have appreciated in value while owned by the trustee. Although these gifts are often marketable securities, it is not unusual for the gifts to be stocks or bonds in a corporation that the donor-trustee owns, controls, or operates. Several problems can arise thereafter. If the value of securities given by a trustee begins to decline, the institution's sale of a large block of the donated securities could contribute to that decline, particularly if the market for those securities is thin. Such a sale would probably be contrary to the donor-trustee's *personal* interests, particularly if the donated securities were in a closely held corporation or a corporation in which the trustee had substantial interest or control. However, failure to sell the securities could harm the institution by reducing the value of its assets. Obviously, if at all possible, donor-trustees should not be responsible for direct management of their gifts. In fact, it is usually unwise to give trustees responsibility for anything except the broad investment philosophy of the institution.

One of the best ways for the board to insulate itself from such potential conflicts, and incidentally to obtain the best investment advice, is to have an independent investment manager, such as a bank or other financial organization, manage or handle such gifts together with the institution's other investments. This completely separates the financial management of the donated securities from the interested donor-trustee. In addition, a truly independent management firm (that is, one not associated with a trustee) would be less hesitant to sell trustee-donated securities than would a fellow trustee. Even independent investment managers, however, are aware that their contracts with the institution are to an extent dependent upon the good graces of the trustees. Thus, it is the president of the institution and the chairman of the governing board who must always be prepared to take major responsibility in explaining to donors the need to dispose of their gift securities. This difficult task is made easier if the trutees have discussed and understood this potential conflict of interest before the actual problem arises.

Many institutions are unable to afford or justify use of the services of an independent investment adviser. Those institutions should remove donor-trustees from the management of donated securities as completely as possible. Furthermore, the institution should establish a clear policy that gives equal treatment to all securities in the institution's portfolio, without regard to how the securities were acquired. Trustees on the institution's investment committee must be prepared to enforce that policy and withstand pressure from fellow trustees who oppose it.

Both large and small institutions should adopt policies that require board ratification of decisions to sell trustee-donated securities, decisions to increase holdings in those securities, or decisions to maintain holdings in those securities if their market value is questionable. However, even if the trustees use such procedures and follow sound investment principles in the management of trustee-donated securities, an institution that suffers losses as a result of its failure to sell trustee-donated securities could face a court challenge from alumni, students, or others who complain that the losses resulted because a conflict of interest interfered with the board's duty to sell.

Trustee Gifts of Property Other than Securities

Trustees often donate works of art, land, library collections, or other property to the institutions they serve. A conflict of interest between the institution and the trustee-donor may arise if they place different valuations on the gift. Obviously, the greater the value placed on the gift, the greater the advantage to the donor-trustee. Yet, the institution and the trustee are both subject to charges of self-dealing and violation of public trust if the valuation placed on the gift is unrealistically high. What may appear in the collegial atmosphere of the boardroom to be a gesture of gratitude for years of volunteer service may be viewed by reporters and judges as self-dealing and a breach of the duty of loyalty. Low valuations are likely to be unacceptable also, both to a donor who has already given an item to the institution and to potential donors if the valuations made by the institution are consistently low.

The best protection from such problems is to insist that all gifts from trustees to the institution be valued by an independent consultant, unrelated to any of its trustees. But this process may itself offend potential trustee-donors, with the result that the art collection eventually goes to an institution willing to accept gifts at the donor's valuation. A more palatable approach might be to average two independent valuations—one supplied by a consultant of the donor-trustee's choosing and one by a consultant chosen by the institution.

Purchase of Services or Goods
from Trustee-Related Businesses

Purchase of services or goods from trustee-related businesses will always appear questionable to some. To repeat the judge's harsh reminder in the *Sibley Hospital* case: "Board membership carries no right to preferential treatment in the placement or handling of . . . business accounts." At the same time, however, trustee-related businesses may supply the best services or goods at the best price in the area where the institution is located. There is nothing wrong with such "favored" transactions *as long as:* (1) The relationship(s) between the institution's trustee(s) and the supplier(s) has (have) been disclosed in the annual reporting system described earlier; *and* (2) The transactions have been ratified by the appropriate committee (or the full board) after such disclosures have been reviewed; *and* (3) The benefits to the institution from trustee-related businesses and the prices paid for those benefits are equal to or better than those the institution could obtain from unrelated businesses.

In some situations it will be difficult to ensure that the last criterion has been met, but the board should be able to substantiate its choice of a "favored" supplier in terms of the best or at least very good market value. As evidenced by the *Sibley Hospital* case, however, such transactions will always carry the appearance of impropriety, and even trustees who carefully follow the criteria outlined above should be prepared to defend lawsuits alleging harm to the institution and a breach of the trustee's fiduciary duty.

Conflicts Caused by a Trustee's Fund-Raising Responsibilities

In addition to contributing their own funds, trustees are more and more often called upon to perform fund-raising services, that is, trustees are asked to seek funds from foundations, corporations, or government sources to which they have particularly close relationships. According to the American Council on Education (Gomberg and Atelsek, 1977), almost 20 percent of the members of governing boards serve on more than one board. Whether the difficulties thus created should be termed conflicts of interest is not clear. We do know, however, that a trustee can go to a potential major donor on behalf of *any* institution the trustee represents only a very few times. Since there is a limited amount of public and private money available for funding colleges, universities, and other nonprofit organizations, it is difficult for a trustee to seek funds from the same source for more than one institution. For example, the trustee who serves on both a college and a museum board may be asked by each to solicit funds from a donor who will contribute to only one institution. Consequently, when trustees are asked to engage in fund-raising activities, they might ideally restrict their efforts for each institution to areas that will not compete with the interests of the other nonprofit institutions they serve.

Questions about fund raising become more difficult for trustees who serve both public and private universities that are seeking public funds. Any position a trustee takes with respect to funding one type of educational institution is likely to conflict with the interests of the other sector, particularly given the state of the economy as the 1980s begin. Accordingly, for a trustee holding positions on the governing boards of both public and independent institutions, it is almost imperative that he or she refrain from fund-raising activities altogether. Charges of conflicts of interest resulting from fund-raising activities are less likely to be raised in the courts or the media than are charges of conflicts in the management of an institution's endowment or other funds. However, such challenges are not impossible, particularly in light of the number of institutions forced to close their doors over the past few years because of inadequate funding. As a minimum, therefore, trustees should not engage in fund raising in which conflicts may arise unless (1) those conflicts are disclosed to the boards of the affected institutions, and (2) the boards determine that the benefits to the institution outweigh the risk of permitting certain quite able fund raisers to continue their activities despite possible conflict-of-interest charges.

Faculty and Student Trustees

A conflict-of-interest problem arises when an institution permits its own faculty members to serve on its board of trustees. Consider, for example, the conflict that arises when the board allocates a portion of the budget for faculty salary increases or votes to grant a faculty member tenure. The potential conflicts between an individual's interests as a representative of the faculty and the interests of the institution *as a whole* are so numerous that they cannot be reasonably remedied by disclosure or nonparticipation.

The potential conflicts raised by the presence of students on boards also seem considerable, although an increasing number of institutions have added student members to governing boards during the last decade. Nonparticipation or disclosure does not eliminate the student's own interests, and his or her often limited perspective makes viewing the interests of the institution as a whole very difficult. To obtain students' points of view, some institutions have added very recent graduates to governing boards while others have invited students to become active members of some of the board's committees. (Also see Chapter Eleven.)

Insurance and Indemnity Provisions

By adopting the procedures outlined in this chapter, by consulting with the institution's legal counsel, and by being mindful of conflict problems, trustees can substantially reduce conflict-of-interest charges. It is also important to remember that, although there are thousands of colleges, universities, museums, and other charitable corporations in the country, the reported number of money judgments finally obtained against individual trustees is insignificant, at least as of today.

Even if the trustees follow all the suggestions made in this chapter, the institution may be sued by those who believe that the institution has been harmed by conflicts of interest. Following good practices does not eliminate lawsuits. The *Sibley Hospital* case gives some indication of the many different people who might be entitled to bring such a lawsuit. The plaintiffs in that case alleged that the overpriced medical services had been caused by the hospital board's self-dealing. It is not difficult to construct a similar theory for a suit brought by a student or employee of an educational institution.

Assuming that trustees and chief executive officers are guided by the admonitions of the court in the *Sibley Hospital* case and by the disclosure and nonparticipation procedures outlined in this chapter, most such suits could be successfully defended. However, the costs of successful defense can be significant, even amounting to a large percentage of a small institution's budget. Both institutions and individual trustees should therefore consider taking advantage either of the indemnity provisions in many state laws or of trustee indemnity insurance.

Indemnity provisions in some state laws—for example, New York's—permit an institution to undertake the cost of defense of suits or claims against trustees. If it is assumed that the trustees acted in good faith and in what they believed to be the best interests of the institution, the indemnity provisions in most state statutes allow the college or university to undertake the cost of the trustee's personal defense. To confirm that responsibility on the part of the institution, a provision authorizing such indemnification should be included in the institution's bylaws. A sample indemnification provision is included in the model bylaws in Resource C of this book.

Such bylaw provisions may be only "cold comfort" to trustees, however, given the limited financial resources of many institutions today. Insuring against the risk of ultimate liability and against the rapidly escalating cost of legal defense may be the only realistic means available to protect the institution and its trustees from serious financial consequences. Forms of trustee indemnity policies vary widely; the most important considerations are the deductible features of the policy and what it excludes from coverage. Therefore, every policy must be examined carefully. Premiums seem to depend upon the size of the board and the institution's assets, but there are no "standard" rates. There is no assurance that such insurance can readily be purchased by every institution, and any history of legal controversy will be relevant. Most policies offer alternate forms of coverage—restricted forms that may cover only the trustees, president, and key administrators and broader forms that include all employees of the institution. Trustees should remember, however, that trustee indemnity insurance does not insure against every risk. For example, insurance does not protect the criminal or the self-dealer who attains personal gain or enrichment. Nor does it protect the dishonest person, nor ordinarily against intentional or willful acts such as libel, slander, assault, or battery. But challenges to matters of management, whether successfully defended or not, would entitle the trustees to indemnity for legal expenses and monetary judgments under the typical indemnity policy. Furthermore, monetary settlement of such suits, subject to approval of the insurance carrier, is authorized under many such policies, and this provision might make possible a more expeditious and practical disposition of a lawsuit than would a protracted court case.

The issue of trustee indemnity insurance therefore may be principally an economic one. It should be evaluated in terms of the magnitude of the risk a college or university can reasonably assume, its ability to pay its lawyers in defense of the actions taken by the administration and countenanced by trustees, and the annual premium paid to a carrier to assume the burdens. Risk and threat to personal assets are nevertheless serious considerations in the minds of many today, both in business and nonprofit corporations. Therefore, if an institution cannot or will not purchase such insurance, individual trustees might consider purchasing it for themselves.

18

James Gilbert Paltridge

Studying
Board Effectiveness

Because trusteeship is a volunteer service, performed in most cases without compensation and by persons who devote only a portion of their time to it, it is important that all trustees have well-founded confidence in their board. They must know its capabilities, its strengths, its weaknesses. Without the security of this knowledge, earning the confidence and maintaining the respect of others may be difficult.

Self-study, conducted periodically and with thoughtful preparation, is a practical tool for refining and improving board performance. Efficiencies of time, both in individual preparation for meetings and in the conduct of meetings, can result from careful examination of procedures that previously have been followed out of custom or tradition. The time that is required to consider long-term goals and policies may emerge from a study of the short-term considerations that so frequently overload the agendas of board meetings. Imaginative leadership of the institution, as well as examination of basic issues of quality and cost, demands thoughtful minds and time-consuming consideration. The board must know whether or not it has the capabilities needed for this kind of leadership—and if not, what can be done to acquire them. The external relations of the board with its various constituencies can be enhanced if the board has found answers to important questions before they are asked. A well-informed board is most likely to be an effective board.

The benefits of periodic, formal, and structured self-study are positive because they usually lead to carefully planned improvements. Informal evaluations, even if they go on continuously, do not always lead to such constructive results. Furthermore, the *process* of a formal evaluation is itself an exercise from which much good can come in the form of improved board morale and rededication to the task of trusteeship.

Programs of self-study must be carefully formulated. Each self-study investigation, however, does not need to cover every facet of board activity in great detail. A board embarking on its first experience might be well advised to make general inquiries with the objective of pinpointing problem areas that could be the subject of subsequent inquiries. A board self-study committee might first define carefully the specific purpose of the investigation and then choose the questions—and the manner in which the questions are to be asked—that will evoke the most useful information. If published or "borrowed" questionnaire instruments are to be used, the committee should study them carefully, dropping less pertinent questions, adding others, and editing still others to fit its own situation. Professional assistance in preparing these inquiries may be valuable.

Methods of Self-Study

There are various ways that a board can conduct a study and evaluation of its own policies, practices, and organizational structures. A board may wish to employ a series of methods over a period of time, allowing the circumstances of each inquiry to dictate the manner in which it is carried out. What follows is a review of various methods that may be employed. They are presented in no particular order or priority of recommendation. They are simply different ways to conduct self-study investigations, and obviously variations of each many be devised.

Periodic Meetings. The time-honored method of gathering everyone together in the same room and talking a problem out has many advantages. The ease of arranging a meeting, however, may not speak to the ease of effecting a productive meeting. The meeting must be skillfully conducted, with discussion directed to specific points of inquiry. It probably should be held at a time or day separate from a regular business meeting so that, free from the concerns of routine or singularly important affairs, the trustees can direct their attention to "the good of the order." Holding such meetings on an occasion separate from a regular board meeting may be the best way of assuring privacy of discussion. If the agenda does not include any official business items, conflicts with "open meeting" regulations may be avoided. An informal social event following the meeting with spouses or families present has been found beneficial.

Gatherings for this purpose may be an ideal way to introduce the idea of self-study and self-evaluation and may encourage members to arrive at the decision to engage in further, more formally structured methods of investigation. Such private gatherings may also be a good way to review the results of a completed questionnaire study, or they may be used to conduct an exhaustive discussion of a single problem area brought out by a previous comprehensive review of board procedures. There are, however, inherent disadvantages, even dangers, in using such a gathering as part of a self-study procedure. The discussion might wander into a reiteration of old or petty grievances and destroy the constructive approach to current problems. The distinctive circumstances of each board's membership and the presence of a skillful discussion leader may determine whether this method will be successful.

Questionnaire Surveys. Ordinarily this type of inquiry is organized around a set of criteria or objectives related to the board's various obligations and functions. It relies upon posing key questions about a number of suggested criteria (each related to a different function or organizational component) so that the multiple responses of all members will produce a composite description of the quality and nature of the board's performance. The lack of unanimity of responses to particular questions may illuminate problem areas. In addition, the same technique may be used in a more restricted way to probe a limited number of problem areas or criteria that a board feels are of particular concern at the time. Thus the board may choose to concentrate the questionnaire effort on board membership and organization, budget reviews, financial management, or financial support.

Resource B of this book contains a questionnaire devised for governing boards of private colleges and universities and published by the Association of Governing Boards (AGB). This is constructed on a set of ten criteria ranging from "Institutional Mission and Educational Policy" to "Financial Support and Management." Each topic suggests four or five pertinent questions that should draw forth answers from the board members about how well their board performs in relation to that criterion. Each topic also contains a summary rating scale calling for responses from "very good" to "poor," along with space for members to comment on their rating response or give suggestions the board might consider. Similar self-study questionnaire forms have been developed for boards of public colleges and universities, community colleges, and multi-campus higher education systems, as well as for boards of state planning and coordinating commissions. Each of these is available through AGB.

These instruments may be used by the various types of boards in their published form, or they may be altered in any manner desired to make the questions related to each criterion more pertinent to particular circumstances or problem areas experienced by the board using them. The use of questionnaire instruments is probably the most thorough method of assessing board performance through self-study. At the same time it requires considerable effort to select or design the proper instrument, to administer it correctly, and to analyze it for correct meanings or valid implications. It is a good method to use for an initial overall evaluation that is followed by programs using the simpler or more pointed investigative techniques that are described in this chapter.

The decision to use the questionnaire technique for self-evaluation should be given careful consideration. In the first place, it is essential that the board reach a very substantial consensus on the use of a questionnaire instrument. Not everyone is willing to give the time and thought necessary for answering a detailed series of questions. This is more frequently the case when the questions involve personal perceptions of problems and introspective judgments. The question of whether to offer anonymity or request signed responses should also be discussed and settled. Decisions should also be reached on how the information from the questionnaires is to be summarized and analyzed, who will prepare the summary report, and who will see the individual responses as well as who will receive copies of a written report.

AGB Board-Mentor Service. AGB has developed a unique mentor-assisted self-study and evaluation program that is available to its member boards. The Board-Mentor Service is designed to help trustees and their chief executives conduct workshops for assessing their organization and performance.

The service is intended to be a one-time, maximum-impact program to help boards develop activities for self-improvement. The workshop is conducted by a volunteer who has been chosen by AGB and the interested board for his or her knowledge and experience—typically an experienced trustee from a similar type of institution. The mentor, who will have completed an orientation program conducted by AGB, helps plan the workshop agenda and serves as a catalyst in leading discussions. The mentor does not make recommendations on specific institutional problems but attempts to guide the discussion towards steps the board may take in solving its own problems.

Prior to the workshop session(s), the board will have provided the mentor with information on how the board views its performance and concerns. This is done by means of the AGB criteria mentioned earlier. A summary of the board members' individual responses is prepared by the institution and made available prior to the mentor's visit. The workshop program usually occupies eight to twelve hours of meeting time, preferably over a two-day period. This gives participants an opportunity to reflect on the discussions and encourages unhurried informality and candor. For longer workshops, two mentors may share responsibility.

The agenda, jointly developed by the participating institution and the mentor, typically includes:

• Introduction and overview of the workshop's purpose and design.
• Showing of the AGB film *College and University Trusteeship* and informal discussion of trustee roles and responsibilities as presented in the film.
• Discussion of highlights of the summary of responses to the board's self-study questionnaire instrument.
• Small group discussions on selected topics such as the distinction between policy and administration, planning strategies, board organization, and one or two specialized issues confronting the board. AGB can make brief filmstrips available on such topics as fund raising, academic tenure, and collective bargaining. These are selected according to the board's interests and needs to stimulate discussion.
• Summary discussion of highlights and major points of consensus.
• Discussion of further actions the board may take toward self-improvement.

To help meet the costs of the program, the participating institution pays a modest service charge to AGB, plus expenses incurred by the board mentor during the period of his or her service.

Checklists. A number of boards periodically use brief checklists to test and reinforce individual members' knowledge of the institution, the board's bylaws or standing orders, basic policies and procedures, committee rules and practices, agreed upon delegations of certain powers, or other predetermined topics. These may serve as interim board self-study techniques. They can also be used to focus on particular subject areas of immediate or possible future concern to the board. They are a useful follow-up on orientation activities for new members.

Instruments of this type also can be used by the board as self-evaluation instruments because summarized responses will provoke discussion of procedures and policies and encourage suggestions for improvements, as well as tell the board how well its established procedures and policies are known and understood by the members. A good example of the checklist technique is the trustee audit instrument that is included in Resource A of this book.

Confidential Meetings. Situations may exist at particular institutions that make formal programs of self-study and board evaluation unwise or inappropriate. These may occur when the board is experiencing an unusually large membership turnover or is facing some critical situation that would make certain evaluative information desirable but difficult or politically unwise to obtain at that time through a formal self-study program.

Under such circumstances, board chairmen have resorted to private meetings or to interviews with the members individually or possibly in small groups according to committee assignments. These are confidential meetings with the chairman or someone delegated by him or her. The discussion content should be structured to solicit suggestions for general board improvement or suggestions related to specific problems. Obviously, great care needs to be exercised in announcing and scheduling the meetings, and they call for tact and diplomacy in their conduct.

Only the board or its chairman can decide if this is a suitable strategy, but it may at times be the only means of communicating the information needed to evaluate past board performances and make improvements. While this may be a valuable interim self-study strategy, it should be followed, after an appropriate lapse of time, with a more structured assessment program.

Private Consultants. Very often an outside viewpoint and professional advice can put a new perspective on board organization and on performance problems that the board itself may not be able to see, diagnose correctly, or remedy. Evaluation by a professional consultant is frequently quicker and perhaps more exacting than a process of evaluation devised by the board members themselves.

Employment of a private consultant may be the best way to avoid the possibility of tensions among members of a board when strongly contrasting viewpoints are known to exist. In cases where serious problems are apparent or suspected, the outside viewpoint of a consultant may also be the best way to find solutions that will be acceptable to the board. A board will be well advised to observe two rules in retaining the professional services of a consultant. First, the board should make sure there is widespread agreement (much more than a simple majority) among its members on the choice of the consultant to be retained. Second, the board should make sure that the consultant is given all the information needed and access to the viewpoints of all members.

Assessment of the Board by Nonmembers. If the self-study program is based upon perceptions and evaluations by the members themselves, should the viewpoints of persons who are not members but closely associated with the board's work also be considered? This question is frequently raised and is usually answered in the negative.

A board's self-study program—self-initiated and self-conducted—is normally considered to be a very private affair. In the absence of glaring problems that are known by outsiders to exist, a board may properly feel that the details of the self-evaluation, and perhaps even the fact that it is being conducted, should be kept private. But there is merit in the inclusion of at least the chief executive officer in the self-study, whether he or she is already a full member of the board or not. Certainly the president's viewpoints are valuable and should be made known to the board.

A board may be genuinely interested in the ideas for self-improvement held by nonmembers with whom the board is closely associated—the alumni association leadership, the institution's managerial staff, faculty administrators, persons associated with principal funding sources, and perhaps student association leaders. Many of these persons may be genuinely flattered to be asked to participate in a self-study program, and their contributions may be very valuable. Their participation need not take the form of the investigatory method used by and for the members themselves; it may consist only of private interviews in which confidential discussion is limited to matters of board activity of concern to the interviewee. These viewpoints could then be summarized and included in the follow-up workshop conferences held by the board.

The disadvantages of this assessment strategy are obvious to most trustees, though in some cases perhaps exaggerated. These need not be labored here. But there are also advantages in obtaining outside viewpoints, just as there are certain disadvantages in relying on only within-the-family viewpoints of where and when improvements in board performance can be made. This is a matter that can only be decided by each board.

Extended Programs of Self-Study

The question of how frequently a board of trustees should engage in studies to evaluate its performance cannot be answered simply by saying "whenever necessary," because need may become evident only when problems have grown to major proportions. Self-studies should be looked upon as a means of forecasting problems and solving them before they become serious. Self-assessments should be made periodically, but frequent exhaustive investigations could become tiresome and arouse suspicions that a sort of organizational hypochondria has set in.

Thought should be given to an extended program of studies for trustees. An annual board retreat that combines a serious conference on issues other than current institutional affairs with a pleasant social event may be an ideal vehicle for reviewing and evaluating the board's performance. One retreat might be preceded by a comprehensive study that would be reported on, analyzed, and discussed at the retreat itself. Another might be preceded only by a brief opinion questionnaire or checklist of knowledge or attitudes—perhaps confined to a single problem area. On still other occasions a loosely structured, free and open discussion of a self-evaluative nature would be appropriate. Annual retreats may not be feasible for some boards for any number of reasons, the so-called sunshine laws relating to open meetings being among them. In place of annual retreats, many boards have used executive sessions or simply more or less private presession or postsession gatherings in connection with scheduled board meetings. Prevailing laws and the traditional practices of individual boards will decide the possibility and practicality, as well as the time and place, of such meetings.

Perhaps an ideal schema would be for a board that has never undertaken a thorough self-study or one that has not done so for several years to start off with a comprehensive, structured questionnaire study of the types previously described, preferably in conjunction with the AGB Board-Mentor Service. Then the next year the board might hold another workshop session to review how well any new practices have worked during the year to improve its effectiveness. If attention has been focused on a particular problem area, perhaps a brief single-subject questionnaire or checklist could be administered before the meeting to crystalize opinions and expedite discussion. If no critical problems have intervened that require a specifically directed assessment, perhaps a few years later the board should schedule a new questionnaire study ranging over a wide list of evaluation criteria. If there has been a significantly large turnover of board membership, this study could follow a previous assessment more closely in time.

Self-study evaluations of the board's performance and organization should be part of a continuing program. In addition, the type of investigation should be varied to suit the circumstances surrounding the board and its activity each time a new assessment is planned.

There is no generally accepted "standard" or "ideal model" by which the performance of every board may be judged. Criteria for assessing the execution of the board's trusts depend on the values and specifications set forth implicitly or explicitly by the constituent publics that created and support the board. The list of criteria that follows is drawn from the literature related to board obligations, organization, and functions. Such a list cannot be exhaustive, nor will each listing be equally important to every board and every institution. This is why each board that is embarking on a program of self-assessment must carefully consider the criteria by which it will be judged and add to or subtract from this list.

Institutional Mission. The institution's statement of mission, purposes, and goals is the rudder that should keep the institution on its determined course. The statement of mission can be refined or adjusted from time to time to keep the institution headed in a desired and appropriate direction. But the important thing is that the direction be thoughtfully plotted, that the institution not be without its necessary steering mechanism. Thus, trustees should periodically evaluate the course of the institution, assess its basic objectives and goals, and decide how well the institution is following its plotted course.

Educational Policy. This needs clear statement, for it is a major determinant of the institution's mission. It is dangerous—to continue the rudder metaphor—if trustees try to "oversteer" the institution in respect to educational policy. The trustee role should be confined to setting the course, not operating the rudder. The former is a function of the governing board in close collaboration with the faculty and administration; the latter is a function of the faculty and administration alone. Trustees should evaluate basic educational policy in the light of the manifest needs of students, as well as assess the institution's adherence to and execution of established policy.

Institutional Planning. Strategic planning for the long term and for intermediate stages is increasingly essential. Keeping close account of current conditions and trends and making meaningful projections of numbers and sources of students, expenses and income, and education program requirements are the essential ingredients of planning. Board members must be knowledgeable about current data and professional projections so that they can participate, review, and assess the institution's planning processes.

Physical Plant. The size and quality of the institution's buildings, equipment, and real estate are a principal fiduciary responsibility of the board. Providing needed facilities and safeguarding the investments in these properties define the board's role. Management of the physical plant, in all its details, should be delegated but periodically reviewed by the board. The board must be aware of physical needs, establish priorities, and direct funds to those needs. It should carefully assess its ability to properly judge requests for expansion. It should be concerned about the extent of deferred maintenance, so that it can be sure that the cost of repairs or rebuilding will not jeopardize the institution's future.

Financial Resources. It is the board's responsibility both to secure adequate financial resources to operate an institution and to supervise its fiscal management. The budget is the policy instrument developed jointly by the administration and faculty and the board. Trustees should carefully assess their ability and that of the institution to attract the favorable attention of various funding resources—students (or parents) who pay tuitions and fees, persons and organizations who provide gifts and endowments, and federal, state, and local governments whose annual budgets contain monies to support students and educational institutions. They must assure themselves that the board, as a unit, has the ability to skillfully devise financial policies, to manage investments, and to supervise the prudent management of funds made available to the institution.

Board Membership. It is the board's own responsibility and that of its leadership to see to it that all members contribute a full share of their abilities and specific expertise to the work of the board. The board should have members who can bring to the board the wide range of experiences and expertise necessary for the complex operation of a modern educational institution. Assessment of individual capabilities for this work and of the capability of the whole board as a working organization is necessary. If selection of board members is a responsibility of the board itself, the board can exercise direct control over the qualities and capabilities of its component membership. If membership selection is the province of an outside authority, the board's personnel needs should be known to the board itself and made known to those who nominate and select or approve new members.

Board-President Relations. The board's long-term effectiveness is heavily dependent on the way it enlists the help of its chief executive in arriving at the decisions and formulating the policies that are the board's responsibility. Careful periodic review of the board's relationships with the executive officer is essential. Processes for selection of the chief executive should be reviewed well in advance of the need for their use.

Board-Faculty Relations. Trustees should periodically examine the line they have drawn between governing policy in academic affairs and operating policy. They share responsibility with the faculty for the quality of the institution, yet most lay board members lack professional experience in this area. The board should carefully examine the role it plays in basic policy formulation and in monitoring its execution to be sure that their decisions are well informed and that they have properly delegated their authority over academic practice.

Board-Student Relations. If the board is to discharge its obligation to provide students with a good learning environment, it needs appropriate lines of communication with students. These are sometimes difficult to establish in the first place, and the constantly changing student body may make them more difficult to maintain. A student representative on the board is not in every case the best channel, other means of communicating information *both ways* between trustees and students need to be devised.

Board-Community-Constituency Relations. Every educational institution has relationships with a number of off-campus constituencies that it serves and that in turn serve the institution—civic leaders in the surrounding community, cultural and educational organizations, commercial enterprises, city, county, and state officials, owners of adjacent or nearby property, and many others whose good will and cooperation the institution needs. While the details of these relationships are generally in the province of the administration and faculty, they can become a worrisome concern of the board.

Quasi-Judicial Role of the Board. Trustees may be called upon to settle disputes arising within the institutional community that are of such importance that only the governing board can adjudicate. In relation to these matters, the board should carefully examine two procedural areas. First, it should be sure that it has properly delegated authority to settle disputes at the lowest possible level, so that it does not have to become involved in operational matters. Second, it should be sure that the institution's due process policies are sound and that the board itself has standby procedures appropriate to the handling of any disputes that unavoidably are brought up to the institution's highest authority.

Self-Assessment as a Demonstration of Accountability

The rationale for periodic self-evaluative studies by boards of trustees is linked strongly to the matter of accountability. Boards must be accountable to themselves for the quality of their performance as trustees. They must at all times know that they are performing their tasks well. They must hold themselves accountable at all times to the institutions they serve—the administrators, the faculty, the alumni, the students. Likewise, they are accountable to the public. The public has a right to expect high quality in the performance of the board, as well as high quality in the educational service that the institution renders. This is true whether the public is supporting the institution through tax dollars, gifts, and endowments or through the direct payment of tuitions and fees for education and training.

Public accountability does not, however, imply unwarranted surveillance. This is destructive of certain freedoms that colleges and universities must jealously guard. Mortimer and McConnell (1978) have addressed this issue clearly: "It will take all the statesmanship the academic community as a whole can muster to enable colleges and universities to serve the broader public interest while preserving the identity, integrity, initiative, and morale of institutions and the intellectual freedom of faculty and students. The balance between the public interest, on the one hand, and institutional independence and initiative, on the other, between central planning and local freedom to act, is a delicate one fraught with tension and sometimes conflict, and it can be maintained only by common commitment and concerted action" (p. 236).

The commitment to effective trusteeship requires a concerted and continuing effort of introspective self-appraisal. For unless the board is sure of the quality of its performance, unwarranted demands for accountability may come to it from other sources.

Barry Munitz

Reviewing
Presidential
Leadership

Much of what commonly passes as leadership—
conspicuous position taking without followers or follow
through, posturing on various public stages, manipulation
without general purpose, authoritarianism—is no more
leadership than the behavior of small boys marching in
front of a parade, who continue to strut along Main Street
after the procession has turned down a side street toward
the fairgrounds. . . . The essence of leadership in any policy
is the recognition of real need, the uncovering and exploit-
ing of contradictions among values and between values and
practice, the realigning of values, the reorganization of institutions where necessary, and the governance of change
[Burns, 1978, p. 283].

The administration of a contemporary college or university
is an increasingly specialized and complex profession, so beset by

varied expectations that it is frequently decried as an unpleasant or even impossible task. Nonetheless, the presidency is an essential role, and a primary charge to those who bear legal and moral responsibility for a college or a university—its trustees—is to help ensure that it can be performed successfully.

Effective leaders in higher education can only be attracted and, once attracted, freed for their constructive work through a healthy governance environment. Yet the interdependence between governing board and chief executive officer has become extremely complicated. For instance, the criteria for presidential appointment that the board announced at the beginning of a search may be quite different from those factors that actually motivate its ultimate choice of candidate and even more different from the measures that a board subsequently uses to assess presidential performance. Moreover, each board member has his or her own understanding of the institution's mission and hence his or her own expectations about presidential responsibilities. The longer a chief executive is in office, the fewer board members remain who were serving at the time of his or her selection or who were involved in defining the actual circumstances that conditioned that selection. Indeed, board members are in an ambiguous position to assess presidential performance because they are being educated by, while simultaneously judging, the one college employee who reports solely to them.

Enhancing the President's Position

The lead editorial in a recent issue of *Change* bemoaned the current status of executive management in higher education: "In corporate management, presidential stress is now generally recognized as a fundamental problem to be dealt with. But in the academic field, the human costs of presidential office are still largely swept under the rug. . . . It remains an unsettling fact that academic leadership, which was once expected to give station and substance to our intellectual enterprises, is now largely in the hands of creative incrementalists. Is this in fact enough? Social imagination may in time make the difference between academic vitality and obscurity, but such requisites for survival are now largely missing" (Bonham, 1979, p. 13).

These comments were far from the first expressions of discontent regarding the particularly precarious position of the contemporary college and university president. Five years earlier, Cohen and March (1974) cynically called for some modest alteration in the status of our chief executive officers: "The world may collapse tomorrow; it may not. The university may survive another ten years; it may not. The differences are important, and the problems are serious. But the outcomes do not much depend on the college president. He is human. His capabilities are limited, and his responsibility is limited by his capabilities. We believe that there are modest gains to be made by making some changes in the perception of his role. We believe presidents can be more effective and more relaxed" (p. 5). I spent several years studying the issues raised by the Cohen and March text. I have worked with a number of institutions to help their presidents serve more successfully and more happily. I remain convinced that a carefully shaped evaluation process can improve the current situation.

Too many chief executives and their boards are not engaging one another in realistic conversations about their performance or about their status in the governance system. Too few institutions have trustees who take pains to make good judgments about the place. Confidence in the traditional process of informal exchanges between chief executive and trustees about administrative questions and subsequent modification when jointly desired, has broken down. If the expectations of the president and board are unclear or are in conflict, relationships with other constituencies are likely to be expedient at best and chaotic at worst; but if these expectations can be clarified, other relationships are more likely to fall into appropriate place. In our current governance climate one important step toward clarity—and thus toward stronger institutional leadership and operations—is for the governing board, acting in partnership with the president, to consider a more deliberate approach to the quality of college or university management.

An awareness of governance assessment issues should not only be evident during the search deliberations but should also be demonstrated at regular intervals during the president's tenure.

Periodic review can provide a candid look at the challenges confronting the chief executive, a more positive context for dealing with those challenges, and a sound basis for a subsequent presidential search whenever it is required. Ad hoc or crisis-generated assessments cannot provide these benefits, nor can they approach in any meaningful way the broader governance issues. However, a continuous analysis of executive progress, based upon the concept of in-service improvement of performance, can make a major contribution to institutional stability.

Concern Regarding the Evaluation Process

From another perspective, however, any attempt at presidential assessment that does not recognize the fragile status of chief executives in higher education or is insensitive to the special circumstances within which they work can create enormous problems. It would be naive to dismiss the critics of formal evaluation programs as simply wanting to prevent public scrutiny of institutions, or to accuse them of wanting to place presidents in a privileged and isolated position. On the contrary, an exclusive, magnified focus upon the chief executive's office can render that position immobile. A belief that detailed review procedures can replace personal qualitative judgments can distort the governance process. Indeed, higher education is in danger of building a search and assessment system in which the absence of controversy will lead to selection and the absence of activity to survival.

The recent introduction of presidential evaluation programs has thus engendered a legitimate and often acrimonious debate regarding their relative merit. Kauffman (1978) has concisely set forth one aspect of the potential problem: "The announcement of the imposition of an evaluation system is often a symbolic act, calculated to give the appearance of tough management or the assertion of greater control by the governing board. . . . The concern about formal *evaluation* is that by institutionalizing we may distract and detract from what *ought* to be done in order to meet the evaluation system's expectations . . . . In the area of higher education, presidential evaluation has been predicated on a governance model that is more a myth than a reality; on decision making that is more political than rational; and on criteria or objectives that are often in the eye of the beholder rather than observable for objective assessment" (p. 63).

In a personal letter, the chairman of a public multicampus system board commented on his institution's brief experience with a "job performance evaluation" by saying that it was "a very traumatic spectre to the presidents and more detailed work must be done to not only assure the president that the board will consider very carefully the source or bias of any presentation but also assure the president that criticisms and comments will be evaluated very, very carefully with those considerations in mind. . . . I would suggest a session with the president or other person being evaluated *first* assuring that person that the board expects to hear more criticism than praise and assuring the person evaluated that it will view such comment very critically."

Others are so skeptical concerning any formal strategy for evaluation or term appointment that they claim such a trend reflects complete insensibility to the realities of the relationship between the chief executive officer and the board. The board chairman of one of this country's most prestigious universities has commented: "The trend toward term appointment and formal, periodic reviews for college and university presidents is a mindless urge which mistakenly assumes that the relationship between the board of directors and the chief executive officer is one of supervision rather than joint responsibility and collaboration. . . . Such an action is not the vote of confidence his appointment should be. It also presumes that his success or failure can best be measured in increments of time rather than in response to complex, interlocked, and overlapping events whose harmonic effects on each other and the organization itself cannot possibly be measured by 'formal periodic reviews.' I cannot imagine anything less appropriate or more erosive of the [chief executive officer's] relationship to his organization or his self-confidence" (Avery, 1978).

The balance between value received and risks taken vis-à-vis the evaluation process, therefore, remains in serious question. A majority of those studying administrative circumstances at our colleges and universities—particularly those at public institutions—believe that there are many situations that require, or at least could strongly benefit from, a more formal approach to assessment. Kauffman (1978) suggests that:

> Our colleges and universities are in desperate need of leadership. Assessment activity must contribute to improve leadership and heightened morale if it is to be worthy of support. While presidents may be on trial, so are our institutions, their governing boards, and faculties. They must nurture the best qualities of leadership that can be found. They must demonstrate that they can treat the leaders humanely and wisely—just as they themselves wish to be treated [p. 68].
>
> I do not deny that public university systems may for political reasons require a visible evaluation system of its top administrators. But if this is necessary, there is all the more reason for a sensitive evaluation process that rewards and reinforces excellent performance and enables the system to get and keep superior executives [p. 65].

In an ideal world, presidential self-assessment might be sufficient, both to identify areas of required emphasis and to provide alternatives for improved performance. But human beings are not given to unbiased self-analysis. Even if they were, the factors that define success are so ambiguous that most individuals need reasonably objective procedures to gain an enhanced measure of self-direction. For the same reasons, the informal daily review of presidential progress by individual board members cannot serve as the sole source of leadership assessment. Nor in our present educational milieu can those indirect judgments substitute for a more equitable and specially identified occasion to analyze the general status of institutional administration. Far from being threatening or disruptive, more formal procedures can create the clarity and generate the support among the institution's constituencies that responsive management requires. If a cure is still conceivable for the breakdown of traditional evaluative relationships, then periodic analysis of a college's governance context must be considered as one possible therapy.

Advantages to the President

There are additional benefits of formal assessment for the president. Academic leadership responsibilities are considerably more complex than they are perceived to be by the general public or than can be suggested by standard assessment criteria. Since too many members of governing boards and of the public at large tend to base their evaluation of executive leadership on oversimplified perceptions of the presidential role, it is essential to provide opportunities for presidents to elaborate upon the actual complexity of their positions. As will be noted in greater detail further on, this is especially true for chief executives at the campus level in multicampus systems.

A capricious environment within which an executive can be placed in a precarious position at any time and on any issue can be turned into one where performance goals, trustee attitudes, and credible options after serving as president are continually clarified. Those presidents who argue privately that their best interests are served by an unenlightened board are doomed to work without a buffer against far less caring external intrusions.

Additionally, the credibility of the administrative process itself can be significantly enhanced if the principal administrator of a campus or a system can personally demonstrate the capacity of his or her institution to address management problems. Such credibility influences the relationship between the president and the governing board as well. Given the nature of the search for chief executives, it is extraordinarily difficult for candidates to confront candidly any gap between the board's expressed expectations and his or her own experience and expertise. Even though a candidate may sense that the board's requirements are unrealistic, or that they do not actually fit the conditions at that institution, or that it is unreasonable to expect someone initially to have the entire range of talents the search committee stipulated, it is extremely difficult to confront honestly such areas of possible "inadequacy."

A person with several years experience in office, and knowing that his employers desire his continued services, usually is willing to identify areas where changing priorities require that staff and board members have different kinds of expertise to work with the president. Such an exchange between board and president also can extend the tenure of an individual at a time when presidents are appointed at an earlier age and serve shorter terms (sometimes creating crises of transition at many institutions). The problem of appropriate longevity and "reentry" for presidents has become exacerbated in situations already complicated by increased financial pressures and collective bargaining. The impact on our institutions of higher education will be devastating if presidents feel that their tenure can be prolonged by noncontroversial decisions that lessen their exposure to constituency pressures.

The evaluation process has been able to prolong productive stay in office by allowing a president and a governing board to refine their priorities and improve their performance in an environment that expects, indeed encourages changing emphases. There have even been critical circumstances where an assessment has enabled a board and a president to reach mutually agreeable conditions for the transition to a new chief executive or has allowed a president to indicate to a governing board that, although it remains confident of his or her performance, the evolving job requirements make the position less attractive to him or her than it formerly was.

Advantages to the Governing Board

Experience demonstrates that the evaluation of institutional management can be as vital to the improvement of trustee stewardship as it is to the enhancement of presidential performance. Faced with the limitations of lay participation in governance, trustees find that a review often provides opportunities to explore leadership obligations and to learn the constraints upon, as well as the incentives available to, institutional managers. The crucial challenge to board members in the 1980s will be to support their chief executive officer by strengthening their own as well as the president's role. They must learn to transform the conflicts that could result from ignoring or misunderstanding current conditions into a firmer relationship achieved through mutual insight and symbiotic caring.

At some of our best colleges and universities a myth prevails that confidence in the president can only be demonstrated by a passive, perhaps even "rubber-stamp" board. Some board members still believe that their finest contribution to the institution is to unconditionally support or to firmly remove a president, just as some presidents still insist that an informed board member usually becomes a troublesome one. In recent years, however, increased public scrutiny, financial constraints, inevitable tensions in educational assumptions, and the advent of conflict-of-interest legislation have made it essential that key board members learn to assume independent but supportive roles. In such a state of mutual respect or skeptical positivism, where institutional problems are dealt with in a relatively calm and often public manner, protection is provided for the president without compromising the ultimate responsibility of the board.

For those who believe that these conditions already exist at most institutions, the following excerpt from Nason's monograph (1979) on the presidential search process is enlightening:

> Surprising, indeed shocking, as sometimes appears the laxity regarding practical terms of employment, the almost complete absence of statements on criteria of performance is the most astounding. The litany of presidential comments is disturbing.
>
> To repeat the obvious and too frequently ignored, the president is the agent of the board of trustees or regents. They set the policies—very often at the president's instigation and always, one hopes, with the president's participation. Within the policy so laid down the president must operate, and it is the board's responsibility to judge whether he or she operates well or ill or somewhere in between. How can the president know what is expected and how can the trustees judge how well the president has lived up to expectations unless there is prior agreement on what the institution needs.
>
> The trend is toward formal assessment of presidential performance at some stated interval, and this is frequently discussed at the time of appointment. The president has a right to know by what criteria he or she will be judged. The trustees have an obligation to state in writing what those standards will be. If they have done the job of analyzing the future needs and problems of the institution, . . . they should be able to convert the results into a set of expectations for presidential performance on which a fair and intelligent appraisal can be based [pp. 76–77].

A board conscious of evaluation objectives will stipulate presidential performance standards as the search process evolves, thereby improving the probability that the roots of any subsequent discontent can be more calmly analyzed. The institutional trauma induced by sudden extreme judgments will also be markedly reduced. If a decision is reached to seek a new president, by the board or by the incumbent, after a carefully focused process, then the college is several steps ahead in the establishment of conditions for the search. In any circumstances, a measured pace for review, for taking a closer look at its own role, as well as at its expectations for the president, encourages the governing board to sharpen the intensity and the quality of its perspective on the institution. Trustees can learn to protect a president's interests even when correct decisions turn out to be unpopular ones.

Alternative Executive Assessment Models

Once a governing board, with its chief executive officer, decides to establish or to undertake a presidential evaluation, there is a range of options available for structuring that process. Those options actually fall along a continuum that is characterized by the following alternatives:

- Will the emphasis be on the questions of hiring or firing or renewal of appointment, or will the focus be on the in-service improvement of executive leadership?
- Will the process be relatively closed—that is, restricted almost exclusively to private involvement of board members, or will the evaluation allow participation by other institutional constituencies?
- Will the evaluation concentrate upon the president alone, or will broader issues of board-president relationships and the status of institutional governance be explored?
- Is there a willingness to invest a reasonable amount of energy and money in the process?
- Is there a determination to seek external advice to assist the governing board and the chief executive officer?

The polarities for this range of alternatives extend from a relatively simple, closed, board-focused assessment that concentrates almost exclusively upon the president, all the way to a comprehensive, public, constituency-involved assessment that explores governance issues with the help of an external consultant.

Choosing the Evaluation Format

The governing board, and more specifically its chairman, must be responsible for selecting the evaluation model. In consultation with the chief executive officer, the chairman must determine the focus, as well as the breadth, of the evaluation perspective required for his or her particular institution. Whatever the pattern preferred, the orientation must always be toward people, not toward a process. An emphasis upon inflexible lockstep procedures, based upon the naive assumption that a "perfect model" will allow any group of evaluators to succeed, will place qualitative judgments in extreme jeopardy. Therefore, the temperament of those involved will be a crucial factor in selecting the format. Other considerations include:

- The reasons for initially contemplating the evaluation.
- The healthiness of the current governance situation.
- The frequency and openness of conversations between the governing board and the president regarding governance issues.
- The size of the board and the complexity of the institution.
- The quality of the search process that led to selection of the current chief executive officer.
- The seniority of the president.
- The degree of politicization currently affecting the institution.
- The traditional strengths of constituency involvement.
- The degree of constituency involvement in how the institution is governed.
- The level of time and money investment acceptable to the institution.
- The existence of internal expertise on governance matters.
- The desire and ability to maintain confidentiality regarding the background for and the results of the assessment.

Assessment Building Blocks

There are certain components of the process that should be considered whatever the format selected for a particular evaluation. The existence of a common framework helps each institution to develop its own assessment process without wasting precious time "reinventing the wheel." However, every college represents a significantly different educational and political context.

The President's Statement. In almost every instance a review should begin with an essay from the president that spells out what his or her objectives were upon assuming office and then analyzes progress toward their achievement. This analysis provides an opportunity for the chief executive officer to present a personal view of the leadership function, to comment upon his or her own working style, and then to analyze how both of these relate to the perceived needs of the institution. It is entirely appropriate that the president serve as initiator of the process and then remain a central figure as the evaluation unfolds. Issues that should be addressed by the president include:

1. Expectations and objectives upon assuming office, including comments on the presidential search process.
2. Assessment of success within the context of those initial objectives.
3. Adequacy of those first expectations, based upon the president's current knowledge.
4. The principal issues now confronting the presidential office.
5. A revision of original objectives in response to those issues.
6. Attitudes toward the nature of academic institutional leadership, based upon the president's past as well as present experience.
7. A comparison of present responsibilities and working style with those in the earlier executive roles of the president.
8. Suggestions concerning those "significant others" whose response to the statement would be most helpful if made part of the evaluation process, and suggestions concerning the types of response that would be most useful to the president.

The Institutional Analysis. While the president is preparing this statement of stewardship, the board should be establishing its frame of reference for the evaluation process. Assumptions regarding the presidential role should be based upon an earlier identification of the institution's social and educational conditions. Nason (1979) among others has consistently urged boards and search committees to appraise the "problems and prospects of their institutions" (p. 29) prior to determining the type of individual their selection process should seek.

Whenever a board attempts to judge a college president, it is also assessing the arena of institutional governance in which that executive performs. That context should be clarified in order to improve the president's performance. Without undertaking an elaborate self-study, boards can examine major current or potential problems and identify the talents that are required to address them. If such an analysis does not exist when the assessment begins—and many institutions lack that type of appraisal—then those in charge of the evaluation must spend some time discussing the highest priority items that would confront any president at their college.

Selecting the Criteria. Extensive consultation with those involved in earlier presidential reviews, along with my own experience in counseling a number of institutions during the past decade, has produced the following comprehensive but general list of performance criteria:

Planning and Administration

1. Are there commonly understood policies and priorities that implement the academic mission of the institution? Is there a broad base of constituency support for those policies, and is there a reasonable indication that the chief executive's educational philosophy is reflected meaningfully in those priorities?
2. Is there an awareness of evolving internal and external expectations? Has that awareness influenced educational planning in such a manner that aspirations can be raised without overextended promises that might go unfulfilled and thus threaten morale?

3. Are the planning, the resource allocation, and the evaluation functions effectively linked to one another so that basic fiscal patterns are meaningfully related to planning priorities and based upon evaluation processes?

4. Is there substantial evidence of sound fiscal management, including the ability to address budgetary issues in a manner that will produce a more efficient and effective use of resources?

5. Has expertise been demonstrated in managing capital as well as operating resources? Have the requirements for new facilities, as well as maintenance, repair, and rehabilitation, been analyzed responsibly?

Decision Making and Problem Solving

6. Can the chief executive officer articulate how fundamental decisions are made? Is there evidence that courageous, tough responses have been given when required?

7. Do mechanisms exist for involving internal constituencies in the decision-making process? If so, do they include a sensitivity to the values of various interest groups?

8. When difficult decisions are required, can the chief executive identify issues confronting the institution in that given problem area? Can he or she perceive the multiple factors that might affect the problem and then consider alternative sources of advice before resolution? Does the president understand the potential interrelatedness of decisions that emerge from seemingly different areas, and is the president capable of interpreting ideas in a context that often involves considerable ambiguity?

9. Are there continuous assessment procedures in place both for programs and personnel? Have they been made credible by a willingness to alter current patterns when the need for revision is indicated?

10. Has a mutually supportive relationship been established between the chief executive and the governing board? Are trustee interests understood, and do they receive timely, constructive responses?

Tone of Presidential Office

11. Has the president selected high quality subordinates and maintained credibility with them? Has the performance of principal

colleagues been reviewed, and have decisive actions been undertaken when sensitive personnel changes are required?

12. Does the president have a demonstrated ability to handle crisis situations that might involve personal criticism, unpopular decisions, or even a public reassessment of earlier recommendations made by the same chief executive?

13. Does the president have an awareness of the distinction between issues that can be delegated and those that require direct action by him or her? For those delegated issues has the president allowed latitude for decision making within a constructive span of control?

14. How has the introduction of new characteristics, such as affirmative action policies or the evolution of a collective bargaining environment, affected the performance and influenced the adaptability of the president?

15. Is there general evidence of the president's commitment to moral and academic excellence? Are the conditions that affect the quality and the pleasantness of day-to-day faculty and student life on the campus ultimately set by the chief executive?

External Relations

16. Have external constituencies related to the institution (for example, the alumni, the local community, and special-interest groups) been educated for political as well as financial support?

17. Can the president respond to the demands for social and intellectual leadership that are made constantly upon her or his office?

18. Does the president understand and enjoy the particular environment in which the campus is located?

19. Have those private, state, and federal agencies that have a significant potential impact on the fiscal and educational policies of the institution been successfully approached?

20. Has the autonomy of the institution been protected wherever possible? In terms of academic programs, physical facilities, compensation patterns, the retention of quality personnel, and so forth has interference by political factions been diminished or minimized?

Refining the Criteria. Each governing board should be able to construct a more particularized set of standards by bringing its own distinctive concerns to bear, even though the basic categories of judgment usually remain remarkably consistent. If those criteria are to remain meaningful, they should:

- Be refined systematically until the board is relatively certain that they are both comprehensive and representative for their particular evaluation. While faculty, students, and staff will provide valuable suggestions regarding the ultimate criteria, only the governing board—working with the president—can establish the actual standards that will constitute their institution's evaluative framework.
- Provide information that will be useful to the ultimate evaluators by asking questions that can be legitimately answered.
- Relate to those high-priority tasks that were identified at the time of the presidential search and appointment.
- Reflect any changes since adoption of primary objectives, and any new priority goals in the identification of presidential responsibilities. This mutual determination of current priorities protects the chief executive against ex post facto application of new criteria, while it educates the board regarding any shifts in management goals.
- Tie directly to the goals and assumptions of the particular evaluation.
- Take account of unpredictable or rapidly changing elements.
- Serve as a reminder for eliciting qualitative responses. Criteria should be used as a guide for talking about performance and never be applied as a report card that substitutes for judgment.
- Undergo a final situational review to ensure that the criteria are useful at a given time. The three following distinctions may be useful to illustrate this point:
  (a) What *any* president should do at *any* institution, (b) what *any* president should do at *this* institution, and (c) what *this* president should do at *this* institution.

Gathering Information. At this stage of the assessment process, that is, when the criteria have been refined, the evaluators must begin to gather the resources for informed judgments. When an evaluation framework has been selected, decisions must be made regarding the involvement of constituencies. Then it is time for those ultimately responsible for studying assessment material and reaching evaluative decisions to hear responses to their criteria.

Although the questions will vary significantly, the essential inquiry remains, "What can you tell us about the way this institution is governed?" The tone of a presidential review will frequently be established by the attitude of the inquirer. For example, most questions should be geared to determining whether the institution is dynamically moving ahead, not whether specific complaints have been registered. In addition, regardless of how limited or how broadly based the request for information is, in almost every instance survey instruments will turn out to be far less important than sophisticated interview procedures and experienced interviewers.

Popularity contests, public opinion polls, and detailed questionnaires that require objective quantification must be avoided wherever possible. Statistical data will be less useful than informal qualitative responses and candid personal impressions. Even a single board member conducting a private review will do more listening then measuring and will participate more in conversation than in examination. The nature of presidential leadership at an academic institution rests more crucially on intangible interpersonal skills than on measurable products. Therefore, the ability to ask the right questions and to gauge the qualitative nature of responses must be among the primary skills required for any coordinator of the evaluation, whether that person comes from inside or outside the institution.

Report for the Governing Board. Ultimately a formal report must be submitted to the chairman of the board. Although, like the criteria themselves, the format as well as the content of these reports will differ substantially, there are basic touchstones that indicate the type of information desired. Each institution will have to determine how extensive the report should be, how widely it will be distributed, and how publicly it will be discussed.

The introduction to the document should contain the rationale for initiating the review. Comments upon the complex role of college chief executive officers are appropriate at this point.

The original objectives of the assessment process should be rehearsed, and some reminder should be provided as to whether the current status of board performance was part of the study. As in the president's statement, reference should be made to the major accomplishments of the chief executive officer, and the most pressing issues currently on his or her desk should be identified.

Recommendations for the president and for the governing board, generally adhering to the categories of criteria developed by the institution, should then be presented. If governance issues were raised by the assessment, then some component of the report should be devoted to the relationship between the chief executive officer and the board, as well as to organizational questions concerning the board itself.

The conclusion should emphasize insights gathered from the evaluation process and propose recommendations for refining that process before the next cycle begins. Specific strategies for implementing the assessment agenda should be outlined. If items on that agenda have been addressed since the assessment began, they should be described. When the evaluation included conversations with internal and/or external constituencies, the interview schedule should be outlined in an appendix. Inevitably there will be issues raised that cannot be formally addressed in a written report. Those should be discussed candidly by the board chairman with the chief executive.

Role of External Consultants

The premise of this chapter is that educational governing boards must make a commitment to reinforce excellence in order to keep first-rate executives. In line with this, some maintain that sensitive, experienced experts can contribute immeasurably to the status of a president. In addition, while the board or system executive must retain ultimate authority for presidential assessment, there can be an essential role for an experienced observer-facilitator-interpreter who encourages objectivity, reconciles areas of dispute, dampens a politicized atmosphere, and exercises the authority of inquiry in a way that leads to constructive trustee recommendations. Those who advocate using such a fact finder or adviser insist that any contemporary president from time to time needs a trusted external observer who can gather a variety of views about his or her performance and suggest a strategy that moves away from confusion and toward resolution.

The decision to hire a consultant undoubtedly complicates and extends the evaluation process. There are both financial and psychological costs involved when the board admits that it cannot or should not undertake the evaluation without external assistance. These disadvantages must be weighed with utmost care. The strongest administrators in higher education usually have the ability to remove themselves occasionally from immediate concerns and use perspective; they serve in effect as their own consultants to the development and the evaluation process by testing informally their own relationship to the institution as if they were special or outside visitors. They instinctively improve the performance of vital colleagues whose potential is evident but whose actual service has suffered from a lack of confidence or initiative. These presidents are constantly fine tuning the institution's objectives, its organizational structure, and its administrative processes. Even these talented individuals, however, occasionally require a respected and disinterested third party to whom they can talk confidentially.

Those supporting the use of consultants argue that time and money often can be saved if a board seeks advice from an experienced professional with broad knowledge of administrative conditions at other colleges and universities, particularly one who is acquainted with the latest developments in leadership assessment and who can translate a mass of material into useful information. A qualified "outsider," chosen with the advice of the executive under review, can keep the evaluation on track. He or she can educate each party as to the expectations of the other and emphasize that at times those requirements must be modified or even altered dramatically in response to changing conditions or new personalities. Such consultants have proven their ability to create trust, provide comfort, relieve tension, and reduce conflict—all necessary conditions for reliable evaluation. Often an incumbent chief executive or a recently retired president from a similar type of institution can ease the minds of both trustees and their own chief executive by serving in such a capacity.

The decision to use a consultant is not an "all or nothing" matter. External advisers can be used to guide the entire evaluation or simply to establish the initial framework. They might spend one day with the board or many days with a variety of constituencies. Often the consultant will be available for occasional guidance but leave specific implementation to campus personnel. The options vary widely, as do the concomitant costs.

Recent Refinements of These Models

During the past five years I have been asked by a number of colleges and universities to assist in the formulation and implementation of presidential evaluation processes. Intriguing patterns have begun to emerge from those experiences, and most recently the following activities took place:

- A chief executive officer of twenty years' standing wanted to leave his institution and begin a new career in another profession. He was very uneasy about even implying to the college that he was rejecting it. At the same time several constituencies on the campus felt that his twenty-year service had been extraordinary but was reaching a reasonable conclusion. However, they were so committed to the person that they were unwilling to suggest that it was time to go. The evaluation led to an amicable shift of responsibility and to a carefully structured search process.
- Several presidents desired an evaluation process for their own professional development but found their governing boards unwilling even to imply that they were dissatisfied with the current performance. Each president and I together convinced her or his board that such conditions provided a splendid opportunity for a meaningful assessment. The assessment in turn provided materials that strengthened the chief executive's role while simultaneously enhancing the trustee's relationship to the institution.
- A president called saying that he was at the conclusion of his fourth year and was feeling substantial pressure to step down. The board chairman agreed that conditions were not good. I learned that the search process that identified the chief executive had been carried out in a most informal manner and so had left

most members of the governing board with very little sense of why the final decision was made or what the institutional priorities were for the new president. By recreating the search process and examining new priorities, both the president and the board put the governance of the institution back on track.

- At a number of institutions the Association of Governing Board's self-study guidelines and criteria were used to analyze the status of campus governance before the evaluation process began. In fact, at several colleges board members translated our evaluation principles into assessment programs for their own corporate responsibilities.

- When I was asked to provide guidance for the chief executive officer of a multicampus system, so many serious questions had to be raised about the structure itself that initial work focused almost exclusively upon reorganization of the system. That activity led in turn to the clarification of assignments for the chief executive officers of each component in the system. A decision was made to postpone the evaluation until he had assessed his own position with the governing board.

- At one campus a major issue that was discussed informally but that never surfaced publicly was the role of the president's spouse. The presidential family had found itself in a number of awkward situations in the community. My own role included working with both the president and his spouse in order to explain the sources of discontent and then to modify slightly their relationship to the campus community.

Lessons Learned

Although my own experiences with the evaluation process have been relatively positive, others have horror stories to tell. It is too early to determine whether the systematic assessment of presidential governance will or should become a permanent fixture for higher education, but it is clear that evaluation is a risky business with plenty of pitfalls. Indeed, enough is known to set forth general caveats and to summarize fundamental values:

1. Seemingly complicated in their permutations and combinations, the alternatives available are relatively few and basically

simple. Either board members carry out their own evaluation, talk-ing with few people but themselves, or they work with other insid-ers and discuss issues with some members of the campus commu-nity, or they use an outside expert to facilitate the process. With that expert—from inside or outside the institution—the board may even undertake a broad-based review of governance concerns with all relevant constituencies. Ironically, in many instances the better the quality of existing relationships between the board and the chief executive officer, the less likely that board is to consider any evaluation at all. Yet, those are the very circumstances that often lead to the most fruitful assessment. They can offer an attrac-tive opportunity for board and executive development, without interfering with a smoothly functioning, more traditional method of "assessment feedback."

2. It is the rare board that can retain the entire process in its own hands. Some discreet, sensible contacts with the leaders of crucial constituencies are virtually required to ensure the quality and the credibility of the assessment. Yet, people on the campus should not be asked their opinion about the current leadership situation unless those inquiring are willing to later indicate how their advice was used. Similarly, the investment in external assis-tance should not be made unless both the president and the board are willing to revise some of their own convictions. The ability to remain flexible, even in the midst of a carefully structured process, is often the key to a successful evaluation.

3. Not surprisingly, as trustees translate their expectations from the corporate or the political sector to the educational one, the focus of evaluation activity shifts subtly but firmly toward the board itself. In almost seven out of ten instances, whereas the orig-inal focus was to have been on the chief executive, a far greater emphasis eventually was placed on members of the governing board as they came to explore their own responsibilities and then strengthen their interaction with the chief executive.

4. The quality of presidential leadership was improved if the president had the opportunity to discuss with the governing board the specific goals toward which his or her office was working, the implications of new situations, and the degree of success that was being achieved.

5. While trustees ultimately are accountable for the quality

of management, they exercise that responsibility through their chief executive, whose effectiveness requires continuity in office, along with the understanding support of the board. The careful but explicit assessment of institutional leadership teaches board members to respect a president for his or her personal and professional dignity, while guarding against capricious action by the board.

6. Chief executives or trustees who insist that they are the subjects or the framers of constant, ongoing informal evaluation and that they therefore do not need any regular periodic assessment are often missing signals that call for the examination of actual working conditions. Such periodic closure is required by both the chief executive and the governing board if they are to focus clearly on current expectations.

7. Unless the basic reasons for a search committee's final selection are clarified for the new chief executive, it will be extremely difficult for the board to provide continuous assistance during his or her tenure in office. Furthermore, after the president has served for several years, it becomes virtually impossible to create from scratch any constructive framework for the examination of current expectations without including a consideration of original performance criteria. Therefore, stating the actual conditions that led to its final decision can be the search committee's major contribution to fruitful assessments during its candidate's tenure.

8. An evaluation restores the balance between internal and external influences on the president's decision-making process and provides that president with a firmer sense of how he or she is viewed by those who depend upon the presidential office. Adversary tendencies are thereby reduced, and a more pleasant and productive climate is created. The completion of such an exercise also permits a president the luxury of an objective reference point at critical moments.

9. The increased expectation concerning public accountability at the highest levels of academic administration can be transformed into a credible procedure for learning about subjective pressures within the institution and thus for minimizing political confrontation by anticipating sources of tension.

10. The president can enjoy work that much more. As

Cleveland (1978) has noted: "Our society has developed many highly effective ways of retarding change and smothering innovation. Some of the most effective have been grown in the hothouse politics of higher education where, as the old canard has it, the stakes are small and the men of honor are often outnumbered by the men of principle. To focus for twelve hours a day on untangling procedural snarls, and neglect to participate in the intellectual excitement that is unleashed by administrative action, is to get mesmerized by the misery and miss all the fun" (p. 16).

Problems of the Multicampus System

An increasing number of colleges are being absorbed by public multicampus systems. Such reorganization frequently occurs in response to pressures for a different combination of political influences and a more cost-effective allocation of financial resources. However, the multilayered organizational configuration makes the issue of executive assessment far more complicated than in single-campus institutions. The role of the campus chief executive officer becomes extremely sensitive. How is that person to be judged? If the system administration is strongly in support of a campus executive, the campus constituencies often feel that he or she has compromised their interests. The campus president often gains credibility with constituencies by confronting the very system administration that must ultimately determine his or her working conditions. Furthermore, the division of responsibilities between campus administration and system administration is not consistent at any two multicampus systems in this country. It frequently depends upon historic and political rather than substantive programmatic factors.

The University of Texas system recently commissioned a study by John Millett, executive vice-president of the Academy of Educational Development. Their charge to him requested that he work out a better distinction between the role of the campus chief executive and that of the system chief executive. Millett began his report by emphasizing that there was "a substantial difference in a multicampus system between the system as an organizational construct and the campus as an educational enterprise. There is some question as to whether or not the substantial difference has been clearly understood by the [University of Texas] Board of Regents as the governing board for a considerable number of separate educational entities" (1978c, p. 1). Millett provided some intriguing background material for this question:

> The organizational issues in a multicampus system are primarily two: (1) how extensive shall be the role of the system administration in providing educational leadership for all campuses; and (2) how extensive shall be the role of system administration in the management of campus support programs.
>
> The multicampus system is an organizational construct for leadership in management. . . . Recognizing that we are dealing here with higher education organization, we can nonetheless suggest that the system chief executive officer should be perceived as having fundamentally an administrative/political role, while the campus chief executive officer should be perceived as having fundamentally an administrative/scholarly role. The campus chief executive officer needs the confidence, the assistance, and the encouragement of the system, but, above all else, the campus chief executive officer needs the support and the cooperation of campus constituencies in realizing the goals of higher education [pp. 8–10].

The three-way interaction among board, system administration, and campus chief executive is likely to heighten the potential for conflict at each level. There are circumstances in which a public challenge to the system administration by a campus executive is the only way for that executive to maintain the support of his or her local constituencies. Most governing boards of multicampus systems delegate to the system executive the responsibility for reviewing leadership on each campus in the system, taking direct board initiatives only on rare occasions. The irony is that large systems require above all that trustees understand the basic needs of their campus components, but they must acquire such insight without undermining the authority of the system executive.

Millett's report provided fine insight into the source of potential difficulties and then suggested guidelines for reducing their frequency and intensity:

> One additional aspect of the multicampus system should be underlined. The governing board of several campuses retains the authority and responsibility of a governing board of a single campus but must of necessity act with some degree of remoteness from campus affairs. If the multicampus governing board tends to act as if it were the governing board of a single campus, its agenda may become unwieldy and time consuming, its actions may be interpreted as undue interference with or favoritism toward a particular campus, and its decisions may appear to be remote from the influence of campus administrators, campus faculty members, and campus students. A multicampus governing board has to learn how to act on broad policy matters and to leave greater areas of discretion to both system administrators and campus administrators than might be the case with the governing board of a single institution [1978c, p. 10].

Conclusion

In this era of fiscal constraints, can the investment of energy and resources for a process of management improvement be justified? In this era of increased pressures upon the president, can this additional responsibility be justified? Experience with thoughtful sympathetic assessment suggests that the answer to both questions is yes. Inevitable tensions between president and governing board must be minimized if an institution is to remain effective. The selection and—of equal importance—the retention of quality executive leadership for higher education are more likely to be achieved successfully when the governing board is willing to analyze openly what it expects of a presidential candidate or incumbent. Most importantly, the board must be willing to provide continued understanding and support for those expectations. It must assess with the president how well the board's original objectives are being met and how many of them remain relevant in the context of current priorities.

The danger is that some of our finest people will be driven away by crude assessment devices. A crucial factor in keeping strong leaders is enhanced stability for the president, the governing board, and the institution itself. More sophisticated selection and review can offer everyone involved a better understanding of the multifaceted forces within which a president must work. By adopting a systematic and thoughtful approach to an evaluation that could be imposed under far less positive circumstances, a president may be freed from rather than paralyzed by cross-expectations. Unfettered somewhat from the claims of countervailing forces, the president can devote greater attention to educational issues and to socially significant ideas. At the same time the more traditional informal evaluation relationship with the board can be restored.

The major issue confronting higher education today is the recruitment and support of good people—those very individuals who are education's scarcest resource. Assessment that focuses on developing philosophers and practitioners of the higher administrative arts is vital to every constituency concerned about the future strength of our country's colleges and universities: "Colleges and universities have their choice of two responses: one, to stand aloof and let those criteria evolve outside the universities, or to assume that it is part of their educational function to develop them. I don't have the foreknowledge that tells me what the future society will be like or whether educational institutions will have the freedom they have now or will serve their constituencies as well as they do now. But I am sure that there will be colleges and universities; and if they are better than they are now, it will be because dedicated trustees labored mightily to build and maintain them and to keep them free" (Alden, 1978, p. 19).

Professional development and formal evaluation probably are inevitable—the only question is whether they will be shaped tenderly by caring professionals who comprehend educational values, or whether they will be forced upon institutions by far less knowledgeable and exceedingly less patient external agents. Although the ultimate concern is institutional governance, the presidents themselves are the key. They must be protected but they cannot be isolated. They must be competent but they cannot expect themselves or be expected by others to begin as experts from the first day on the job. Any assessment program introduced to improve their performance must do just that, not place additional burdens upon individuals in an already complex position.

Many people claim that we do not even have an adequate general description of the presidency of a college or university. Yet, in the last fifth of the twentieth century, leaders must be attracted who will shape imaginative and courageous responses to difficult issues. Once hired, they must receive understanding and support. A creative assessment process, tailored to fit the particular requirements of a given institution, can provide for its constituencies unique insights into the responsibilities of their chief executive officer. Those with the power to appoint and to remove presidents must learn to appreciate a variety of administrative subtleties. An enlightened evaluation can enhance presidential stability and prolong presidential service while it redresses college grievances. Governance by inadvertence has never been acceptable to the finest of boards and presidents; the potential for strengthened leadership is in their hands.

20

J. L. Zwingle

Assessing
Institutional
Performance

Among the major responsibilities of governing boards in higher education, institutional assessment is one of the three most important, though it may also be the most neglected. The other two highest priorities, comprehensive planning and selection of the president, are usually placed ahead of institutional assessment. But consider: weakness in planning and in assessment will almost certainly then leave complete initiative to the president in these matters. Where then will trustees find guidelines when it becomes necessary to select another president? How will they manage to evaluate past presidential performance? It can thus be seen that shortcomings in assessment have considerable bearing on the turnover in presidents. Expectations are poorly defined at the outset. Subsequent evaluations become individualistic and subjective among all the parties involved.

Planning and evaluation are but opposite sides of the same coin. Neglect of these two central functions is perhaps attributable to the notion that a competent president should be able to meet all the demands of the office, while the board stands by to judge the results. The occasional success of exceptionally strong presidents reinforces this misconception. The successors to such presidents, along with the trustees, are of course wrong in supposing that they themselves are not implicated in the course of events that they attribute to the president. This is a failure of perception and at the same time a failure of procedure.

One form of assessment to which governing boards are attracted is essentially financial, and it comes about in two recurring items on the agenda: the annual budget and the annual audit. In general it is assumed that, if the financial situation is sound, other matters can be left to the administration and the faculty. Apparently successful institutions are sometimes lulled into complacency for years on end, while trends may be developing that with seeming suddenness threaten the future of the institution. Then comes a great outcry and an effort to quickly make a change of direction. Certain great universities offer grim reminders of just such conditions, not to mention many small colleges. Other institutions, on the contrary, appear to exist in a permanent state of emergency, which itself becomes taken for granted and prevents people from seeking new directions for the institution.

Recent studies emphasize two shortcomings that bear directly on institutional assessment: first, inadequacy of institutional research, that is, data collection and its interpretation; second, failure to check up on the achievement of goals once they have been adopted. Although both should rank high among priorities for administrators and trustees alike, both stand near the bottom of the scale. (See, however, the studies by Romney, 1978, and by Kells and Kirkwood, 1979.)

Two underlying factors may explain this rather strange state of affairs. Foremost among them is the old problem of effective education itself. If it were possible to ascertain the precise elements that would assure results, what a change for everyone! But the elusive nature of effective education continues to baffle even the most serious inquirers. To recognize education when it happens is one thing. To make it happen is another. But there is a second factor that inhibits the formulation and assessment of educational policies, that is, the abdication of trustees from responsibility for academic policy. Administrators and faculty members are of divided opinion about trustees. They look to trustees for protection and for support, but they fear the possible meddling in academic matters by those unprepared for such a role. In consequence, each group has tacitly or even explicitly agreed to a separation of duties. Such a separation can be made to work as long as there is no serious conflict between fiscal affairs and the academic program. But if a financial crisis forces a review of academic policy, emergency measures are likely to be taken by necessity rather than on the basis of prior contingency planning. The harvest then is a rich mixture of outrage and recrimination.

If a board is to be serious about this responsibility, it should recognize the difference between institutional assessment and two apparently similar functions: the financial audit on the one hand, and quality control on the other. The financial audit is of course an important exercise. Properly treated it may be useful as part of institutional assessment. Like the annual budget, it reflects certain aspects of policy—or at least of practice. With rare exceptions, however, concern for the audit is limited to worry over the so-called bottom line, especially if it is red. Since state-related institutions operate on direct appropriations and usually on line-item budgets, variations in expenditure are more limited than in the private sector. But life for state-related institutions is not necessarily simpler on this account. Fiscal affairs are basic to everything else. Shortfalls there mean shortfalls everywhere. The picture is even more beclouded in these times of inflation and energy shortages. Add these to problems of shrinkage in enrollment, and it becomes difficult to think about any other problems. In good times or bad, however, administrators and trustees should maintain sound balance among conflicting claims. The financial audit is one indicator of institutional health, but only one (see Chapter Fifteen). For example, Quality control is another exercise that might easily be identified as the equivalent of institutional assessment. The renewed emphasis on competency is an attempt to achieve quality control. The trend toward some form of core curriculum is another indication of a growing concern for standards.

Institutional assessment, however, is both more inclusive and more difficult than either a financial audit or tests for competency. Assume for a moment that an institution is financially solvent and is graduating students with high scores on national tests. What then would be left for institutional assessment? Virtually everything. The first and most basic question is this: How much does the institution know about itself? Over what span of time does this knowledge extend? Consider the following examples:

A four-year college enrolling 1,500 students may find that more than 50 percent are dropping out between the end of the first year and the beginning of the third year. Those remaining for the fourth year may show high achievement academically and the college may not be suffering financially. But before assuming that such attrition is acceptable, the governing board should inquire into the causes for this attrition, as well as its implications for the admissions program, for student counseling, and for the future.

A university may find that, among its fifteen colleges and special programs, college A or program B consistently incurs heavy deficits, while college C consistently produces substantial surpluses. College C may then claim that "its" revenue is being used as a subsidy for other programs and insist that it be allowed to retain "its" revenue. But should every tub stand on its own bottom? Is every unit entitled to the revenues produced by its own enrollment?

An institution may have benefited at one point from an exceptionally large gift, one that undergirded its programs for many years. In such circumstances administrators and trustees may neglect cultivating other prospective donors, and then after years of seeming security and stability find that the institution faces financial stringency. Again, a college may have benefited for years from the excellence of a strong senior faculty, only to find that retirements have suddenly changed the profile of the faculty, with years of rebuilding ahead. Such examples could easily be multiplied, each one demonstrating the need for comprehensive institutional research as the first requirement for both sound planning and sound assessment.

However, these illustrations might also mislead a trustee into thinking that institutional assessment is after all quite commonsensical, largely a two-plus-two sort of arithmetic, with a dash of judgment thrown in. But such a simplistic view would overlook one crucial factor, that is, the peculiar nature of a college. Beyond the basic aims of a college to convey knowledge and skills and to advance knowledge, there is the large and more difficult task of providing an atmosphere in which students will be able to mature intellectually and emotionally, gain a broad sense of citizenship and cultural sensitivity, and project and revise their personal goals. These aspects of a college are by all counts the most important. Achievement of these goals involves a complex of relationships. The spirit and motivation of faculty members, along with their sense of shared goals, will affect their relations with students and will determine the prevailing mood of the institution. In the same way, the relationships between students and faculty on the one hand and between them and the administration and trustees on the other will also affect the tone of the institution. While these are largely subjective factors, they are nonetheless amenable to assessment.

Preliminary Considerations

With all its difficulties, periodic evaluation is not only feasible but essential. Timing and preparation are central to the success of the effort. Too frequent and too intense programs of assessment lead to a level of self-consciousness that will impede an institution's program rather than stimulate improvement. Data can be compiled regularly and systematically, but a campus-wide review and interpretation of data is best done at intervals of three to five years. Development of trend lines and the perspective of a large time frame for judgment make for better interpretation of accumulated facts.

It is not as if the governing board must take on the task of assessment with nothing in hand. It must rather ask the administration to organize and present material either already available or at any event needed for competent administration. A reservoir of available information is in fact provided through the periodic evaluations of an institution by its regional accrediting association. In each region of the country, procedures have been in effect for decades for the review of institutions at regular intervals. Formerly the cycle was ten years in length, but interim reports are now requested at five-year intervals in some regions. Where the region itself does not require the five-year report, the institution should take the initiative and use the regional self-study program for its own benefit at shorter intervals. Given the rapid changes in modern life, ten years is much too long a period between formal reviews.

The accrediting (or reaffirmation) process begins with a program of self-study that should require about a year's work by committees of the faculty and administration. The formal review is carried out by a team of persons from other institutions who represent the special areas to be analyzed. The report of that team, with recommendations, is then given double scrutiny by committees of the regional association. Thereafter the commission on higher education of the regional association determines whether more information is needed or whether additional improvements should be made by the institution before final action by the commission.

Although accreditation is well established among leading colleges and universities, certain shortcomings in the process call for fresh attention. Especially notable is the almost total lack of trustee involvement at any stage of the self-study process, not to mention the rather cavalier attitude that some presidents adopt toward it. Strong institutions, assuming that accreditation is not in jeopardy, fail to make the most of this opportunity to address unresolved questions already well recognized on campus. It may be embarrassing at times to have visiting teams bring out matters of critical importance, though at the end the institution is well served in just this way.

Think again about the financial audit. Occasionally an institution will find that, despite all normal precautions, the financial situation is not as represented. With the least suggestion of error or misrepresentation in financial matters trustees spring to the alert, persist in tracing the problem to the source, and then make sure that corrections are made. By contrast, the program of the institution (which after all is its reason for being) is left to the staff, with little trustee reaction except for rejoicing over success or (frequently ill-informed) concern over signs of weakness or misdirection. The obligation of the board is not to leap from extreme to extreme but to make sure by all reasonable means that educational policies and performance receive top priority in trustee deliberations. Institutional assessment is one ready means of achieving this result.

As an introduction to this process, one regional association has adopted a statement entitled "Characteristics of Excellence and Standards for . . . Accreditation" (Middle States Association of Colleges and Schools, 1978). The same group has also published a *Handbook for Institutional Self-Study* (1977). The two publications follow roughly the same outline, although the second is more detailed. The major points included serve to inform the lay trustee about the nature of the review and also indicate its potential value to the board:

- Goals and objectives
- Outcomes (educational effectiveness)
- Program
- Students and student life
- Faculty
- Teaching
- Instructional resources and equipment
- Organization and governance
- Financial planning

Not every institution will undertake a full-scale review of every one of these categories on every occasion but by agreement with the association may choose a more limited focus and concentrate on matters of immediate interest or concern. It has been known to happen, however, that when the limited study is reviewed by a visiting team, other matters emerge as being more urgent than those studied. In any event, a board of trustees should be aware of the evaluation beforehand, be informed as the procedure develops, and take seriously the final recommendations. Failure of the board in this respect is a serious flaw in responsible trusteeship. By contrast, positive results will flow from alert and reasonable participation by trustees as this exercise proceeds.

This trustee involvement can take one or more of several courses: (1) the trustee committee on academic affairs can be asked to approve initial plans for institutional self-study; (2) the president can invite selected trustees to review certain sections of the self-study itself; (3) selected trustees can be invited to confer with the visiting team from the accrediting association; (4) the trustees or selected committees of the board can study and respond to recommendations of the visiting team; (5) the board can ask the president to report on recommendations made by the visiting team; and (6) the board can request follow-up reports on actions flowing from recommendations of the visiting team.

Speaking as we are about regional accreditation as a ready-made opportunity for trustees to take more interest in educational activities and to capitalize on the results for further benefits for the institution, we should not fail to speak of those types of accreditation that have become increasingly burdensome. Specialized accrediting agencies now press upon departments and also upon professional schools. These special forms of accreditation may well strengthen education in various fields, but there is also a tendency toward proliferation and overextension of this kind of activity. The effort to reduce this spread of specialized activities has led to the formation of a national Council on Postsecondary Accreditation in Washington, D.C. While the organization is still young and unproved, its aims are important to all who are concerned for the future of higher education, and it forms a new resource for institutional assessment.

Other organizations provide various kinds of useful information for the benefit of administrators of all sizes and types of colleges and universities, from small to large, from simple to complex, from two-year colleges to graduate research institutions. Trustees certainly cannot deal with the flood of technical information available from all these sources, but the point is for governing boards to understand that periodic assessment can be supported by activities and information already at hand or reasonably within reach. In addition to the resources of the various collegiate and specialized associations, there is a growing body of professionals who have adopted institutional review as a field of their own.

Thus far we have emphasized two aspects of assessment: the kinds of data already available or needed by the central administration for sound direction, and the additional sources of data and personnel available outside the institution in organizations having a natural relationship to it.

But this development of information is only the starting point. More important is the next stage, the use of information for practical purposes. Compilations of data are notorious as dust gatherers. They become fertile only when used to change the course of events either in the classroom and the laboratory or in administration. Assessment must be a prelude to action; otherwise it is a waste of money and energy. It may be better not to undertake an assessment if there is not also a commitment to apply its results and to sustain a schedule of periodic reviews. Granted that institutions cannot thrive if everything is constantly under scrutiny and under threat of change, colleges and universities are also well known for resistance to change and for honoring the established ways.

One method of increasing the energy for assessment is the use of special advisory groups, made up of a judicious mixture of interested persons with special reasons for involvement—trustees, administrators, faculty members, even certain key alumni or friends of the institution drawn from various fields of study or of practice. While many colleges list advisory groups of one sort or another, they are rarely taken seriously and instead are treated as honorific. If such groups are to become useful, they require the services of a competent staff person, an assignment that should not be a casual addition to other full-time duties. Service to advisory groups need not become a full-time job, but it is too important to be left marginal. The only way to utilize advisory groups effectively is to establish a schedule of meetings as part of the annual calendar and to take the administration of such events as seriously as that of other important meetings. Otherwise invitation to membership will correctly be seen as simply a gesture, and the result will probably prove to be mutual embarrassment.

Failure of the institution to broaden the base of public interest in and concern for the institution will eventually become a handicap in the process of assessment itself. However, effective utilization of advisory groups will make possible a special kind of reinforcement among various complementary and overlapping functions in the institution—planning as the first stage, development as the second, assessment as the third. In fact any failure to maintain relationship among these three will almost assure some form of distress in the management of institutional affairs.

Implementing these suggestions might seem to create a mountain of new work. Some things doubtless must be added to the normal staff load. More important, however, is a change of emphasis in the normal flow of work. For example, if the president and the board adopt a cycle of special reports covering a period of two or three years, such a schedule will ensure that all major aspects of the institution have had close attention during this period, as distinct from the once-over-lightly typical of many reports to the board. The reports being urged here should have long and careful preparation, and each in turn should be presented to the board in the name of a board committee or some ad hoc group that includes both trustees and others (such as academic affairs or athletics). Incidentally, this suggestion will not necessarily lead to longer board meetings. Not every committee of the board needs to report every time, and many reports can simply be noted for the record when nothing out of the ordinary is involved. At times these special reports can be used as a basis for communication with the full constituency of the college, an important additional benefit requiring little in the way of additional effort or expense. If it is understood that a particular report is intended ultimately for the widest possible readership, the quality of the report should improve.

The process of assessment can also be enlivened by special occasions for considering matters that bear on the institution's future. Institutions are usually eager to hold special events to gain public attention, but the result is more often ceremonial or social than substantial. While the general public will not be interested in the minutiae of institutional programs, selected persons of proved or of potential value to the college will respond to serious treatments of serious issues, especially when they can be convinced that the public interest is involved in what otherwise might appear to be a private concern of a small group.

Many public relations programs, however, rely on well-known public figures or on other promotional devices. In retrospect it can often be seen that these events had little to do with the program of the college or its outreach toward the future. This is not a subtle point, but it is one that is often ignored. While it is not necessary to be deadly serious about everything all the time, there is a curious gap between much of what passes for good public relations and the ever-present problem of institutional development. Those who are actually or potentially interested in the college include at least some persons who are concerned about fundamental issues of education. Such people will respond to programs that demonstrate the sober, persistent efforts of an institution to deal with these matters, including a careful assessment of its own performance.

Beware of the Undertow

In all institutions there is something like an undertow that wears down the energies of those attempting either an innovation or an assessment. All institutions and the persons associated with them tend to have all sorts of justifications for whatever is habitually done. Assessment is automatically seen as a threat, an intrusion, a hint of meddling by the uninitiated. Faculty members rightly consider themselves to be authorities in their several fields, and they tend not to welcome the judgment of others. Administrators too are supposed to be in command of their posts and are not likely to welcome assessment. Members of governing boards, most of all, are not quick to adopt a program of assessment for themselves. They are the ones who assess others. What with one thing and another, regular and systematic assessment is often accepted in principle as a good thing for somebody else, but it suffers from both resistance and neglect. Let enrollments or program quality decline, or let the flow of money be reduced, however and suddenly assessment becomes urgent—just when the atmosphere is least conducive to it and just when time is most pressing. All the more reason to be foresighted and to accept a schedule of periodic assessments as a normal way to conduct the institutional business.

Structure and Schedule

What decisions are to be made? By whom? The answer to the latter question is clear: by the president and the board. The former question requires a range of considerations. The first of these is the projection of major topics for review and assessment, listed in order of priority for the college (or the system). Adoption of such a list (subject to change from time to time) will make possible a plan for board meetings over a period of two or three years in advance. The result of this decision to adopt a schedule will be to set the tasks for committees of the board, including auxiliary representation from groups that should be party to the early stages of preparation. Such a plan makes possible the accumulation of significant data, analyses, and projections that in turn will reveal the feasibility of certain intermediate decisions. This kind of periodic but continuous and sequential work should reduce the tendency to confront problems only when they have become emergencies. Emergencies will arise, no matter what. But institutions cannot sustain momentum by surviving from crisis to crisis.

The second major decision requires improved attention to the annual budget. The budget for any year is part of a progression of yearly budgets. The judicious consideration of any budget necessitates a study of trend lines reflecting experience of the last three, four, or five years, together with a projection for the next two or three years. In addition, it requires a study of the educational policies reflected in the budget—the balance or imbalance among such major elements as instructional salaries, library appropriations, student services, admissions, public relations, and maintenance of properties. Of almost equal importance is the development of a "shadow budget"—a set of figures reflecting improvements in the various components of the institution.

The third major decision involves a change in trustee committee reports. Much of a typical agenda consists of validating actions taken by administrators or perhaps by the executive committee of the board or of matters that should not, but often do, take up a disproportionate amount of time. This last problem usually indicates that trustees have not prepared adequately for the meeting. They then impose on other trustees by asking them about details already covered in preliminary documents. Correction of this abuse calls for a chairman with a firm hand, a chairman who is himself or herself well prepared and who sets a high standard for the other members. One common reason for lack of time to discuss important long-range issues of a college is simply that these items are placed late on the agenda and then are easily deferred when time has been extravagantly used on less important factors.

The combination of planning and assessment is a potential means of maintaining the interest and constructive involvement of trustees, who will gain not only a sense of participation but an improved grasp of the institution, not to mention a greater sense of the basic responsibilities belonging to trusteeship. Of the two, planning and assessment, it is hard to say which offers the greater challenge, although it does appear that assessment is the more difficult. Since both functions are often neglected by trustees, the opportunity for improvement in both is open and inviting.

One of the lively debates involving evaluation these days concerns the use of "student satisfaction" as a basis for judgment about the institution. A review of the arguments would take up too much space here, but it is easy to see that there are prior questions to be answered. Widespread student dissatisfaction is a clear indication of trouble, but a high degree of student satisfaction might require some probing too. All such matters lead back to questions about the aims of the institution and the other factors we have been discussing.

One of the more interesting yet controversial treatments of the subject may be found in Astin's *Four Critical Years* (1977). In this volume, the author reviews the outcome of tests administered over a period of fifteen years. Based on this information, he comes to the startling conclusion that, in seven major areas of educational policy, decisions underlying educational development in the past twenty years have been wrong—wrong in the sense that the mainstream of educational and institutional development has run contrary to the best interests of students and to the conditions favoring student achievement. Certainly it is not to be expected that everyone responsible for all these decisions will agree with Astin's conclusions. It would be interesting to know, however, the response of educators to his statement that most policy decisions are made not on the basis of research data but rather in response to economic pressures. That debate belongs to another area of thought, but trustees who are interested in institutional assessment would do well to examine at least the concluding chapters of his book.

Trustees who want a full-scale treatment of the subject will find many volumes and articles available to them, some of which are listed in Resource E of this volume. One such book is Dressel's *Handbook of Academic Evaluation* (1976). Although perhaps not many trustees will choose to work their way through the entire volume, certain sections of the text will attract the interest of one or another type of trustee. Dressel views the totality of assessment in three large segments: first, he examines those general considerations that affect the exercise as a whole, especially the use of evaluation as a basis for making decisions and for projecting change; second, he concentrates on students, their experience, and educational progress as a basis for institutional evaluation; and, third, he examines programs and personnel as the means for educational achievement.

Dressel and other writers on the subject provide various checklists conforming generally to this pattern: (1) academic departments, (2) administration, (3) finance, (4) plant operation and maintenance, (5) student services, (6) admissions and counseling, (7) financial aid, and (8) institutional development (as an inclusive term). A summary that I have found useful recasts the procedure in another fashion, using the same information: (1) history, (2) data, (3) projections, (4) opinions, (5) options, and (6) decision. Each of these items deserves elaboration, but most of them are self-explanatory. It may seem strange to begin with "history," but any set of data should be put in context if it is to be understood. Even when radical change is under consideration, a clear view of the historical factors will prove useful. And so as one proceeds through the various stages listed, each one in turn will clarify the next in line. Neglect of any one of the first five steps will weaken the quality of the ultimate decision.

Each of these items is treated separately elsewhere in the *Handbook*. The purpose here is to emphasize the need for periodic soundings and sightings to determine whether the institution is in safe waters and is on course. Example: A university may invest heavily in a revision of engineering curricula, only to find that enrollments are low and that deficits are high. (Or the reverse may be true in that there has been no revision in recent times with the same consequence.) What to do? The tendency is to press for an immediate decision one way or the other, to hammer away at the symptoms rather than to do the correct thing—to conduct a careful assessment of the problem, following a sequence of analyses that should clarify the situation and point toward certain options.

The same kind of problem will appear in every type of institution. A four-year college may from year to year increase its offerings to broaden its appeal, only to find that both human and financial resources are overstrained—time for assessment. Or, to put things in a different frame, everything may seem to be going just right for an institution at the moment, but unrecognized trends may be developing that if brought to focus may call for basic change in one sector or another.

Such practical wisdom might seem not to require extended comment. Unfortunately, however, any person of broad experience among colleges can testify to the contrary. All too frequently institutions are caught by surprise (when there should be no surprise) in a crisis that only seems to be a sudden development. Often the crisis will have developed over a period of years with indications that might have been identified if a program of assessment had been in place.

To summarize, an approach that I have found quite useful is to cast the procedure for assessment along these lines. First, recapture a sense of the historical context. Whatever may be the current profile, the origins of the program or procedure should be understood. Lest this be thought a waste of time, it is well to recognize that whatever is being done now was started at some earlier time by someone for some reason. Whoever established the program or procedure or their successors may still be around, and they may consider proposed changes as a personal reflection. One need not be extravagant in time spent on this preliminary stage, but it is too often overlooked at the cost of much time later.

The next major step is the collection of adequate data to ensure that the ultimate recommendations are well based on pertinent facts. At times the logic may be reversed, facts being assembled to support a prior decision (or private intent) on the part of one or more persons in the administration or on the board. Ongoing institutional research will prove invaluable, though it is sometimes viewed as too expensive or too slow to justify the cost. Ultimately more may be lost by the spotty work sometimes passing for institutional research. Further, regular analysis of data within the institution (enrollment, retention, tenure rates, cost-benefit studies, major allocations of funds, plant maintenance, and all such) should be supplemented by comparable data from comparable institutions, and placed against information on national trends. Here a warning must be entered: Every institution has its own personality and program. Some succeed where others fail even in comparable circumstances. One cannot or should not leap from data to decision. The factor of judgment and of institutional differences must make the difference for better or worse.

After the collection of data, and the study of data, what next? The formulation of recommendations, which itself requires three activities for which there may be too little patience or understanding: gathering opinions, studying projections, and weighing options. Whatever assessment is being made, subjective elements must be considered along with objective data. The final recommendation need not represent a consensus but should take into account the range of opinion among those qualified to understand the problem.

Whatever recommendations are being studied, an attempt should be made to project the probable consequences of the ultimate decision. And these projections should reveal at least two, perhaps more, options for consideration—whether to cut back on (or expand) administration, whether to reduce (or expand) intercollegiate sports, whether or not to build a new library, whether the board of trustees needs new procedures (or new blood), and so on. Ultimately the decision comes: If all factors have been carefully developed, answers will usually present themselves so clearly as to prevent serious division of opinion. If division does occur, at least the process will give strength to the administration and the board in carrying out the final choice of action.

The need for continuing, systematic assessment, either by

sections or throughout the institution, appears to be self-evident. Yet even casual reading of the daily news will reveal the surprise announcement that some institution—large or small, public or private—discovers to its dismay that some unforeseen crisis has befallen. Funds may be in disarray, investments gone wrong, embezzlement discovered. Faculty unrest may have reached the boiling point; academic freedom is seen to be threatened; the president (or someone else) is struck with a vote of no confidence; the governor may be disaffected. Occasionally such misfortunes can come on overnight, but rarely so. The roots of disaster usually go deep.

Examination of successful institutions will reveal that whether by formal or informal means, the administration and the board have maintained a steady view of the whole institution, and even in times of stress have been able to handle problems. The greater the knowledge about the institution's intentions and performance, the more probable its stability.

In the assessment process, the board's role is to insist that an adequate program is mounted, financed, and maintained on schedule. Trustees and regents are reminded that there are but few major points for sound practice in discharging trustee responsibilities:

1. To place the board on record as supporting the importance of systematic assessment.
2. To establish a calendar of review that the president and staff accept as most feasible and useful. Larger institutions in particular may require a plan (on an annual basis, for example) to review one fifth of program offerings so that the entire institution is covered over a five-year period.
3. To authorize personnel and budget for institutional research and for outside evaluators.
4. To make sure that resources already available are utilized.
5. To ensure adequate time on the board agenda for considering evaluations when completed and to ensure regular and systematic follow-up.

In sum, institutional assessment as a total enterprise is important in determining the future as well as in measuring the past.

Instruments for assessment are available, as are a growing body of qualified professionals to provide assistance from the outside. Administrative support for assessment is the key to its effectiveness, and trustee participation at various stages and in various ways will have a good effect on policy. Altogether, institutional assessment offers one of the best possible avenues for strengthening trustee performance.

Resource A

Trustee Audit

Some students of trusteeship contend that it takes two years for a new board member to become fully productive. Others believe that experience can be readily transferred from various voluntary or vocational endeavors to trusteeship. The truth lies in between. Most individuals can become effective trustees in fairly short order, *provided* they give deliberate thought to their responsibilities and are willing to learn from the experience of others. All trustees can surely profit from taking stock of themselves from time to time, a task that the following checklist is designed to encourage.

The list of questions may be disconcerting at first glance, but it is not intended to cause acute trustee or presidential anxiety. Rather, it is designed to point up the breadth of the trustee's responsibilities and the need for a wide grasp of his or her institution. The checklist may be modified and adapted to a particular institutional setting as part of a periodic review process, and the addition of "yes," and "no," and "sometimes" or "somewhat" response categories may improve it as a survey instrument. Whatever the categories, however, a "perfect score" is an unreasonable expectation. The chief executive is urged to review them with a small committee of trustees to develop a final version.

Responses may be made anonymously or by name to strengthen orientation programs for new trustees or to suggest agendas for future board workshops or retreats. The results can be useful in determining whether specific programs are necessary to improve trustee understanding and knowledge and in assessing the board's needs for certain areas of expertise and interest.

Background

1. Do you feel that you have had adequate opportunity to understand your obligations, responsibilities, and possibilities for growth *as a trustee?*
2. Have you a clear grasp of *your board's* responsibilities?
3. If you have answered yes to either or both of the first two questions, what has been the primary source of your information (for example, an orientation program, a particular individual, a book, prior service as a board member)?
4. Are you familiar with your institution's stated mission, institutional plan, and current policies?
5. Do you stay abreast of higher education trends, legislation, and other public policy by reading *AGB News Notes,* the *Chronicle of Higher Education, AGB Reports,* or other material?
6. Have you recently taken an opportunity to meet with trustees and educators from other institutions?
7. Do you have adequate opportunities to know your fellow trustees?
8. Do you find any conflict between your responsibility for the welfare and advancement of your institution and your responsibility to the citizens of your region, state, or nation?
9. What do you feel is your strongest area or areas of *expertise* based on your background and experience (x):

_____ Budget/Finance	_____ Student Affairs
_____ Investments	_____ Faculty Affairs
_____ Management	_____ Fund Raising
_____ Planning	_____ Public Relations
_____ Legal Affairs	_____ Marketing
_____ Plant Management	_____ Government Relations
_____ Real Estate	_____ Other: _____
_____ Education	

10. Now go back and indicate any primary areas of *interest* outside of your areas of expertise (+).

Knowledge of the Institution

11. Are you familiar with your institution's recent history and what makes it distinctive from neighboring colleges and universities?

12. Cite three of its special strengths:
    a. _____
    b. _____
    c. _____

13. Cite three of its greatest needs:
    a. _____
    b. _____
    c. _____

14. Do you feel well informed about the type and quality of your institution's educational programs?

15. Have you attended a campus event within the past year?

16. Do you regularly read the campus newspaper or faculty or student organization minutes?

17. Do you know the names of your institution's:
    a. key administrators
    b. faculty leaders
    c. student leaders

18. Have you met some of them apart from board meetings?

19. Are you acquainted with the physical plant and maintenance needs of your institution?

Board and Committee Meetings

20. Are you satisfied with your attendance at board and committee meetings?

21. Do you read the minutes of meetings to determine whether they faithfully represent the proceedings and decisions as you recall them?

22. Do you prepare for board meetings by reading agendas and supporting materials?

23. Do you sometimes suggest agenda items?

24. Do you help board and committee meetings to steer clear of nonpolicy matters better left to the administration?

Fund Raising and Public Relations

25. Do you contribute to your institution, according to your means, for: (a) annual operations? (b) capital campaigns?
26. Within the past year or two, have you helped to secure a gift from an individual, a corporation, or other source?
27. Have you recently taken advantage of an opportunity to say a good word about your institution to a policy maker or organization at the state level?
28. Do you take advantage of opportunities to inform other groups or persons about your institution or higher education generally?

Trustee Concerns

29. Do you understand the concept of "fund accounting"?
30. Do you find your institution's financial statements intelligible?
31. Are you mindful of your institution's stated mission, its plan and goals, and its current policies when you vote on proposals presented to the board?
32. Do you feel that you are sensitive to the concerns of students and faculty while maintaining impartiality and a total institutional perspective?
33. Do you help to meet the needs of your chief executive for occasional counsel and support in his or her often difficult relationships with groups on and off campus?
34. Do you appreciate the importance of keeping your chief executive informed in event you establish personal communication lines with individuals on campus and of the need to avoid prejudiced judgments on the basis of such relationships?
35. Have you ever suggested to the board's nominating committee or to the appointing authority someone who would make an outstanding new board member?
36. Are you satisfied that there are no real or apparent conflicts of interest in your service as a trustee?
37. Do you avoid asking special favors of the administration, including requests for information without the knowledge of at least the board or committee chairman?
38. If you have not already done so, would you be willing to serve as a committee chairman or board officer?

Why (or why not?) _____

_____

39. Have you found your trusteeship to be stimulating and rewarding thus far?
    Why (or why not?) _____

    _____

40. How would you rate yourself as a trustee at this time?
    _____ Above Average
    _____ Average
    _____ Below Average

Resource B

Self-Study Criteria
for Private College
and University Boards

Self-study criteria are also available in booklet form from the Association of Governing Boards of Universities and Colleges (AGB) for other types of institutions: community colleges, public colleges and universities, multicampus boards, state postsecondary planning and coordinating agencies. Designed to be completed by each board member, the questions provide a means of summarizing judgments concerning a wide range of board policies and practices as suggested in Chapter Eighteen. They can be adapted to meet the distinctive characteristics of particular boards and institutions through adding or deleting items. Responses that require clarification or qualification can be explained in the "comment" section for each criterion.

What follows is the result of a project sponsored by AGB and conducted by the Center for Research and Development in Higher Education at the University of California, Berkeley. It was made possible through the interest and support of the Ford Foundation.

The materials contained here were developed by James Gilbert Paltridge, research educator, with the assistance of Frances LaVonne White, research assistant at the Center for Research and Development in Higher Education, and with the collaboration of Richard T. Ingram, vice-president of AGB.

A national advisory committee of ten chief executives and ten members of various types of postsecondary education boards contributed significantly to this project. AGB and the authors express their appreciation to the committee, as well as to the trustees of several institutional boards who participated in field testing of early versions of the criteria.

Any viewpoints implied or expressed about the performance standards of boards of higher education are the sole responsibility of the authors, and not those of the project's advisory committee, the Ford Foundation, AGB, or the Center for Research and Development in Higher Education.

AGB will welcome reports from institutions using these materials and suggestions for improving both the criteria and the suggested procedures.

Criterion 1: Institutional Mission and Educational Policy

No institution can be all things to all people. Each institution must decide what its particular mission is—its *real purpose*—if it is to have sound direction. The mission must be clearly defined so students will know the institution's purposes and objectives, faculty members will know how to direct their efforts, and the several publics on whom the campus community depends will know what they are supporting.

An official statement setting forth the specific mission of a college or university should be a cooperative effort of the administration, the faculty, and the governing board. Acting alone, the board lacks the professional experience to define educational goals in detail. Its role is to ensure that the mission is clearly stated; and because it stands apart from day-to-day operations, administrative preoccupations, and faculty special interests, the board is in a unique position to lead, seek consensus, and stimulate action.

	Yes	No	Don't Know or Can't Judge
1. Is there a written and officially adopted statement of the institution's mission or purpose?	___	___	___
2. In your opinion is this statement sufficiently clear and useful to serve as a guide to the board, administration, and faculty?	___	___	___
3. Does the board periodically review its statement of purpose and educational goals, and examine the policies that implement them?	___	___	___
4. Does the board assume a role in helping to determine whether educational programs are viable and consistent with the institution's mission?	___	___	___
5. Do you feel that the institution lives up to its stated mission?	___	___	___

Summary: In relation to this criterion I feel that the board's overall performance has been:

Very Good ___   Good ___   Barely Adequate ___

Poor ___   Don't Know or Cannot Judge ___

Further comments or suggestions related to this criterion:

Criterion 2: Institutional Planning

In the difficult period stretching ahead for higher education, effective planning is increasingly essential. The number and future sources of students should be anticipated. Projections of expenses and income need to be studied. The character of the educational program and student services must be considered. The size of the faculty and its distribution by rank and tenured status are matters to be carefully plotted.

The board should be involved in the planning process, and adopted plans should be used by the board as a guide to decision making.

	Yes	No	Don't Know or Can't Judge
1. Does the board require, participate in, review, and approve comprehensive institutional planning regarding:			
a. enrollments?	___	___	___
b. staffing?	___	___	___

	Yes	No	Don't Know or Can't Judge
c. physical facilities?	⎯	⎯	⎯
d. availability of resources?	⎯	⎯	⎯
e. educational programs?	⎯	⎯	⎯
2. Has the board approved a comprehensive institutional plan within the past five years?	⎯	⎯	⎯
3. Does the board have a schedule for reviewing and, if desirable, revising the plan at regular intervals?	⎯	⎯	⎯
4. Was the faculty involved in the plan's development?	⎯	⎯	⎯

Summary: In relation to this criterion I feel that the board's overall performance has been:

Very Good ⎯⎯⎯ Good ⎯⎯⎯ Barely Adequate ⎯⎯⎯
Poor ⎯⎯⎯ Don't Know or Cannot Judge ⎯⎯⎯

Further comments or suggestions related to this criterion:

Criterion 3: Physical Plant

It is the board's responsibility to create and maintain a physical environment that is conducive to learning and consistent with reasonable expectations of future funds and enrollment trends. Decisions that involve the campus master plan and the capital outlay budget request are the major concerns. Prudence demands that maximum use be made of the present physical plant before construction or remodeling is considered. And maintenance should not be deferred to the possible peril of the institution's future. Efficient use of the board's time and effort requires that it be concerned only with those matters that cannot properly be delegated to the staff.

	Yes	No	Don't Know or Can't Judge
1. Has the board approved a master plan for the physical campus that includes both present and anticipated needs?	⎯	⎯	⎯
2. Within the past two years, has the board received and reviewed a report on physical plant utilization—classroom, laboratory, dormitory, office, and other building space?	⎯	⎯	⎯

3. Prior to its consideration of requests
for remodeling or new construction has
the board satisfied itself that present
spaces are being used effectively and instructional areas are scheduled for op-
timum utilization?   _____ _____   _____
4. Is the board satisfied that maintenance
programs are adequate and that they are
not being unreasonably deferred?   _____ _____   _____
5. Do you feel that the board makes deci-
sions on details related to buildings and
grounds that really should be delegated to
the administrative staff?   _____ _____   _____

Summary: In relation to this criterion I feel that the board's overall per-
formance has been:
Very Good _____   Good _____   Barely Adequate _____
Poor _____   Don't Know or Cannot Judge _____
Further comments or suggestions related to this criterion:

Criterion 4: Financial Support and Management

In the financial affairs of the institution the board has a dual responsibility. It must secure the financial resources sufficient to meet
operating costs and maintain the institution in a manner consistent with its
stated mission and goals. It must be sure that the institution has prudent
fiscal management. The collective effort of all board members is essential
to the first responsibility. The second responsibility calls upon the expertise of those board members who are experienced in devising financial
policies, managing investments, or have other financial skills. The board
must see to it that sound financial policies are followed, yet refrain from
personal involvement in execution of policies and administration of financial programs.

| | | Don't Know or |
| | Yes | No | Can't Judge |

1. Do you feel that the *resource development*
program is well organized into a continuing and coordinated effort of the board
and the president?   _____ _____   _____

2. Do you feel there is an adequate financial commitment on the part of the individual members to:
   a. personal giving?   _____ _____   _____
   b. influencing other persons or organizations to give?   _____ _____   _____
3. Does the board have within its membership persons with special expertise who give their advice and leadership in the following areas:
   a. long-range fiscal planning?   _____ _____   _____
   b. investment practices?   _____ _____   _____
   c. fiscal management?   _____ _____   _____
   d. budget review?   _____ _____   _____
   e. analyses of reports and recommendations of the auditor?   _____ _____   _____
4. Does the board understand "fund accounting" and the data presented in regular financial reports?   _____ _____   _____
5. Do you feel that the board fully accepts its responsibility for prudent fiscal management?   _____ _____   _____

Summary: In relation to this criterion I feel that the board's overall performance has been:

Very Good _____   Good _____   Barely Adequate _____
Poor _____   Don't Know or Cannot Judge _____

Further comments or suggestions related to this criterion:

Criterion 5: Board Membership

A primary requisite for effective governance is to be sure that the men and women responsible for the institution's policy direction have the skills, knowledge, and background necessary for effective decision making. The complex operation of modern educational institutions requires that boards have available to them a wide range of experiences and expertise. The larger society to which these institutions are now linked more closely than ever before requires that the board's membership be more diverse in terms of geographic, social, or occupational origins and viewpoints. Such diversity does not require that members be representatives of special groups or interests unless this is specified in the bylaws or charter. Each member must be willing to serve the interests of the institution as a whole.

	Yes	No	Don't Know or Can't Judge
1. Do you feel that the board now contains a sufficient range of expertise, attitudes, and external relationships to make it an effective board?	____	____	____
2. Does the board have a committee that assesses its needs in the way of qualifications of new members and that maintains a roster of prospective members?	____	____	____
3. Does the board have a committee that reviews the performance of its individual members?	____	____	____
4. Does the board have an established procedure for orienting new members to their institution and to their duties and responsibilities?	____	____	____
5. Do you feel that the board should alter its policies and practices with respect to:			
a. size of board?	____	____	____
b. length of term?	____	____	____
c. number of successive terms?	____	____	____
d. age limit or honorary retirement?	____	____	____
e. age composition?	____	____	____
f. sex composition?	____	____	____
g. minority composition?	____	____	____
h. geographical composition?	____	____	____
i. persons with educational experience?	____	____	____
j. persons with financial management experience?	____	____	____
k. requiring a minimum attendance record?	____	____	____

Summary: In relation to this criterion I feel that the board's overall performance has been:

Very Good ____   Good ____   Barely Adequate ____

Poor ____   Don't Know or Cannot Judge ____

Further comments or suggestions related to this criterion:

Criterion 6: Board Organization

The effectiveness of a board greatly depends on the structure of its organization and the conduct of its meetings. A productive board is usually one that has periodically taken the time to thoughtfully sort out its duties, critically review its organizational structure and rules of procedure, and update its bylaws, policy or operations documents. Committee structure depends upon the board's size, the frequency of meetings, and the workload that can be placed on individual members. Periodic critical review should also determine, among other things, if a few persons in fact are making most of the board's decisions, if responsible minority opinions have the opportunity for full board consideration, and if communication between the campus community and the public is open.

	Yes	No	Don't Know or Can't Judge
1. Within the past two or three years, has the board in some formal way reviewed its organization, committee practices, and bylaws?	___	___	___
2. Do meeting agendas:			
a. put before you issues of *policy* the board should consider?	___	___	___
b. include appropriate supporting information in the right amount?	___	___	___
c. reach you sufficiently in advance of the meeting?	___	___	___
3. Do you believe that the number and duration of board meetings are sufficient to properly take care of the institution's business?	___	___	___
4. Are board meetings effectively conducted and reasonably stimulating?	___	___	___
5. Do you feel that the present committee structure:			
a. efficiently handles the board's work?	___	___	___
b. Gives the *full board* the opportunity to consider all matters of key importance?	___	___	___
c. allows constituencies to be heard before recommendations are formed?	___	___	___
6. Do board policies governing board and committee membership afford sufficient opportunity for rotating leadership?	___	___	___

Summary: In relation to this criterion I feel that the board's overall performance has been:

Very Good ___   Good ___   Barely Adequate ___

Poor ___   Don't Know or Cannot Judge ___

Further comments or suggestions related to this criterion:

Criterion 7: Board-Chief Executive Relations

Trustees and the chief executive officer share at least one major characteristic: they have a total institutional perspective. The quality of the "working relationship" between the board and the executive officer is of critical importance to the effectiveness of each. While the board must take responsibility for basic policies and their consequences, it must also give the chief executive the authority and flexibility to act decisively.

Selection of the chief executive officer is a major responsibility of the governing board. This selection should be preceded by a clear definition of his or her qualifications and expected accomplishments.

	Yes	No	Don't Know or Can't Judge
1. Is there a climate of mutual trust and support between the board and chief executive?	____	____	____
2. Has the board or some of its members counseled with the chief executive to provide guidelines or strengthen certain areas of performance?	____	____	____
3. Do you feel that the board has delegated to the chief executive the authority he or she needs to administer the institution successfully?	____	____	____
4. Is there a written statement of role and responsibility for the chief executive that clearly defines his or her functions and the board's expectations?	____	____	____
5. Is there a clear understanding of the respective responsibilities between the executive and the board concerning their fund-raising roles?	____	____	____
6. Should the board or a board committee formally assess the chief executive's performance in some systematic way from time to time?	____	____	____

Summary: In relation to this criterion I feel that the board's overall performance has been:

Very Good _____   Good _____   Barely Adequate _____
Poor _____   Don't Know or Cannot Judge _____

Further comments or suggestions related to this criterion:

Criterion 8: Board-Faculty Relations

In academic affairs a measure of the board's success is the nature of its relationship with the faculty. Most lay board members lack the professional expertise to legislate in this area, yet they share the burden of responsibility for the quality of the institution and for the manner in which the institution fulfills its academic goals. Therefore, the board must trust the professionals for advice, and delegate to them authority to carry out educational policies and procedures.

The line between governing policy and operating policy is not easily drawn but it must be established with reasonable clarity. The institution needs to be given academic direction, yet the faculty must be free to perform its professional work.

	Yes	No	Don't Know or Can't Judge
1. Does the board have effective means of two-way communication with the faculty?	____	____	____
2. Does the board, through the chief executive, seek the advice and recommendations of faculty leaders in formulating basic educational policies?	____	____	____

3. Do you feel that the board exercises authority over:
    a. ____ more aspects of educational affairs than it needs to?
    b. ____ fewer aspects of educational affairs than it should?
    c. ____ neither. Its participation in educational affairs is about right.

	Yes	No	Don't Know or Can't Judge
4. Does the board delegate to the chief executive and faculty full responsibility for implementing educational policies?	____	____	____
5. Has the board adopted adequate policies concerning:			
a. grievance procedures?	____	____	____
b. process for selection, promotion, retention, tenure?	____	____	____
c. standards for faculty performance?	____	____	____

Summary: In relation to this criterion I feel that the board's overall performance has been:
Very Good ____   Good ____   Barely Adequate ____
Poor ____   Don't Know or Cannot Judge ____
Further comments or suggestions related to this criterion:

Criterion 9: Board-Student Relations

The board has ultimate responsibility to protect the welfare of students and to provide a healthy campus environment that is conducive to scholarship and personal development. The students' health and comfort are essential to learning. The students' freedom to learn independently is a basic tenet of academic freedom, and like other freedoms it must be exercised under the obligation to protect the welfare of the community as a whole. The board should have good communication with students.

	Yes	No	Don't Know or Can't Judge
1. Does the board have a satisfactory means for continuing two-way communication with students?	___	___	___
2. Has the board approved policies that make adequate provision for the students' health, welfare, and noncurricular (cultural, educational, recreational) activities?	___	___	___
3. Has the board set adequate policies for student appeal of perceived injustices (academic or other)?			
4. Are students and student organizations free to examine and discuss questions or issues of interest to them and to express opinions publicly, so long as it is made clear that they speak only for themselves?	___	___	___

Summary: In relation to this criterion I feel that the board's overall performance has been:
Very Good ___   Good ___   Barely Adequate ___
Poor ___   Don't Know or Cannot Judge ___
Further comments or suggestions related to this criterion:

Criterion 10: Court of Appeal

Governing boards may be called upon to fulfill a quasi-judicial function in the settlement of disputes arising within the institutional community, though generally disputes should be settled at the lowest possible administrative level to avoid inappropriate board involvement in operational matters. The board should carefully develop due process policies and delegate authority.

	Yes	No	Don't Know or Can't Judge

1. Has the board developed procedural due process or "fair hearing" requirements that delegate the management of conflict situations to the chief executive and to academic administrators or faculty leaders? _____ _____ _____

2. Are the disputes that have been brought to the board:
   a. accurately and concisely briefed for your study? _____ _____ _____
   b. brought to the board before they have escalated to crisis proportions? _____ _____ _____
   c. settled without unduly prolonged debate? _____ _____ _____

3. Do you feel that disputes have been settled with sympathetic understanding of the human and institutional issues involved? _____ _____ _____

4. Do you feel that the board has been called upon to adjudicate cases of conflict that should have been settled before they came to the board? _____ _____ _____

Summary: In relation to this criterion I feel that the board's overall performance has been:

Very Good _____   Good _____   Barely Adequate _____
Poor _____   Don't Know or Cannot Judge _____
Further comments or suggestions related to this criterion:

General Assessment

1. What issues have most occupied the board's time and attention during the past year?

2. What were the one or two successes during the past year for which the board feels special satisfaction?

3. What particular shortcomings do you see in the board's organization or performance that need attention?

4. Other comments or suggestions?

Resource C

Bylaws for Independent Colleges

These bylaws were developed for the Association of Governing Boards of Universities and Colleges (AGB) by the Washington, D.C., law firm of Zuckert, Scoutt, and Rasenberger after consultation with attorneys, board members, and administrators representing a number of institutions. They should *not* be adopted verbatim. The bylaws are intended to provide a basis for discussion on the form of governance an institution may wish to establish. Furthermore, although the model is not designed to be used by public colleges or universities—state laws vary too widely—some of its provisions could be useful for tax-supported institutions as well. Several other points should be kept in mind:

First, the masculine pronoun has been used throughout strictly for simplicity's sake.

Second, the bylaws of any institution of higher learning provide the basis upon which that institution is governed and should not be viewed merely as a legal formality. Therefore, the adoption or amendment of bylaws demands serious attention to ensure that the provisions are clearly written and, more important, appropriate to the particular institution.

Third, state laws governing colleges and universities, along with other charitable or educational corporations, vary. Although an attempt has been made in the model to conform to the requirements states generally place upon institutions of higher learning, no attempt has been made to take account of the nuances of every state. Therefore, before the suggestions in these or any other bylaws are adopted, an attorney should be consulted to ensure compliance with local law.

Finally, since a wide variety of options are available to a college or university for determining how its governing board is organized, any model necessarily involves a number of somewhat arbitrary choices. Comments received from attorneys, trustees, and chief executives on drafts of the model have underscored the possible divergence of approaches. There was general agreement that bylaws should be kept as simple as possible to allow for flexibility and to avoid need for frequent amendment. (Need for additional specificity or clarification could be covered in a board "policy manual" or separate board document.)

Several provisions stand out as being particularly appropriate for attention:

1. *Article II, Section 2.* The model provides that the members of the board of trustees shall all be elected by the incumbent trustees. Some universities and colleges take a different approach and provide for classes of trustees and election by class; for example, three alumni trustees nominated by the alumni.
2. *Article II, Section 6.* The minimum (eighteen) or maximum (seventy) age limits placed on trustees may be found inappropriate and may be altered or eliminated.
3. *Article IV.* To avoid the sometimes cumbersome distinction between "officers of the board" and "officers of the college," it is suggested that the bylaws refer only to the "officers of the college." These would include the chairman and vice-chairman of

the board of trustees, the president (ex officio board member, without power to vote), one or more vice-presidents, and a secretary and a treasurer (who may or may not be trustees). Some institutions may prefer to retain the distinction, however.

4. *Article VII.* The model does not specify the number of vice-presidents or their particular duties. This approach gives the board flexibility in creating new offices or duties as the need arises without requiring amendment of the bylaws. Some institutions may prefer to specify in the bylaws duties assigned to particular vice-presidents; for example, vice-president for academic affairs and vice-president for public relations and development.

5. *Article XII.* The bylaws provide for ten standing committees charged with specific duties. Committees may be consolidated or changed for better definition of role.

6. *Article XII, Section 6.* The model provides that the executive committee shall consist of the chairman and vice-chairman of the board, as well as the chairman of each standing committee. A board may wish to elect additional members from "at large" or include the chairmen of specified committees.

7. *Article XIV.* It is good practice to include a provision on conflicts of interest in the bylaws in addition to a more detailed policy statement adopted by resolution of the board—a statement that includes the possibility of a formal financial disclosure procedure to be conducted perhaps annually. The latter allows for greater flexibility to add or modify specific provisions based upon experience.

8. *Article XV, Section 1.* Certain special types of colleges and universities—for example, single-sex or sectarian institutions—may wish to modify this provision on discrimination. However, legal counsel should be consulted before changes are made.

Additional modifications may be made, of course, in a number of other provisions. AGB is eager to receive comments and suggestions from those who have adopted any part of these bylaws.

[Name of Institution]

BYLAWS

Adopted by Board of Trustees

[insert date of adoption and
most recent amendment dates]

Article I: Powers of Trustees

The Board of Trustees shall have the power to manage the property and business of the corporation (referred to in this and the following articles as "College"), and shall have the power to carry out any other functions which are permitted by the articles of incorporation, or these bylaws, except insofar as such powers may be limited by law. These powers shall include but shall not be limited to the following:

1. Appoint or remove the President and other Officers and administrative officials of the College in accordance with these bylaws; the power to appoint or remove administrative officials, but not Officers of the College, may, in the discretion of the Board, be delegated to the President of the College;
2. Approve degrees in course and honorary degrees upon recommendations of the faculty;
3. Establish and review the educational programs of the College;
4. Establish annually the budget of the College, which shall be submitted to it upon recommendation of the Finance Committee;
5. Authorize the construction of new buildings and major renovations of existing buildings;
6. Authorize the sale and purchase of land, buildings, or major equipment for the use of the College;
7. Institute and promote major fund-raising efforts of the College;
8. Authorize any changes in tuition and fees within the College;

9. Authorize Officers or agents of the College to accept gifts for the College;
10. Authorize the incurring of debts by the College and securing thereof by mortgage and pledge of real and personal property, tangible and intangible.

Article II: Membership of Board of Trustees

Section 1. The Board of trustees shall consist of not less than twenty-one (21), nor more than thirty-five (35) persons.

Section 2. New members of the Board of Trustees shall be elected by a majority of the Trustees then in office at each annual meeting of the Board.

Section 3. Trustees shall serve for three-year terms and until their successors are elected and qualified and may succeed themselves in office. However, if a Trustee has served for three consecutive terms (including any partial term), he shall not be eligible for re-election until one year has elapsed after the end of his third term.

Section 4. Any member of the Board of Trustees may be removed from office, for cause, at any meeting of the Board by affirmative vote of two thirds of the Trustees then in office.

Section 5. Any vacancy in the Board of Trustees may be filled by the remaining Trustees by election at any regular meeting of the Board.

Section 6. No person shall be eligible for election prior to attaining the age of eighteen (18) years, nor shall any Trustee be elected to serve a term commencing after he has attained the age of seventy (70) years.

Article III: Trustees Emeriti

A Trustee who has served for a minimum of three terms or has served for a minimum of two terms and attained the age of seventy years may, upon recommendation of the Membership Committee, be elected by a majority of the Board as a Trustee Emeritus. This position shall be reserved for those Trustees with records of unusual and distinctive service. Trustees Emeriti shall be elected for three-year terms and may be reelected without limit.

They shall be entitled to receive notices of all meetings of the Board, to attend and speak at all such meetings, to receive minutes of all meetings of the Board and Executive Committee, and to be members of all committees except the Executive Committee. They shall have the power to vote in meetings of any committee on which they may serve, but shall not have voting powers in meetings of the Board of Trustees. A Trustee Emeritus shall not be counted as a member of the Board of Trustees for any purpose.

Article IV: Officers of the College

Section 1. The Officers of the College shall be the Chairman and Vice-Chairman of the Board of Trustees, the President, one or more Vice-Presidents, a Secretary, and a Treasurer. All Officers shall be approved by the Trustees. Unless a vacancy in an office occurs at another time, appointment of Officers shall be held at the annual meeting of the Board. The Chairman and the Vice-Chairman shall serve for terms of two years and until their successors are appointed and qualified. The other Officers of the College shall serve such terms as may be determined by the Board of Trustees.

Section 2. The Chairman and Vice-Chairman shall be members of the Board of Trustees. The President shall be ex officio a member of the Board without power to vote and shall not be counted as a member of the Board or any committee on which he may serve for any purpose. No other Officer need be a member of the Board of Trustees.

Section 3. The Board may approve one or more Vice-Presidents, Assistant Treasurers, Assistant Secretaries, and such other Officers as may be deemed necessary for the proper management of the College.

Section 4. All Officers of the College shall hold office at the discretion of the Boad of Trustees and shall be subject to removal by affirmative vote of a majority of the entire membership of the Board of Trustees, without prejudice to any contract rights such Officer may have against the College.

Section 5. In the event of a vacancy in the office of the President, the Board shall appoint a special Presidential Search Committee to submit nominations for candidates for that office. A vacancy in any of the offices of the College may be filled at any meeting of the Board of Trustees.

Article V: Powers and Duties of the Chairman
and Vice-Chairman of the Board of Trustees

The Chairman shall preside at all meetings of the Board of Trustees, shall have a right to vote on all questions, shall appoint to all committees the members who are not appointed by the Board of Trustees, and shall have such other powers and duties as the Board from time to time may prescribe. In the absence of the Chairman, the Vice-Chairman shall perform the duties of the office of the Chairman.

Article VI: Powers and Duties of the
President of the College

The President of the College shall be the Chief Executive Officer of the College and the official adviser to and executive agent of the Board of Trustees and its Executive Committee. He shall, as educational and administrative head of the College, exercise a general superintendence over all the affairs of the institution, and bring such matters to the attention of the Board as are appropriate to keep the Board fully informed to meet its policy-making responsibilities. He shall have power, on behalf of the Trustees, to perform all acts and execute all documents to make effective the actions of the Board or its Executive Committee. Except as otherwise provided in these bylaws, he shall be ex officio a member of all committees of the Board without power to vote.

Article VII: Powers and Duties of the Vice-President(s)

Each Vice-President shall have such powers and shall perform such duties as may be assigned to him by the President. In case of the absence or disability of the President, the duties of that office shall be performed by any Vice-President designated by the Board of Trustees, or in the absence of any such designation, by the most senior Vice-President available, which, in the absence of other criteria established by the Board, shall be the Vice-President with the greatest length of service to the College.

Article VIII: Powers and Duties of the Secretary

The Secretary shall have custody of the seal of the College and shall attest to and affix said seal to such documents as required in the business of the College, including but not limited to deeds, bonds, mortgages, agreements, contracts, diplomas, evidences of the award of degrees, transcripts, abstracts of resolutions, certificates, minutes, and bylaws issued pursuant to the authority of the College. He shall give proper notice of all meetings of the Board of Trustees and shall keep a record of the appointment of all committees of the Board of Trustees and members of the administrative and teaching staffs. He shall keep or cause to be kept a record of the minutes of all meetings of the Board of Trustees and each of its committees. Any of the duties or powers of the Secretary may be performed by an Assistant Secretary who shall be responsible to and report to the Secretary.

Article IX: Powers and Duties of the Treasurer

The Treasurer shall be the Chief Financial Officer of the College. He shall have the duty to keep or cause to be kept full and accurate accounts of all receipts and disbursements and to obey all lawful orders of the Trustees, the President of the College, and the Finance, Audit, and Investment Committees respecting funds, property, and accounts of the College. He shall be responsible for the preparation of any corporate financial reports as may be required by departments of government, including but not limited to [the applicable state authority]. The Treasurer shall, in the name of the College, give receipts for monies or property as shall be required, deposit funds in accordance with resolution and direction of the Finance Committee or the Board of Trustees, and safeguard the money of the College. He shall not pay out any money unless by order of the Board of Trustees or under such regulations or with such approval as the Finance Committee or Investment Committee may prescribe. He shall cooperate with any independent auditors or certified public accountants retained by the Board of Trustees for the purpose of conducting audits of the accounts of the College, and shall make reports at meetings of the Board of Trustees or the Finance and Audit Committees with respect to the financial condition of the College at such time and in such form as the Board or the Committees may duly require. The Treasurer shall give a bond to the College faithfully to perform the duties of his office, and to account for all monies and other matters and things which may come into his hands and possession by virtue of said office, in such amount as the Audit Committee shall direct.

Article X: Meetings

Section 1. There shall be four regular meetings of the Board of Trustees annually, which shall be held in the winter, spring, summer, and fall on such date and place as may be designated either by the Board or by any two of the Chairman, the President, and the Secretary. The annual meeting of the Board shall be the meeting each year.

Section 2. Special meetings may be held at the call of any two of the Chairman, the President, and the Secretary; and it shall be the duty of the Chairman or the Secretary to call such special meetings on the request of five Trustees, setting forth the objects of the meeting.

Section 3. Written notice of all meetings of the Board of Trustees shall be sent by the Secretary to each Trustee at least ten days before the date of the meeting. In the case of special meetings, the notice shall state the purposes of the meeting, and no business shall be transacted at such meeting that does not relate to the purposes stated.

Section 4. Whenever notice is required to be given under the provisions of statutes or of the articles of incorporation or of these bylaws, a waiver thereof in writing signed by the persons entitled to said notice, whether before or after the time stated therein, shall be deemed equivalent thereto. Attendance at any meeting by a Trustee shall be conclusively deemed a waiver of notice of that meeting unless objection be made thereto at such meeting.

Section 5. A majority of the Trustees shall be necessary and sufficient to constitute a quorum for the transaction of business, and the act of a majority of the Trustees present and voting at a duly called meeting of the Board or any committee shall be the act of the Board of Trustees or that committee, except as may be provided by statute or by the articles of incorporation, or by these bylaws.

Article XI: Action Without Formal Meeting

Any action required or permitted to be taken by the Board of Trustees or by any committee thereof may be taken without a formal meeting. Meetings may be conducted by mail, telegram, cable, or in any other way the Trustees shall decide. However, a written consent setting forth the action so taken and signed by all members of the Board or of a committee, as the case may be, must be filed with the minutes of the proceedings of the Board or the committee.

Article XII: Committees

Section 1. There may be such special or ad hoc committees as the Board of Trustees may from time to time establish for the discharge of particular duties.

Section 2. There shall be the standing committees specified in this Article. Members of standing committees shall be appointed by the Chairman, after consultation with the Board, annually, at or following the annual meeting of the Board of Trustees. Except as provided in these bylaws, the Chairman of the Board and the President of the College shall be ex officio members of all standing committees, and each standing committee shall include at least three additional Trustees. Except where otherwise provided in this Article, additional members, including persons who are not on the Board of Trustees, may be appointed. The chairman of each standing committee and a majority of its members shall be Trustees.

Section 3. The Board of Trustees may at any time discontinue any of its standing committees for such time as may be determined, and the duties of any committee so discontinued shall be performed during such discontinuance by the Executive Committee.

Section 4. The chairman of any committee, with the consent of the Chairman of the Board, may request the President of the College to appoint an Officer of the College or a member of the administrative staff to serve as a liaison between the committee and the office of the President. Such liaison person shall assist the committee in the carrying out of its duties.

Section 5. Except as provided in this section, all standing committees shall meet at least two times annually.

Section 6. Executive Committee

a. The Executive Committee shall be composed of members, all of whom shall be Trustees. The Chairman of the Board of Trustees shall be the chairman of the Executive Committee. The Vice-Chairman of the Board and the chairman of each standing committee of the Board shall be members of the Executive Committee. The President shall be ex officio a member of the Executive Committee, without power to vote, and shall not be counted as a member of that committee for any purpose.

b. Between meetings of the Board of Trustees, the Executive Committee shall have general supervision of the administration and property of the College except that unless specifically empowered by the Board of Trustees to do so, it may not take any action inconsistent with a prior act of the Board of Trustees, award degrees, alter bylaws, locate permanent buildings on tax-exempt property held for College purposes, remove or appoint the President of the College, or take any action which has been reserved by the Board.

c. The Executive Committee shall meet regularly at least times a year in the months of   ,   ,   , and Special meetings shall be called by the Secretary on the written request of the Chairman or at least three of the members.

d. A majority of the members of the Executive Committee shall constitute a quorum for the transaction of business.

e. The minutes of the meetings of the Executive Committee shall be distributed promptly after each meeting to each member of the Board of Trustees. At each and every meeting of the Board of Trustees, the proceedings and actions taken by the Executive Committee since the last meeting of the Board shall be reported to the Board.

Section 7. Committee on Membership. The Committee on Membership shall be composed of   members. It shall present to the Board of Trustees nominations for Trustees to be elected by the Board, and for Chairman, Vice-Chairman, Secretary and Treasurer. The Committee shall furnish information relating to the background and qualifications of all such nominees at least two weeks prior to the Board meeting at which an election or appointment is scheduled to take place. The Committee shall develop and administer a program of orientation for newly elected Trustees. The Committee shall also, subject to the requirements as set forth in these bylaws, nominate Trustees Emeriti. It shall report to the Board of Trustees at the annual meeting.

Section 8. Educational Affairs Committee. The Educational Affairs Committee shall be composed of   members. It shall, in cooperation with the President, study and appraise the quality of the academic program; measure the program relative to other comparable institutions in terms of teaching load, class size, student-faculty ratios, instructional expenditures, research programs, and other relevant factors; formulate desirable short- and long-range enrollment goals; advise the Finance Committee on the specifications and requirements for financing the academic programs; recommend salary, pension, and other personnel policies concerning the academic personnel; and make such reports and recommendations to the Board of Trustees relative to the forgoing as may be required.

Section 9. Faculty Affairs Committee. The Faculty Affairs Committee shall be composed of   members. It shall review matters affecting the faculty of the College, other than those affecting the academic program; consider proposals on such matters; and report and make recommendations thereon to the Board of Trustees as may be required.

Section 10. Student Affairs Committee. The Student Affairs Committee shall be composed of   members. It shall review matters affecting students of the College, other than those relating to the academic program; consider proposals on such matters; and report and make recommendations thereon to the Board of Trustees as may be required.

Section 11. Finance Committee. The Finance Committee shall be composed of   members. It shall review annual operating and capital budgets prepared and presented under the direction of the President and make recommendations with respect thereto to the Board of Trustees. It shall review major financial transactions not provided for in the budget and submit proposed variances with recommendations to the Board of Trustees or Executive Committee. The Treasurer of the College shall be an ex officio member of the Finance Committee, without power to vote, and shall not be counted as a member of the Committee for any purpose.

Section 12. Audit Committee. The Audit Committee shall be composed of   members. It shall periodically appraise the financial control and accounting systems of the College and recommend any changes it deems appropriate. It shall recommend the designation of an independent auditor each year and shall cause to be prepared and submitted to the Board of Trustees at least once a year an audited statement of the financial condition of the College as of the close of the fiscal year and of the receipts and expenditures for each year. The Committee may request any designated independent auditor, or any officer or employee of the College, to appear before it to report on the financial condition of the College and answer any questions the Committee might have. The President of the College shall not be an ex officio member of the Audit Committee, but may, upon invitation of the Committee, attend any meeting.

Section 13. Development Committee. The Development Committee shall be composed of   members. It shall review and recommend fund-raising and public relations programs and report to the Finance Committee on fund-raising progress and estimates of income to be received therefrom. It shall report on its activities to the Board of Trustees at the annual meeting.

Section 14. Investment Committee. The Investment Committee shall be composed of   members. Acting within the scope of investment policy guidelines established by the Board of Trustees, the Committee shall have charge of the investment of all funds of the College, including the power to effect purchases, sales, or exchanges of securities and other investment assets of the College. The Committee may employ investment counsel and may delegate authority to purchase or sell securities for the account of the College to such investment counsel or to any Officer of the College subject to such limitations as the Committee may impose. The Committee shall report changes in investments to the Board of Trustees at each Board meeting. It shall from time to time prepare and submit to the Finance Committee estimates of expected endowment income.

Section 15. Building and Grounds Committee. The Building and Grounds Committee shall be composed of   members. It shall review and analyze maintenance and operations policy, recommend improvements, review and recommend approval of plans and cost estimates for new facilities, review the annual operating and capital budgets of the Department of Buildings and Grounds, and recommend approval to the Finance Committee. It shall report on its activities at the annual meeting of the Board of Trustees and at such other times as it may be requested to do so by the Board of Trustees.

Article XIII: Indemnification

Each Trustee and Officer of the College shall be indemnified by it against all expenses actually and necessarily incurred by such Trustee or Officer in connection with the defense of any action, suit, or proceeding to which he has been made a party by reason of his being or having been such Trustee or Officer except in relation to matters as to which such Trustee or Officer shall be adjudicated in such action, suit, or proceeding to be liable for gross negligence or willful misconduct in the performance of duty.

Article XIV: Conflicts of Interest

A Trustee shall be considered to have a conflict of interest if (a) such Trustee has existing or potential financial or other interests which impair or might reasonably appear to impair such member's independent, unbiased judgment in the discharge of his responsibilities to the College, or (b) such Trustee is aware that a member of his family (which for purposes of this paragraph shall be a spouse, parents, siblings, children, and any other relative if the latter reside in the same household as the Trustee), or any organization in which such Trustee (or member of his family) is an officer, director, employee, member, partner, trustee, or controlling stockholder has such existing or potential financial or other interests. All Trustees shall disclose to the Board any possible conflict of interest at the earliest practicable time. No Trustee shall vote on any matter, under consideration at a Board or committee meeting, in which such Trustee has a conflict of interest. The minutes of such meeting shall reflect that a disclosure was made and that the Trustee having a conflict of interest abstained from voting. Any Trustee who is uncertain whether he has a conflict of interest in any matter may request the Board or committee to determine whether a conflict of interest exists, and the Board or committee shall resolve the question by majority vote.

Article XV: Discrimination Prohibited

Section 1. In administering its affairs, the College shall not discriminate against any person on the basis of race, creed, color, national or ethnic origin, sex, or age.

Section 2. In interpreting these bylaws, all masculine pronouns shall be deemed to refer equally to the feminine gender.

Article XVI: Review and Amendment of Bylaws

Section 1. These bylaws may be changed or amended at any meeting of the Trustees by a two thirds vote of those present, provided notice of the substance of the proposed amendment is sent to all the Trustees at least ten days before the meeting.

Section 2. Prior to each annual meeting of the Board of Trustees, the Executive Committee shall review these bylaws and suggest any necessary changes thereto.

Resource D

Statement on Conflicts of Interest

Potential conflicts of interest have become a source of increasing concern in all branches of trusteeship. Many governing boards of colleges and universities have adopted statements of policy to make public the position of their institutions in this complex matter. In response to a growing number of requests, the board of directors of the Association of Governing Boards of Universities and Colleges (AGB) has adopted the following statement to assist institutions in arriving at a general statement that can be adapted to particular circumstances. The statement is not intended to cover all possible conditions and is confined to broad considerations rather than to details, but it covers the issues most likely to arise.

AGB acknowledges with gratitude the various institutions that have shared their adopted statements with it, and a number of member trustees and chief executives who have given the benefit of their review.

Preliminary Considerations

Institutions of postsecondary education, both public and private, continue to be involved in programs affecting the public interest. Their trustees have adopted and published guidelines for themselves and administrators at all levels to ensure that the highest possible degree of probity is observed. Among these concerns is the problem of potential conflicts of interest.

At the same time, it should be recognized that members of governing boards are likely to be, and indeed should be, persons of responsible involvement in affairs other than trusteeship of postsecondary education. A competent board can scarcely be recruited from persons entirely free from potential conflicts of interest. To a degree, the same can be said for administrators.

The term *trustee* itself indicates that members of a board are acting for others, not for themselves, and are legally appointed for that purpose. Disclosure of potential conflicts of interest is therefore but reasonable a step to be taken by reasonable persons, and it does not imply dubious practice. Concern for the letter of the law is but the first stage. Equally important is a demonstrated awareness of broad ethical considerations.

The policy adopted by a board should ensure that both trustees and staff members place the welfare of the institution above personal interests or the interests of family members or others who may be personally involved in substantial affairs affecting the institution, including not only fiscal transactions but any other matters affecting the institution's program, personnel, or auxiliary enterprises. It should provide for systematic, continuous disclosure of potential conflicts and the means for resolving them. The individual trustee and the board as a whole should maintain current records of potential conflicts for review and evaluation by persons appointed by the board.

To ensure that the statement of policy has the full force of the institution behind it, the bylaws of the institution should include reference to the statement. The policy statement itself need not be included in the bylaws, since the policy may require occasional modification based on experience. Change is usually accomplished most easily when it does not involve the bylaws. Public and private institutions should also review pertinent statutes bearing on conflict of interest to make sure that the institutional policy conforms in all respects to their requirements.

Because trustees are responsible for the total well-being of an institution, their responsibility extends beyond financial aspects into all matters bearing on the progress, stability, and effectiveness of the institution. Thus the board should be alert to all relationships that could be seen as affecting its integrity. These may not always be issues of legality but of self-imposed standards.

In formulating its own statement, a board may feel it necessary to identify specific danger zones without attempting to be overprescriptive. For example, nepotism is a practice to be avoided. Whether to be specific on such a point is a matter of judgment. For another: a board member may be sought as lecturer in some field of specialization or may be needed as a consultant for a short period. It is the responsibility of both the individual involved, and of the board as a whole, to determine in advance the limitations to be accepted by the trustee during such a period of double function, if indeed such double function is deemed permissible at all.

In more general terms, it has been argued that a president should not serve as a voting member of his or her own board, a point worthy of consideration. If the president is not to have the vote, the board should certainly take care to specify the role of the president in meetings of the board and to ensure particularly that the board will not act on institutional affairs without the recommendations of the president and without his or her full participation, unless under most unusual circumstances.

Boards having student and faculty representation from within the institution need to consider, as indeed the students and faculty should consider, whether certain restrictions on the role of these members should be adopted to avoid the conflict of interest implicit in this arrangement.

An attempt to compile an inventory of potential conflicts of interest, however, would be futile. There can be no substitute for sensitivity on the part of individual trustees and of the board as a whole. Overzealous pursuit of the issue can ultimately hamper the sensible performance of duty. Legal determinations may prove fairly easy. The more delicate issues may simply require the intelligence and judgment to raise necessary questions in a timely fashion and to dispose of them one way or another~as the board itself may see fit.

Sample Conflict-of-Interest Policy
for Trustees, Officers, and Other Key Employees

1. *Scope.* The following statement of policy applies to each member of the Board and to all officers of [college or university]. Further, it is intended to serve for the guidance of all persons employed by the institution, regardless of position.

2. *Fiduciary Responsibility.* Members of the Board, officers, and staff serve a public interest role and thus have a clear obligation to conduct all affairs of the institution in a manner consistent with this concept. All decisions of the Board and officers of administration of the [college or university] are to be made solely on the basis of a desire to promote the best interests of the institution and the public good.

3. *Disclosure.* The policy of the Board of [college or university] requires that in the event the Board or officers must consider any transaction for the institution which also involves (1) a member of the Board or any officer of the institution or a member of his or her family (which shall be a spouse, parents, siblings, children, and any other relative), or (2) an organization with which a member of the Board or any officer of the institution is affiliated, such trustee or officer, at the first knowledge of the transaction, shall disclose fully the precise nature of the interest or involvement.

Disclosure is further required of Board members and officers of the institution concerning all *relationships and business affiliations* that reasonably could give rise to a conflict of interest involving the institution. This disclosure shall be continuously reported and kept current, as set forth below. For the purpose of this policy, affiliation is understood to prevail if the trustee or officers, or a member of the family:

a. Is an officer, director, trustee, partner, employee, or agent of such organization; or
b. Is either the actual or beneficial owner of more than [for example, 1 percent to 5 percent] of the voting stock or controlling interest of such an organization; or

c. Has any other direct or indirect dealings with such organization from which he or she knowingly is materially benefited (for example, through receipt directly or indirectly of cash or other property in excess of [$] a year—including [or exclusive of] dividends or interest).

All disclosures required under this policy must be directed in writing to the Secretary of the Board or to   , who together with the [college or university] counsel, shall be responsible for the administration of this policy. Matters under this policy concerning trustees shall be reported initially to the Chairman of the Board for appropriate action; those concerning staff will be referred initially to the President. Information disclosed to the Secretary (or Chairman or President) shall be held in confidence except when the best interest of the institution would be served by disclosing the information to the Board in executive session.

4. *Restraint on Participation.* Trustees or officers who have declared or been found to have conflict of interest in any matter before the administration or the Board shall refrain from participating in consideration of the proposed transaction, unless for special reasons the Board or administration requests information or interpretation from the person or persons involved. The person or persons involved should *not* vote on such matters and should not be present at the time of vote.

Any Board member who is uncertain about possible conflict of interest in any matter may request the Board to determine whether a possible conflict prevails; the Board shall resolve the question by majority vote. When possible, the question of potential conflict should be referred to counsel for an opinion prior to the Board's vote.

Adopted by the (Board of Trustees)

_____

(Institution)

_____

(Date)

Sample Record Forms

Following are two possible options for developing and maintaining adequate records. Either option can be modified or adapted with advice of legal counsel to institutional circumstances and the judgment of the board. Neither form is presented as a perfect device. Boards that elect to adopt a version of either form are urged to require each board member to complete and update it annually. Further, the forms should be formally reviewed on a schedule and by an official or officials determined by the board.

Option I: Conflict-of-Interest Questionnaire

_____
(Institution Name)

_____   _____
(Name)   (Date)

_____
Office Held (Trustee, Vice-President for Administration, and so forth)

1. Are you an officer or director of any corporation with which [institution name] has business dealings? Yes _____ No _____
   If the answer to the forgoing question is yes, please list the names of such corporations, the offices held, and the approximate dollar-amount of business involved with the [college or university] last year.

   _____
   _____
   _____
   _____

2. Do you, or does any member of your family, have a financial interest in, or receive any remuneration or income from, any business organization with which [institution name] has business dealings? Yes _____ No _____
   If the answer to the forgoing question is yes, please supply the following information:
   a. Names of the business organizations in which such interest is held and the person(s) by whom such interest is held:

   _____
   _____
   _____
   _____

b. Nature and amount of each such financial interest, remuneration, or income:

_____

_____

_____

_____

3. Did you, or any member of your family, receive, during the past twelve months, any gifts or loans from any source from which [institution name] buys goods or services or with which [institution name] has significant business dealings? Yes _____ No _____

If the answer to the forgoing questions is yes, list such gifts or loans as follows:

Name of Source	*Item*	*Approximate Value*

I certify that the forgoing information is true and complete to the best of my knowledge.

_____   _____

Date   Signature

Option II: Disclosure Letter

Board Secretary [or other designated official]
[Name and address of college or university]
Dear _____ :

I have received and read the statement of "Policy on Conflicts of Interest" approved by the Board on [date], and I am in compliance with the ¦olicy except as specifically set forth below.

For the information of the [college or university], I am listing on the reverse all of my "associates" as defined, and the position and/or interest that I or a member of my family has in each "associate."

Sincerely,

_____   _____

(Date)   (Signature)

Exceptions
(Note: If there are none, please write "none.")

	*Associates**	
*Trustee or Family Member***	*Associate*	*Position and/or Interest*

*An associate of an individual includes any person, trust, organization, or enterprise (of a business nature or otherwise) with respect to which the individual or any member of his or her family (1) is a director, officer, employee, member, partner, or trustee, or (2) has financial interest as described in the Board's policy on conflict of interest adopted on [date], or any other interest that enables him or her to exercise control or significantly influence policy.

**The family of an individual includes his or her spouse, parents, siblings, children, and any other blood relative.

Resource E

Recommended Readings

Chapter One: Toward Effective Trusteeship for the Eighties

The most valuable essay on the future of college and university trusteeship was done by John W. Nason (1975). For good reason it is the most frequently cited and quoted reference in this book and other current literature on institutional governance. In addition, J. L. Zwingle's *Effective Trusteeship: Guidelines for Board Members* (1979) provides helpful suggestions for new and experienced trustees.

For an interesting historical perspective on the respective roles of trustees, administrators, faculties, and students in academic decision making, read the *Statement on Government of Colleges and Universities* (American Association of University Professors, 1966). Written in the midst of the unsettling period of student activism and the calls for "shared governance," the *Statement* was a joint effort of the American Association of University Professors (AAUP), the American Council on Education (ACE), and the Association of Governing Boards of Universities and Colleges (AGB). Among other principles, it recommends that institutional policies recognize that matters of faculty status (appointments, reappoint-ments, decisions not to reappoint, promotions, the granting of tenure, and dismissal) are primarily a faculty responsibility. Although many educators and trustees still subscribe to the principles of institutional governance espoused in this document, especially the principles of academic freedom, due process, and the rights and responsibilities of faculty members, many others see need for revision. Critics hold that a very changed academic landscape, particularly the advent of statewide boards and multicampus institutions in the 1970s and the fiscal and enrollment crunch anticipated in the 1980s, invalidate many of its recommendations. Contrary to popular belief, and for the record, the 1966 *Statement* was never formally "endorsed" by AGB or ACE as official policy. Rather it was "commended" to the attention of their members as a resource for discussion in developing their own policy statements. Disclaiming any intention to press this document on boards of trustees, AGB welcomes comment from interested readers.

Intended especially for community college trustees, *Trusteeship: Handbook for Community College and Technical Institute Trustees* (Potter, 1979) may also be useful to the members of boards and administrators of other institutions. Published by the Association of Community College Trustees (ACCT), this 177 page reference includes sections on the "selection, use, and evaluation of the college attorney" and "political action." ACCT also publishes a periodical, *ACCT Trustee Quarterly,* and offers other publications on specialized topics in community college governance.

A good reference particularly valuable for new trustees and regents of public colleges and universities is Heilbron's, *The College and University Trustee: A View from the Board Room* (1973). Its anecdotes about how public higher education in California contended with the turbulent sixties are object lessons for the present time. Heilbron's views on how to improve the selection of public institution trustees are enlightened and enlightening.

Chapter Two: Evolution of Lay Governing Boards

Besse's "A Comparison of the University with the Corporation" (1973) is a short treatise by an experienced lay trustee, who is also a lawyer and utility executive. It is an exceptionally concise and instructive chapter in a volume entitled *The University as an Organization*. Various other chapters are also valuable, but Besse's comments are especially useful for the lay trustee who feels a certain misgiving about the academy's claim to be a unique kind of organization.

Most trustees would profit from the ownership of a brief but comprehensive history of education, especially if they wish to gain perspective on trusteeship itself. One such volume is *The History of Western Education* by Boyd (1966). A classic in its field, it is now in its eighth edition. Mentioned elsewhere in this volume are many other commentators on trusteeship in the perspectives of history and the current scene. Among the more rewarding are those by Corson (1975), Kerr (1974), Nason (1975), and Rauh (1969).

Chapter Three: Responsibilities of the Governing Board

The Governance of Colleges and Universities by Corson (1960 and 1975) is the best treatment of the subject as a whole. Chap. 13 deals with the role of trustees, but the entire book is well worth reading. Rauh's *The Trusteeship of Colleges and Universities* (1969) concentrates on the trustees' place and performance in higher education. Zwingle, elder statesman in the field of academic governance, has produced three excellent brochures on trustees—*The Lay Governing Board* (1970), *Effective Trusteeship: Guidelines for Board Members* (1979), and (with Mayville) *College Trustees: A Question of Legitimacy* (1974). Nason's *The Future of Trusteeship* (1975) is an attempt to deal with the "Role and Responsibilities of College and University Boards," to use the words of the subtitle.

In a report to the Carnegie Commission on Higher Education, Perkins (1973) edited a highly useful volume entitled *The University as an Organization*. Chap. 2 by Duryea presents a clear, brief historical account of the evolution of college and university governance. In chap. 9 Corson analyzes the structure of the university, and in chap. 11 Perkins examines in brilliant fashion the "Conflicting Responsibilities of Governing Boards."

Among special studies of interest are the brief and provocative examination of selected state university boards by Paltridge, Hurst, and Morgan (1973) entitled *Boards of Trustees: Their Decision*

Patterns; the ERIC report by Hodgkinson (1971) called *Campus Governance—The Amazing Thing Is That It Works at All;* Greenleaf's short treatise on *Trustees as Servants* (1974), one in a series of his thoughtful and imaginative discussions on the place in our society of institutions and trustees; and Trow's "Reflections on the Transition from Mass to Universal Higher Education" (1970). The examples Trow uses belong to the period in which the article was written. As an analysis, however, of what has happened to postsecondary education since the Second World War and how the changes have affected governance, the article is both current and important.

Chapter Four: Selecting and Deploying Trustees

The resources on trustee selection, enlistment, and deployment are limited. Much of what does exist is published by the Association of Governing Boards of Universities and Colleges (AGB) in the form of journal articles, studies, and special publications. However, Nason's *The Future of Trusteeship* (1975) is must reading for any new trustee—the major characteristics that comprise the effective board are discussed, including the need for a new sense of responsibility and commitment.

The AGB Pocket Publication series offers trustees concise and readable summary information on a variety of subjects and issues with which they are likely to be concerned. Of particular interest to new trustees are *The Fund-Raising Role* by Radock (1977); *Resource Management Responsibilities* by Nelson (1977); and *A Guide for New Trustees* by Axelrod (1977).

A useful article on board effectiveness is Zwingle's "Build a Better Board" (1976). Among other things, it centers on unhurried recruitment, systematic orientation, and judicious deployment of trustees. Thompson and Miller (1979) introduce the concept of the trustee committee in their article "A Board Self-Improvement Tool."

Chapter Five: Organizing the Board

Greenleaf's *Trustees as Servants* (1974) provides a refreshing and sometimes unorthodox treatment of trusteeship in the not-for-profit sector. Especially with regard to his call for professional staffing for boards and, in large institutions, for chairmen who are full-time and salaried, Greenleaf offers an interesting alternative to prevailing practice. Also on the subject of staffing is an article by Summers and Smotony (1979) entitled "What Do Board Secretaries Do?" It reports a national survey of professional staff board secretaries, their backgrounds, and typical duties.

Frantzreb (1970) offers some useful suggestions for board structure and management with emphasis on committees in *Operational Imperatives for a College Board of Trustees in the 1970s*. This booklet also provides a checklist for bylaw provisions and an approach to monitoring trustee assignments. Another solid reference is Rauh's chapter on the "Internal Organization of the Board" in Perkins (Ed.), *The University as an Organization* (1973).

An important relationship is discussed in Gies and Anderson's *The Board Chairperson and the President* (1977), including suggestions on how they can support one another's leadership role. Frantzreb (1976) also has sound suggestions in "Secret Ingredients of a Chairperson." An article on advisory boards by Gale (1976) entitled "Lay Advisory Boards as an External Relations Tool" suggests ideas on how to establish, operate, and staff them.

One of the very best articles on conducting meetings is Jay's "How to Run a Meeting" (1976), delightfully written with wit and wisdom: "Almost everyone is in some way pleased and proud to be made chairman of something. And that is three quarters of the trouble (p. 51)." And for those who find themselves depressed over meetings required by state sunshine laws, ammunition with a sense of humor can be found in Cleveland's "The Cost of 'Openness'" (1975).

Chapter Six: Assuring Trustee Orientation and Development

Trustees need regular access to timely information that is free of jargon and economizes their time. Every board member can benefit from reading the *Chronicle of Higher Education, AGB Reports,* and *AGB News Notes*. Items in these publications can also stimulate discussion at regular meetings or special workshops.

AGB offers for purchase or rental a film entitled "College

and University Trusteeship" that provides an overview of board responsibilities for use in trustee orientation programs and in workshop settings. AGB (in Washington, D. C.) will provide upon request a complimentary list of its publications.

Chapter Seven: Participating in Policy Making and Management

Valuable works that appeared more than a decade ago include: Ruml and Morrison's *Memo to a College Trustee* (1959); Rauh's *The Trusteeship of Colleges and Universities* (1969); Henderson's *The Role of the Governing Board* (1967); and Corson's *The Governance of Colleges and Universities* (1960; rev. ed., 1975). An article by Bush (1961), noted scientist and trustee of three educational institutions, is included in Learned, Christenson, and Andrews (Eds.), *Problems of General Management.*

Four recent studies have supplied a body of fact to underpin our knowledge of the functioning of college and university boards. The earliest were Hartnett's *College and University Trustees: Their Backgrounds, Roles, and Educational Attitudes* (1969) and *The New College Trustee: Some Predictions for the 1970s* (1970). These were followed by Davis and Batchelor (1974), *The Effective College and University Board: A Report of a National Survey of Trustees and Presidents;* and Paltridge, Hurst, and Morgan (1973), *Boards of Trustees: Their Decision Patterns.* The latter was based on analyses of the official records of 100 meetings of boards of twenty four-year institutions in California.

Three other works warrant mention. In Perkins (Ed.), *The University as an Organization* (1973), chaps. 6 and 11 to 13 merit the attention of trustees. The second is Nason (1975), *The Future of Trusteeship.* The third is Baldridge, and others (1978), *Policy Making and Effective Leadership.* This work will help trustees understand the uniqueness of the university as an institution and of the environment in which it functions.

Finally, one old and three recent works are useful, if difficult to classify. Davis' "More to be Desired Are They than Gold. . . ." (1958) is an inspirational piece that has been quoted many times. On a more philosophical level, Greenleaf's *The Institution as Servant* (1972) and *Trustees as Servants* (1974) offer stimulating food for thought. The third recent work illuminates the practices and the thinking of community college trustees: Dziuba and Meardy (Eds.), *New Directions for Community Colleges: Enhancing Trustee Effectiveness* (1976).

Chapter Eight: Selecting the Chief Executive

Kauffman's *The Selection of College and University Presidents* (1974) is an excellent contemporary study of the subject. *How College Presidents Are Chosen* by Bolman (1965) is an older study full of wit and wisdom. Both have the additional merit of being brief. *The Leaning Ivory Tower* by Bennis (1973) is an amusing account of his uprisings and downsittings as a university administrator, including his reactions to the selection procedures that he endured. Pattillo's "Choosing a College President" (1973) is another brief summary of the major steps in the process.

Kerr's chapter on "Presidential Discontent" in *Perspectives on Campus Tensions* (1970), Cole's article on "The Reeling Presidency" (1976), and two articles by McKenna, "Recycling College Presidents" (1972) and "Ten Lessons of a Recycled President" (1977), deal with some of the pressures under which presidents work, the human cost of being a president, and ways of ameliorating the situation. A thorough discussion of the role and problems of a president's wife is to be found in Corbally's *The Partners* (1977a) and "The Problem of the President's Wife" (1977b).

For those interested in the legislative and administrative regulations surrounding equal opportunity and affirmative action, a good source is Hanson and Pondrum's section in *Federal Regulations and the Employment Practices of Colleges and Universities* (1974).

Search and selection committee members should understand the nature of the president's job—a subject on which there has been extensive writing. Two thoughtful and perceptive treatments from the 1960s are Kerr's *The Uses of the University* (1963) and Perkins' *The University in Transition* (1966). A more recent study was prepared by Cohen and March (1974) for the Carnegie Commission on Higher Education; their *Leadership and Ambiguity: The American College President* is, as its title suggests, provocative and controversial. *The Multiple Roles of the College and University Presi-*

dent by Millett (1976) is an overview by an experienced and wise administrator.

The most recent and probably the most detailed treatment of the topic of this chapter is Nason's *Presidential Search: A Guide to the Process of Selecting and Appointing College and University Presidents* (1979). Those wanting more detailed advice than this chapter affords will find it in the results of the nationwide study conducted by Nason.

Chapter Nine: Engaging in Institutional Planning

An excellent introduction to the subject of planning for institutions of higher education is Eurich and Tickton's *Long-Range Planning and Budgeting at Colleges and Universities* (1973), which reviews the history of recent institutional planning in the United States, stresses the reasons why it should be done, and describes the general character of the process. *Alternatives,* a series of ten articles by higher education administrators (American Association of State Colleges and Universities, 1978), is a lively, nontechnical consideration of many aspects of the planning process. Millett (1978a) discusses the ways in which planning may be employed to help an institution manage change and make thoughtful decisions about the way it will meet and deal with the social, political, and economic conditions of the future.

Parekh's *Long-Range Planning* (1977) is a more technical manual describing in considerable detail the actual implementation of an institution-wide planning process. Its sample of goal statements and questions designed to elicit concrete information for planning is particularly useful in illustrating the scope and details that planning should encompass. *A College Planning Cycle* (National Association of College and University Business Officers, 1975) gives a somewhat less technical approach to planning. Of special worth is an appendix containing sample planning forms that show the data that a planning process should generate.

Fenske's *New Directions for Institutional Research: Using Goals in Research and Planning* (1978) is aimed chiefly at those concerned with institutional research and the use of institutional goals in such research. For the more general reader, however, it contains helpful chapters on the assessment of institutional goals and on the Institutional Goals Inventory.

The literature on the role of board members in institutional planning is not extensive. Most of it has appeared in *AGB Reports.* Cornett (1977) in "Masterly Planning" presents a general description of the trustee role and responsibilities; Miller (1978) describes the planning process at Stanford University and comments briefly on trustees' participation in that process. An article by Armacost and the Young Presidents' Organization Team (1976) contains a list of questions for trustees to ask to help improve institutional management and policy making. These questions go beyond planning, but the planning section is comprehensive and provocative. Bowman in "Defer Maintenance, Invite Disaster" (1977) writes about the perils inherent in deferred maintenance of which trustees need to be aware. Also noteworthy is "A Planning Model for Small Colleges" by Vaccaro (1979).

Two recent talks also addressed the subject of trustees and the planning process. Nelson (1975), in a paper presented at AGB's National Conference on Trusteeship, stressed the importance of trustee involvement in planning and gave special attention to the role of trustees in public institutions. Ingram (1977a) presented to the Society for College and University Planning ways in which chief executives and planning administrators can encourage greater trustee participation in planning. Both the articles and the talks cited speak directly, practically, and concretely to the issue at hand and should be of invaluable assistance to trustees.

Chapten Ten: Overseeing Academic Programs

In the literature on academic governance, works of direct relevance to the role of the trustee in overseeing academic programs are few. From an earlier period, Wildersmith (1949) in "A University Trustee Views the Academic Profession" presents the traditional case for trustee restraint in academic matters. But a case for the activist trustee is made by Ruml and Morrison in the classic *Memo to a College Trustee* (1959).

In *Academic Power in the United States,* Clark and Youn (1976) capture the historical roots of our peculiarly American system of academic governance. Rauh's *The Trusteeship of Colleges and Universities* (1969) provides a comprehensive picture of trusteeship in the late 1960s. The report from the Carnegie Commission (1973), *Governance of Higher Education,* provides a valuable and tightly summarized context of academic governance and trusteeship in addition to summaries of the work of other commissions and associations.

General works on governance that also give insights into the trustee role include those by Corson (1960 and 1975) and Millett (1978b)—both distinguished long-time observers of American higher education. Among the useful recent articles on trustees, each of which refers to their role in academic programs, are those by Gould (1973), Martin (1974), Perkins (1973), and Riley (1977).

Chapter Eleven: Working with Faculty and Students

The writings about governance of higher education, including faculty and student participation, are too numerous to list. Historically, major items of interest are Jencks and Riesman (1968), *The Academic Revolution;* Corson (1975), *Governance of Colleges and Universities;* and Millett (1962), *The Academic Community.* The *Statement on Government of Colleges and Universities* (1966), developed jointly by the American Association of University Professors, the American Council on Education, and AGB, is a major document, as is the report by the American Association for Higher Education (1967) entitled *Faculty Participation in Academic Governance.*

More recent studies of university governance include books by Baldridge (1971); Baldridge and others (1978); Blau (1973); Millett (1978b); and Mortimer and McConnell (1978). The report by the Carnegie Commission on Higher Education (1973) would be especially useful for board members.

Among many commentaries about faculty members, papers and books by Blackburn (1977), Duryea (1978), Dykes (1968), and Hermann (1973) are particularly helpful. On student participation in governance, the following deserve particular attention: American Association of University Professors (1970), Kellems (1975), McGrath (1970), Morrison (1970), Robinson and Shoenfeld (1970), and Wren (1975). Finally, Nason and Wood's "Student-Faculty Trusteeship: A Short Debate" (1977) is worth careful consideration.

Chapter Twelve: Setting Tenure and Personnel Policies

Although now twenty years old, *Tenure in American Higher Education* by Byse and Joughin (1959) still provides a valuable overview of academic tenure. Of the numerous more recent volumes on tenure, the report of the American Association of University Professors and Association of American Colleges Commission on Academic Tenure (1973) offers the most comprehensive and balanced study, complete with forty-seven specific recommendations on policy and practice. It also includes an eloquent history of tenure by Metzger. Chait and Ford in *Tenure and the Alternatives* (forthcoming) survey and evaluate experiences with alternatives and modifications to conventional tenure practices and amplify the suggestions sketched in this chapter about improving the management of tenure sytems.

In *Steady-State Staffing in Tenure-Granting Institutions and Related Papers*, Furniss (1973) presents some useful approaches to planning and analysis. For an excellent illustration of the potential and specific application of a computer-based planning model on faculty flow, see the study completed by the Institute for Educational Development (1973) for twelve private colleges in Pennsylvania. Blackburn's *Tenure* (1972) offers a very informative and sometimes surprising summary of studies that examined the relationship between tenure status and such questions as research productivity and teaching effectiveness.

On legal questions, both Edwards and Nordin's *Higher Education and the Law* (1979) and Kaplin's *The Law of Higher Education* (1978) serve well as reference volumes. Edwards and Nordin provide the text of more cases; Kaplin considers the administrative implications of various decisions. Policy recommendations of the American Association of University Professors (1977) should be read in conjunction with Furniss' articles on the status of AAUP policy generally (1978) and the wisdom of AAUP retrenchment policies more particularly (1976).

Making Affirmative Action Work in Higher Education by the Carnegie Council on Policy Studies (1975) represents the most valuable work to date. Especially helpful are the concrete suggestions on progam implementation and the many excerpts from actual affirmative action plans. For a provocative critique of affirmative action, see Lester (1974), *Antibias Regulations of Universities.*

Chapter Thirteen: Responding to Unionism

For a comprehensive examination of the critical issues faced in collective bargaining, see the *Handbook of Faculty Bargaining* by Angell, Kelley, and Associates (1977). Trustees in the public sector faced with legislative issues should consider Angell's monograph, *Legislatures, Collective Bargaining, and the Public University* (1978a), while trustees of private institutions should review the materials prepared for the Association of Governing Boards by Mortimer (1977) in *Academic Collective Bargaining* and familiarize themselves with the arguments presented to the U.S. Supreme Court in the *Yeshiva University* case (1978). Those trustees concerned with governance and the impact of collective bargaining on that process are referred to Adler's *Governance and Collective Bargaining in Four-Year Institutions 1970–1971* (1978) and Mortimer and Richardson's *Governance in Institutions with Faculty Unions: Six Case Studies* (1977).

Where dispute settlement is of concern, trustees should read selected chapters of *The Effective Administrator: A Practical Approach to Problem Solving, Decision Making, and Campus Leadership* by Walker (1979), as well as *Grievance Arbitration in Higher Education: Recent Experiences with Arbitration of Faculty Status Disputes* by Weisberger (1979). And, for continuing current information on all facets of faculty employment relations, see *ACBIS Fact Sheet,* a monthly newsletter produced by the Academic Collective Bargaining Information Service/Project on Educational Employment Relations.

Chapter Fourteen: Securing Resources

One of the best and easiest to read compilations of the concept, function, and challenge of obtaining resources, and the trustee role in this endeavor, is presented in the collection of articles called *On Development* and edited by Stuhr (1977).

Historical context is provided by Cutlip's *Fund Raising in the United States* (1965) and Curti and Nash's *Philanthropy in the Shaping of Higher Education* (1965). In addition, the trustee who wishes to keep in touch with current developments and future trends will find valuable information in publications of leading consulting firms and organizations in the areas of educational management and fund raising: *Giving USA*, American Association of Fund-Raising Counsel; *Bulletin on Public Relations and Development for Colleges and Universities*, Gonser Gerber Tinker Stuhr; *Foundation News*, Council on Foundations; *Fund-Raising Management*, Hoke Communications; *Grantsmanship Center News; Philanthropic Digest*, Brakeley, John Price Jones, Inc.; and *Taxwise Giving*. Articles about obtaining resources appear periodically in *AGB Reports* and *CASE Currents*.

Persons wishing to pursue the detail of measurement and cost will learn about selection and application of indicators in the work of J. W. Leslie (1978–79), whose conclusions and assorted sources of data are summarized in "Selected Indicators Chart Trends" in *New Directions for Institutional Advancement: Evaluating Advancement Programs*. The topic of cost effectiveness in educational fund raising has been addressed in a book edited by Heeman (1978–79), *New Directions for Institutional Advancement: Analyzing the Cost Effectiveness of Fund Raising*.

Trustees in the smaller, independent colleges will be especially interested in *The President's Role in Development*, published by the Association of American Colleges (1975). Included are perspectives by and for board members. Trustees in public, two-year colleges will benefit from reading *Community College Development: Alternative Fund-Raising Strategies*, by Luck and Tolle (1978) and *Philanthropic Support for Public Junior Colleges* by Bremer (1965).

A thirteen-minute filmstrip on "Trustee's Role in Fund Raising" (Radock, 1975) is available from AGB for its member boards that participate in the Board-Mentor Service. An eight-page publication by Radock (1977) entitled *The Fund-Raising Role* is also available.

Chapter Fifteen: Reporting Finances

The interested trustee or regent will find an extended discussion of financial reporting in *Financial Responsibilities of Governing Boards of Colleges and Universities* published by the AGB and the National Association of College and University Business Officers (1979). A number of informative books on financial and accounting practice in institutions of higher education are available, one of the more readable being the *Financial and Accounting Guide for Nonprofit Organizations* by Gross (1974), who has long been a crusader for simplified financial reporting.

For the trustee or regent who wishes more insight into the complex world of internal and institutional administration and management, a quick scan of *College and University Business Administration* published by the National Association of College and University Business Officers (1974) can be most enlightening. The depth and breadth of activity and the requirements for the reporting structure—in which the board reports are only the tip of the iceberg—are made immediately apparent by this work. A quick browse through this substantial volume may thus inspire a sense of restraint in the trustee whose board is seeking to clarify or develop its own financial reporting apparatus.

Chapter Sixteen: Managing Resources

The National Association of College and University Business Officers (NACUBO) and the Association of Governing Boards of Universities and Colleges (AGB) are the two chief sources of definitive information on the subjects of this chapter. Their jointly produced *Financial Responsibilities of Governing Boards of Colleges and Universities* (1979) is current and useful. NACUBO's *College and University Business Administration* (1974) is aimed at the business officer and is therefore more detailed than necessary for general trustee enlightenment; however, the chapters on budgeting and investment management will be especially helpful to members of board finance committees.

Funds for the Future, a study sponsored by the Twentieth-Century Fund (1975), summarizes much of what is currently available on educational endowments. An especially interesting recent addition to the literature is Ennis and Williamson (1976) on *Spending Policy for Educational Endowments.* The subject of social policy in relation to investments has not yet received definitive treatment. Recent articles have expressed a variety of viewpoints. Two that appeared in *AGB Reports* are Murray (1978), "Framing a South African Policy Statement" and Olswang (1978), "Trustees, Divestiture, and the Law."

New ground is being broken in the development of performance measures to enable the trustee or administrator to compare results for his or her institution with the higher education sector as a whole or with selected peer institutions. Minter and Bowen's annual studies of the private sector represent the most advanced work to date in this field.

Chapter Seventeen: Contending with Conflicts of Interest and Liability

Several publications have featured information about conflicts of interest or potential liability of members of governing boards. Among them are Welles' monograph on *Conflicts of Interest: Nonprofit Institutions* for the Twentieth-Century Fund (1977) and two shorter pieces, "Trustee Responsibility" by Anderson (1979) and an open letter from President Bok (1979) to the Harvard Community about the ethical problems of accepting gifts. Although Welles' piece is controversial and has been criticized by many, it provides worthwhile analysis. A background paper on endowment policy by Williamson (1975) entitled *Funds for the Future* also provides a good study of the various options to trustees responsible for their institution's financial resources.

Finally, this note would not be complete without a special acknowledgement to Margaret J. Gillis, of the law firm of Nixon, Hargrave, Devans, and Doyle, whose research and writing made this chapter possible.

Chapter Eighteen: Studying Board Effectiveness

Contemporary literature relevant to board evaluation and self-study is found under two closely related subject areas, one dealing with the responsibilities and expectations of trustees and the other with the processes of evaluation and self-study. Boards, and individual trustees, will do well to thoroughly review the former and use the latter as a planning guide to their own self-study projects.

Nason (1975), after conducting a national study of the characteristics and operating policies of collegiate governing boards, set forth in *The Future of Trusteeship* a concise and definitive statement of the major responsibilities of trustees in the years ahead. These are grouped in two classifications: (1) the standard expectations or requirements of trusteeship and (2) the additional responsibilities created by new demands upon trustee boards. This is followed by his statement defining the effective board. Greenleaf (1974), who defines trustees as servants of their institution and its various publics, suggests alternatives to the conventional wisdom related to trustee responsibilities and suggests ways to improve board performance. In *The College and University Trustee,* Heilbron (1973) writes from the perspective of an experienced trustee of public colleges and offers a list of warnings to trustees about frequent abuses of their powers. The list is equally applicable to trustees of any institution. Dugger (1975–1976), a frequent commentator on social and political issues, wrote "If I Were a Trustee," an article that draws upon an earlier paper entitled "The University Regent: Responsibilities of the Philosopher-King" (1975).

Two research studies have contributed to this literature by investigating the decision-making practices of trustees. In *College and University Trustees,* Hartnett (1969) explored the manner in which certain decisions are made by trustees or delegated to administrators. Paltridge (1973) analyzed the degree and detail of attention boards devoted to various types of decisions and concluded that better management of agendas and more time-efficient conduct of board meetings were needed.

The processes of self-evaluation are discussed by various authors in papers available through AGB. Two instruments are presented in the Resources section of this book: the trustee audit (Resource A) offers a checklist technique for individual trustee review, and the AGB self-study criteria (Resource B) is intended for board assessment. Pray (1965) offers a "report card" rating procedure for trustee self-study, and Shark (1977) describes the AGB Board-Mentor Service for self-evaluation and follow-up planning in "Now in Action." The National Association of Independent Schools (1978) has provided their members with a self-evaluation formula in *Evaluating Our Performance*. Polk and Coleman (1976) direct their writing to community college trustees and discuss self-evaluation as a key to public accountability.

Chapter Nineteen: Reviewing Presidential Leadership

The material available analyzing the assessment of presidential performance is sparse. *AGB Reports* from time to time during the past few years has carried a number of significant articles, particularly by Hays (1976a, 1976b), chancellor of the Minnesota State College System. Kauffman's (1978) article, although it focuses more on the search process, contains insightful references to the problems and values of performance assessment. Similarly, Nason's *Presidential Search: A Guide to the Process of Selecting and Appointing College and University Presidents* (1979) is full of valuable comments upon the status of higher education's chief executive officers. AGB has also published a companion book by Nason, *Presidential Assessment: A Challenge to College and University Leadership* (1980).

Bennis (1973) has written entertainingly on the problem of finding and evaluating presidents in *The Leaning Ivory Tower*. There is a growing literature analyzing the more general problem of institutional leadership, and Burns' *Leadership* (1978) contains a number of comments upon the leadership problems at nonprofit institutions. Kerr's writing on the presidency always casts an important light upon management and leadership issues and his essay on "Presidential Discontent" (1970) remains a very significant reference point.

Chapter Twenty: Assessing Institutional Performance

The literature on evaluation has grown rapidly in recent years. Much of it is technical and statistical, dealing with research methods and special investigations. While these studies are of interest mainly to members of the profession, the lay trustee needs to know that such resources are available and can profit from occasional reference to them. A recent and very commendable publication of this type is *The Assessment of College Performance* by Miller (1979). Another is the *Handbook of Academic Evaluation* by Dressel (1976), itself an adequate guide to the entire subject and written by a senior scholar in the field.

Shorter but enlightening statements about institutional assessment will be found in *AGB Reports:* "Who Killed These Four Colleges?" by Healy and Peterson (1977); "Our Best Defense Against Regulation" by Roger Heyns (1977), former president of the American Council on Education; and "Leave Education to the Faculty?" by Kenneth Young (1978). Arnstein (1979) also offers interesting perspectives in "Two Cheers for Accreditation." Also noteworthy is a brief statement by Selden and Porter (1977) entitled *Accreditation: Its Purposes and Uses.*

References

Adler, D. L. *Governance and Collective Bargaining in Four-Year Institutions 1970–1971*. Monograph 3. Washington, D.C.: Academic Collective Bargaining Information Service, 1978.

Alden, V. "Corporate Boss, University President." *AGB Reports,* 1978, *20* (3), 14–19.

American Association of Fund-Raising Counsel. *Giving USA: 1977 Annual Report.* New York: American Association of Fund-Raising Counsel, 1977.

American Association for Higher Education, Task Force on Faculty Representation and Academic Negotiations, Campus Governance Programs. *Faculty Participation in Academic Governance.* Washington, D.C.: American Association for Higher Education, 1967.

American Association of State Colleges and Universities, Resource Center for Planned Change. *Alternatives.* Washington, D.C.: American Association of State Colleges and Universities, 1978.

American Association of University Professors. "Draft Statement on Student Participation in College and University Government." *AAUP Bulletin,* 1970, *56* (1), 33–35.

American Association of University Professors. "Surviving the

481

Seventies, Part III: Tenuring-In." *AAUP Bulletin,* 1973, *59* (2), 198–203.

American Association of University Professors. *Policy Documents and Reports.* Washington, D.C.: American Association of University Professors, 1977.

American Association of University Professors and Association of American Colleges Commission on Academic Tenure. *Faculty Tenure: A Report and Recommendations.* San Francisco: Jossey-Bass, 1973.

American Association of University Professors, American Council on Education, Association of Governing Boards of Universities and Colleges. "Statement on Government of Colleges and Universities." *AAUP Bulletin,* 1966, *52* (4), 375–379.

American College Public Relations Association. "A Joint Legislative Relations Program to Increase Tax Support." *28 Case Studies of Institutional Public Relations and Development Programs,* 1964, *2,* 31.

American College Public Relations Association. "Information Programs: State-wide Information Program in Florida." *Award Winning Case Studies in College Advancement Programs,* 1965, *3,* 51–54.

Anderson, G. L. *The Evaluation of Academic Administrators: Principles, Processes, and Outcomes.* University Park: Pennsylvania State University, 1975.

Anderson, G. P. "Trustee Responsibility: Conflict of Interest." *Lex Collegii,* 1979, *2* (4), 6–7.

Angell, G. W. "Q and A on State Bargaining Laws." *AGB Reports,* 1977, *19* (4), 29–32.

Angell, G. W. *Legislatures, Collective Bargaining, and the Public University.* Monograph 4. Washington, D.C.: Academic Collective Bargaining Information Service, 1978a.

Angell, G. W. *Trustees and Collective Bargaining—Two Reports.* Monograph 5. Washington, D.C.: Academic Collective Bargaining Information Service, 1978b.

Angell, G. W. "The Trustees' Guide to Faculty Bargaining." *AGB Reports,* 1978c, *20* (1), 39–43.

Angell, G. W., and Kelley, E. P., Jr. *Faculty Bargaining Under Trustee Policy.* Monograph 7. Washington, D.C.: Academic Collective Bargaining Information Service/Project on Educational Employment Relations, 1979.

Angell, G. W., Kelley, E. P., Jr., and Associates. *Handbook of Faculty Bargaining: Asserting Administrative Leadership for Institutional Progress by Preparing for Bargaining, Negotiating and Administering Contracts, and Improving the Bargaining Process.* San Francisco: Jossey-Bass, 1977.

Armacost, P. M., and the Young Presidents' Organization Team. "Questions for a Board of Trustees." *AGB Reports,* 1976, *18* (4), 3–6.

Arnstein, G. "Two Cheers for Accreditation." *AGB Reports,* 1979, *21* (4), 35–41.

Assembly on University Goals and Governance. *A First Report.* Sponsored by the American Academy of Arts and Sciences, January 1971.

Association of American Colleges. *The President's Role in Development.* Washington, D.C.: Association of American Colleges, 1975.

Association of Governing Boards of Universities and Colleges. *AGB Survey of Board Chairmen Opinion.* Washington, D.C.: Association of Governing Boards of Universities and Colleges, 1973.

Association of Governing Boards of Universities and Colleges. *AGB Survey of Board Chairmen Opinion.* Washington, D.C.: Association of Governing Boards of Universities and Colleges, 1974.

Association of Governing Boards of Universities and Colleges and National Association of College and University Business Officers. *Financial Responsibilities of Governing Boards of Colleges and Universities.* Washington, D.C.: Association of Governing Boards of Universities and Colleges and National Association of College and University Business Officers, 1979.

Astin, A. W. *Four Critical Years: Effects of College on Beliefs, Attitudes, and Knowledge.* San Francisco: Jossey-Bass, 1977.

Avery, R. S. Letter to John W. Nason, Keene, N. Y., October 24, 1978.

Axelrod, N. R. *A Guide for New Trustees.* Washington, D.C.: Association of Governing Boards of Universities and Colleges, 1977.

Baldridge, J. V. *Power and Conflict in the University.* New York: Wiley, 1971.

Baldridge, J. V., and others. *Policy Making and Effective Leadership: A National Study of Academic Management.* San Francisco: Jossey-Bass, 1978.

Barnard, C. I. *Functions of the Executive.* Cambridge, Mass.: Harvard University Press, 1938.

Bean, A. "Fund Raising and the Trustee." *AGB Reports,* 1973, *15* (7), 6–12.

Bean, A. "The Liberal Arts College Trustee's Next 25 Years." *AGB Reports,* 1975, *17* (6), 34–43.

Bell, L. "From the Trustees' Corner." *Association of American Colleges Bulletin,* 1956, *42,* 353–361.

Bennis, W. *The Leaning Ivory Tower.* San Francisco: Jossey-Bass, 1973.

Besse, R. "A Comparison of the University with the Corporation." In J. A. Perkins (Ed.), *The University as an Organization.* New York: McGraw-Hill, 1973.

Blackburn, R. T. *Tenure: Aspects of Job Security on the Changing Campus.* Atlanta, Ga.: Southern Regional Education Board, 1972.

Blackburn, R. T. *Research on Governing Boards and Some Problem-Solving Tactics and Strategies Involving a Professor as Trustee.* Ann Arbor: Center for the Study of Higher Education, University of Michigan, 1977.

Blau, P. M. *The Organization of Academic Work.* New York: Wiley, 1973.

Blount, C. W. "When You Meet Your Legislator. . . ." *AGB Reports,* 1976, *18* (2), 15–17.

Bok, D. C. "Reflections on the Ethical Problems of Accepting Gifts: An Open Letter to the Harvard Community." *Harvard University Gazette,* Supplement, May 4, 1979.

Bolman, F. de W. *How College Presidents Are Chosen.* Washington, D.C.: American Council on Education, 1965.

Bonham, G. W. "The Stresses of Leadership." *Change,* 1979, *11* (3), 12–13.

Boswell, J. W. "Leaves of Absence in a Complex University." Unpublished doctoral dissertation, University of Michigan, 1970.

Bowman, W. W. "Defer Maintenance, Invite Disaster." *AGB Reports,* 1977, *19* (6), 12–17.

Boyd, W. *The History of Western Education.* New York: Barnes & Noble, 1966.

Boyd, W. B. "The Impact of Collective Bargaining on University Governance." *AGB Reports,* 1973, *16* (3), 26–31.

Brademas, J. Remarks on panel in U.S. House of Representatives, National Assembly of the American College Public Relations Association, Washington, D.C., July 20, 1971.

Brakeley, John Price Jones, Inc. "Where Did All the Women Go?" *Chairman's Letter,* July–August, 1978, p. 8.

Bremer, F. H. *Philanthropic Support for Public Junior Colleges.* Unpublished doctoral dissertation, University of Texas, 1965.

Brubacher, J. S., and Rudy, W. *Higher Education in Transition.* New York: Harper & Row, 1968.

Budig, G. A. "Gubernatorial Opinion of Higher Education." *Educational Record,* 1977, *58* (4), 373–377.

Burke, E. *Speech to the Electors of Bristol,* November 3, 1774.

Burns, J. M. *Leadership.* New York: Harper & Row, 1978.

Bush, V. "Of What Use Is a Board of Directors?" In E. P. Learned, C. R. Christenson, and K. R. Andrews (Eds.), *Problems of General Management.* Homewood, Ill.: Irwin, 1961.

Byse, C., and Joughin, L. *Tenure in American Higher Education: Plans, Practices, and Law.* Ithaca, N.Y.: Cornell University Press, 1959.

Carnegie Commission on Higher Education. *Governance of Higher Education: Six Priority Problems.* New York: McGraw-Hill, 1973.

Carnegie Council on Policy Studies in Higher Education. *Making Affirmative Action Work in Higher Education: An Analysis of Institutional and Federal Policies with Recommendations.* San Francisco: Jossey-Bass, 1975.

Carr, R. K., and Van Eyck, D. K. *Collective Bargaining Comes to the Campus.* Washington, D.C.: American Council on Education, 1973.

Cartter, A. M. *Ph.D.s and the Academic Labor Market.* New York: McGraw-Hill, 1976.

Chait, R. "Nine Alternatives to Tenure Quotas." *AGB Reports,* 1976, *18* (2), 38–43.

Chait, R. "Much To Do About Tenure." In G. W. Bonham (Ed.), *Three Views: Tenure.* New York: Change Magazine Press, 1979.

Chait, R., and Ford, A. T. *Tenure and the Alternatives.* San Francisco: Jossey-Bass, forthcoming.

Clark, B. R., and Youn, T. K. *Academic Power in the United States.* Washington, D.C.: American Association for Higher Education, 1976.

Cleveland, H. "The Cost of 'Openness.' " *AGB Reports,* 1975, *17* (5), 7–10.

Cleveland, H. *The Education of Administrators for Higher Education.* Urbana: University of Illinois Press, 1978.

Cohen, M. D., and March, J. G. *Leadership and Ambiguity: The American College President.* New York: McGraw-Hill, 1974.

Cole, C. C., Jr. "The Reeling Presidency." *Educational Record,* 1976, *57* (2), 71–78.

Collier, D. J. *Program Classification Structure.* Technical Report 106. Boulder, Colo.: National Center for Higher Education Management Systems, 1978.

Cook, J. "Is Charity Obsolete?" *Forbes,* 1979, *123* (3), 45–51.

Corbally, M. W. *The Partners.* Danville, Ill.: Interstate Printers and Publishers, 1977a.

Corbally, M. W. "The Problem of the President's Wife." *AGB Reports,* 1977b, *19* (5), 6–8.

Cornett, R. O. "Masterly Planning." *AGB Reports,* 1977, *19* (3), 36–38.

Corson, J. J. *The Governance of Colleges and Universities.* New York: McGraw-Hill, 1960.

Corson, J. J. "Perspectives on the University Compared with Other Institutions." In J. A. Perkins (Ed.), *The University as an Organization.* New York: McGraw-Hill, 1973.

Corson, J. J. *The Governance of Colleges and Universities.* (rev. ed.) New York: McGraw-Hill, 1975.

Coughlin, E. K. "States Appropriate $17 Billion in Tax Funds for Higher Education." *Chronicle of Higher Education,* October 10, 1978, pp. 13–16.

Council for Financial Aid to Education. *Voluntary Support of Education, 1970–71.* New York: Division of Research, Council for Financial Aid to Education, 1972.

Council for Financial Aid to Education. *Voluntary Support of Education, 1973–74.* New York: Division of Research, Council for Financial Aid to Education, 1975.

Council for Financial Aid to Education. *Voluntary Support of Education, 1976–77.* New York: Division of Research, Council for Financial Aid to Education, 1978.

Crawford, E. M. "Improving Your Public Appropriations." *AGB Reports,* 1975, *17* (4), 28–33.

Curti, M., and Nash, R. *Philanthropy in the Shaping of Higher Education.* New Brunswick, N.J.: Rutgers University Press, 1965.

Cutlip, S. *Fund Raising in the United States.* New Brunswick, N.J.: Rutgers University Press, 1965.

Davis, J. S., and Batchelor, S. A. *The Effective College and University Board: A Report of a National Survey of Trustees and Presidents.* Research Triangle Park, N.C.: Research Triangle Institute, Center for Educational Research and Evaluation, 1974.

Davis, P. H. "More to be Desired Are They than Gold. . . ." *Association of American Colleges Bulletin,* 1958, *44* (3), 391–398.

Drake, S. L. *Research Report: A Study of Community and Junior College Boards of Trustees.* Washington, D.C.: American Association of Community and Junior Colleges, Association of Governing Boards of Universities and Colleges, and Association of Community College Trustees, 1977.

Dressel, P. L. *Handbook of Academic Evaluation: Assessing Institutional Effectiveness, Student Progress, and Professional Performance for Decision Making in Higher Education.* San Francisco: Jossey-Bass, 1976.

Dugger, R. "The University Regent: Responsibilities of the Philosopher-King." *Planning for Higher Education,* 1975, *4* (6), 1–3.

Dugger, R. "If I Were a Trustee." *Change Magazine,* December–January, 1975–1976, *7* (10), 8–9.

Duncan, R. F. *College Trustees, Fund-Raising, and Public Relations.* New York: Kersting, Brown, 1960.

Dunseth, W. B. "Giving That Doesn't Hurt." *AGB Reports,* 1978a, *20* (5), 23–25.

Dunseth, W. B. Speech given at national conference on trusteeship, Association of Governing Boards, San Francisco, April 17, 1978.

Duryea, E. D. "Evolution of University Organization." In J. A. Perkins (Ed.), *The University as an Organization.* New York: McGraw-Hill, 1973.

Duryea, E. D. *Perceptions of Faculty-Governing Board Relations, 1900–1969.* Buffalo: Department of Higher Education, State University of New York, 1978.

Duryea, E. D., and Neddy, J. C. *Collective Bargaining: Impact on Governance.* Washington, D.C.: Association of Governing Boards of Universities and Colleges, 1977.

Dykes, A. R. *Faculty Participation in Academic Decision Making.* Washington, D.C.: American Council on Education, 1968.

Dziuba, V., and Meardy, W. (Eds.). *New Directions for Community Colleges: Enhancing Trustee Effectiveness,* no. 15. San Francisco: Jossey-Bass, 1976.

Edwards, H. T., and Nordin, V. D. *Higher Education and the Law.* Cambridge, Mass.: Institute for Educational Management, Harvard University, 1979.

Eliot, C. W. *University Administration.* Boston: Houghton Mifflin, 1908.

Ennis, R. M., and Williamson, J. P. *Spending Policy for Educational Endowments.* New York: The Common Fund, 1976.

Epstein, L. D. *Governing the University: The Campus and the Public Interest.* San Francisco: Jossey-Bass, 1974.

Eurich, A. C., and Tickton, S. G. *Long-Range Planning and Budgeting at Colleges and Universities.* Washington, D.C.: Academy for Educational Development, 1973.

Fenske, R. H. (Ed.). *New Directions for Institutional Research: Using Goals in Research and Planning,* no. 19. San Francisco: Jossey-Bass, 1978.

Fields, C. M. "Higher Education's Washington Lobbyists." *Chronicle of Higher Education,* March 19, 1979, pp. 1, 11–13.

Fisher, C. F. (Ed.). *New Directions for Higher Education: Developing and Evaluating Administrative Leadership,* no. 22. San Francisco: Jossey-Bass, 1978.

Folger, J. K. "Community Colleges and Legislative Relations." *Peabody Journal of Education,* 1976, *53* (3), 157–161.

Fouts, D. E. "Picking a President the Business Way." *AGB Reports,* 1977, *19* (1), 6–10.

Frantzreb, A. C. *Operational Imperatives for a College Board of Trustees in the 1970s.* New York: Frantzreb and Pray Associates, 1970.

Frantzreb, A. C. "Secret Ingredients of a Chairperson." *AGB Reports,* 1976, *18* (5), 48.

Frantzreb, A. C. "Management of Volunteers." In A. W. Rowland (Ed.), *Handbook of Institutional Advancement: A Practical Guide to College and University Relations, Fund Raising, Alumni Relations, Government Relations, Publications, and Executive Management for Continued Advancement.* San Francisco: Jossey-Bass, 1977.

Froeschle, H. O. "Community Support for the College Budget." *Techniques,* 1972, 7 (5), 10.

Fulton, O., and Trow, M. "Research Activity in American Higher Education." *Sociology of Education,* 1974, *47* (1), 29–73.

"Fund-Raising Progress on 107 Campuses." *Chronicle of Higher Education,* May 30, 1978, p. 13.

Furniss, W. T. *Steady-State Staffing in Tenure-Granting Institutions and Related Papers.* Washington, D.C.: American Council on Education, 1973.

Furniss, W. T. "The 1976 AAUP Retrenchment Policy." *Educational Record,* 1976, *57* (3), 133–139.

Furniss, W. T. "Status of AAUP Policy." *Educational Record,* 1978, *59* (1), 7–29.

Gale, R. L. "Lay Advisory Boards as an External Relations Tool." *Peabody Journal of Education,* 1976, *53* (3), 162–165.

Gardner, J. W. *Self-Renewal: The Individual and the Innovative Society.* New York: Harper & Row, 1965.

Gies, J. C., and Anderson, W. W. *The Board Chairperson and the President.* Washington, D.C.: Association of Governing Boards of Universities and Colleges, 1977.

Gomberg, I. L., and Atelsek, F. J. *Composition of College and University Governing Boards,* Higher Education Panel Report no. 35. Washington, D.C.: American Council on Education, 1977.

Gould, S. B. "Trustees and the University Community." In J. A. Perkins (Ed.), *The University as an Organization.* New York: McGraw-Hill, 1973.

Gove, S. K., and Carpenter, J. "State Lobbying for Higher Education." *Educational Record,* 1977, *58* (4), 357–372.

Greenleaf, R. K. *The Institution as Servant.* Cambridge, Mass.: Center for Applied Studies, 1972.

Greenleaf, R. K. *Trustees as Servants.* Cambridge, Mass.: Center for Applied Studies, 1974.

Gross, M. J., Jr. *Financial and Accounting Guide for Nonprofit Organizations.* New York: Ronald Press, 1974.

Hanson, D. J., and Pondrum, C. N. "Executive Order 11246, as Amended." In *Federal Regulations and the Employment Practices of Colleges and Universities: A Guide to the Interpretation of Federal Regulations Affecting Personnel Administration on Campus.* Washington, D.C.: National Association of College and University Business Officers, 1974.

Harris, L. "Harris Survey: Confidence in Institutions." *Chicago Tribune,* September 25, 1978.

Hartnett, R. T. *College and University Trustees: Their Backgrounds, Roles, and Educational Attitudes.* Princeton, N.J.: Educational Testing Service, 1969.

Hartnett, R. T. *The New College Trustee: Some Predictions for the 1970s.* Princeton, N.J.: Educational Testing Service, 1970.

Haslam, C. L. "The Locus of Decision Making in Colleges and Universities: The Broad Perspective." *Journal of College and University Law,* 1974, *1,* 241–248.

Hays, G. D. "Evaluating a President: The Minnesota Plan." *AGB Reports,* 1976a, *18* (5), 5–9.

Hays, G. D. "Evaluating a President: Criteria and Procedures." *AGB Reports,* 1976b, *18* (6), 41–46.

Healy, R. M., and Peterson, V. T. "Who Killed These Four Colleges?" *AGB Reports,* 1977, 19 (3), 14–18.

Healy, T. S. "1978 Annual Report." Washington, D.C.: Georgetown University, 1978.

Heeman, W. (Ed.). *New Directions for Institutional Advancement: Analyzing the Cost Effectiveness of Fund Raising,* no. 3. San Francisco: Jossey-Bass, 1978–79.

Heilbron, L. H. *The College and University Trustee: A View from the Board Room.* San Francisco: Jossey-Bass, 1973.

Henderson, A. *The Role of the Governing Board.* Washington, D.C.: Association of Governing Boards of Universities and Colleges, 1967.

Hermann, B. R. *An Evaluation of Faculty Representation on College and University Governing Boards in the United States.* Unpublished doctoral dissertation, Texas A & M University, 1973.

Heyns, R. W. "Our Best Defense Against Regulation." *AGB Reports,* 1977, *19* (3), 9–13.

Hodgkinson, H. L. *Campus Governance—The Amazing Thing Is That It Works at All.* Research Report no. 11, ERIC Clearinghouse on Higher Education. Washington, D.C.: American Association for Higher Education, 1971.

Howe, R. A. "Collective Bargaining: A Short Advanced Course." *AGB Reports,* 1975, *17* (5), 26–30.

Ingram, R. T. "Trusteeship: An Overview." *Community and Junior College Journal,* 1973, *44,* 7–9.

Ingram, R. T. "How Can Governing Boards Assure Better Planning?" Paper presented at 12th annual meeting of Society for College and University Planning, Seattle, August 17, 1977a.

Ingram, R. T. *Trustee Workshops and Retreats.* Washington, D.C.: Association of Governing Boards of Universities and Colleges, 1977b.

Ingram, R. T. "The Marriage of Presidents and Boards." In R. E. Lahti (Ed.), *New Directions for Community Colleges: Managing in a New Era,* no. 28. San Francisco: Jossey-Bass, 1979.

Institute for Educational Development. *The Twelve College Faculty Appointment and Development Study.* New York: Institute for Educational Development, 1973.

Jacobson, H. K. "A Report on North Dakota's WISE Program." Paper presented at annual convention of American College Public Relations Association, Dallas, July 26, 1967.

Jacobson, H. K. (Ed.). *New Directions for Institutional Advancement: Evaluating Advancement Programs,* no. 1. San Francisco: Jossey-Bass, 1978–79.

Jay, A. "How to Run a Meeting." *Harvard Business Review,* 1976, *54,* 43–57.

Jencks, C., and Riesman, D. *The Academic Revolution.* New York: Doubleday, 1968.

Kaplin, W. A. *The Law of Higher Education: Legal Implications of Administrative Decision Making.* San Francisco: Jossey-Bass, 1978.

Kauffman, J. F. *The Selection of College and University Presidents.* Washington, D.C.: Association of American Colleges, 1974.

Kauffman, J. F. "The New College President: Expectations and Realities." *Educational Record,* 1977, *58* (2), 146–168.

Kauffman, J. F. "The Selection of College and University Presidents." In C. F. Fisher (Ed.), *New Directions for Higher Education: Developing and Evaluating Administrative Leadership,* no. 22. San Francisco: Jossey-Bass, 1978.

Kellems, S. E. *Emerging Sources of Student Influence.* Research Report no. 5, ERIC Clearinghouse on Higher Education. Washington, D.C.: American Association for Higher Education, 1975.

Kelley, E. P., Jr. *Institutions and Campuses with Faculty Collective Bargaining Agents,* Special Report no. 12, Update. Washington, D.C.: Academic Collective Bargaining Information Service, 1978.

Kells, H., and Kirkwood, R. "Institutional Self-Evaluation Processes." *Educational Record,* 1979, *60* (1), 15–45.

Kemerer, F. R., and Baldridge, J. V. *Unions on Campus: A National Study of the Consequences of Faculty Bargaining.* San Francisco: Jossey-Bass, 1975.

Kerr, C. *The Uses of the University.* Cambridge, Mass.: Harvard University Press, 1963.

Kerr, C. "Presidential Discontent." In D. C. Nichols (Ed.), *Perspectives on Campus Tensions.* Washington, D.C.: American Council on Education, 1970.

Kerr, C. "Trustees: Job Assignments." *AGB Reports,* 1974, *16* (4), 2.

Ketchum, D. Letter to Michael Radock, University of Michigan, February 1979.

Kirkwood, R. "Institutional Responsibilities in Accreditation." *Educational Record,* 1978, *59* (4), 297–304.

Kohr, R. V. "Capital Campaigning." In A. W. Rowland (Ed.), *Handbook of Institutional Advancement: A Practical Guide to College and University Relations, Fund Raising, Alumni Relations, Government Relations, Publications, and Executive Management for Continued Advancement.* San Francisco: Jossey-Bass, 1977a.

Kohr, R. V. "Checklist of Institutional Data." In A. W. Rowland (Ed.), *Handbook of Institutional Advancement: A Practical Guide to College and University Relations, Fund Raising, Alumni Relations, Government Relations, Publications, and Executive Management for Continued Advancement.* San Francisco: Jossey-Bass, 1977b.

Ladd, E., Jr., and Lipset, S. *Professors, Unions, and American Higher Education.* Berkeley, Calif.: Carnegie Commission on Higher Education, 1973.

Lamson, G., and others. *Steady-State Staff Planning: The Experience of a "Mature" Liberal Arts College and Its Implications.* Washington, D.C.: Educational Resources Information Clearinghouse, Document Ed. 111 297m, March 1974.

Lavine, J. M., and Lemon, W. L. *Collective Bargaining.* Washington, D.C.: Association of Governing Boards of Universities and Colleges, 1975.

Leslie, D. W. (Ed.). *New Directions for Institutional Research: Employing Part-Time Faculty,* no. 18. San Francisco: Jossey-Bass, 1978.

Leslie, J. W. "Selected Indicators Chart Trends." In H. K. Jacobson (Ed.), *New Directions for Institutional Advancement: Evaluating Advancement Programs,* no. 1. San Francisco: Jossey-Bass, 1978–79.

Lester, R. *Antibias Regulations of Universities.* New York: McGraw-Hill, 1974.

Luck, M. F., and Tolle, D. J. *Community College Development: Alternative Fund-Raising Strategies.* Indianapolis: R & R Newkirk, 1978.

Luecke, D. S. "An Alternative to Quotas: A Model for Controlling Tenure Proportions." *Journal of Higher Education,* 1974, *45* (4), 273–284.

Lyman, R. W. Remarks made to Stanford University alumni, San Francisco, May 7, 1973.

McGrath, E. J. *Should Students Share the Power?* Philadelphia: Temple University Press, 1970.

McKenna, D. L. "Recycling College Presidents." *Liberal Education,* 1972, *58* (4), 456–463.

McKenna, D. L. "Ten Lessons of a Recycled President." *Liberal Education,* 1977, *63* (3), 423–434.

Magarrell, J. "Fewer Private Colleges? Not So, an Analyst Charges." *Chronicle of Higher Education,* July 23, 1979, pp. 1, 6.

Martin, H. C. "Trustees and Academic Policy." *AGB Reports,* 1974, *17* (2), 10–20.

Maryland State Board for Higher Education. *Maryland Statewide Plan for Postsecondary Education.* Annapolis: Maryland State Board for Higher Education, 1978.

Means, H. B., and Semas, P. W. (Eds.). *Faculty Collective Bargaining.* Washington, D.C.: Editorial Projects for Education, 1976.

Middle States Association of Colleges and Schools. *Handbook for Institutional Self-Study.* Philadelphia: Middle States Association of Colleges and Schools, 1977.

Middle States Association of Colleges and Schools. Statement on "Characteristics of Excellence and Standards for . . . Accreditation." Philadelphia: Middle States Association of Colleges and Schools, 1978.

Miller, R. I. *The Assessment of College Performance: A Handbook of*

Techniques and Measures for Institutional Self-Evaluation. San Francisco: Jossey-Bass, 1979.

Miller, W. F. "How Stanford Plans." *AGB Reports,* 1978, *20* (5), 26–30.

Millett, J. D. *The Academic Community.* New York: McGraw-Hill, 1962.

Millett, J. D. *The Multiple Roles of the College and University President.* Washington, D.C.: American Council on Education, 1976.

Millett, J. D. *Higher Education Planning: A Report of Experience and a Forecast of Strategies for Change.* Washington, D.C.: Academy for Educational Development, 1978a.

Millett, J. D. *New Structures of Campus Power: Success and Failures of Emerging Forms of Institutional Governance.* San Francisco: Jossey-Bass, 1978b.

Millett, J. D. "Report to University of Texas System Governing Board." Austin: October 1978c.

Minter, W. J., and Bowen, H. R. *Independent Higher Education: Fourth Annual Report on Financial and Educational Trends in the Independent Sector of American Higher Education.* Washington, D.C.: National Association of College and University Business Officers, 1978.

The Missouri Statement: A Student Call to Action. Columbia: Associated Students of the University of Missouri, 1977.

"Monitor Spotlights: Harriet Naylor." Interview in *Monitor of Philanthropy,* 1978, *8* (9), 97, 105.

Morgan, J. N., Dye, R. F., and Hybels, J. H. "Results from Two National Surveys of Philanthropic Activity." *Research Papers Sponsored by the Commission on Private Philanthropy and Public Needs.* Vol. I: *History, Trends, and Current Magnitudes.* Washington, D.C.: U.S. Department of the Treasury, 1977.

Morrison, R. S. *Students and Decision Making.* Washington, D.C.: Public Affairs Press, 1970.

Mortimer, K. P. *What Trustees Should Know About Faculty Collective Bargaining.* An unpublished study prepared for the Association of Governing Boards of Universities and Colleges, Washington, D.C., 1976.

Mortimer, K. P. *Academic Collective Bargaining.* Washington, D.C.: Association of Governing Boards of Universities and Colleges, 1977.

Mortimer, K. P., and McConnell, T. R. *Sharing Authority Effectively: Participation, Interaction, and Discretion.* San Francisco: Jossey-Bass, 1978.

Mortimer, K. P., and Richardson, R. C., Jr. *Governance in Institutions with Faculty Unions: Six Case Studies.* University Park: Center for the Study of Higher Education, Pennsylvania State University, 1977.

Munitz, B. "Measuring a President's Performance." *AGB Reports,* 1976, *18* (1), 36–40.

Munitz, B. *Leadership in Colleges and Universities: Assessment and Search.* Oak Brook, Ill.: Johnson Associates, 1977.

Munitz, B. "Strengthening Institutional Leadership." In C. F. Fisher (Ed.), *New Directions for Higher Education: Developing and Evaluating Administrative Leadership,* no. 22. San Francisco: Jossey-Bass, 1978.

Murray, R. F. "Framing a South African Policy Statement." *AGB Reports,* 1978, *20* (4), 5–8.

Nason, J. W. *The Future of Trusteeship: The Role and Responsibilities of College and University Boards.* Washington, D.C.: Association of Governing Boards of Universities and Colleges, 1975.

Nason, J. W. *Presidential Search: A Guide to the Process of Selecting and Appointing College and University Presidents.* Washington, D.C.: Association of Governing Boards of Universities and Colleges, 1979.

Nason, J. W. *Presidential Assessment: A Challenge to College and University Leadership.* Washington, D.C.: Association of Governing Boards of Universities and Colleges, 1980.

Nason, J. W., and Wood, G. P. "Student-Faculty Trusteeship: A Short Debate." *AGB Reports,* 1977, *19* (2), 12–14.

National Association of College and University Business Officers. *College and University Business Administration.* Washington, D.C.: National Association of College and University Business Officers, 1974.

National Association of College and University Business Officers. *A College Planning Cycle—People, Resources, Process—A Practical Guide.* Washington, D.C.: National Association of College and University Business Officers, 1975.

National Association of Independent Schools. *Evaluating Our Performance.* Boston: National Association of Independent Schools, 1978.

National Center for Education Statistics. *Salaries, Tenure, and Fringe Benefits of Full-Time Instructional Faculty in Institutions of Higher Education, 1975–76.* Washington, D.C.: U.S. Government Printing Office, 1977.

National Center for Education Statistics. *The Condition of Education.* Washington, D.C.: U.S. Government Printing Office, 1978a.

National Center for Education Statistics. *Digest of Education Statistics, 1977–78.* Washington, D.C.: U.S. Government Printing Office, 1978b.

National Center for Education Statistics. *Financial Statistics of Institutions of Higher Education.* Washington, D.C.: U.S. Government Printing Office, 1979a.

National Center for Education Statistics. *Selected Statistics on the Salaries, Tenure, and Fringe Benefits of Full-Time Instructional Faculty for the 1978–79 Academic Year.* Washington, D.C.: U.S. Department of Health, Education, and Welfare, Education Division, March 1979b.

Nelson, C. A. "The Board's Role in Mission Setting and Long-Range Planning." Paper presented at Association of Governing Boards of Universities and Colleges' National Conference on Trusteeship, Washington, D.C., April 21, 1975.

Nelson, C. A. *Resource Management Responsibilities.* Washington, D.C.: Association of Governing Boards of Universities and Colleges, 1977.

Nelson, C. A. "Wanted: Strong Trustees for Strong Boards." *Trustee,* 1978, *31* (11), 21–25.

Nelson, C. A., and Turk, F. J. "Some Facts About Trustees." *AGB Reports,* 1974, *16* (7), 3–9.

New York Civil Service Laws, Sections 200–214.

North Carolina General Statutes, Section 116–36(b), Vol. 3a, Pt. 2.

Olswang, S. G. "Trustees, Divestiture, and the Law." *AGB Reports,* 1978, *20* (4), 9–14.

O'Neil, J. *Resource Use in Higher Education.* Berkeley, Calif.: Carnegie Commission on Higher Education, 1971.

Ottley, A. H. *Funding Strategies for Community Colleges.* Chicago: Advanced Institutional Development Program Consortium, Central YMCA Community College, 1978.

Paltridge, J. G., Hurst, J., and Morgan, A. *Boards of Trustees: Their*

Decision Patterns. Berkeley, Calif.: Center for Research and Development in Higher Education, 1973.

Parekh, S. B. *Long-Range Planning: An Institution-Wide Approach to Increasing Academic Vitality.* New Rochelle, N.Y.: Change Magazine Press, 1977.

Parsons, C. "Academia for Sale." *Christian Science Monitor,* February 20, 1979.

Pattillo, M. M. "Choosing a College President." *AGB Reports,* 1973, *15* (5), 2–8.

Patton, C. V. *Academia in Transition: Mid-Career Change or Early Retirement.* Cambridge, Mass.: Abt Books, 1979.

Perkins, J. A. *The University in Transition.* Princeton, N.J.: Princeton University Press, 1966.

Perkins, J. A. (Ed.). *The University as an Organization.* New York: McGraw-Hill, 1973.

Peterson, R. E., and Uhl, N. P. *Formulating College and University Goals: A Guide for Using the IGI.* Princeton, N.J.: Educational Testing Service, 1977.

Polk, C. H., and Coleman, J. D., Jr. "Self-Evaluation, Key to Accountability." In V. Dzuiba and W. Meardy (Eds.), *New Directions for Community Colleges: Enhancing Trustee Effectiveness,* no. 15. San Francisco: Jossey-Bass, 1976.

Potter, E. G. *Trusteeship: Handbook for Community College and Technical Institute Trustees.* Washington, D.C.: Association of Community College Trustees, 1979.

Potter, G. F. "Collective Bargaining: A Primer for Trustees." *AGB Reports,* 1975, *17* (5), 21–25.

Pray, F. C. *Report Card for College Trustees.* New York: Frantzreb and Pray Associates, 1965.

Radock, M. "Trustee's Role in Fund Raising." Filmstrip available to members of the Association of Governing Boards of Universities and Colleges, Washington, D.C., 1975.

Radock, M. *The Fund-Raising Role.* Washington, D.C.: Association of Governing Boards of Universities and Colleges, 1977.

Radock, M. "A Position Report on Philanthropy, 1978: Highlights of Problems and Trends in Educational Fund Raising." Paper presented at 24th annual conference of National Council on Philanthropy, Washington, D.C., November 29, 1978.

Ramsden, R. J. "Guidelines to Good Operations—Analysis of the Standards Achieved by 25 Institutions in Their University Relations and Development Operations." Speech at annual assembly of the Council for Advancement and Support of Education, San Francisco, July 11, 1977.

Rauh, M. A. *The Trusteeship of Colleges and Universities.* New York: McGraw-Hill, 1969.

Rauh, M. A. "Internal Organization of the Board." In J. A. Perkins (Ed.), *The University as an Organization.* New York: McGraw-Hill, 1973.

Research and Forecasts. *Survey on the Changing Nature of the Corporate Board.* New York: Research and Forecasts, 1978.

Riley, G. L. "The Changing Role of Trustees in Academic Governance." In G. L. Riley and J. V. Baldridge (Eds.), *Governing Academic Organizations.* Berkeley, Calif.: McCutchan, 1977.

Robinson, L. H., and Shoenfeld, J. D. *Student Participation in Academic Governance.* Washington, D.C.: ERIC Clearinghouse on Higher Education, George Washington University, 1970.

Romney, L. *Measures of Institutional Goal Achievement.* Boulder, Colo.: National Center for Higher Education Management Systems, 1978.

Rowland, A. W. (Ed.). *Handbook of Institutional Advancement: A Practical Guide to College and University Relations, Fund Raising, Alumni Relations, Government Relations, Publications, and Executive Management for Continued Advancement.* San Francisco: Jossey-Bass, 1977.

Rudolph, F. *The American College and University.* New York: Knopf, 1965.

Ruml, B., and Morrison, D. H. *Memo to a College Trustee.* New York: McGraw-Hill, 1959.

Schneiter, P. H. *The Art of Asking: A Handbook for Successful Fund Raising.* New York: Walker, 1978.

Selden, W. K., and Porter, H. V. *Accreditation: Its Purposes and Uses.* Washington, D.C.: Council on Postsecondary Accreditation, 1977.

Seymour, H. J. *Designs for Fund Raising.* New York: McGraw-Hill, 1966.

Shark, A. R. "Now in Action: The Board-Mentor Service." *AGB Reports,* 1977, *19* (5), 26–27.

Shark, A. R., Brouder, K., and Associates. *Students and Collective Bargaining.* Washington, D.C.: National Student Educational Fund, 1976.

Shea, J. M. "Organization and Structure." In A. W. Rowland (Ed.), *Handbook of Institutional Advancement: A Practical Guide to College and University Relations, Fund Raising, Alumni Relations, Government Relations, Publications, and Executive Management for Continued Advancement.* San Francisco: Jossey-Bass, 1977.

Simpson, W. A. "Tenure: A Perspective View of Past, Present, and Future." *Educational Record,* 1975, *56* (1), 48–54.

Smallwood, S. J. "Measuring Fund-Raising Costs." *CASE Currents,* 1979, *5* (1), 18–21.

Smallwood, S. J., and Levis, W. C. "First Draft: Model for Financial Reporting of Fund-Raising Activities." *Philanthropy Monthly,* 1977, *10* (10), 8–28.

Statement on Government of Colleges and Universities. Washington, D.C.: American Association of University Professors, American Council on Education, and Association of Governing Boards of Universities and Colleges, 1966.

Stuhr, R. L. *On Development.* Chicago: Gonser Gerber Tinker Stuhr, 1977.

Summers, B. J., and Smotony, B. M. "What Do Board Secretaries Do?" *AGB Reports,* 1979, *21* (2), 33–36.

"Survey of Board Chairmen Opinion." Washington, D.C.: Association of Governing Boards of Universities and Colleges, 1974.

Thompson, H. L., and Miller, J. E. "A Board Self-Improvement Tool." *AGB Reports,* 1979, *21* (2), 44–47.

Trow, M. "Reflections on the Transition from Mass to Universal Higher Education." *Daedalus,* 1970, *99* (1), 1–42.

Twentieth Century Fund, Inc. *Funds for the Future.* New York: McGraw-Hill, 1975.

Vaccaro, L. C. "A Planning Model for Small Colleges." *AGB Reports,* 1979, *21* (4), 30–34.

Walker, D. E. *The Effective Administrator: A Practical Approach to Problem Solving, Decision Making, and Campus Leadership.* San Francisco: Jossey-Bass, 1979.

Weisberger, J. M. *Grievance Arbitration in Higher Education: Recent Experiences with Arbitration of Faculty Status Disputes,* Monograph

6. Washington, D.C.: Academic Collective Bargaining Information Service, 1979.

Welles, C. *Conflicts of Interest: Nonprofit Institutions.* New York: The Twentieth-Century Fund, 1977.

West, R. R. "Tenure Quotas and Financial Flexibility in Colleges and Universities." *Educational Record,* 1974, *55* (2), 96–100.

Wildersmith, O. L. "A University Trustee Views the Academic Profession." *American Association of University Professors Bulletin,* 1949, *35,* 233–239.

Williamson, J. P. *Funds for the Future.* New York: McGraw-Hill, 1975.

Wilson, E. G. "Excerpts from Notes of AGB National Conference on Trusteeship." Sharon, Conn., 1979.

Wren, S. C. *The College Student and Higher Education Policy: What Stake and What Purpose?* Berkeley, Calif.: Carnegie Council on Policy Studies in Higher Education, 1975.

Yoder, S. L., and May, J. A. "Going Public: The Michigan Awareness Program." *CASE Currents,* 1980, *6* (1), 18–20.

Young, K. E. "Leave Education to the Faculty?" *AGB Reports,* 1978, *20* (4), 31–35.

Yuker, H. "Faculty Workloads and Productivity." In T. Tice (Ed.), *Campus Employment Relations.* Ann Arbor, Mich.: Institute of Continuing Legal Education, 1976.

Zwingle, J. L. *The Lay Governing Board.* Washington, D.C.: Association of Governing Boards of Universities and Colleges, 1970.

Zwingle, J. L. "Build a Better Board." *AGB Reports,* 1976, *18* (3), 32–36.

Zwingle, J. L. *Effective Trusteeship: Guidelines for Board Members.* Washington, D.C.: Association of Governing Boards of Universities and Colleges, 1979.

Zwingle, J. L., and Mayville, W. *College Trustees: A Question of Legitimacy.* Research Report no. 10, ERIC Clearinghouse on Higher Education. Washington, D.C.: American Association for Higher Education, 1974.

Court Cases

AAUP v. *Bloomfield College,* 322 A.2d 846 (1974); 346 A.2d 615 (1975).

Board of Regents v. *Roth,* 408 U.S. 564 (1972).

Browzin v. *Catholic University of America,* 527 F.2d 843 (1975).

Chance v. *Board of Examiners,* 11FEP 1450 (1976).

Cornell University, 74 LRRM 1269 (1970). *Cornell University* is also known as 183 NLRB 329 (1970).

Jersey Central Power & Light Co. v. *Local Union 327 etc. of International Brotherhood of Electrical Workers,* 508 F.2d 687 (1975).

Johnson v. *Board of Regents of the University of Wisconsin System,* 377 F. Supp. 230 (1974).

Levitt v. *Board of Trustees of Nebraska State Colleges,* 376 F. Supp. 946 (1974).

Lumpert v. *University of Dubuque,* 255 N.W.2d 168 (1977).

National Labor Relations Board and Yeshiva University Faculty Association v. *Yeshiva University,* 582 F.2d 686 (2nd Cir. 1978).

Perry v. *Sinderman,* 408 U.S. 593 (1972).

Scheur v. *Creighton University,* 260 N.W.2d 595 (1977).

Stern v. *Lucy Webb Hayes National Training School for Deaconesses and Missionaries, et al.,* 381 F. Supp. 1003 (D.D.C., 1974).

Waters v. *Wisconsin Steelworkers,* 502 F.2d 1309 (1974).

Watkins v. *United States Steelworkers of America, Local 2369,* 516 F.2d 41 (1975).

Index